HTML

Your visual blueprint for
designing effective Web pages

Visual

From
maranGraphics™

&

IDG Books Worldwide, Inc.
An International Data Group Company
Foster City, CA • Indianapolis • Chicago • New York

HTML

Published by
IDG Books Worldwide, Inc.
An International Data Group Company
919 E. Hillsdale Blvd., Suite 400
Foster City, CA 94404

Copyright© 2000 by maranGraphics Inc.
5755 Coopers Avenue
Mississauga, Ontario, Canada
L4Z 1R9

Library of Congress Catalog Card No.: 00-103130

ISBN: 0-7645-3471-8

Printed in the United States of America
10 9 8 7 6 5 4 3 2

1V/RV/QX/QQ/MG

Distributed in the United States by IDG Books Worldwide, Inc.

Distributed by CDG Books Canada Inc. for Canada; by Transworld Publishers Limited in the United Kingdom; by IDG Norge Books for Norway; by IDG Sweden Books for Sweden; by IDG Books Australia Publishing Corporation Pty. Ltd. for Australia and New Zealand; by TransQuest Publishers Pte Ltd. for Singapore, Malaysia, Thailand, Indonesia, and Hong Kong; by Gotop Information Inc. for Taiwan; by ICG Muse, Inc. for Japan; by Intersoft for South Africa; by Eyrolles for France; by International Thomson Publishing for Germany, Austria and Switzerland; by Distribuidora Cuspide for Argentina; by LR International for Brazil; by Galileo Libros for Chile; by Ediciones ZETA S.C.R. Ltda. for Peru; by WS Computer Publishing Corporation, Inc. for the Philippines; by Contemporanea de Ediciones for Venezuela; by Express Computer Distributors for the Caribbean and West Indies; by Micronesia Media Distributor, Inc. for Micronesia; by Chips Computadoras S.A. de C.V. for Mexico; by Editorial Norma de Panama S.A. for Panama; by American Bookshops for Finland.
For corporate orders, please call maranGraphics at 800-469-6616.
For general information on IDG Books Worldwide's books in the U.S., please call our Consumer Customer Service department at 800-762-2974.
For reseller information, including discounts and premium sales, please call our Reseller Customer Service department at 800-434-3422.
For information on where to purchase IDG Books Worldwide's books outside the U.S., please contact our International Sales department at 317-572-3993 or fax 317-572-4002.
For consumer information on foreign language translations, please contact our Customer Service department at 800-434-3422, fax 800-550-2747, or e-mail rights@idgbooks.com.
For information on licensing foreign or domestic rights, please phone 650-653-7000 of fax 650-653-7500.
For sales inquiries and special prices for bulk quantities, please contact our Sales department at 650-655-3200.
For information on using IDG Books Worldwide's books in the classroom or for ordering examination copies, please contact our Educational Sales department at 800-434-2086 or fax 317-572-4005.
For press review copies, author interviews, or other publicity information, please contact our Public Relations department at 650-653-7000 or fax 650-653-7500.
For authorization to photocopy items for corporate, personal, or educational use, please contact maranGraphics at 800-469-6616.

Trademark Acknowledgments

Permissions

U.S. Corporate Sales	U.S. Trade Sales
Contact maranGraphics at (800) 469-6616 or fax (905) 890-9434.	Contact IDG Books at (800) 434-3422 or (650) 655-3000.

ABOUT IDG BOOKS WORLDWIDE

Welcome to the world of IDG Books Worldwide.

IDG Books Worldwide, Inc., is a subsidiary of International Data Group, the world's largest publisher of computer-related information and the leading global provider of information services on information technology. IDG was founded more than 30 years ago by Patrick J. McGovern and now employs more than 9,000 people worldwide. IDG publishes more than 290 computer publications in over 75 countries. More than 90 million people read one or more IDG publications each month.

Launched in 1990, IDG Books Worldwide is today the #1 publisher of best-selling computer books in the United States. We are proud to have received eight awards from the Computer Press Association in recognition of editorial excellence and three from Computer Currents' First Annual Readers' Choice Awards. Our best-selling *...For Dummies*® series has more than 50 million copies in print with translations in 31 languages. IDG Books Worldwide, through a joint venture with IDG's Hi-Tech Beijing, became the first U.S. publisher to publish a computer book in the People's Republic of China. In record time, IDG Books Worldwide has become the first choice for millions of readers around the world who want to learn how to better manage their businesses.

Our mission is simple: Every one of our books is designed to bring extra value and skill-building instructions to the reader. Our books are written by experts who understand and care about our readers. The knowledge base of our editorial staff comes from years of experience in publishing, education, and journalism — experience we use to produce books to carry us into the new millennium. In short, we care about books, so we attract the best people. We devote special attention to details such as audience, interior design, use of icons, and illustrations. And because we use an efficient process of authoring, editing, and desktop publishing our books electronically, we can spend more time ensuring superior content and less time on the technicalities of making books.

You can count on our commitment to deliver high-quality books at competitive prices on topics you want to read about. At IDG Books Worldwide, we continue in the IDG tradition of delivering quality for more than 30 years. You'll find no better book on a subject than one from IDG Books Worldwide.

John J. Kilcullen
Chairman and CEO
IDG Books Worldwide, Inc.

Eighth Annual Computer Press Awards ⋙ 1992

Ninth Annual Computer Press Awards ⋙ 1993

Tenth Annual Computer Press Awards ⋙ 1994

Eleventh Annual Computer Press Awards ⋙ 1995

IDG is the world's leading IT media, research and exposition company. Founded in 1964, IDG had 1997 revenues of $2.05 billion and has more than 9,000 employees worldwide. IDG offers the widest range of media options that reach IT buyers in 75 countries representing 95% of worldwide IT spending. IDG's diverse product and services portfolio spans six key areas including print publishing, online publishing, expositions and conferences, market research, education and training, and global marketing services. More than 90 million people read one or more of IDG's 290 magazines and newspapers, including IDG's leading global brands — Computerworld, PC World, Network World, Macworld and the Channel World family of publications. IDG Books Worldwide is one of the fastest-growing computer book publishers in the world, with more than 700 titles in 36 languages. The "...For Dummies®" series alone has more than 50 million copies in print. IDG offers online users the largest network of technology-specific Web sites around the world through IDG.net (http://www.idg.net), which comprises more than 225 targeted Web sites in 55 countries worldwide. International Data Corporation (IDC) is the world's largest provider of information technology data, analysis and consulting, with research centers in over 41 countries and more than 400 research analysts worldwide. IDG World Expo is a leading producer of more than 168 globally branded conferences and expositions in 35 countries including E3 (Electronic Entertainment Expo), Macworld Expo, ComNet, Windows World Expo, ICE (Internet Commerce Expo), Agenda, DEMO, and Spotlight. IDG's training subsidiary, ExecuTrain, is the world's largest computer training company, with more than 230 locations worldwide and 785 training courses. IDG Marketing Services helps industry-leading IT companies build international brand recognition by developing global integrated marketing programs via IDG's print, online and exposition products worldwide. Further information about the company can be found at www.idg.com.

1/26/00

maranGraphics is a family-run business
located near Toronto, Canada.

At *maranGraphics*, we believe in producing great computer books–one book at a time.

Each maranGraphics book uses the award-winning communication process that we have been developing over the last 25 years. Using this process, we organize screen shots and text in a way that makes it easy for you to learn new concepts and tasks.

We spend hours deciding the best way to perform each task, so you don't have to!

Our clear, easy-to-follow screen shots and instructions walk you through each task from beginning to end.

We want to thank you for purchasing what we feel are the best computer books money can buy. We hope you enjoy using this book as much as we enjoyed creating it!

Sincerely,

The Maran Family

Please visit us on the Web at:
www.maran.com

CREDITS

Visual Architect:
Cathy Benn

Writer:
Eric Kramer

Copy Editors:
Roxanne Van Damme
Stacey Morrison

Screen Flow Structuring:
Ruth Maran

Project Manager:
Judy Maran

Editors:
Raquel Scott
Janice Boyer
Stacey Morrison
Teri Lynn Pinsent
Andrea Carere
Luis Lee

Screen Captures & Editing:
James Menzies

Layout Designers:
Treena Lees
Sean Johannesen
Ted Sheppard

Cover Illustration:
Russ Marini

Screen Artist:
Jimmy Tam

Indexer:
Cathy Benn

Post Production:
Robert Maran

**Senior Vice President,
Technology Publishing
IDG Books Worldwide:**
Richard Swadley

**Editorial Support
IDG Books Worldwide:**
Barry Pruett
Martine Edwards

ACKNOWLEDGMENTS

Thanks to the dedicated staff of maranGraphics, including
Jennifer Amaral, Cathy Benn, Janice Boyer, Andrea Carere,
Sean Johannesen, Wanda Lawrie, Luis Lee, Treena Lees,
Jill Maran, Judy Maran, Robert Maran, Ruth Maran,
Russ Marini, James Menzies, Suzana Miokovic, Stacey Morrison,
Teri Lynn Pinsent, Steven Schaerer, Raquel Scott, Ted Sheppard,
Jimmy Tam, Roxanne Van Damme, Kelleigh Johnson and
Paul Whitehead.

Finally, to Richard Maran who originated the easy-to-use
graphic format of this guide. Thank you for your
inspiration and guidance.

TABLE OF CONTENTS

HTML:
Your visual blueprint for
designing effective Web Pages

4) ADD IMAGES

5) WORK WITH IMAGES

6) CREATE LINKS

TABLE OF CONTENTS

7) CREATE TABLES

8) ADD SOUNDS AND VIDEOS

9) CREATE FORMS

HTML:
Your visual blueprint for
designing effective Web Pages

10) CREATE FRAMES

11) USING JAVASCRIPT

12) WEB PAGE EXTRAS

TABLE OF CONTENTS

12) WEB PAGE EXTRAS (CONTINUED)

13) SET UP STYLE SHEETS

14) FORMAT TEXT USING STYLE SHEETS

15) LAY OUT WEB PAGES USING STYLE SHEETS

HTML:
Your visual blueprint for
designing effective Web Pages

16) PUBLISH WEB PAGES

17) INTRODUCTION TO XML

18) REFERENCE

APPENDIX

INDEX

HOW TO USE THIS BOOK

HTML: Your visual blueprint for designing effective Web pages uses straightforward examples to teach you how to create and design amazing Web pages.

To get the most out of this book, you should read each chapter in order, from beginning to end. Each chapter introduces new ideas and builds on the knowledge learned in previous chapters. Once you become familiar with HyperText Markup Language (HTML), this book can be used as an informative desktop reference.

Who This Book Is For

If you are looking for a resource that will help you quickly get started creating Web pages, *HTML: Your visual blueprint for designing effective Web pages* is the book for you. This book will walk you through the basics you need to get started and familiarize you with the essentials of Web page design. The book also demonstrates advanced HTML related technologies, such as JavaScript and XML, for more experienced Web page designers.

What You Need To Use This Book

To perform the tasks throughout this book, you need a text editor—we use WordPad—and a Web browser, such as Microsoft Internet Explorer 5 or Netscape Navigator 4.7.

Keep in mind that new versions of the popular Web browsers are continually being released. It is a good idea to make sure that you are using the latest version of a Web browser. Also, since each Web browser displays Web pages in a slightly different way, you may want to use more than one Web browser to view your pages.

The Conventions In This Book

A number of typographic and layout styles have been used throughout *HTML: Your visual blueprint for designing effective Web pages* to distinguish different types of information.

Courier Font

Indicates the use of HTML code such as tags or attributes.

Bold

Indicates information that must be typed by you.

Italics

Indicates a new term being introduced.

Apply It

An Apply It section usually contains a segment of code that takes the lesson you just learned one step further. Apply It sections offer inside information and pointers that can be used to enhance the functionality of your code.

Extra

An Extra section provides additional information about the task you just accomplished. Extra sections often contain interesting tips and useful tricks to make working with HTML easier and more efficient.

HTML:
Your visual blueprint for
designing effective Web pages

The Organization Of This Book

HTML: Your visual blueprint for designing effective Web pages contains 18 chapters and an appendix.

The first chapter, Getting Started, introduces you to the Internet, the World Wide Web and HTML. This chapter also helps you plan the content of your Web pages.

Chapter 2, Web Page Basics, shows you how to set up a Web page by adding items such as paragraphs and headings. In Chapter 3, Format Text, you will learn how to change the appearance of text to enhance the appearance of your Web page.

In Chapter 4, Add Images, and Chapter 5, Work With Images, you will learn how to add images to your Web pages and adjust the images to suit your needs.

Chapter 6, entitled Create Links, teaches you how to connect your Web pages to information on the Internet, such as other Web pages and files.

Chapters 7 through 10 provide detailed explanations of how to create and use several types of popular Web page elements, including tables, forms and frames. You will also learn how to create more entertaining Web pages by adding sounds and videos.

Chapter 11, Using JavaScript, and Chapter 12, Web Page Extras, show you techniques for creating Web pages that are interactive and attractively designed.

Chapters 13 through 15 explain how to use style sheets to quickly format and lay out your HTML documents.

Chapter 16, entitled Publish Web Pages, guides you step-by-step through the process of making your pages available for other people to view on the World Wide Web.

Chapter 17, Introduction to XML, offers an overview of a technology that may eventually change the way we use HTML.

The final chapter contains a reference section. Once you become familiar with the contents of this book, you can use the HTML Tag Summary and Style Sheet Property Summary as a quick reference when creating your Web pages.

What Is On The CD-ROM Disc

The CD-ROM disc included in this book contains sample code from each of the lessons. This saves you from having to type the code and helps you quickly get started creating HTML documents.

The CD-ROM disc also contains several shareware and evaluation versions of programs that can be used to work with HTML. An e-version of the book and all the URLs mentioned in the book are also available on the disc.

THE INTERNET AND
THE WORLD WIDE WEB

THE INTERNET

The Internet is the largest computer network in the world. More than 275 million people worldwide use the Internet to access information, exchange electronic mail (e-mail), participate in discussion groups, shop online and more.

The Internet began as a military research project in the late 1960s. The U.S. Defense Department created a network, called ARPANET, that covered a large geographic area and that would continue to function even if part of the network failed. The improved, high-speed network that developed from this technology became the Internet. In the 1980s, most of the people accessing the Internet were scientists and researchers. In the early 1990s, companies began to offer Internet access to home users and the Internet eventually grew to include organizations and individuals around the world.

Structure of the Internet

The Internet consists of thousands of connected networks around the world. Each government agency, company, college, university and organization on the Internet is responsible for maintaining its own network. When you transfer information over the Internet, these organizations allow the information to pass through their networks.

Computers on the Internet use a collection of protocols called Transmission Control Protocol/Internet Protocol (TCP/IP) to transfer information over the Internet. A protocol is a set of rules controlling the transfer of information between computers. TCP/IP allows computers on the Internet to communicate as if they were directly connected.

Internet Connections

There are several types of Internet connections available. The type of connection a person uses determines how quickly information can transfer to their computer.

Modem	Cable Modem
Most people use a modem to connect to the Internet through a regular telephone line. When browsing the Web using a modem, a modem speed of 56 Kilobits per second (Kbps) is recommended.	A cable modem can transfer information at a speed of up to 3,000 Kbps using the same type of cable that attaches to a television set. Contact your local cable company to determine if they offer cable Internet services.
ISDN	**DSL**
An Integrated Services Digital Network (ISDN) line is a digital phone line offered by telephone companies in most cities. An ISDN line can transfer information at speeds from 64 Kbps to 128 Kbps.	Digital Subscriber Line (DSL) is a service offered by telephone companies in many cities. DSL can transfer information at speeds from 1,000 Kbps to 9,000 Kbps.

THE WORLD WIDE WEB

The World Wide Web is a part of the Internet and consists of a huge collection of documents stored on computers around the world. The World Wide Web is commonly known as the Web.

A Web page is a document on the Web. Web pages can include information such as text, images, pictures, sounds and videos. Web pages are stored on computers called Web servers. Once a Web page is stored on a Web server, it is available for other people to view. Many colleges, universities, government agencies, companies, organizations and individuals create and maintain collections of Web pages called Web sites.

Web Browsers

A Web browser is a program that lets people view and explore information on the Web. A Web browser retrieves Web pages and other files from a Web server and displays them on a user's computer. Two popular Web browsers include Microsoft Internet Explorer and Netscape Navigator. The latest versions of these two programs are available at the www.microsoft.com/ie and www.netscape.com Web sites.

URLs

Each page on the Web has a unique address, called a Uniform Resource Locator (URL). People can instantly display a Web page if they know its URL.

A Web page URL consists of a scheme, a Web server name and a path. The scheme identifies the language, or protocol, used to access the Web page. The Web server name, also known as a domain name, indicates the name of the server that stores the Web page. The path specifies the location of the Web page on the Web server. For example, the URL http://www.maran.com/books/promo.html has the scheme http, the Web server name www.maran.com and the path /books/promo.html.

Although Web page URLs usually use the http (HyperText Transfer Protocol) scheme, there are other common schemes used on the Internet. For example, an FTP (File Transfer Protocol) site uses the ftp scheme. FTP sites store files that people can download.

Links

Web pages contain highlighted text or images, called links, that connect to other pages on the Web. Links are also known as hyperlinks. Links save people from having to enter the URL of each Web page they want to view. This allows people to move through a vast amount of information by jumping from one Web page to another.

Links are easily identifiable on a Web page. Text links appear underlined and in color and image links usually display a colored border.

PLAN YOUR WEB SITE

Plan your Web site carefully before you begin creating individual Web pages for the site. This can help you avoid having to reorganize your Web pages later. Decide how many Web pages you want your Web site to contain and consider how the pages will link to each other.

When users visit your Web site, they should be able to easily access information in the site. Sketching a layout of your Web site can help you organize the site. Once you have determined a layout for your Web site, you should plan the main page, or home page, for the site.

WEB SITE LAYOUT

Linear

A linear layout organizes Web pages in a straight line. This layout is ideal for Web pages that people should read in a specific order, such as pages containing a story or step-by-step instructions. Each Web page in a linear layout usually links to the next and previous page in the Web site, allowing users to move both forwards and backwards through the Web pages.

Web

A Web layout has no overall structure. Each Web page in a Web layout contains multiple links to other Web pages in the site. This type of layout is ideal for Web pages that people do not need to read in a specific order.

Hierarchical

In a hierarchical layout, all Web pages branch off a home page. The home page provides a general summary of the information in the Web site, while the other pages provide more specific information. Users select links on the home page to access Web pages that contain detailed information.

Combination

Combining layouts provides you with the most flexibility when creating your Web site. For example, combining a hierarchical layout with a Web layout lets you create a Web site that has an overall structure, yet still allows users to randomly browse through information.

PLAN YOUR HOME PAGE

The home page is usually the first page users will see when they visit your Web site. The home page is usually named index.html or index.htm.

Your home page should contain a brief summary of your Web site, a table of contents and links that users can select to quickly access information of interest.

When planning your home page, make sure the home page will work well with the layout of your Web site. For example, the home page for a Web site with a linear layout should contain a link to the next page in the Web site.

STEPS FOR CREATING WEB PAGES

Before you begin creating Web pages, decide what you want to accomplish with your Web pages. Decide on a main topic or theme for your Web pages and then determine the type of information you want to include. For example, you may want to create personal Web pages to share information about your family, interests or

an area of expertise. Commercial Web pages allow you to share information about your business, such as press releases, online catalogs and job postings.

Use the following steps as a guideline to help you create attractive and useful Web pages.

STEPS FOR CREATING WEB PAGES

1) Gather Information

Collect the information you want to include on your Web pages, such as text, images, diagrams and contact numbers. Make sure that the information you gather directly relates to the main topic or theme of your Web pages and will appeal to your intended audience. When gathering information, keep in mind that you must have permission to use any information that you did not create yourself.

2) Organize Information

Divide the information you gathered into different sections. Each section will be a separate Web page that discusses a different concept or idea. Each Web page should contain enough information to fill a single screen. When organizing your information, consider that adding many elements to a single Web page will increase the file size of the Web page. A larger file size can increase the time it takes for the page to transfer to a user's computer.

3) Enter Information

Enter the text you want to appear on your Web pages in a text editor or word processor. Each Web page should be a separate document. Then add HTML tags to convert the documents into Web pages. HTML tags also allow you to add elements such as images, sounds, videos and tables to your Web pages.

4) Add Links

Adding links is an important step in creating Web pages. Links are text or images that users can select to display pages on the Web. The links you add to your Web pages should allow users to easily move through information of interest.

5) Publish Web Pages

When you finish creating your Web pages, you can have a company called a Web Presence Provider (WPP) publish your pages. A Web presence provider will store your pages on a Web server to make the pages available for other people to view. After you publish your Web pages, you should test the pages to ensure that your links work properly and your information appears the way you want.

WEB PAGE CONTENT CONSIDERATIONS

W hen creating your Web pages, carefully consider the content you want the pages to include. The following suggestions can help you design well-organized Web pages that contain useful information.

EMPHASIZE IMPORTANT INFORMATION

Always display the most important information at the top of each Web page. Some users will not scroll through a Web page to read all the information. These users will miss important information if you do not display the information at the top of each page.

Including a table of contents that contains links to important areas of a Web page can help users access any important information that appears later in the page.

Headings can also help emphasize important information, allowing users to glance through a Web page and quickly find information of interest.

CONSIDER FILE SIZES

When determining the content for a Web page, keep in mind that including many elements with large file sizes, such as embedded sounds and videos, will increase the time it takes for the page to transfer to a user's computer. Whenever possible, you should limit the number of large files you include on a Web page.

AVOID "UNDER CONSTRUCTION" LABELS

Avoid using "under construction" labels for Web pages that are not complete. Users will become frustrated when they visit a Web page that does not contain useful information. You should not make Web pages available on the Web until the pages are complete.

PAGE LENGTH

Web pages should not be too short or too long. If a Web page is shorter than half a screen of information, try to combine the information with another page. If a Web page is longer than five screens, you may want to break up the page into several shorter pages. Users may become frustrated if they have to scroll through a large amount of information on a page.

AVOID SPECIFIC WEB BROWSER INSTRUCTIONS

Avoid giving detailed instructions on how to perform a task using a specific Web browser. People who use a different Web browser may not be able to perform the task using the instructions you provide. For example, adding a Web page to your list of favorite Web pages is a different process in Internet Explorer than in Netscape Navigator.

COPYRIGHT CONSIDERATIONS

If you plan to use text, images or other information you did not create, make sure that the information is not copyrighted. Many pages on the Web offer information and images that do not have copyright restrictions. If you want to use copyrighted information, you must obtain permission from the author.

INCLUDE CONTACT INFORMATION

Always include your name and e-mail address on Web pages you create. This allows users to contact you if they have questions or comments.

When providing contact information, you may want to set up a separate e-mail address for messages about your Web site. This will help prevent your personal e-mail inbox from becoming overloaded with queries and comments if your Web site becomes popular.

WEB PAGES WITHOUT IMAGES

Some users turn off the display of images to browse the Web more quickly, while others use Web browsers that cannot display images. Always design your Web pages so that users who do not see images will still get valuable information from your pages. It is also important to make sure you provide text that will appear for users who do not see images.

USE WARNINGS

If your Web pages display information that some users may consider offensive, place a warning on your home page. When users visit your Web site, they will see the warning and can then decide if they want to view your Web pages.

If you want to prevent certain people, such as children, from entering your Web site, ask your Web presence provider about setting up password protection for your Web site.

PROVIDE A FAQ

A FAQ is a list of Frequently Asked Questions about a topic. A FAQ can help answer questions that people have about your Web pages and help prevent people from sending you e-mail messages asking the same questions over and over.

If you are not sure what information to include in your FAQ, you may want to wait until you have received some questions and comments about your site before creating the FAQ. This can help you determine what information to include in your FAQ.

INTRODUCTION TO HTML

HyperText Markup Language (HTML) is a computer language used to create Web pages. Web pages are HTML documents that consist of text and HTML tags. HTML documents have the .html or .htm extension (example: index.html). A Web browser interprets the tags in an HTML document and displays the document as a Web page.

You do not have to create different HTML documents for different types of computers. Any computer that has a Web browser installed can display Web pages, including computers running a Unix, Windows or Macintosh operating system.

HTML ESSENTIALS

HTML Tags

HTML tags tell a Web browser about the structure and formatting of a Web page. Each tag gives a specific instruction and is surrounded by angle brackets < >. Most tags have an opening tag and a closing tag that affect the text between the tags. Some tags have only an opening tag. Although tags can display uppercase or lowercase letters, most people use uppercase letters to make the tags stand out.

Many tags have attributes that offer options for the tags. For example, the <FONT> tag has a COLOR attribute that lets you change the color of text. Most attributes have values that you can specify. For example, the COLOR attribute can have a value of red.

Web Browsers

A Web page may not look the same when displayed in different Web browsers. Each Web browser may interpret HTML tags differently and many Web browsers do not support all of the features of HTML.

Some companies that make Web browsers, such as Netscape and Microsoft, have developed additional tags and attributes that Web browsers made by other companies may not understand. When a Web browser does not understand a tag or attribute, the information is usually ignored. These tags and attributes are commonly known as extensions and are not part of the HTML standard.

HTML Versions

There are several versions of HTML. The HTML specification, also known as the HTML standard, is constantly evolving and a new version of HTML is released every few years. Each version offers new features to give people more control when creating Web pages. An organization called the World Wide Web Consortium (W3C) regulates the versions of HTML. HTML version 4.01 is the latest version of HTML. Information about HTML and its versions is available at the www.w3.org Web site.

VIEW HTML CODE FOR A WEB PAGE

Viewing the HTML code used to create other pages on the Web is a great way to get ideas for your own Web pages. You can find popular Web sites at the coolsiteoftheday.com and www.100hot.com Web sites.

Viewing the HTML code for a Web page allows you to see how other people use HTML tags. This can help you learn HTML techniques and can improve your understanding of HTML.

Examining the HTML code used to create other Web pages can also help you troubleshoot problems you are experiencing with your own Web pages. For example, if you are having a problem creating a table, you should view the HTML code for a Web page that contains a table.

Although you can use the HTML code you find on the Web, you should never copy any content on a Web page without first obtaining permission from the author.

VIEW HTML CODE FOR A WEB PAGE

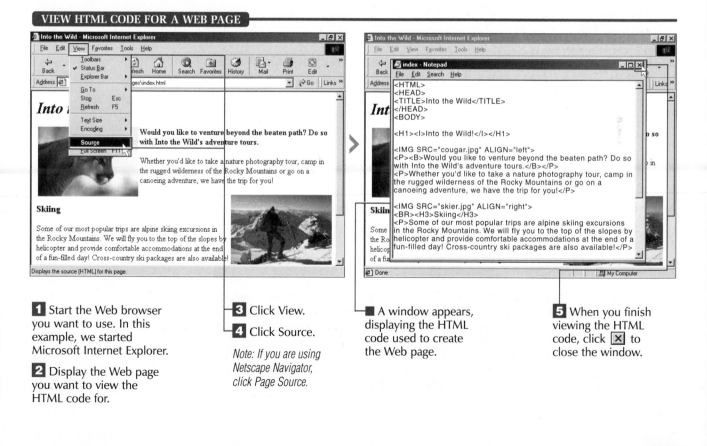

■1 Start the Web browser you want to use. In this example, we started Microsoft Internet Explorer.

■2 Display the Web page you want to view the HTML code for.

■3 Click View.

■4 Click Source.

Note: If you are using Netscape Navigator, click Page Source.

■ A window appears, displaying the HTML code used to create the Web page.

■5 When you finish viewing the HTML code, click ☒ to close the window.

SET UP A WEB PAGE

Many people create Web pages using a text editor or word processor. Popular text editors include Notepad for Windows and SimpleText for Macintosh. Microsoft WordPad, Microsoft Word and Corel WordPerfect are popular word processors.

To set up a Web page, first enter the text you want to appear on the Web page. Do not format the text using your text editor or word processor. You must add HTML tags to change the appearance of the text. HTML tags provide instructions for formatting and structuring a Web page.

After entering the text for the Web page, save the Web page as a text document and specify a name for the Web page with the .html or .htm extension. A Web page name can contain letters and numbers, but no spaces. The main Web page, or home page, in a Web site is usually named index.html.

1 Start the word processor or text editor you want to use to create a Web page. In this example, we started Microsoft WordPad.

2 Type the text you want to appear on the Web page.

3 Click 🖫 to save the Web page.

■ The Save As dialog box appears.

4 Type a name for the Web page. Make sure you add the .html or .htm extension to the Web page name.

*Note: A Web page name can contain letters and numbers, but no spaces. The home page is usually named **index.html**.*

■ This area shows the location where the program will store the Web page. You can click this area to change the location.

Extra

If the text you type for your Web page scrolls off the screen in your text editor or word processor, you can have the program wrap the text to fit on the screen. To wrap text in Microsoft WordPad, select the View menu and then click Options. In the Options dialog box, click the Wrap to window option (○ changes to ⊙).

HTML editors such as BBEdit and HomeSite are also useful for creating Web pages. These programs offer menus and toolbars that help you add HTML tags to a Web page. BBEdit is available at the www.barebones.com Web site and HomeSite is available at the www.allaire.com Web site.

Visual editors such as Microsoft FrontPage and HoTMetaL PRO allow you to create Web pages without having to enter HTML tags. Visual editors enter the tags for you as you create a Web page. Microsoft FrontPage is available at the www.microsoft.com/frontpage Web site and HoTMetaL PRO is available at the www.softquad.com Web site.

---

5 Click this area to list the ways you can save the Web page.

6 Click Text Document.

7 Click Save.

■ A dialog box appears, stating that all formatting will be removed from the Web page.

8 Click Yes to save the Web page.

CONTINUED ▶

SET UP A WEB PAGE (CONTINUED)

There are some basic HTML tags you should add to every Web page you create.

The <HTML> tag should appear at the top of every Web page you create. This tag identifies your document as a Web page containing HTML code.

The <HEAD> tag should appear directly below the <HTML> tag. The <HEAD> tag identifies the head section of your Web page, which contains information about the Web page, such as the title.

The <TITLE> tag appears in the head section of your Web page. This tag allows you to give your Web page a descriptive title. Every Web page you create must have a title. Titles usually appear in the title bar of a Web browser window. A Web page title should contain only letters and numbers.

The <BODY> tag identifies the body section of your Web page. This section contains the content of your Web page, including the text, images, tables and other elements you want users to see when they visit your Web page.

SET UP A WEB PAGE (CONTINUED)

```
index - WordPad
File  Edit  View  Insert  Format  Help

<HTML>

Fruit and Flowers, Inc.
No garden? No problem!
Our special, patented fertilizer lets you grow lush flowers and healthy fruit
INDOORS!
Grow beautiful, exotic flowers and impress your friends!
Grow your own fruit and save on your grocery bills!
Our fruit selection includes:
Popular berries such as strawberries, raspberries and blueberries.
Exotic fruit such as mangos, papayas and kiwis.
Our flower selection includes:
Seasonal plants such as poinsettias, holly and mistletoe.
Tropical flowers such as orchids, birds of paradise and yellow jasmine.

</HTML>
```

```
index - WordPad
File  Edit  View  Insert  Format  Help

<HTML>
<HEAD>

</HEAD>

Fruit and Flowers, Inc.
No garden? No problem!
Our special, patented fertilizer lets you grow lush flowers and healthy fruit
INDOORS!
Grow beautiful, exotic flowers and impress your friends!
Grow your own fruit and save on your grocery bills!
Our fruit selection includes:
Popular berries such as strawberries, raspberries and blueberries.
Exotic fruit such as mangos, papayas and kiwis.
Our flower selection includes:
Seasonal plants such as poinsettias, holly and mistletoe.
Tropical flowers such as orchids, birds of paradise and yellow jasmine.

</HTML>
```

HTML TAGS

1 Type **<HTML>** before all the text on the Web page.

2 Type **</HTML>** after all the text on the Web page.

Note: Although the <HTML> and </HTML> tags are optional, it is considered proper form to include these tags.

HEAD TAGS

1 Type **<HEAD>** directly below the <HTML> tag.

2 Press Enter twice.

3 Type **</HEAD>**.

Note: Although the <HEAD> and </HEAD> tags are optional, it is considered proper form to include these tags.

Extra

The HTML standard also includes the `<!DOCTYPE>` tag, which you can use to provide Web browsers with information about the HTML version you are using. For example, type **<!DOCTYPE HTML PUBLIC "-//W3C// DTD HTML 4.0 Transitional//EN">** before the `<HTML>` tag on your Web page to indicate that you are using HTML version 4.0. Many people choose not to use the `<!DOCTYPE>` tag since Web browsers do not require the tag.

To save time when creating Web pages, create a document that contains only the `<HTML>`, `<HEAD>`, `<TITLE>` and `<BODY>` tags and then use this document as a template each time you create a Web page.

Choose the title for your Web page carefully since search tools will use the title to catalog the Web page. A search tool is a Web site that helps people quickly find information on the Web. When users enter words in a search tool, your Web page will be more likely to appear in the search results if the words match your Web page title. Popular search tools include Infoseek (www.infoseek.com) and Yahoo! (www.yahoo.com).

TITLE TAGS

1 Type **<TITLE>** directly below the `<HEAD>` tag.

2 Type the title of the Web page, using only letters and numbers.

3 Type **</TITLE>**.

BODY TAGS

1 Type **<BODY>** directly below the `</HEAD>` tag.

2 Type **</BODY>** directly above the `</HTML>` tag.

Note: Although the `<BODY>` and `</BODY>` tags are optional, it is considered proper form to include these tags.

DISPLAY A WEB PAGE IN A WEB BROWSER

D isplaying your Web page in a Web browser allows you to see how the page will appear on the Web.

You need a Web browser program, such as Microsoft Internet Explorer or Netscape Navigator, before you can display your Web page in a Web browser. The most recent versions of Microsoft Internet Explorer and Netscape Navigator are available at the www.microsoft.com/ie and www.netscape.com Web sites.

A Web browser reads the HTML code used to create a Web page and then displays the Web page in the Web browser window. As a Web browser reads

each section of HTML code, the browser displays the resulting information on the screen. This means that a Web browser can display part of a Web page before it has completely finished processing the page.

You should display your Web page in several Web browsers to see how each browser will display the Web page. Each Web browser may interpret HTML tags differently and many Web browsers do not support all of the features of HTML. For example, the most current Web browsers may recognize HTML features offered by the latest version of HTML, while older Web browsers may not be able to properly display the features.

DISPLAY A WEB PAGE IN A WEB BROWSER

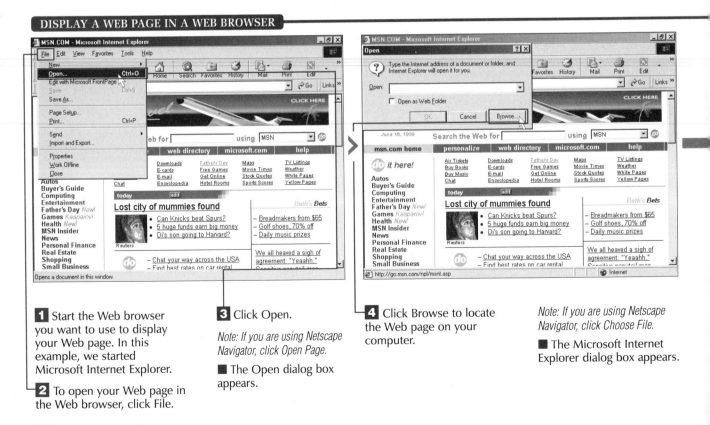

1 Start the Web browser you want to use to display your Web page. In this example, we started Microsoft Internet Explorer.

2 To open your Web page in the Web browser, click File.

3 Click Open.

Note: If you are using Netscape Navigator, click Open Page.

■ The Open dialog box appears.

4 Click Browse to locate the Web page on your computer.

Note: If you are using Netscape Navigator, click Choose File.

■ The Microsoft Internet Explorer dialog box appears.

Extra

If you cannot locate the Web page you want to open, you may not have saved your Web page properly. When saving a Web page, you must save the page in a text only format and add the .html or .htm extension to the name of the page (example: index.html).

Refreshing the display of your Web page in a Web browser allows you to see how changes you have made will appear on the Web. After saving your changes in your text editor or word processor, click the Refresh or Reload button in the Web browser window. If you are using Netscape Navigator, you may need to press the Shift key as you click Reload to properly refresh your Web page.

Although Microsoft Internet Explorer and Netscape Navigator are the two most popular Web browsers, there are several other Web browsers available, such as Opera and Lynx. For information on Opera, visit the www.opera.com Web site. For information on Lynx, visit the lynx.browser.org Web site.

Even though you can display your Web page in a Web browser on your computer, other people on the Web will not be able to view your page until you transfer the page to a Web presence provider's Web server.

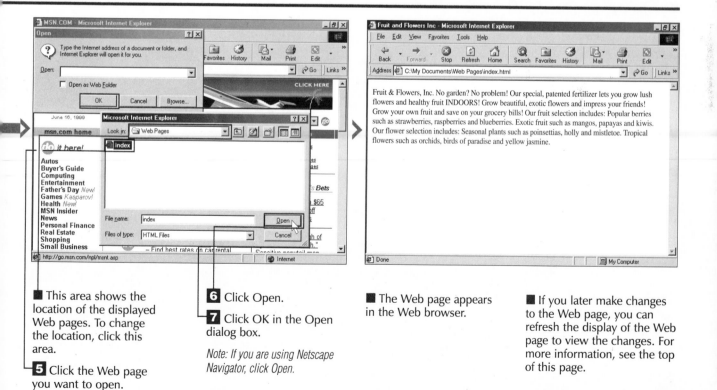

■ This area shows the location of the displayed Web pages. To change the location, click this area.

5 Click the Web page you want to open.

6 Click Open.

7 Click OK in the Open dialog box.

Note: If you are using Netscape Navigator, click Open.

■ The Web page appears in the Web browser.

■ If you later make changes to the Web page, you can refresh the display of the Web page to view the changes. For more information, see the top of this page.

START A NEW PARAGRAPH

Web browsers usually ignore returns you type in your text editor or word processor. You must use the <P> tag to specify where you want each new paragraph to begin.

When you display your Web page in a Web browser, a blank line will appear between each paragraph you defined using the <P> tag. This can help improve the layout and readability of your Web page by breaking up large sections of text.

By default, most Web browsers left align paragraphs. The ALIGN attribute allows you

to change the alignment of a paragraph. Paragraphs can be left aligned, centered, right aligned or justified. Changing the alignment of an important paragraph can make the paragraph stand out from the rest of your Web page.

While the ALIGN attribute is still supported by Web browsers, the use of *style sheets* is now preferred. For information on style sheets, see page 196.

START A NEW PARAGRAPH

```
<HTML>
<HEAD>
<TITLE>Bird Watchers Home Page</TITLE>
</HEAD>
<BODY>

Bird Watchers' Home Page

<P>Bird watchers appreciate the beauty and wonder of birds and are always
interested in ways to attract them. One of the best and easiest ways to draw
birds to your backyard is to build a birdhouse. On this page, I will introduce you
to steps you can follow to construct a simple birdhouse</P>

<P>STEP ONE: PREPARATION
Decide what type of bird you want to attract. This decision will influence the
dimensions of the house and the size of the entry hole you must drill. Purchase
wood. Pine is my favorite choice, but other types of wood are fine</P>

<P>STEP TWO: CUTTING, DRILLING AND ASSEMBLING
Cut the boards so they are the correct dimensions. Select the board that will be
the front of the house and drill an entry hole. Carefully assemble the boards to
complete the house</P>

</BODY>
```

Bird Watchers' Home Page

Bird watchers appreciate the beauty and wonder of birds and are always interested in ways to attract them. One of the best and easiest ways to draw birds to your backyard is to build a birdhouse. On this page, I will introduce you to steps you can follow to construct a simple birdhouse.

STEP ONE: PREPARATION Decide what type of bird you want to attract. This decision will influence the dimensions of the house and the size of the entry hole you must drill. Purchase wood. Pine is my favorite choice, but other types of wood are fine.

STEP TWO: CUTTING, DRILLING AND ASSEMBLING Cut the boards so they are the correct dimensions. Select the board that will be the front of the house and drill a hole. Carefully assemble the boards to complete the house.

1 Type **<P>** in front of each paragraph on your Web page.

2 Type **</P>** after each paragraph on your Web page.

Note: Although the </P> tag is optional, you should include the tag if you plan to format paragraphs using style sheets. For information on style sheets, see page 196.

■ The Web browser displays a blank line between each paragraph.

Apply It

Web browsers automatically wrap the text in your paragraphs to fit on a user's screen. To make sure certain words or phrases on your Web page will appear on the same line, use the <NOBR> tag.

TYPE THIS:

```
<P>Controlling line breaks is
useful when you want certain
text, such as a name or phone
number, to always appear on
the same line. In this example,
I want the text <NOBR>Jennifer
Stewart, Sales Director</NOBR>
to always appear on the same
line.</P>
```

RESULT:

Controlling line breaks is useful when you want certain text, such as a name or phone number, to always appear on the same line. In this example, I want the text Jennifer Stewart, Sales Director to always appear on the same line.

---

align - WordPad

File Edit View Insert Format Help

```
<HTML>
<HEAD>
<TITLE>Change Paragraph Alignment</TITLE>
</HEAD>
<BODY>

<P ALIGN="left">This paragraph is left aligned. This paragraph is left aligned.
This paragraph is left aligned. This paragraph is left aligned.</P>

<P ALIGN="center">This paragraph is centered. This paragraph is centered.
This paragraph is centered. This paragraph is centered.</P>

<P ALIGN="right">This paragraph is right aligned. This paragraph is right
aligned. This paragraph is right aligned. This paragraph is right aligned.</P>

<P ALIGN="justify"> This paragraph is justified. This paragraph is justified. This
paragraph is justified. This paragraph is justified. This paragraph is justified. This
paragraph is justified. This paragraph is justified. This paragraph is justified. </P>

</BODY>
</HTML>
```

For Help, press F1   NUM

Change Paragraph Alignment - Microsoft Internet Explorer

File Edit View Favorites Tools Help

Back Forward Stop Refresh Home Search Favorites History Mail Print Edit

Address C:\My Documents\Web Pages\align.html

This paragraph is left aligned. This paragraph is left aligned. This paragraph is left aligned. This paragraph is left aligned.

This paragraph is centered. This paragraph is centered. This paragraph is centered. This paragraph is centered.

This paragraph is right aligned. This paragraph is right aligned. This paragraph is right aligned. This paragraph is right aligned.

This paragraph is justified. This paragraph is justified. This paragraph is justified. This paragraph is justified. This paragraph is justified. This paragraph is justified. This paragraph is justified. This paragraph is justified.

Done   My Computer

CHANGE PARAGRAPH ALIGNMENT

1 In the <P> tag for the paragraph you want to change, type **ALIGN="?"** replacing **?** with the way you want to align the paragraph (**left**, **center**, **right** or **justify**).

■ The Web browser displays the paragraph with the alignment you specified.

START A NEW LINE

The <BR> tag instructs a Web browser to stop placing text and other elements on the current line and begin a new line in the Web browser window. The <BR> tag is useful for separating short lines of text, such as the text in a mailing address or poem. Unlike many HTML tags, the <BR> tag does not have a closing tag.

Many people use the <BR> tag to place inline elements on their own line in a Web browser window. An inline element is an element that Web browsers do not automatically place on a new line, such as an image.

The <BR> tag is also useful for increasing the amount of space between elements on your Web page. For example, you can use the <BR> tag to add an extra blank line between two paragraphs. Each <BR> tag you add will create an extra line of space.

START A NEW LINE

```
<HTML>
<HEAD>
<TITLE>My Poetry Web Page</TITLE>
</HEAD>
<BODY>

My Poetry Web Page
<P>Welcome to my Web page. Here, you will find a collection of my favorite
poems.
Here is the poem of the week:</P>

<BR>The sun
<BR>shines through the
<BR>green leaves
<BR>reflecting the sunshine
<BR>of this summer afternoon.
<BR>I watch the child
<BR>as he runs through the sprinkler
<BR>carefree, without worries
<BR>remembering my own childhood
<BR>memories I can always carry with me.

</BODY>
</HTML>
```

My Poetry Web Page

Welcome to my Web page. Here, you will find a collection of my favorite poems. Here is the poem of the week:

The sun
shines through the
green leaves
reflecting the sunshine
of this summer afternoon.
I watch the child
as he runs through the sprinkler
carefree, without worries
remembering my own childhood
memories I can always carry with me.

1 Type **
** in front of each element you want to appear on a new line.

■ You can type several <BR> tags in a row to increase the amount of vertical space that will appear between two elements.

■ The Web browser displays each element you specified on a new line.

INSERT BLANK SPACES

Web browsers usually ignore extra spaces you add when typing the text for your Web page. If you want to include extra blank spaces on your Web page, use the   code.

Inserting blank spaces is useful for indenting the first line of a paragraph. Blank spaces are also useful for separating elements on a Web page, such as images. For example, inserting blank spaces between two images that are side by side can prevent the images from appearing as one large image.

The   code creates a non-breaking space. Typing   instead of typing a space between two words will prevent the words from being separated when a Web browser wraps text to fit in the window. This ensures that the two words will always appear on the same line.

The <PRE> tag provides another way to add blank spaces to your Web page. The <PRE> tag retains the spacing of text you type. For information on the <PRE> tag, see page 22.

INSERT BLANK SPACES

index - WordPad

File Edit View Insert Format Help

```
<HTML>
<HEAD>
<TITLE>Classical Music Composers</TITLE>
</HEAD>
<BODY>

<H2>Beethoven</H2>
<P>        Ludwig van Beet
Bonn, Germany in 1770. He spent most of his life in Vienna, where he earned
teaching piano and selling his compositions.
<BR>One of the most fascinating aspects of Beethoven's life was his triumph o
struck him during adulthood. In fact, he composed some of his most powerful w
hearing.</P>

</BODY>
</HTML>
```

Classical Music Composers - Microsoft Internet Explorer

File Edit View Favorites Tools Help

Back Forward Stop Refresh Home Search Favorites History Mail Print Edit

Address C:\My Documents\Web Pages\index.html

Beethoven

Ludwig van Beethoven was born in Bonn, Germany in 1770. He spent most of his life in Vienna, where he earned a living giving concerts, teaching piano and selling his compositions. One of the most fascinating aspects of Beethoven's life was his triumph over deafness, which struck him during adulthood. In fact, he composed some of his most powerful works after losing his hearing.

1 Type ** ** where you want a blank space to appear on your Web page.

■ To insert multiple blank spaces, type ** ** for each space you want to add.

■ The Web browser displays the blank space(s) on your Web page.

ADD A HEADING

Headings can help organize the information on your Web page. Users can glance through the headings on a Web page to quickly find information of interest.

There are six heading levels you can use. Heading level 1 (<H1>) is the largest and heading level 6 (<H6>) is the smallest. <H1>, <H2> and <H3> headings are often used for Web page and section titles, while <H5> and <H6> headings are useful for disclaimers and copyright information. <H4> headings are usually the same size as the main text on a Web page.

Using heading levels consistently will help your users understand the structure of your Web page. To avoid confusion, do not use more than three different heading levels on a single Web page.

Web browsers usually display headings in bold text with a blank line above and below the headings. In most Web browsers, headings are left aligned by default. The ALIGN attribute allows you to change the alignment of a heading. While the ALIGN attribute is still supported by Web browsers, the use of *style sheets* is now preferred. For information on style sheets, see page 196.

ADD A HEADING

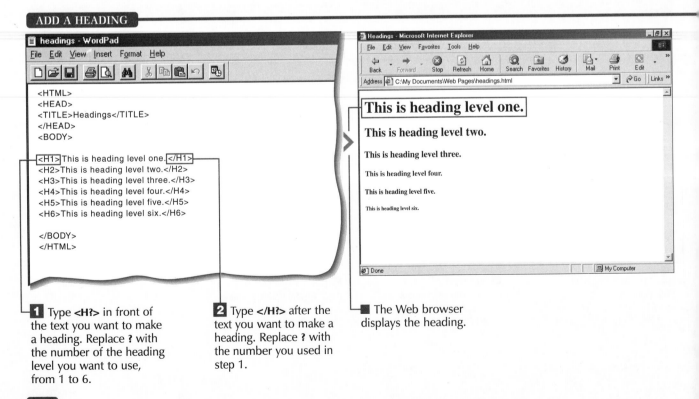

1 Type **<H?>** in front of the text you want to make a heading. Replace **?** with the number of the heading level you want to use, from 1 to 6.

2 Type **</H?>** after the text you want to make a heading. Replace **?** with the number you used in step 1.

■ The Web browser displays the heading.

Apply It

Style sheets can help ensure that the headings on your Web page are consistent. A style sheet allows you to specify in one location how you want your headings to appear. For example, you can have all of your <H2> headings display the Arial font and appear underlined.

TYPE THIS:

```
<HEAD>
<TITLE>My Web Page</TITLE>
<STYLE>
H2 {font-family:"Arial";text-decoration:underline}
</STYLE>
</HEAD>
<BODY>
<H2>First Heading</H2>
Style sheets can help you quickly format the headings on your Web page.
<H2>Second Heading</H2>
This saves you from having to format each heading separately.
```

RESULT:

First Heading

Style sheets can help you quickly format the headings on your Web page.

Second Heading

This saves you from having to format each heading separately.

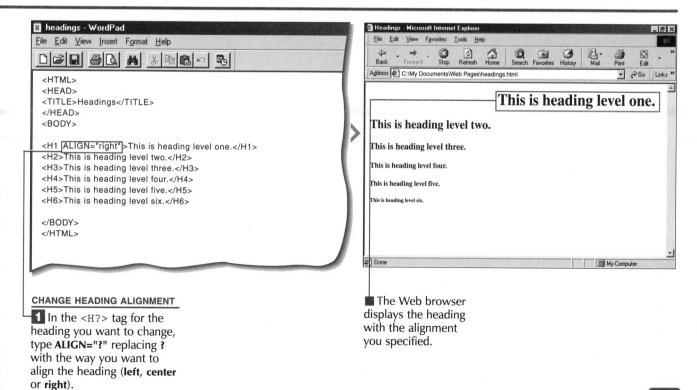

CHANGE HEADING ALIGNMENT

1 In the <H?> tag for the heading you want to change, type **ALIGN="?"** replacing **?** with the way you want to align the heading (**left**, **center** or **right**).

■ The Web browser displays the heading with the alignment you specified.

PREFORMAT TEXT

A Web browser usually ignores blank lines and extra spaces you add when typing the text for your Web page. The <PRE> tag instructs Web browsers to retain the spacing you type in your text editor or word processor.

Web browsers display preformatted text in a monospaced font, such as Courier. A monospaced font is a font in which each character takes up the same amount of space. When typing text you plan to preformat, use a monospaced font so you can see the text exactly as it will appear in a Web browser.

When you preformat text, Web browsers will display the text with the exact spacing you typed and will not wrap the text to fit the size of the Web browser window. When typing the text, consider that long lines of text may extend beyond the edge of a Web browser window.

Preformatting text is useful for creating simple tables. Type the text for your table using spaces to line up columns of information and then preformat the text. Using spaces instead of tabs will help ensure that your table will appear correctly in a Web browser, since the spacing for tabs differs among Web browsers.

PREFORMAT TEXT

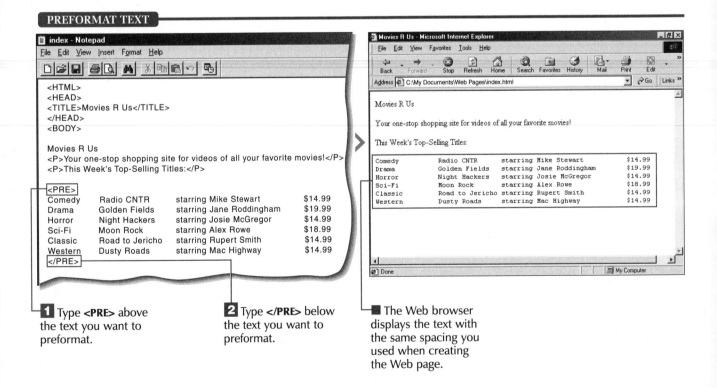

1 Type **<PRE>** above the text you want to preformat.

2 Type **</PRE>** below the text you want to preformat.

■ The Web browser displays the text with the same spacing you used when creating the Web page.

ADD A COMMENT

Adding a comment to your Web page is useful when you want to remind yourself to update a section of text or indicate why you used a specific tag.

A comment must be surrounded by the <!-- and --> delimiters. Web browsers will ignore the information between the delimiters. This prevents your comments from appearing on your Web page.

Keep in mind that users who view the HTML code for your Web page will be able to read your comments. For information on viewing the HTML code for a Web page, see page 9.

Many people use comment delimiters to hide Web page elements that some Web browsers may not recognize. For example, using comment delimiters allows you to hide *JavaScript* on your Web pages from older Web browsers that do not recognize JavaScript. This will prevent the Web browsers from displaying the code for the JavaScript on your Web page. For information on JavaScript, see page 158.

Comment delimiters are also useful for temporarily hiding parts of your Web page. For example, you may want to temporarily hide a Web page area you are revising.

ADD A COMMENT

```
<HTML>
<HEAD>
<TITLE>Fruit and Flowers Inc</TITLE>
</HEAD>
<BODY>

<H3>Fruit & Flowers, Inc.</H3>

<P><I>No garden? No problem!</I></P>
<P>Our special, patented fertilizer lets you grow lush flowers and healthy f
INDOORS!</P>

<P>Our fruit selection includes:
<BR>Popular berries such as strawberries, raspberries and blueberries.
<BR>Exotic fruit such as mangos, papayas and kiwis.</P>

<!-- Add a photograph of berries here -->

<P>Our flower selection includes:
```

Fruit & Flowers, Inc.

No garden? No problem!

Our special, patented fertilizer lets you grow lush flowers and healthy fruit INDOORS!

Our fruit selection includes:
Popular berries such as strawberries, raspberries and blueberries.
Exotic fruit such as mangos, papayas and kiwis.

Our flower selection includes:
Seasonal plants such as poinsettias, holly and mistletoe.
Tropical flowers such as orchids and yellow jasmine.

1 Type <!-- where you want to add a comment.

2 Type the comment.

3 Type --> to complete the comment.

Note: Adding a space on either side of a comment can help make the comment easier to read.

■ The Web browser does not display the comment on your Web page.

INSERT SPECIAL CHARACTERS

The HTML standard provides character encoding for adding special characters to your Web page. This lets you include characters that do not appear on your keyboard, such as mathematical symbols.

When adding a special character, you must specify a number code or name code for the character. A number code, also known as a numeric character reference, consists of an ampersand, a number sign, the number of the character and a semicolon. A name code, also known as a character entity reference, consists of an ampersand, the name of the character and a semicolon.

Character encoding is useful for adding characters that are used for creating Web pages, such as <, >, " and &, since Web browsers may misinterpret these characters. For example, Web browsers may interpret the < character as the beginning of a tag.

Keep in mind that the appearance of special characters you add to your Web page will depend on the configuration of a user's Web browser and the fonts installed on the user's computer.

INSERT SPECIAL CHARACTERS

```
index - WordPad
File  Edit  View  Insert  Format  Help

<HTML>
<HEAD>
<TITLE>Music</TITLE>
</HEAD>
<BODY>

<H1><CENTER>Jay's Music Web Site</CENTER></H1>

<P ALIGN="center">&#169; 2000 Jay Hanlen</P>

<P>Welcome to my Web site, where you can download many songs th
recorded.
<BR>I have been a musician for more than 20 years, and through this
learned to play many instruments.
<BR>Today, I create sound files for my Web site and perform in a ba

</BODY>
```

Music - Microsoft Internet Explorer
File Edit View Favorites Tools Help

Back   Forward   Stop   Refresh   Home   Search   Favorites   History   Mail   Print   Edit

Address C:\My Documents\Web Pages\index.html

Jay's Music Web Site

© 2000 Jay Hanlen

Welcome to my Web site, where you can download many songs that I have recorded.
I have been a musician for more than 20 years, and through this time, I have learned to play many instruments.
Today, I create sound files for my Web site and perform in a band.

Done   My Computer

1 Click where you want the special character to appear on your Web page.

2 Type the number code or name code for the special character (example: © or ©).

■ The Web browser displays the special character.

■ The appearance of the special character depends on a user's Web browser and font settings.

SPECIAL CHARACTERS

CHARACTER	NUMBER CODE	NAME CODE	CHARACTER	NUMBER CODE	NAME CODE	CHARACTER	NUMBER CODE	NAME CODE
"	&#34;	&quot;	¿	&#191;	&iquest;	à	&#224;	&agrave;
&	&#38;	&amp;	À	&#192;	&Agrave;	á	&#225;	&aacute;
<	&#60;	&lt;	Á	&#193;	&Aacute;	â	&#226;	&acirc;
>	&#62;	&gt;	Â	&#194;	&Acirc;	ã	&#227;	&atilde;
¡	&#161;	&iexcl;	Ã	&#195;	&Atilde;	ä	&#228;	&auml;
¢	&#162;	&cent;	Ä	&#196;	&Auml;	å	&#229;	&aring;
£	&#163;	&pound;	Å	&#197;	&Aring;	æ	&#230;	&aelig;
¤	&#164;	&curren;	Æ	&#198;	&AElig;	ç	&#231;	&ccedil;
¥	&#165;	&yen;	Ç	&#199;	&Ccedil;	è	&#232;	&egrave;
¦	&#166;	&brvbar;	È	&#200;	&Egrave;	é	&#233;	&eacute;
§	&#167;	&sect;	É	&#201;	&Eacute;	ê	&#234;	&ecirc;
¨	&#168;	&uml;	Ê	&#202;	&Ecirc;	ë	&#235;	&euml;
©	&#169;	&copy;	Ë	&#203;	&Euml;	ì	&#236;	&igrave;
ª	&#170;	&ordf;	Ì	&#204;	&Igrave;	í	&#237;	&iacute;
«	&#171;	&laquo;	Í	&#205;	&Iacute;	î	&#238;	&icirc;
¬	&#172;	&not;	Î	&#206;	&Icirc;	ï	&#239;	&iuml;
®	&#174;	&reg;	Ï	&#207;	&Iuml;	ð	&#240;	&eth;
¯	&#175;	&macr;	Ð	&#208;	&ETH;	ñ	&#241;	&ntilde;
°	&#176;	&deg;	Ñ	&#209;	&Ntilde;	ò	&#242;	&ograve;
±	&#177;	&plusmn;	Ò	&#210;	&Ograve;	ó	&#243;	&oacute;
²	&#178;	&sup2;	Ó	&#211;	&Oacute;	ô	&#244;	&ocirc;
³	&#179;	&sup3;	Ô	&#212;	&Ocirc;	õ	&#245;	&otilde;
´	&#180;	&acute;	Õ	&#213;	&Otilde;	ö	&#246;	&ouml;
µ	&#181;	&micro;	Ö	&#214;	&Ouml;	÷	&#247;	&divide;
¶	&#182;	&para;	×	&#215;	&times;	ø	&#248;	&oslash;
·	&#183;	&middot;	Ø	&#216;	&Oslash;	ù	&#249;	&ugrave;
¸	&#184;	&cedil;	Ù	&#217;	&Ugrave;	ú	&#250;	&uacute;
¹	&#185;	&sup1;	Ú	&#218;	&Uacute;	û	&#251;	&ucirc;
º	&#186;	&ordm;	Û	&#219;	&Ucirc;	ü	&#252;	&uuml;
»	&#187;	&raquo;	Ü	&#220;	&Uuml;	ý	&#253;	&yacute;
¼	&#188;	&frac14;	Ý	&#221;	&Yacute;	þ	&#254;	&thorn;
½	&#189;	&frac12;	Þ	&#222;	&THORN;	ÿ	&#255;	&yuml;
¾	&#190;	&frac34;	ß	&#223;	&szlig;			

EMPHASIZE TEXT

To emphasize text on your Web page, you may want to bold, italicize, underline or strike out the text.

The <B> tag allows you to bold text, while the <I> tag lets you italicize text. Bold text and italicized text are useful for introducing new terms and highlighting important phrases on a Web page.

The <U> tag underlines text. Be careful when underlining text since users may mistake the text for a *link*. For information on links, see page 74.

The <STRIKE> tag places a line through text. The <STRIKE> tag is useful for showing changes to information on a Web page. For example, striking out a price is an effective way to show the price has been reduced.

While the <U> and <STRIKE> tags are still supported by Web browsers, the use of *style sheets* is now preferred. For information on style sheets, see page 196.

EMPHASIZE TEXT

```
<HTML>
<HEAD>
<TITLE>Bold or Italicize Text</TITLE>
</HEAD>
<BODY>

<P>This is plain text.</P>

<P><B>This is bold text.</B></P>

<P><I>This is italicized text.</I></P>

</BODY>
</HTML>
```

This is plain text.

This is bold text.

This is italicized text.

BOLD TEXT

1 Type **<B>** in front of the text you want to bold.

2 Type **</B>** after the text you want to bold.

ITALICIZE TEXT

1 Type **<I>** in front of the text you want to italicize.

2 Type **</I>** after the text you want to italicize.

■ The Web browser bolds or italicizes the text.

Extra

The <STRONG> and <EM> tags are also used to emphasize text. In most Web browsers, the <STRONG> tag bolds text and the <EM> tag italicizes text.

Example:

```
<STRONG>This is bold text.</STRONG>
<EM>This is italicized text.</EM>
```

The <DEL> and <INS> tags let you emphasize updates to your Web page. Use the <DEL> tag to emphasize text you want to delete and the <INS> tag to emphasize text you have inserted. Internet Explorer currently strikes out deleted text and underlines inserted text. The <INS> and <DEL> tags are not yet fully supported by Web browsers.

Example:

```
Network Cards: <DEL>$50</DEL><INS>$45</INS>
```

The <CENTER> tag allows you to horizontally center text on your Web page. Centering short lines of text, such as a title or heading, can help emphasize the text.

Example:

```
<H1><CENTER>Fruit & Flowers Inc.</CENTER></H1>
```

Using multiple tags lets you combine effects when emphasizing text. For example, using both the <I> tag and the <U> tag lets you italicize and underline text at the same time. When typing the end tags, switch the order of the tags.

Example:

```
<H1><I><U>How to Create an Exciting Web Page</U></I></H1>
```

```
<HTML>
<HEAD>
<TITLE>Underline or Strike Out Text</TITLE>
</HEAD>
<BODY>

<P>This is plain text.</P>

<P><U>This text is underlined.</U></P>

<P><STRIKE>You can strike out this text.</STRIKE></P>

</BODY>
</HTML>
```

This is plain text.

This text is underlined.

~~You can strike out this text.~~

UNDERLINE TEXT

1 Type **<U>** in front of the text you want to underline.

2 Type **</U>** after the text you want to underline.

STRIKE OUT TEXT

1 Type **<STRIKE>** in front of the text you want to strike out.

2 Type **</STRIKE>** after the text you want to strike out.

■ The Web browser displays a line under or through the text.

SUPERSCRIPT OR SUBSCRIPT TEXT

The <SUP> tag allows you to create superscript text on your Web page. Superscript text appears slightly higher than the main text on a Web page.

The <SUB> tag allows you to create subscript text on your Web page. Subscript text appears slightly lower than the main text on a Web page.

Superscript text and subscript text are ideal for displaying mathematical equations, chemical formulas, scientific notation and footnotes.

Web browsers may display superscript and subscript text in a smaller font size than the main text on your Web page. If you are using a small font size for the main text, your superscript and subscript text may be too small to read. Make sure the font size you use is large enough to properly display superscript and subscript text. For information on changing the font size of text, see page 30.

SUPERSCRIPT OR SUBSCRIPT TEXT

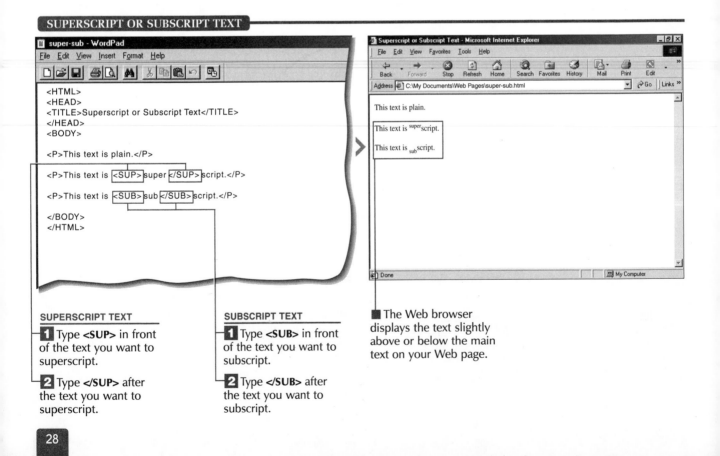

SUPERSCRIPT TEXT

1 Type **<SUP>** in front of the text you want to superscript.

2 Type **</SUP>** after the text you want to superscript.

SUBSCRIPT TEXT

1 Type **<SUB>** in front of the text you want to subscript.

2 Type **</SUB>** after the text you want to subscript.

■ The Web browser displays the text slightly above or below the main text on your Web page.

CHANGE THE FONT

Using the <FONT> tag with the FACE attribute lets you change the font for a section of text on your Web page. You can specify a new font by name, such as Courier, or by type, such as monospace.

If you specify a font by name, you should specify more than one font in case your first choice is not available on a user's computer. One of the fonts you specify should be a common font, such as Arial, to increase the probability that a computer will display one of your font choices.

Keep in mind that the fonts you specify may not appear the way you expect on some computers,

since some users can set their Web browsers to display the fonts they prefer.

Although there is no limit to the number of fonts your Web page can contain, using multiple fonts may distract users and draw their attention away from the content of your Web page.

While the <FONT> tag and FACE attribute are still supported by Web browsers, the use of *style sheets* is now preferred. For information on style sheets, see page 196.

For information on style sheets, see page 196.

CHANGE THE FONT

```
<HTML>
<HEAD>
<TITLE>Classical Music Composers</TITLE>
</HEAD>
<BODY>

<H2>Beethoven</H2>
<P><FONT FACE="Old English Text MT, Arial">Ludwig van Beethoven wa
Bonn, Germany in 1770. He spent most of his life in Vienna, where he ea
living giving concerts, teaching piano and selling his compositions.
<BR>One of the most fascinating aspects of Beethoven's life was his triu
deafness, which struck him during adulthood. In fact, he composed some
most powerful works after losing his hearing.</FONT></P>

<H2>Bach</H2>
<P>Johann Sebastian Bach was born into a family of musicians in 1685 in
Eisenach, Germany. Bach's works include church organ and choral music
for chamber orchestras and over 200 cantatas. Although he was more re
as an organist during his lifetime, Bach's compositions influenced ma
```

Beethoven

Ludwig van Beethoven was born in Bonn, Germany in 1770. He spent most of his life in Vienna, where he earned a living giving concerts, teaching piano and selling his compositions.
One of the most fascinating aspects of Beethoven's life was his triumph over deafness, which struck him during adulthood. In fact, he composed some of his most powerful works after losing his hearing.

Bach

Johann Sebastian Bach was born into a family of musicians in 1685 in Eisenach, Germany. Bach's works include church organ and choral music, music for chamber orchestras and over 200 cantatas. Although he was more respected as an organist during his lifetime, Bach's compositions influenced many later composers, including Beethoven and Mozart.

1 Type **<FONT FACE="?">** in front of the text you want to change. Replace **?** with the name (example: Arial) or type (**serif**, **sans-serif** or **monospace**) of the font you want to use.

Note: To specify more than one font name, separate each name with a comma (,) and a space.

2 Type **</FONT>** after the text you want to change.

■ The Web browser displays the text in the font you specified.

CHANGE THE FONT SIZE

The SIZE attribute lets you change the size of text on your Web page. Increasing the size of text makes the text easier to read, while decreasing the size of text allows you to fit more information on a screen.

Using the SIZE attribute with the <BASEFONT> tag allows you to change the size of all the text on your Web page. Using the SIZE attribute with the <FONT> tag lets you change the size of a section of text.

There are 7 font sizes you can use. The smallest font size is 1 and the largest font size is 7. Keep in mind that the font size you use may not appear the way you expect on some computers, since some users can set their Web browsers to display the font size they prefer.

While the SIZE attribute, <BASEFONT> tag and <FONT> tag are still supported by Web browsers, the use of *style sheets* is now preferred. For information on style sheets, see page 196.

CHANGE THE FONT SIZE

```
<HTML>
<HEAD>
<TITLE>Fruit and Flowers Inc</TITLE>
</HEAD>
<BODY>

<BASEFONT SIZE="5">
<P>Fruit and Flowers, Inc.</P>
<P>Our fruit selection includes:
<BR>Popular berries such as strawberries, raspberries and blueberries.
<BR>Exotic fruit such as mangos, papayas and kiwis.</P>
<P>Our flower selection includes:
<BR>Seasonal plants such as poinsettias, holly and mistletoe.
<BR>Tropical flowers such as orchids, birds of paradise and yellow jasmin

</BODY>
</HTML>
```

Fruit and Flowers, Inc.

Our fruit selection includes:
Popular berries such as strawberries, raspberries and blueberries.
Exotic fruit such as mangos, papayas and kiwis.

Our flower selection includes:
Seasonal plants such as poinsettias, holly and mistletoe.
Tropical flowers such as orchids, birds of paradise and yellow jasmine.

CHANGE ALL TEXT

1 Type **<BASEFONT SIZE="?">** before the text on your Web page. Replace ? with a number from 1 to 7. The smallest font size is 1; the largest font size is 7.

■ The Web browser displays the text in the new size.

■ The <BASEFONT> tag will not affect the size of headings on your Web page. For information on headings, see page 20.

30

Extra

The <BIG> and <SMALL> tags also allow you to change the size of text. The <BIG> tag makes text larger than the surrounding text and the <SMALL> tag makes text smaller than the surrounding text.

Example:

```
<P>Come to our <BIG>SALE</BIG> on Saturday!
<SMALL>No rain checks.</SMALL></P>
```

Changing the size of individual characters on your Web page can create interesting text effects. For example, you may want to show a large capital letter at the beginning of a paragraph.

Example:

```
<P><FONT SIZE="7">O</FONT>nce upon a time,
there was a princess who lived in a castle.</P>
```

In most cases, the 7 font sizes correspond to the point sizes in the following chart. The point sizes may vary depending on the configuration of a user's Web browser.

Font Size 1	8 points
Font Size 2	10 points
Font Size 3	12 points
Font Size 4	14 points
Font Size 5	18 points
Font Size 6	24 points
Font Size 7	36 points

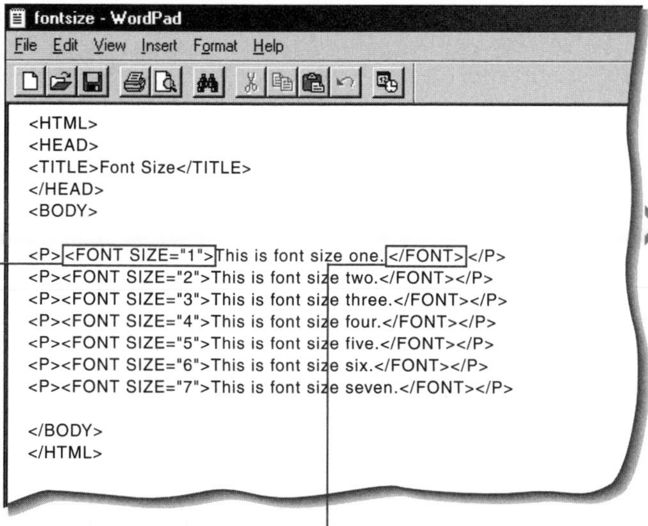

```
<HTML>
<HEAD>
<TITLE>Font Size</TITLE>
</HEAD>
<BODY>

<P><FONT SIZE="1">This is font size one.</FONT></P>
<P><FONT SIZE="2">This is font size two.</FONT></P>
<P><FONT SIZE="3">This is font size three.</FONT></P>
<P><FONT SIZE="4">This is font size four.</FONT></P>
<P><FONT SIZE="5">This is font size five.</FONT></P>
<P><FONT SIZE="6">This is font size six.</FONT></P>
<P><FONT SIZE="7">This is font size seven.</FONT></P>

</BODY>
</HTML>
```

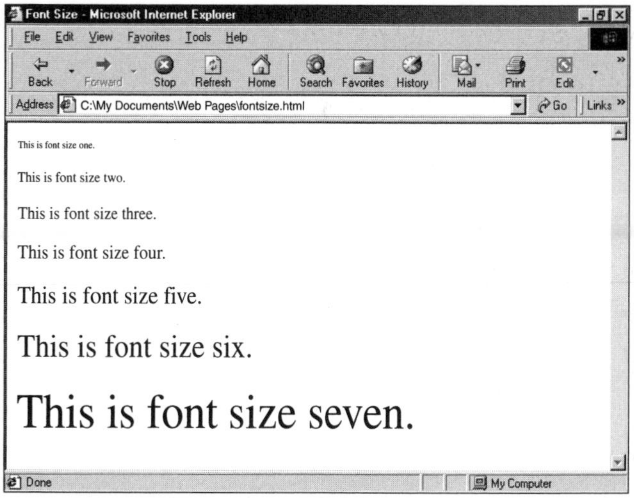

CHANGE SECTION OF TEXT

1 Type **<FONT SIZE="?">** in front of the text you want to change. Replace **?** with a number from 1 to 7. The smallest font size is 1; the largest font size is 7.

*Note: Type a plus (+) or minus (-) sign before the number to specify a size relative to the surrounding text. For example, type **+2** to make the text two sizes larger than the surrounding text.*

2 Type **</FONT>** after the text you want to change.

■ The Web browser displays the text in the new size.

CHANGE TEXT COLOR

C hanging the color of text on all or part of your Web page can help add visual interest to your Web page.

Using the TEXT attribute with the <BODY> tag allows you to change the color of all the text on your Web page. Using the COLOR attribute with the <FONT> tag lets you change the color of a section of text.

When changing the color of text, you must specify the name or hexadecimal value for the color you want to use. A hexadecimal value is a code that tells Web browsers which color to display. The code is composed of a number

sign (#) followed by the red, green and blue (RGB) components of the color. There are only 16 colors you can specify by name.

The colors you choose may not appear the way you expect on some computers since some users can set their Web browsers to display the colors they prefer.

While the TEXT attribute, COLOR attribute and the <FONT> tag are still supported by Web browsers, the use of *style sheets* is now preferred. For information on style sheets, see page 196.

CHANGE TEXT COLOR

index - Notepad

File Edit View Insert Format Help

```
<HTML>
<HEAD>
<TITLE>Fruit and Flowers Inc</TITLE>
</HEAD>
<BODY TEXT="#0000FF">

<P>Fruit and Flowers, Inc.</P>
<P>No garden? No problem!</P>
<P>Our special, patented fertilizer lets you grow lush flowers and health
INDOORS!</P>
<P>Grow beautiful, exotic flowers and impress your friends!
<BR>Grow your own fruit and save on your grocery bills!</P>

<P>Our fruit selection includes:
<BR>Popular berries such as strawberries, raspberries and blueberries.
<BR>Exotic fruit such as mangos, papayas and kiwis.</P>

<P>Our flower selection includes:
```

Fruit and Flowers Inc - Microsoft Internet Explorer

File Edit View Favorites Tools Help

Back Forward Stop Refresh Home Search Favorites History Mail Print Edit

Address C:\My Documents\Web Pages\index.html

Fruit and Flowers, Inc.

No garden? No problem!

Our special, patented fertilizer lets you grow lush flowers and healthy fruit INDOORS!

Grow beautiful, exotic flowers and impress your friends!
Grow your own fruit and save on your grocery bills!

Our fruit selection includes:
Popular berries such as strawberries, raspberries and blueberries.
Exotic fruit such as mangos, papayas and kiwis.

Our flower selection includes:
Seasonal plants such as poinsettias and mistletoe.
Tropical flowers such as orchids and yellow jasmine.

Done   My Computer

CHANGE ALL TEXT

1 In the <BODY> tag, type **TEXT="?"** replacing **?** with the name or hexadecimal value for the color you want to use (example: blue or #0000FF).

Note: For a list of colors, see the color chart at the front of this book.

■ The Web browser displays all the text on the Web page in the color you specified.

Note: The TEXT attribute will not affect the color of links on your Web page. For information on links, see page 74.

Extra

Here are the 16 colors you can specify by name and their corresponding hexadecimal values.

aqua	#00FFFF	navy	#000080
black	#000000	olive	#808000
blue	#0000FF	purple	#800080
fuchsia	#FF00FF	red	#FF0000
gray	#808080	silver	#C0C0C0
green	#008000	teal	#008080
lime	#00FF00	white	#FFFFFF
maroon	#800000	yellow	#FFFF00

Colors you specify using the COLOR attribute with the <FONT> tag will override colors you specify using the TEXT attribute with the <BODY> tag. This allows you to change the color of all the text on your Web page and also specify a different color for a section of text.

Example:
```
<BODY TEXT="navy">
<P>This text will be navy.</P>
<P><FONT COLOR="purple">This text
will be purple.</FONT></P>
<P>This text will be navy.</P>
```

---

textcolor - WordPad

File Edit View Insert Format Help

```
<HTML>
<HEAD>
<TITLE>Font Color</TITLE>
</HEAD>
<BODY>

<P><FONT COLOR="#FF0000">This text is red.</FONT></P>
<P><FONT COLOR="#0000FF">This text is blue.</FONT></P>
<P><FONT COLOR="#008000">This text is green.</FONT></P>
<P><FONT COLOR="#000000">This text is black.</FONT></P>
<P><FONT COLOR="#FFFF00">This text is yellow.</FONT></P>

</BODY>
</HTML>
```

Font Color - Microsoft Internet Explorer

File Edit View Favorites Tools Help

Back Forward Stop Refresh Home Search Favorites History Mail Print Edit

Address C:\My Documents\Web Pages\textcolor.html

This text is red.

This text is blue.

This text is green.

This text is black.

This text is yellow.

Done My Computer

CHANGE SECTION OF TEXT

1 Type **<FONT COLOR="?">** in front of the text you want to change. Replace **?** with the name or hexadecimal value for the color you want to use (example: red or #FF0000).

Note: For a list of colors, see the color chart at the front of this book.

2 Type **</FONT>** after the text you want to change.

■ The Web browser displays the text in the color you specified.

CHANGE BACKGROUND COLOR

The BGCOLOR attribute allows you to change the background color of your Web page.

When changing the background color, you must specify the name or hexadecimal value for the color you want to use. A hexadecimal value is a code that tells Web browsers which color to display. The code is composed of a number sign (#) followed by the red, green and blue (RGB) components of the color. There are only sixteen colors you can specify by name. For more information, see the top of page 33.

Choose a background color that works well with the color of your text. For example, red text on a blue background can be difficult to read.

Keep in mind that the colors you use may not appear the way you expect on some computers since some users can set their Web browsers to display the colors they prefer.

While the BGCOLOR attribute is still supported by Web browsers, the use of *style sheets* is now preferred. For information on style sheets, see page 196.

CHANGE BACKGROUND COLOR

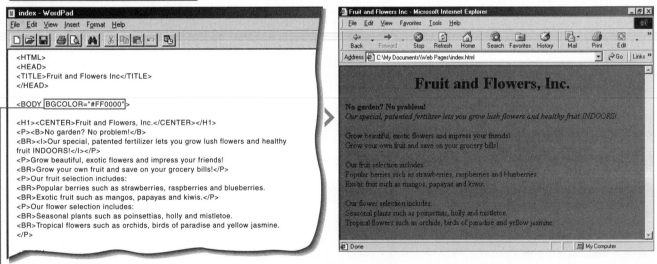

1 In the <BODY> tag, type **BGCOLOR="?"** replacing ? with the name or hexadecimal value for the color you want to use (example: red or #FF0000).

Note: For a list of colors, see the color chart at the front of this book.

■ The Web browser displays the background color you specified.

CHANGE THE MARGINS

Changing the margins of a Web page allows you to adjust the amount of space that appears between the contents of the page and the edges of a Web browser window. This can help improve the appearance of your Web page.

By default, most Web browsers display Web page margins of approximately 10 pixels. The LEFTMARGIN, RIGHTMARGIN, TOPMARGIN and BOTTOMMARGIN attributes allow you to change the margins that appear when a user displays your Web page in Internet Explorer. These attributes are not part of the HTML standard and are not supported by other Web browsers.

To change the margins that appear when a user displays your Web page in Netscape Navigator, use the MARGINWIDTH attribute to change the left and right margins and the MARGINHEIGHT attribute to change the top and bottom margins. These attributes are not part of the HTML standard and are only supported by Netscape Navigator.

You should specify the attributes for both Internet Explorer and Netscape Navigator to ensure that the margins you specify appear the way you want in both Web browsers.

CHANGE THE MARGINS

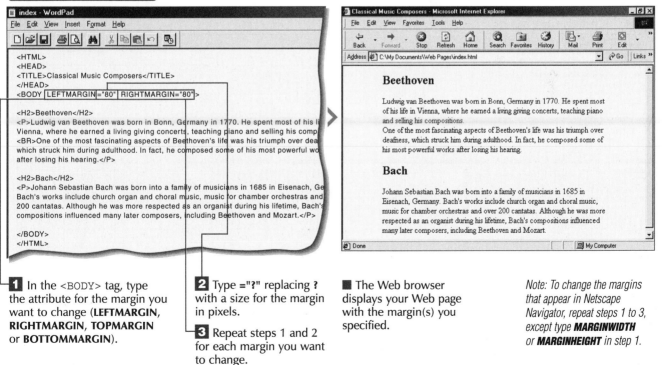

1 In the <BODY> tag, type the attribute for the margin you want to change (**LEFTMARGIN**, **RIGHTMARGIN**, **TOPMARGIN** or **BOTTOMMARGIN**).

2 Type ="?" replacing **?** with a size for the margin in pixels.

3 Repeat steps 1 and 2 for each margin you want to change.

■ The Web browser displays your Web page with the margin(s) you specified.

*Note: To change the margins that appear in Netscape Navigator, repeat steps 1 to 3, except type **MARGINWIDTH** or **MARGINHEIGHT** in step 1.*

USE A MONOSPACED FONT

Use the `<TT>`, `<CODE>`, `<KBD>` or `<SAMP>` tag to display text on your Web page in a monospaced font. A monospaced font is a font, such as Courier, in which each character takes up the same amount of space.

The `<TT>` tag is the most commonly used tag for displaying text in a monospaced font. This tag is useful for visually separating words or phrases that you want to emphasize but that do not have a specific purpose, such as instructions.

If your text has a specific purpose, use the `<CODE>`, `<KBD>` or `<SAMP>` tag to display the text in a monospaced font. Use the `<CODE>` tag for text

that represents computer code. The `<KBD>` tag is useful for emphasizing text you want users to type. Use the `<SAMP>` tag for displaying sample text, such as output from a computer program.

The text that uses the `<TT>`, `<CODE>`, `<KBD>` or `<SAMP>` tag will display the monospaced font that is set in a user's Web browser. The default monospaced font is usually Courier New.

Some Web browsers may apply additional formatting to text that uses the `<CODE>`, `<KBD>` or `<SAMP>` tag. For example, Web browsers may bold text that uses the `<KBD>` tag.

USE A MONOSPACED FONT

1 Before the text you want to display a monospaced font, type the tag you want to use (**<TT>**, **<CODE>**, **<KBD>** or **<SAMP>**).

2 After the text you want to display a monospaced font, type the end tag that corresponds to the tag you used in step 1 (**</TT>**, **</CODE>**, **</KBD>** or **</SAMP>**).

■ The Web browser displays the text in a monospaced font.

CREATE A BLOCK QUOTE

The <BLOCKQUOTE> tag allows you to create a block quote on your Web page. A block quote is a section of text that is separated from the rest of the text on your Web page. Block quotes usually appear indented from both sides of a Web page and are often used for displaying long quotations.

There is no limit to the amount of text you can include in a block quote. If a block quote is very long, consider using the <P> tag to break up the text in the block quote into paragraphs. For information on the <P> tag, see page 16.

If you want to display short quotations within a paragraph on your Web page, the HTML standard recommends using the <Q> tag. According to the HTML standard, placing the <Q> and </Q> tags around the text will enclose the text in quotation marks (""). The <Q> tag is not yet supported by most Web browsers.

CREATE A BLOCK QUOTE

mathquiz - WordPad

File Edit View Insert Format Help

```
<HTML>
<HEAD>
<TITLE>Madison Toys Limited</TITLE>
</HEAD>
<BODY>

<H3>MADISON WINS GOLD</H3>
<P>Madison Toys Limited is pleased to announce that The Super Math Quiz, one
our best-selling products, received the Gold Medal for Educational Toys. Upon
presenting the award, International Toy Conference chairperson J.C. White offe
the following words of praise:

<BLOCKQUOTE>
The Super Math Quiz is one of the finest educational toys I have ever seen. This
toy is both challenging and entertaining. It also reflects the latest research of
mathematics educators around the world.
</BLOCKQUOTE>

Madison Toys Limited is also pleased to announce that sales of The Super Math
tripled since the presentation of the Gold Medal.</P>
```

Madison Toys Limited - Microsoft Internet Explorer

File Edit View Favorites Tools Help

Back Forward Stop Refresh Home Search Favorites History Mail Print Edit

Address C:\My Documents\Web Pages\mathquiz.html

MADISON WINS GOLD

Madison Toys Limited is pleased to announce that The Super Math Quiz, one of our best-selling products, received the Gold Medal for Educational Toys. Upon presenting the award, International Toy Conference chairperson J.C. White offered the following words of praise:

> The Super Math Quiz is one of the finest educational toys I have ever seen. This toy is both challenging and entertaining. It also reflects the latest research of mathematics educators around the world.

Madison Toys Limited is also pleased to announce that sales of The Super Math Quiz have tripled since the presentation of the Gold Medal.

Done — My Computer

1 Type **<BLOCKQUOTE>** above the text you want to display as a block quote.

2 Type **</BLOCKQUOTE>** below the text you want to display as a block quote.

■ The Web browser displays the text as a block quote. Block quotes are usually indented from both sides of the Web page.

CREATE AN ORDERED LIST

An ordered list is useful for displaying items that are in a specific order, such as a set of instructions or a table of contents.

When creating an ordered list, there are two main tags you must use. The <OL> tag marks the beginning of the ordered list and the <LI> tag marks the beginning of each item in the list.

While there is no limit to the amount of text an item in an ordered list can contain, try to limit each item to one or two lines of text. This will help improve the readability of your list.

By default, a number (1, 2, 3...) appears beside each item in an ordered list. The TYPE attribute lets you change the number style of your list. While the TYPE attribute is still supported by Web browsers, the use of *style sheets* is now preferred. For information on style sheets, see page 196.

After creating an ordered list, you can add a new item to the ordered list at any time. A Web browser will automatically renumber the items in the list.

CREATE AN ORDERED LIST

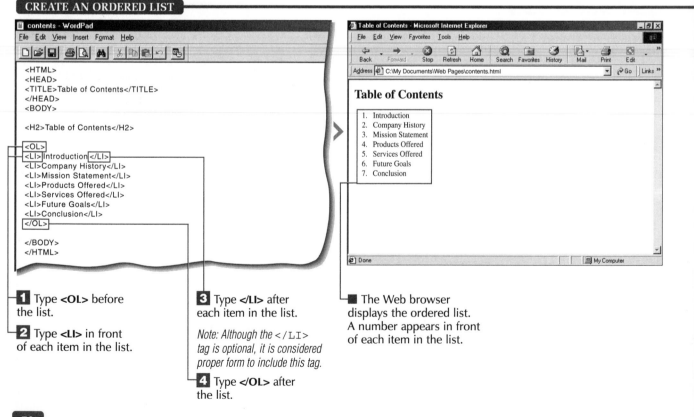

1 Type **<OL>** before the list.

2 Type **<LI>** in front of each item in the list.

3 Type **</LI>** after each item in the list.

Note: Although the </LI> tag is optional, it is considered proper form to include this tag.

4 Type **</OL>** after the list.

■ The Web browser displays the ordered list. A number appears in front of each item in the list.

Apply It

The START and VALUE attributes allow you to customize your ordered lists. The START value lets you start your ordered list with a number other than 1. The VALUE attribute lets you skip a number by assigning a new number to a list item.

TYPE THIS:

```
<H3>Honorable Mentions</H3>
<OL START="4">
<LI>P. Robinson</LI>
<LI>K. Faulkner and R. Benton</LI>
<LI VALUE="7">J. Smith</LI>
<LI>A. Canton</LI>
<LI>B. Gifford</LI>
</OL>
```

RESULT:

Honorable Mentions

4. P. Robinson
5. K. Faulkner and R. Benton
7. J. Smith
8. A. Canton
9. B. Gifford

---

contents - WordPad

File Edit View Insert Format Help

```
<HTML>
<HEAD>
<TITLE>Table of Contents</TITLE>
</HEAD>
<BODY>

<H2>Table of Contents</H2>

<OL TYPE="A">
<LI> Introduction </LI>
<LI>Company History</LI>
<LI>Mission Statement</LI>
<LI>Products Offered</LI>
<LI>Services Offered</LI>
<LI>Future Goals</LI>
<LI>Conclusion</LI>
</OL>

</BODY>
</HTML>
```

Table of Contents - Microsoft Internet Explorer

File Edit View Favorites Tools Help

Back · Forward · Stop · Refresh · Home · Search · Favorites · History · Mail · Print · Edit

Address C:\My Documents\Web Pages\contents.html

Table of Contents

A. Introduction
B. Company History
C. Mission Statement
D. Products Offered
E. Services Offered
F. Future Goals
G. Conclusion

Done   My Computer

CHANGE NUMBER STYLE

1 In the <OL> tag, type **TYPE="?"** replacing **?** with one of the following number styles.

A – A, B, C
a – a, b, c
I – I, II, III
i – i, ii, iii
1 – 1, 2, 3

■ The Web browser displays the ordered list with the number style you specified.

CREATE AN UNORDERED LIST

An unordered list is useful when you want to display items that are in no particular order, such as a list of products or Web sites.

When creating an unordered list, there are two main tags you must use. The <UL> tag marks the beginning of an unordered list and the <LI> tag marks the beginning of each item in the list.

To improve the readability of your unordered list, try to limit each item in the list to one or two lines of text.

Web browsers usually indent the items in an unordered list from the left edge of the Web browser window. A bullet appears beside each item in the list.

By default, Web browsers display unordered lists with the disc (●) bullet style. The TYPE attribute allows you to change the bullet style of your list. While the TYPE attribute is still supported by Web browsers, the use of *style sheets* is now preferred. For information on style sheets, see page 196.

For information on style sheets, see page 196.

CREATE AN UNORDERED LIST

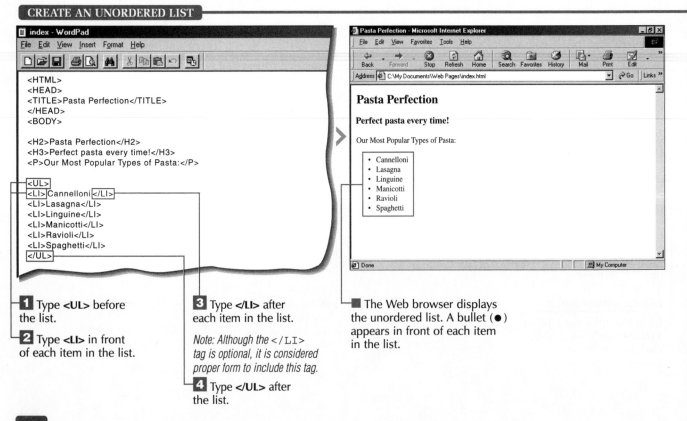

1 Type **<UL>** before the list.

2 Type **<LI>** in front of each item in the list.

3 Type **</LI>** after each item in the list.

Note: Although the </LI> tag is optional, it is considered proper form to include this tag.

4 Type **</UL>** after the list.

■ The Web browser displays the unordered list. A bullet (●) appears in front of each item in the list.

Apply It

An unordered list can use more than one bullet style. This is useful for grouping related items in the list. Using more than one bullet style may not work properly in Netscape Navigator.

TYPE THIS:

```
<UL TYPE="circle">
<LI>Apples</LI>
<LI TYPE="disc">Carrots</LI>
<LI>Pears</LI>
<LI>Oranges</LI>
<LI TYPE="disc">Corn</LI>
</UL>
```

RESULT:

○ Apples
● Carrots
○ Pears
○ Oranges
● Corn

---

index - WordPad

File Edit View Insert Format Help

```
<HTML>
<HEAD>
<TITLE>Pasta Perfection</TITLE>
</HEAD>
<BODY>

<H2>Pasta Perfection</H2>
<H3>Perfect pasta every time!</H3>
<P>Our Most Popular Types of Pasta:</P>

<UL TYPE="square">
<LI>Cannelloni</LI>
<LI>Lasagna</LI>
<LI>Linguine</LI>
<LI>Manicotti</LI>
<LI>Ravioli</LI>
<LI>Spaghetti</LI>
</UL>
```

Pasta Perfection - Microsoft Internet Explorer

File Edit View Favorites Tools Help

Back Forward Stop Refresh Home Search Favorites History Mail Print Edit

Address C:\My Documents\Web Pages\index.html

Pasta Perfection

Perfect pasta every time!

Our Most Popular Types of Pasta:

- Cannelloni
- Lasagna
- Linguine
- Manicotti
- Ravioli
- Spaghetti

Done   My Computer

CHANGE BULLET STYLE

1 In the <UL> tag, type **TYPE="?"** replacing **?** with the bullet style you want to use.

circle (○)

disc (●)

square (■)

■ The Web browser displays the list with the bullet style you specified.

CREATE A NESTED LIST

A nested list is a list within a list. Nested lists allow you to provide additional information about an item in a list. This lets you create lists with several levels of items, such as a project outline.

To create a nested list, add a new ordered or unordered list to an existing list on your Web page. A nested list can include both ordered and unordered lists. This is useful when only some items in your list are in a specific order. For information on ordered and unordered lists, see pages 38 to 41.

When creating a nested list in your text editor or word processor, indent each level so that you can clearly see the structure of the list. Web browsers will automatically indent each item in your list regardless of the indents you add when creating the list.

The formatting you can apply to a nested list is the same as the formatting for an ordered or unordered list. For example, you can change the start number, number style or bullet style as shown on pages 38 to 41.

CREATE A NESTED LIST

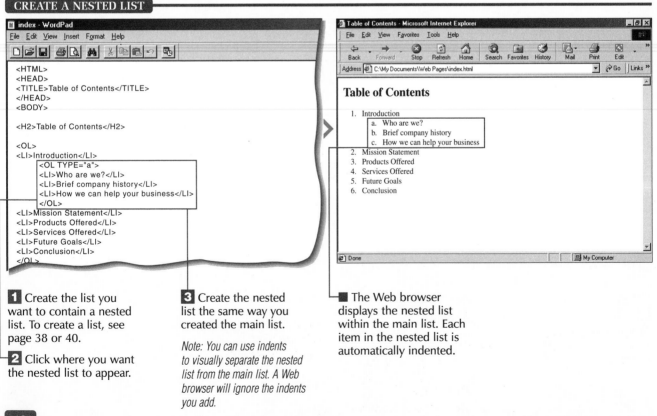

1 Create the list you want to contain a nested list. To create a list, see page 38 or 40.

2 Click where you want the nested list to appear.

3 Create the nested list the same way you created the main list.

Note: You can use indents to visually separate the nested list from the main list. A Web browser will ignore the indents you add.

■ The Web browser displays the nested list within the main list. Each item in the nested list is automatically indented.

CREATE A DEFINITION LIST

A definition list displays terms and their definitions. This type of list is ideal for a glossary.

There are three main tags used for creating definition lists. The <DL> tag marks the beginning of a definition list, the <DT> tag marks the beginning of each term in the list and the <DD> tag marks the beginning of each definition in the list.

Web browsers automatically left align the terms in a definition list. The definitions

appear below the terms and are indented from the left side of the Web page.

You do not have to alternate the <DT> and <DD> tags in a definition list. If you want to specify several terms for one definition, use the <DT> tag several times in a row. Similarly, to specify several definitions for one term, use the <DD> tag several times in a row.

CREATE A DEFINITION LIST

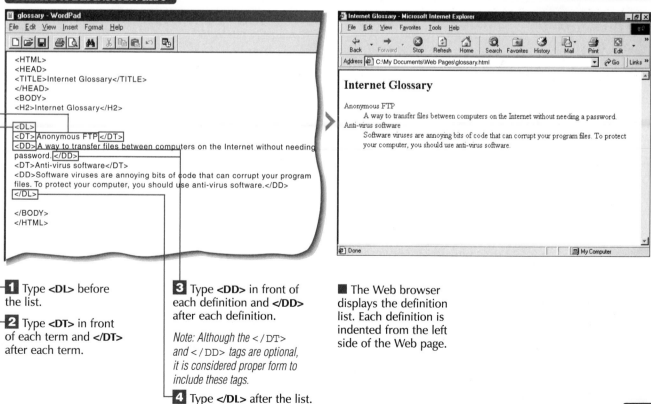

1 Type **<DL>** before the list.

2 Type **<DT>** in front of each term and **</DT>** after each term.

3 Type **<DD>** in front of each definition and **</DD>** after each definition.

Note: Although the </DT> and </DD> tags are optional, it is considered proper form to include these tags.

4 Type **</DL>** after the list.

■ The Web browser displays the definition list. Each definition is indented from the left side of the Web page.

ADD AN IMAGE

The `<IMG>` tag allows you to add an image to your Web page. Images are inline elements, which means Web browsers will automatically display images within the flow of text rather than on a new line.

There are many places that offer images you can use on your Web pages, such as Web sites and computer stores. You can also use a scanner to scan images into a computer or use an image editing program to create your own images. Make sure you have permission to use any images you did not create yourself.

Images increase the time it takes for a Web page to appear on a screen. Whenever possible, use images

with small file sizes since these images will transfer faster.

Images you add to your Web pages should be in the *GIF* or *JPEG* format. For more information on image formats, see page 56.

Some users have Web browsers that cannot display images, while others turn off the display of images to browse the Web more quickly. Use the `ALT` attribute to provide text that will be displayed if an image does not appear on your Web page. This will give users who do not see images information about the missing image.

ADD AN IMAGE

```
<HTML>
<HEAD>
<TITLE>Foster City Zoo</TITLE>
</HEAD>
<BODY>

<H1><CENTER>FOSTER CITY ZOO</CENTER></H1>

<IMG SRC="tiger.jpg">

</BODY>
</HTML>
```

1 Type **<IMG SRC="?">** where you want the image to appear, replacing **?** with the location and name of the image on your computer.

Note: For information on specifying the location and name of an image, see the top of page 45.

■ The Web browser displays the image on your Web page.

Extra

When adding an image, you must specify the location and name of the image on your computer. If an image you want to add to a Web page is stored in the same folder as the Web page, specify just the name of the image (example: castle.jpg). If an image is stored in a subfolder, specify the name of the subfolder and the name of the image (example: images/castle.jpg).

Example:

`<IMG SRC="images/tiger.gif">`

Many people add banners across the top of their Web pages to display information such as a company logo or advertisement. When adding a banner to your Web page, use an image that is approximately 450 pixels wide to ensure it will fit across the screen when displayed in a Web browser. Banner images are usually in the GIF format and are commonly 100 pixels high.

Example:

`<IMG SRC="banner.gif">`

Use the `<CENTER>` tag to horizontally center an image on your Web page. If the image is on the same line as another element, such as a line of text or another image, use the `<P>` or `<BR>` tag to have the image appear on its own line.

Example:

`<BR><CENTER><IMG SRC="logo.jpg"></CENTER>`

PROVIDE ALTERNATIVE TEXT

```
<HTML>
<HEAD>
<TITLE>Foster City Zoo</TITLE>
</HEAD>
<BODY>

<H1><CENTER>FOSTER CITY ZOO</CENTER></H1>

<IMG SRC="tiger.jpg" ALT="Image of Tiger">

</BODY>
</HTML>
```

FOSTER CITY ZOO

Image of Tiger

1 Type **ALT="?"** in the `<IMG>` tag, replacing **?** with the text you want to display if the image does not appear.

■ If the image does not appear, the Web browser will display the text you specified.

ADD A BACKGROUND IMAGE

Using the BACKGROUND attribute with the <BODY> tag allows you to add a background image to your Web page. A background image is a small image that repeats to fill an entire Web page. Interesting background images are available at the www.nepthys.com/textures and imagine.metanet.com Web sites.

When adding a background image, use an image that creates an interesting background design without overwhelming your Web page. A good background image will have invisible edges so when the image repeats to fill your Web page, it will have a seamless background.

Since background images increase the time it takes for a Web page to appear on a screen, you should try to use a background image with a small file size.

Make sure the background image you use does not affect the readability of your Web page. You may need to change the color of text to help make the text on your Web page easier to read. To change the color of text, see page 32.

While the BACKGROUND attribute is still supported by Web browsers, the use of *style sheets* is now preferred. For information on style sheets, see page 196.

ADD A BACKGROUND IMAGE

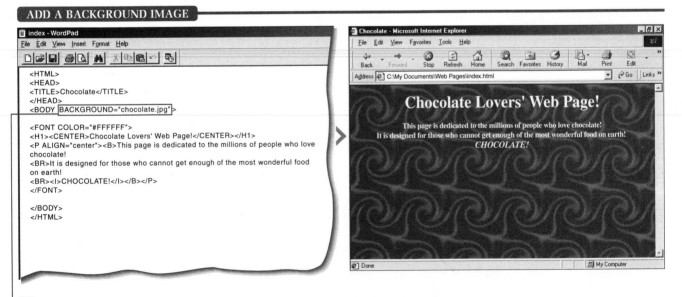

1 In the <BODY> tag, type **BACKGROUND="?"** replacing **?** with the location and name of the background image on your computer.

Note: For information on specifying the location and name of an image, see the top of page 45.

■ The Web browser repeats the image to fill the entire Web page.

ADD A BORDER

The BORDER attribute allows you to add a border to an image on your Web page. A border can make an image stand out and can improve the appearance of your Web page.

When adding a border, you must specify a thickness for the border in pixels. The border you add should be large enough to be visible, but small enough that it will not draw attention away from your image.

The BORDER attribute is also useful for removing the border that automatically appears around an

image link. To remove the border from an image link, specify a border thickness of 0 pixels. After removing the border, make sure that it is still clear that the image is a link, since many users expect image links to display borders. For more information on image links, see page 74.

While the BORDER attribute is still supported by Web browsers, the use of *style sheets* is now preferred. For information on style sheets, see page 196.

ADD A BORDER

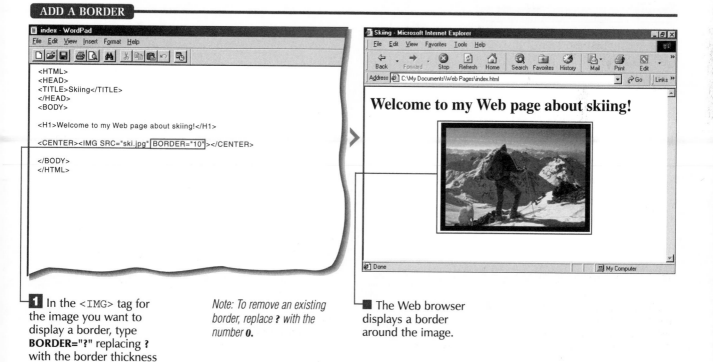

1 In the < IMG> tag for the image you want to display a border, type **BORDER="?"** replacing **?** with the border thickness you want to use in pixels.

Note: To remove an existing border, replace ? with the number 0.

■ The Web browser displays a border around the image.

WRAP TEXT AROUND AN IMAGE

The ALIGN attribute allows you to wrap text around an image. This can help give your Web page a professional look.

If you have already used the ALIGN attribute to align an image with text, you cannot wrap text around the image. For information on aligning an image with text, see page 50.

When wrapping text around an image, use the left or right value to specify how you want the text to wrap around the image. The left value places the image on the left side of the text and the right value places the image on the right side of the text.

If you want only some text to wrap around an image, use the CLEAR attribute with the <BR> tag to mark where you want to stop wrapping text around the image. Use the left, right or all value to have the text continue when the left margin, right margin or both margins are clear of images.

While the ALIGN and CLEAR attributes are still supported by Web browsers, the use of *style sheets* is now preferred. For information on style sheets, see page 196.

WRAP TEXT AROUND AN IMAGE

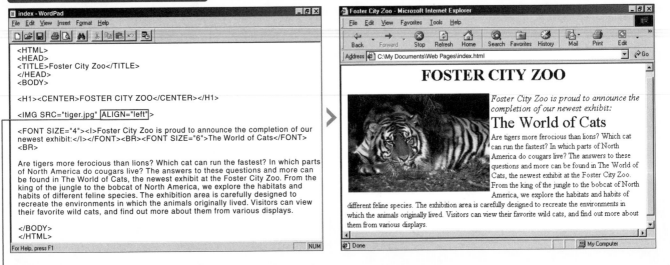

1 To wrap text around the right side of an image, type **ALIGN="left"** in the <IMG> tag for the image.

■ To wrap text around the left side of an image, type **ALIGN="right"** in the <IMG> tag for the image.

■ The Web browser displays the text wrapped around the image.

Apply It

The `ALIGN` attribute also lets you wrap text between two images on your Web page. The images must appear directly above the text you want to wrap between them.

TYPE THIS:

```
<IMG SRC="image1.gif" ALIGN="left">
<IMG SRC="image2.gif" ALIGN="right">
A Web browser will wrap this text between the two images. Wrapping text
between two images can improve the layout of your Web page.
```

RESULT:

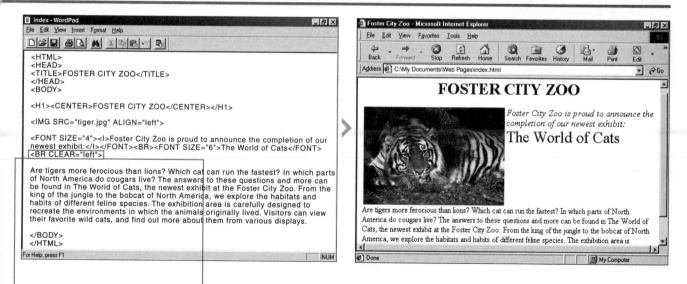

A Web browser will wrap this text between the two images. Wrapping text between two images can improve the layout of your Web page.

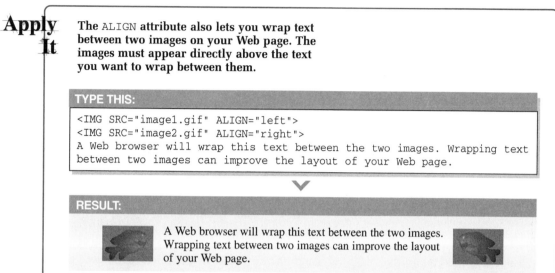

STOP TEXT WRAP

1 Click where you want to stop text from wrapping around an image.

2 Type **<BR CLEAR="?">** replacing **?** with the margin(s) you want to be clear of images before the text continues (**left**, **right** or **all**).

■ The Web browser stops the text wrap where you specified.

ALIGN AN IMAGE WITH TEXT

Use the ALIGN attribute with the top, middle or bottom value to vertically align an image with a line of text. By default, Web browsers align the bottom of an image with the bottom of a line of text.

If you have more than one image on the same line, the alignment you specify may not turn out the way you expect. View your Web page in several Web browsers to make sure you are satisfied with the results.

If you have wrapped text around an image, you cannot align the image with text. For

information on wrapping text around an image, see page 48.

While the ALIGN attribute is still supported by Web browsers, the use of *style sheets* is now preferred. For information on style sheets, see page 196.

The texttop, absmiddle and absbottom values produce results similar to the top, middle and bottom values, though they are not part of the HTML standard. The texttop, absmiddle and absbottom values are not supported by all Web browsers.

ALIGN AN IMAGE WITH TEXT

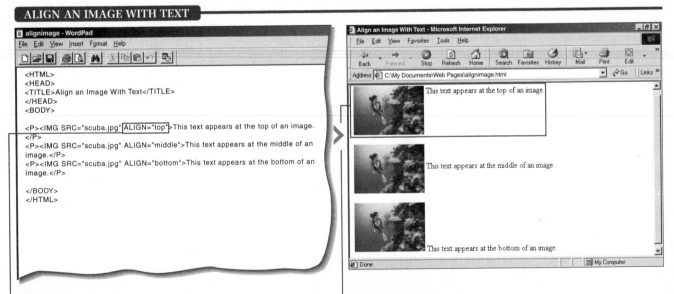

1 In the <IMG> tag for the image you want to align with text, type **ALIGN="?"** replacing **?** with the way you want to align the image with the text (**top, middle** or **bottom**).

■ The texttop, absmiddle and absbottom values allow you to achieve similar results, though some Web browsers may not recognize these values.

■ The Web browser aligns the image with the text.

ADD SPACE AROUND AN IMAGE

B y default, most Web browsers display only a few pixels of space between images and other Web page elements. Increasing the amount of space around an image can enhance the overall appearance of your Web page.

Adding space between an image and the surrounding text will make the text easier to read. Increasing the amount of space between two images that appear side by side will prevent the images from appearing as one large image.

The HSPACE attribute allows you to add space to both the left and right sides of an image. The

VSPACE attribute allows you to add space to both the top and bottom of an image.

You cannot add space to only one side of an image using the HSPACE or VSPACE attribute. To add space to only one side of an image, modify the image using an image editing program.

While the HSPACE and VSPACE attributes are still supported by Web browsers, the use of *style sheets* is now preferred. For information on style sheets, see page 196.

ADD SPACE AROUND AN IMAGE

```
<HTML>
<HEAD>
<TITLE>Foster City Zoo</TITLE>
</HEAD>
<BODY>

<H1><CENTER>FOSTER CITY ZOO</CENTER></H1>

<IMG SRC="tiger.jpg" ALIGN="left" HSPACE="30" VSPACE="20"> Are tigers more
ferocious than lions? Which cat can run the fastest? In which parts of North
America do cougars live? The answers to these questions and more can be found
in The World of Cats, the newest exhibit at the Foster City Zoo. From the king of
the jungle to the bobcat of North America, we explore the habitats and habits of
different feline species. The exhibition area is carefully designed to recreate the
environments in which the animals originally lived. Visitors can view their favorite
wild cats, and find out more about them from various displays. Learn how the wild
cats hunt and how mothers rear their cubs. The World of Cats is open six days a
week during regular zoo hours.

</BODY>
</HTML>
```

■ The Web browser adds space around the image.

LEFT AND RIGHT SIDES

1 In the <IMG> tag for the image you want to add space around, type **HSPACE="?"** replacing **?** with the amount of space you want to add in pixels.

TOP AND BOTTOM

1 In the <IMG> tag for the image you want to add space around, type **VSPACE="?"** replacing **?** with the amount of space you want to add in pixels.

ADD A HORIZONTAL RULE

The <HR> tag allows you to add a horizontal rule to your Web page. A horizontal rule is a line that visually separates sections of a Web page. For example, you may want to use a horizontal rule to separate sections of text or set off headings on your Web page.

Avoid overusing horizontal rules on your Web page since this can be distracting and can make your Web page difficult to read. Try not to place more than one horizontal rule on each screen.

By default, a horizontal rule you add to your Web page displays a thickness of 2 pixels. The SIZE

attribute allows you to change the thickness of a horizontal rule.

If you do not want a horizontal rule to extend across your entire Web page, use the WIDTH attribute to change the width of the horizontal rule. You should specify a new width as a percentage to have the width vary according to the size of the Web browser window.

While the SIZE and WIDTH attributes are still supported by Web browsers, the use of *style sheets* is now preferred. For information on style sheets, see page 196.

ADD A HORIZONTAL RULE

```
horizontalrule - WordPad
File  Edit  View  Insert  Format  Help

<HTML>
<HEAD>
<TITLE>Horizontal Rule</TITLE>
</HEAD>
<BODY>

This text appears above the horizontal rule.

<HR>

This text appears below the horizontal rule.

</BODY>
</HTML>
```

Horizontal Rule - Microsoft Internet Explorer
File Edit View Favorites Tools Help

Back Forward Stop Refresh Home Search Favorites History Mail Print Edit

Address C:\My Documents\Web Pages\horizontalrule.html

This text appears above the horizontal rule.

This text appears below the horizontal rule.

Done   My Computer

1 Type **<HR>** where you want a horizontal rule to appear on your Web page.

Note: To add space between a horizontal rule and the surrounding text, use the <P> tag. For information on the <P> tag, see page 16.

■ The Web browser displays the horizontal rule.

Extra

When you change the width of a horizontal rule using the WIDTH attribute, the horizontal rule will appear centered on your Web page. Use the ALIGN attribute to change the alignment of the horizontal rule. In the <HR> tag, type **ALIGN="?"** replacing **?** with the way you want to align the horizontal rule (**left**, **center** or **right**).

Example:

```
<HR WIDTH="50%" ALIGN="left">
```

Using the NOSHADE attribute with the <HR> tag allows you to remove the three-dimensional effect from a horizontal rule. The horizontal rule will appear as a solid, two-dimensional bar with no shading.

Example:

```
<HR NOSHADE>
```

To add a more elaborate horizontal rule to your Web page, use an image as a horizontal rule. Create your own horizontal rule images in an image editing program or obtain images on the Internet. Interesting horizontal rule images are available at the www.coolgraphics.com/gallery and www.mediabuilder.com/graphicsline.html Web sites.

When adding a horizontal rule image to your Web page, use the <P> or <BR> tag to have the image appear on its own line.

Example:

```
<P><IMG SRC="line.gif"></P>
```

---

horizontalrule - WordPad

File Edit View Insert Format Help

```
<HTML>
<HEAD>
<TITLE>Horizontal Rule</TITLE>
</HEAD>
<BODY>

This horizontal rule is 10 pixels.
<HR SIZE="10">

This horizontal rule extends across half of the page.
<HR WIDTH="50%">

</BODY>
</HTML>
```

Horizontal Rule - Microsoft Internet Explorer

File Edit View Favorites Tools Help

Back Forward Stop Refresh Home Search Favorites History Mail Print Edit

Address C:\My Documents\Web Pages\horizontalrule.html

This horizontal rule is 10 pixels.

This horizontal rule extends across half of the page.

Done   My Computer

CHANGE THICKNESS

1 In the <HR> tag, type **SIZE="?"** replacing **?** with the thickness you want the horizontal rule to display in pixels.

CHANGE WIDTH

1 In the <HR> tag, type **WIDTH="?%"** replacing **?** with the percentage of the Web page you want the horizontal rule to extend across.

■ The Web browser displays the horizontal rule with the new thickness or width.

USE IMAGES IN A LIST

Creating a list that uses images instead of bullets lets you include an eye-catching list on your Web page. For example, you may want to add a small version of your company logo to each item in a list of products.

The image you use for a list should be a small image that will fit neatly beside each item in the list. Interesting bullet images are available on the Internet at the www.grapholina.com/Graphics and www.theshockzone.com Web sites. To create your own bullet images, use an image editing program such as Jasc Paint Shop Pro or Adobe Photoshop.

When adding a bullet image, use the ALIGN attribute with the top, middle or bottom value to specify how you want to align the image with the text in your list. The top value aligns the top of an image with text. The middle value aligns the middle of an image with text and the bottom value aligns the bottom of an image with text.

While the ALIGN attribute is still supported by Web browsers, the use of *style sheets* is now preferred. For information on style sheets, see page 196.

USE IMAGES IN A LIST

```
index - WordPad
File  Edit  View  Insert  Format  Help

<HTML>
<HEAD>
<TITLE>Pasta Perfection</TITLE>
</HEAD>
<BODY>

<H2>Pasta Perfection</H2>
<H3>Perfect pasta every time!</H3>
<P>Our Most Popular Types of Pasta:</P>

<UL>
<BR>Cannelloni
<BR>Lasagna
<BR>Linguine
<BR>Manicotti
<BR>Ravioli
<BR>Spaghetti
</UL>

</BODY>
</HTML>
```

```
index - WordPad
File  Edit  View  Insert  Format  Help

<HTML>
<HEAD>
<TITLE>Pasta Perfection</TITLE>
</HEAD>
<BODY>

<H2>Pasta Perfection</H2>
<H3>Perfect pasta every time!</H3>
<P>Our Most Popular Types of Pasta:</P>

<UL>
<BR><IMG SRC="pasta.jpg">Cannelloni
<BR><IMG SRC="pasta.jpg">Lasagna
<BR><IMG SRC="pasta.jpg">Linguine
<BR><IMG SRC="pasta.jpg">Manicotti
<BR><IMG SRC="pasta.jpg">Ravioli
<BR><IMG SRC="pasta.jpg">Spaghetti
</UL>

</BODY>
</HTML>
```

1 Type **<UL>** before the list.

2 Type **
** in front of each item in the list.

3 Type **</UL>** after the list.

4 To add the image you want to use as a bullet, type **<IMG SRC="?">** after the <BR> tag for each item. Replace **?** with the location and name of the image on your computer.

Note: For information on specifying the location and name of an image, see the top of page 45.

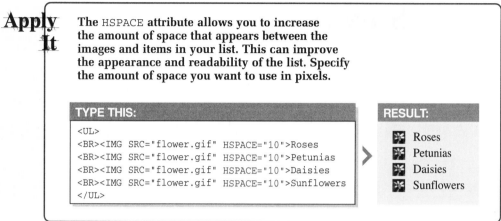

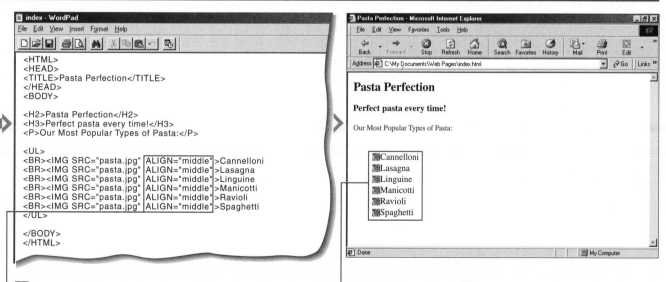

5 To specify how you want to align the image with each item, type **ALIGN="?"** in each <IMG> tag. Replace ? with the alignment you want to use (**top**, **middle** or **bottom**).

Note: For more information on aligning images with text, see page 50.

■ The Web browser displays the list. The image you specified appears in front of each item in the list.

Note: If the image is too large, see page 60, to reduce the size of the image.

CONVERT AN IMAGE TO GIF OR JPEG

If an image you want to add to your Web page is not a GIF or JPEG image, you can convert the image to the GIF or JPEG format. The GIF and JPEG formats are the most popular image formats on the Web.

GIF (Graphics Interchange Format) images are limited to 256 colors and are often used for logos, banners and computer-generated art. GIF images support features such as *animation* and *transparency*. For information on animation and transparency, see pages 180 and 68. GIF images have the .gif extension (example: logo.gif).

JPEG (Joint Photographic Experts Group) images can contain approximately 16.7 million colors and are often used for photographs and very large images. A JPEG image can contain millions of colors but still maintain a small file size, allowing the image to transfer quickly over the Internet. JPEG images usually have the .jpg extension (example: stonehenge.jpg).

To convert an image to the GIF or JPEG format, you need an image editing program such as Jasc Paint Shop Pro or Adobe Photoshop. For information on Paint Shop Pro, visit the www.jasc.com Web site. For information on Photoshop, visit the www.adobe.com Web site.

CONVERT AN IMAGE TO GIF OR JPEG

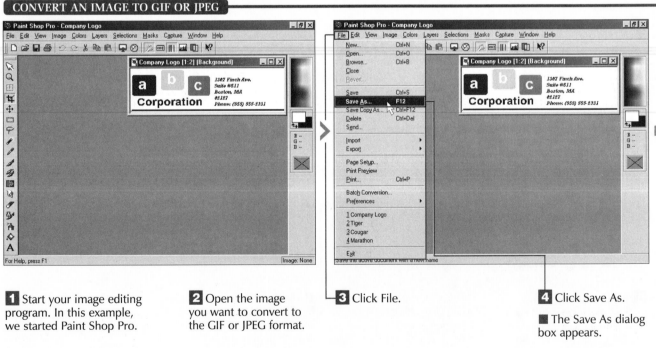

1 Start your image editing program. In this example, we started Paint Shop Pro.

2 Open the image you want to convert to the GIF or JPEG format.

3 Click File.

4 Click Save As.

■ The Save As dialog box appears.

Extra

When you convert an image to the GIF or JPEG format, the image is automatically compressed. Compression decreases the file size of the image so the image will transfer over the Internet more quickly.

You should only convert an image to the JPEG format once you have finished making changes to the image in your image editing program. When a JPEG image is compressed, the image file loses some information. Each time you edit and save a JPEG image, the image compresses and loses more information. Eventually, this will reduce the quality of the image.

The PNG (Portable Network Graphics) format is an image format that has recently been gaining popularity on the Web. PNG images can include millions of colors and support some of the same features as GIF images, such as transparency. Unlike JPEG images, PNG images do not lose information when compressed. While most Web browsers can display PNG images, they do not yet fully support PNG features. To convert an image to the PNG format, perform the steps below, except select the Portable Network Graphics format in step 7.

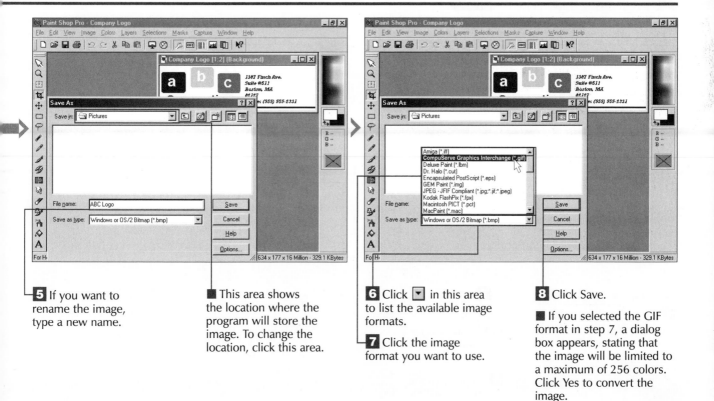

5 If you want to rename the image, type a new name.

■ This area shows the location where the program will store the image. To change the location, click this area.

6 Click ▼ in this area to list the available image formats.

7 Click the image format you want to use.

8 Click Save.

■ If you selected the GIF format in step 7, a dialog box appears, stating that the image will be limited to a maximum of 256 colors. Click Yes to convert the image.

DEFINE IMAGE SIZE

D efining the size of an image on your Web page can help the Web page appear on a screen more quickly since Web browsers will not have to calculate the size of the image.

To define the size of an image, you must first determine the size of the image using an image editing program. Once you know the dimensions of the image in pixels, use the WIDTH and HEIGHT attributes to define the size of the image.

When you define the size of images on your Web page, Web browsers can determine how much

space the images will take up on your Web page before the images transfer to a computer. This prevents Web browsers from having to change the layout of your Web page each time a new image transfers. As a result, users can easily read the text on your Web page as your images transfer.

Defining the size of images also ensures that users who turn off the display of images will see your Web page with the layout you intended. A Web browser will leave a space for each image using the size you defined.

DEFINE IMAGE SIZE

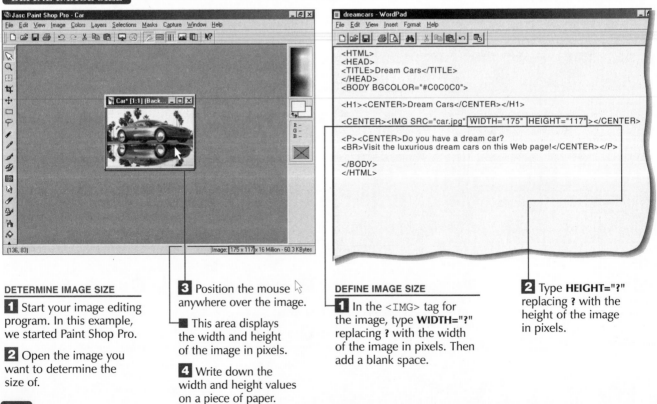

DETERMINE IMAGE SIZE

1 Start your image editing program. In this example, we started Paint Shop Pro.

2 Open the image you want to determine the size of.

3 Position the mouse anywhere over the image.

■ This area displays the width and height of the image in pixels.

4 Write down the width and height values on a piece of paper.

DEFINE IMAGE SIZE

1 In the <IMG> tag for the image, type **WIDTH="?"** replacing ? with the width of the image in pixels. Then add a blank space.

2 Type **HEIGHT="?"** replacing ? with the height of the image in pixels.

INCREASE IMAGE SIZE

The WIDTH and HEIGHT attributes allow you to increase the size of an image on your Web page without increasing the file size of the image. This lets you include a large image on your Web page without increasing the time it takes for the Web page to transfer to a computer.

When increasing the size of an image, specify a new size for the image in pixels or as a percentage of the Web browser window. Avoid making the image too large, since the image may appear grainy.

When specifying a new size for an image in pixels, use both the WIDTH and HEIGHT attributes. To

avoid distorting the image, keep the width and height values proportional. When specifying a new size as a percentage of the Web browser window, you do not need to specify both a width and a height. A Web browser will automatically calculate the other percentage to ensure the image will not be distorted.

While the WIDTH and HEIGHT attributes can also be used to reduce the size of an image, using an image editing program is more effective. For more information, see page 60.

INCREASE IMAGE SIZE

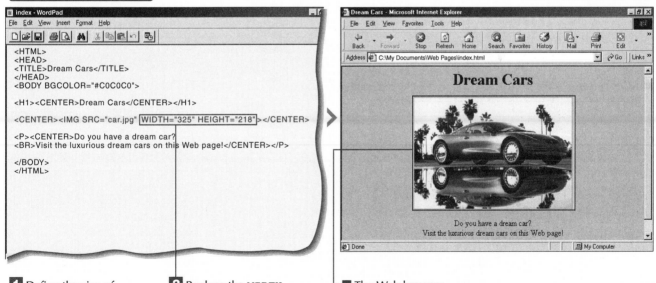

1 Define the size of the image you want to change. To define the size of an image, see page 58.

2 Replace the WIDTH and HEIGHT values with the new width and height you want to use in pixels.

■ You can also specify a WIDTH or HEIGHT value as a percentage of the Web browser window (example: 30%).

■ The Web browser displays the image with the new size.

REDUCE IMAGE SIZE

You may want to reduce the size of a large image so that it will take up less space on your Web page. Reducing the size of an image decreases the file size of the image. This allows the image to transfer faster and appear on a user's screen more quickly.

You should use an image editing program such as Jasc Paint Shop Pro or Adobe Photoshop to reduce the size of an image.

Most image editing programs allow you to specify a new size for an image in pixels. When

you specify a new width for an image in Paint Shop Pro, the program will automatically calculate the height for you to keep the image in proportion.

After reducing the size of an image, you should save your changes in a new file rather than replacing the original image. This lets you keep the original image on your computer in case you need the image at a later time. For example, you may want to use the original image for creating *thumbnail images*. For information on thumbnail images, see the top of page 61.

see the top of page 61.

REDUCE IMAGE SIZE

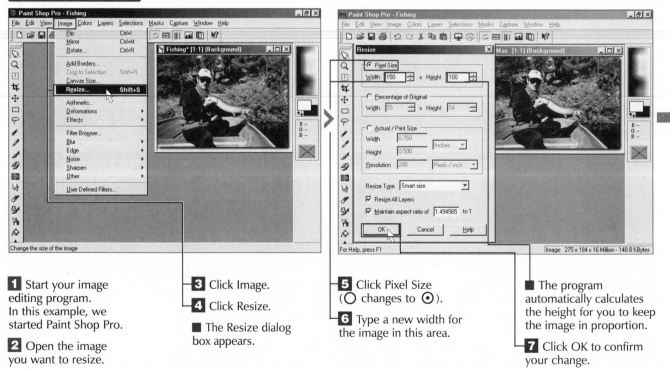

1 Start your image editing program. In this example, we started Paint Shop Pro.

2 Open the image you want to resize.

3 Click Image.

4 Click Resize.

■ The Resize dialog box appears.

5 Click Pixel Size (○ changes to ⊙).

6 Type a new width for the image in this area.

■ The program automatically calculates the height for you to keep the image in proportion.

7 Click OK to confirm your change.

15

Extra

Paint Shop Pro also allows you to specify a new size for an image as a percentage of its original size. In the Resize dialog box, click the Percentage of Original option (○ changes to ⦿). Then type the percentage you want to use in the Width area.

Many people reduce the size of images to create thumbnail images. A thumbnail image is a small version of an image that users can select to display the larger image. This lets users decide if they want to wait for the larger image to transfer to their computer. Create a thumbnail image by linking the smaller image to the larger version.

Example:
`<A HREF="largeimage.jpg"><IMG SRC="smallimage.jpg"></A>`

If you do not have an image editing program, use the WIDTH and HEIGHT attributes to reduce the size of an image. This will reduce the amount of space the image takes up on your Web page, but will not reduce the file size of the image. In the <IMG> tag for the image, type **WIDTH="?" HEIGHT="?"** replacing **?** with a new width and height for the image in pixels.

Example:
`<IMG SRC="photo.jpg" WIDTH="120" HEIGHT="60">`

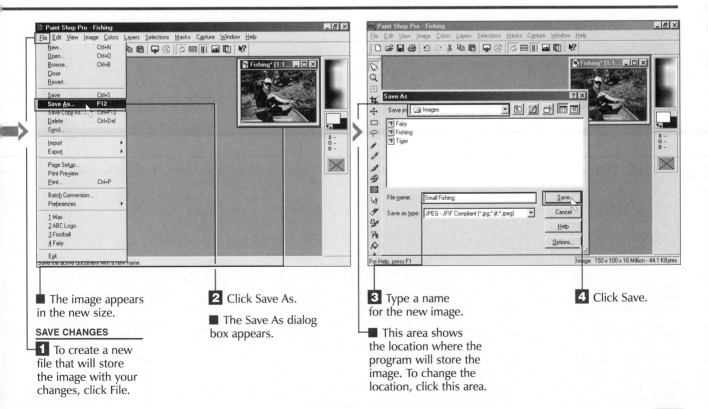

■ The image appears in the new size.

SAVE CHANGES

1 To create a new file that will store the image with your changes, click File.

2 Click Save As.

■ The Save As dialog box appears.

3 Type a name for the new image.

■ This area shows the location where the program will store the image. To change the location, click this area.

4 Click Save.

CROP AN IMAGE

Cropping an image lets you remove parts of the image that you do not need. This is useful when you want to focus a user's attention on an important part of an image.

When you crop an image, the file size of the image is reduced. This allows the image to transfer faster and appear on a screen more quickly.

Many image editing programs, such as Jasc Paint Shop Pro and Adobe Photoshop, have a tool you can use to crop an image. If your image editing program does not have a cropping tool, you may be able to crop the image using a different method.

Refer to the documentation that came with your image editing program for more information.

After cropping an image, you should save your changes in a new file rather than replacing the original image. This lets you keep the original image on your computer in case you need the image at a later time. Saving the original image on your computer also allows you to crop the image again later if you are unsatisfied with the results.

CROP AN IMAGE

1 Start your image editing program. In this example, we started Paint Shop Pro.

2 Open the image you want to crop.

3 Click ⊞.

4 Position the mouse ⊞ over the top left corner of the image area you want to keep.

5 Drag the mouse ⊞ over the image area you want to keep.

6 Double-click within the area you selected.

■ The areas of the image you did not select disappear.

7 To create a new file that will store the cropped image, perform steps 1 to 4 on page 61.

REDUCE IMAGE RESOLUTION

Reducing the resolution of an image will decrease the file size of the image. This will allow the image to transfer faster and appear on a user's screen more quickly.

The resolution of an image refers to the clarity of the image. Higher resolution images are sharper and more detailed. Most computer monitors display images at a resolution of 72 dots per inch (dpi). Images you include on your Web pages do not need to display a resolution higher than 72 dpi unless users will be printing the images.

To reduce the resolution of an image you will need an image editing program such as Jasc Paint Shop Pro or Adobe Photoshop.

After reducing the resolution of an image, you should save your changes in a new file rather than replacing the original image. This allows you to keep both a low resolution and a high resolution version of the image on your computer. You will need to use both versions if you want your Web page to display the low resolution version of the image while the higher resolution image transfers. For more information, see page 64.

REDUCE IMAGE RESOLUTION

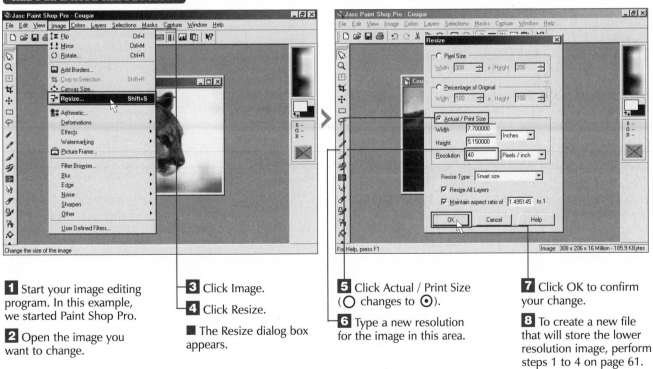

1 Start your image editing program. In this example, we started Paint Shop Pro.

2 Open the image you want to change.

3 Click Image.

4 Click Resize.

■ The Resize dialog box appears.

5 Click Actual / Print Size (○ changes to ⊙).

6 Type a new resolution for the image in this area.

7 Click OK to confirm your change.

8 To create a new file that will store the lower resolution image, perform steps 1 to 4 on page 61.

USE LOW RESOLUTION IMAGES

Use the LOWSRC attribute to have a low resolution version of an image appear on a user's screen while the higher resolution version of the image transfers to the user's computer.

Before you can use the LOWSRC attribute, you must create a low resolution version of your image as shown on page 63. The low resolution version of the image will have a smaller file size, allowing it to transfer quickly over the Internet.

The low resolution version of an image may have smaller dimensions than the

high resolution version. Use the WIDTH and HEIGHT attributes to specify the width and height of the high resolution version of your image in pixels. If you do not specify a width and height, both images may display the dimensions of the low resolution image. To determine the width and height of an image, see page 58.

The LOWSRC attribute is not part of the HTML standard and is not supported by many Web browsers. Web browsers that do not support the LOWSRC attribute will only display the high resolution image.

USE LOW RESOLUTION IMAGES

index - WordPad

File Edit View Insert Format Help

```
<HTML>
<HEAD>
<TITLE>Foster City Zoo</TITLE>
</HEAD>
<BODY>

<IMG SRC="cougar.gif">

<H1>Foster City Zoo</H1>
<P>The spacious grounds of Foster City Zoo were established in 1960 on 350 acres of
and farmland located five miles west of Foster City, NY. Our primary commitment is to e
the public about the animal kingdom.</P>
<P>Foster City Zoo is proud to announce the completion of our newest exhibit, The Wor
Cats. Are tigers more ferocious than lions? Which cat can run the fastest? In which parts
North America do cougars live? The answers to these questions and more can be found
World of Cats exhibit.</P>

</BODY>
</HTML>
```

index - WordPad

File Edit View Insert Format Help

```
<HTML>
<HEAD>
<TITLE>Foster City Zoo</TITLE>
</HEAD>
<BODY>

<IMG SRC="cougar.gif"  LOWSRC="cougar_lowres.gif">

<H1>Foster City Zoo</H1>
<P>The spacious grounds of Foster City Zoo were established in 1960 on 350 acres of
and farmland located five miles west of Foster City, NY. Our primary commitment is to e
the public about the animal kingdom.</P>
<P>Foster City Zoo is proud to announce the completion of our newest exhibit, The Wor
Cats. Are tigers more ferocious than lions? Which cat can run the fastest? In which parts
North America do cougars live? The answers to these questions and more can be found
World of Cats exhibit.</P>

</BODY>
</HTML>
```

1 Create a low resolution version of the image you want to include on your Web page as shown on page 63.

2 Type **<IMG SRC="?"** where you want the image to appear, replacing **?** with the location and name of the high resolution image on your computer. Then add a blank space.

Note: For information on specifying the location and name of an image, see the top of page 45.

3 Type **LOWSRC="?"** replacing **?** with the location and name of the low resolution image on your computer. Then add a blank space.

Extra

The image you add using the LOWSRC attribute does not need to be a low resolution version of the image you add using the SRC attribute. Specifying a different image can create an animated effect, with the image you specify for the LOWSRC attribute changing to the image you specify for the SRC attribute.

Example:

```
<IMG SRC="cat.gif" LOWSRC="dog.gif"
WIDTH="300" HEIGHT="200">
```

If you want to use only a low resolution version of an image without having the high resolution version appear later, do not use the LOWSRC attribute. Add the low resolution version of the image using the SRC attribute. Using only low resolution images can decrease the file size of your Web pages.

Example:

```
<IMG SRC="images/lowresolution.gif"
WIDTH="200" HEIGHT="135">
```

You should use the ALT attribute each time you add an image to your Web page to provide text that will appear for users who do not see images. Some users have Web browsers that cannot display images, while others turn off the display of images to browse the Web more quickly. These users will see neither the high nor low resolution version of an image on your Web page.

Example:

```
<IMG SRC="car.gif" LOWSRC="car_lowres.gif"
WIDTH="240" HEIGHT="200" ALT="Image of
corvette">
```

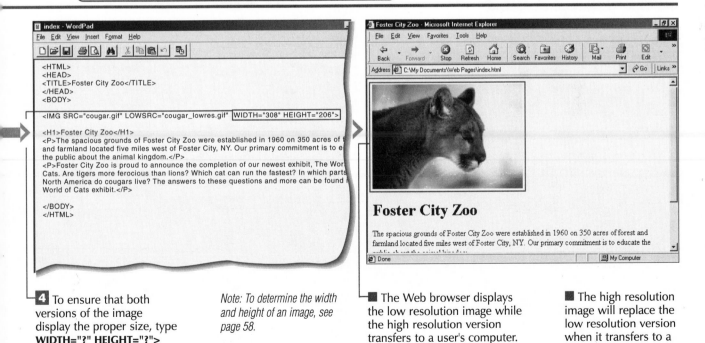

4 To ensure that both versions of the image display the proper size, type **WIDTH="?" HEIGHT="?">** replacing **?** with the width and height of the high resolution image in pixels.

Note: To determine the width and height of an image, see page 58.

■ The Web browser displays the low resolution image while the high resolution version transfers to a user's computer.

■ The high resolution image will replace the low resolution version when it transfers to a user's computer.

REDUCE COLORS IN AN IMAGE

Although a GIF image can contain up to 256 colors, many simple images can be accurately displayed with fewer colors. Reducing the number of colors in a GIF image will decrease the file size of the image, allowing the image to transfer more quickly over the Internet.

To reduce the number of colors in an image, you need an image editing program such as Jasc Paint Shop Pro or Adobe Photoshop.

After you reduce the number of colors in an image, you can view the image with the new number of colors. If you are satisfied with the results, save your changes in a new file. If the quality of the image has been significantly affected, do not save your changes. Try reducing the number of colors in the original image again, choosing a slightly higher number of colors.

Do not reduce the number of colors in a JPEG image. The JPEG format was specifically designed to store images containing millions of colors using small file sizes. In many cases, reducing the number of colors in a JPEG image will increase the file size of the image.

REDUCE COLORS IN AN IMAGE

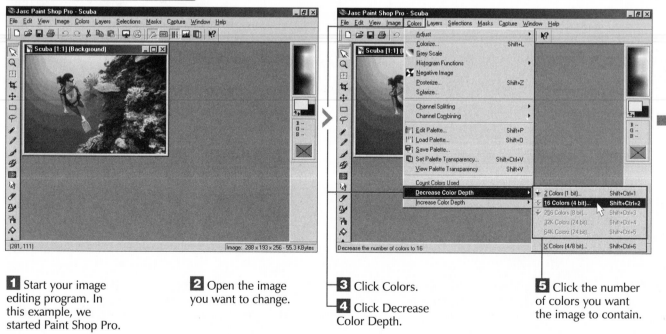

1 Start your image editing program. In this example, we started Paint Shop Pro.

2 Open the image you want to change.

3 Click Colors.

4 Click Decrease Color Depth.

5 Click the number of colors you want the image to contain.

Extra

Paint Shop Pro allows you to view the number of colors an image contains. This can help you determine whether you should reduce the number of colors in the image. Open the image you want to view the number of colors for, select the Colors menu and then click Count Colors Used.

If an image contains 16 or more colors, Paint Shop Pro allows you to specify the maximum number of colors you want the image to contain. Perform steps 1 to 5 below, except select the X Colors option in step 5. In the Palette area of the dialog box that appears, type the maximum number of colors you want the image to contain.

The available options for reducing the number of colors in an image depend on the image editing program you use. For example, some image editing programs allow you to choose the colors you want an image to keep. Other programs may reduce the number of colors in an image by combining colors. Consult the documentation that came with your image editing program to determine which options your program offers.

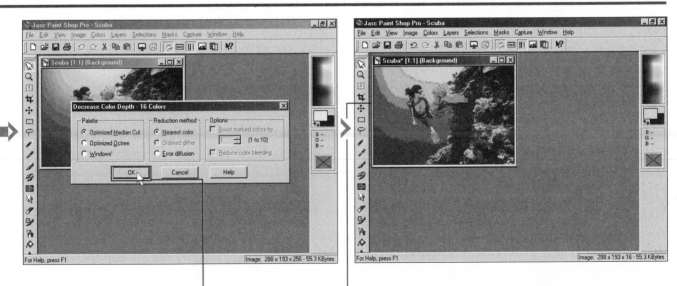

■ The Decrease Color Depth dialog box appears.

Note: The dialog box that appears on your screen may offer different options.

6 Click OK to confirm your change.

■ The image displays the new number of colors.

7 To create a new file that will store the image with the new number of colors, perform steps 1 to 4 on page 61.

MAKE IMAGE BACKGROUND TRANSPARENT

You may want to make the background of a GIF image transparent so the background will blend into your Web page.

You need an image editing program such as Jasc Paint Shop Pro or Adobe Photoshop to make the background of a GIF image transparent.

In order to make the background of a GIF image transparent, the entire background must contain only one color. Your image editing program will make each pixel that contains the color transparent. If the background of an image is multicolored, only the pixels that contain the color you specify will

become transparent, giving the image background a speckled look.

In some cases, an image background you want to make transparent may appear to be one color when it actually contains several colors. This is due to a process called dithering. Dithering combines several colors within a pixel of an image to simulate another color.

The image you use should be saved in GIF version 89a rather than version 87a. GIF version 89a is a more recent GIF version that supports advanced features such as transparency. To save an image in GIF version 89a, see the top of page 71.

MAKE IMAGE BACKGROUND TRANSPARENT

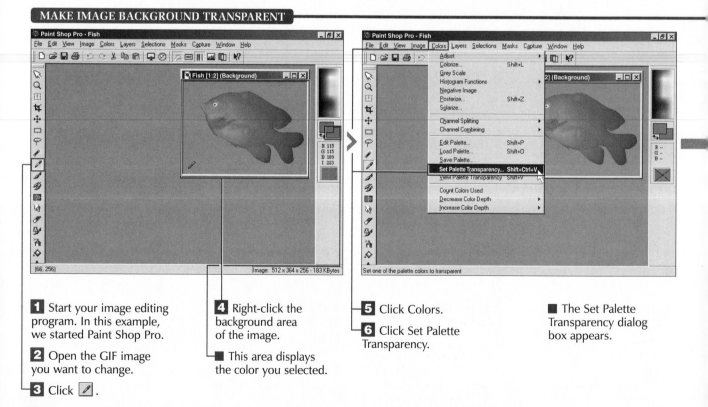

1 Start your image editing program. In this example, we started Paint Shop Pro.

2 Open the GIF image you want to change.

3 Click 🖊.

4 Right-click the background area of the image.

■ This area displays the color you selected.

5 Click Colors.

6 Click Set Palette Transparency.

■ The Set Palette Transparency dialog box appears.

Extra

If the background of a GIF image is multicolored, change the background to one color before making the background transparent. Open the image in Paint Shop Pro and then click 🖉 . Hold down the Shift key and click the background until a dotted line appears around the entire background. Then press the Delete key to change the background to one color. If you have difficulty changing the background to one color using this method, try using a paint tool to manually color the background.

When making the background of an image transparent, make sure the background color does not appear in the image itself. When you make the background of an image transparent, every pixel in the image that contains the same color as the background will also become transparent.

If you have used an image on your Web page for a link, you may want to remove the colored border that remains even after you make the background of the image transparent. To remove the border from an image link, type **BORDER="0"** in the `<IMG>` tag for the image.

Example:

```
<A HREF="http://www.bakery.com">
<IMG SRC="cake.jpg" BORDER="0"></A>
```

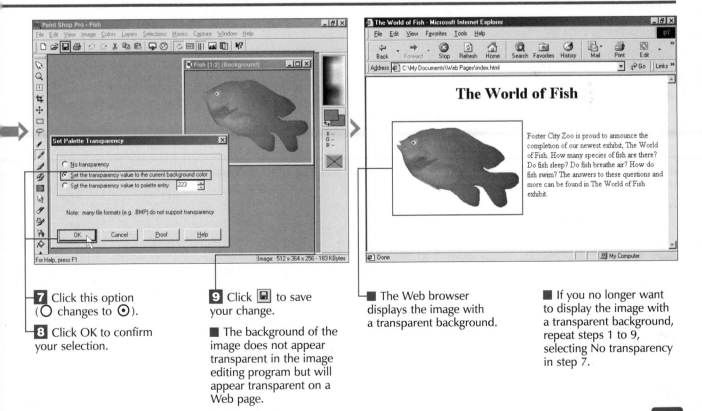

7 Click this option (○ changes to ⊙).

8 Click OK to confirm your selection.

9 Click 🖫 to save your change.

■ The background of the image does not appear transparent in the image editing program but will appear transparent on a Web page.

■ The Web browser displays the image with a transparent background.

■ If you no longer want to display the image with a transparent background, repeat steps 1 to 9, selecting No transparency in step 7.

INTERLACE A GIF IMAGE

Interlacing a GIF image allows the entire image to appear on a screen as it transfers to a computer.

A noninterlaced GIF image transfers to a computer one row at a time, from the top of the image to the bottom. Users must wait until the image fully transfers to see the entire image. An interlaced GIF image transfers to a computer by skipping alternate rows. This allows users to quickly see the entire image. The image will first appear blurry and then gradually sharpen as it transfers.

To interlace a GIF image, you need an image editing program such as Jasc Paint Shop Pro or Adobe Photoshop.

Interlacing GIF images is particularly useful when you use large images or have many images on your Web page. Since users can see the images as they transfer, they will have a better idea of what the final Web page will look like.

Some older Web browsers do not support interlaced GIF images. If a Web browser does not support interlacing, the images will appear on a screen as though they were noninterlaced GIF images.

INTERLACE A GIF IMAGE

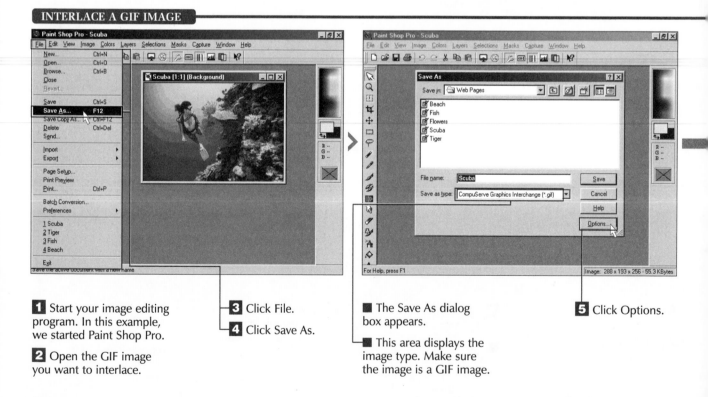

1 Start your image editing program. In this example, we started Paint Shop Pro.

2 Open the GIF image you want to interlace.

3 Click File.

4 Click Save As.

■ The Save As dialog box appears.

■ This area displays the image type. Make sure the image is a GIF image.

5 Click Options.

Extra

To remove the interlacing from an image, repeat steps 1 to 9 below, except select the Noninterlaced option in step 6 (○ changes to ⊙).

In Paint Shop Pro, the Save Options dialog box allows you to select the GIF version you want to use to save your image. GIF version 87a was the first version developed. While saving a GIF image in version 87a may result in a slightly smaller file size, using the more recent version 89a will allow you to take advantage of advanced features such as *animation* and *transparency*.

Many image editing programs allow you to change your default settings so that all new GIF images you create will automatically be interlaced. Refer to the documentation that came with your image editing program for more information.

If you want a JPEG image on your Web page to appear on a screen as it transfers, make the image a progressive JPEG image. Like an interlaced GIF image, a progressive JPEG image will initially appear blurry and then gradually sharpen as it transfers to a computer. To make a JPEG image progressive, perform steps 1 to 9 below, except select the Progressive encoding option in step 6 (○ changes to ⊙).

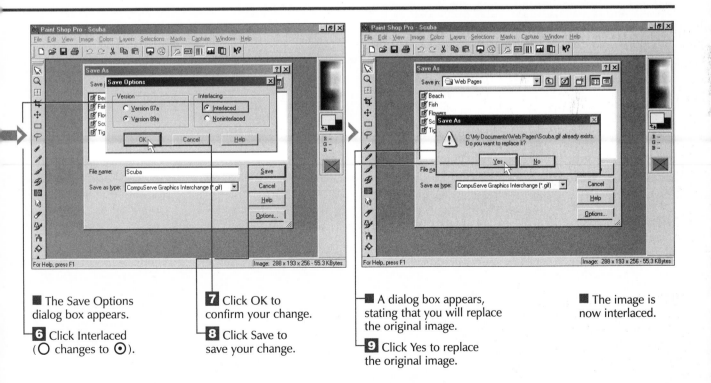

■ The Save Options dialog box appears.

6 Click Interlaced (○ changes to ⊙).

7 Click OK to confirm your change.

8 Click Save to save your change.

■ A dialog box appears, stating that you will replace the original image.

9 Click Yes to replace the original image.

■ The image is now interlaced.

CONVERT IMAGE TO WEB BROWSER SAFE COLORS

Converting an image to Web browser safe colors helps ensure that the image will appear the way you expect when displayed in a Web browser.

Web browser safe colors are a set of 216 colors that can be accurately displayed on computers that display only 256 colors. The remaining 40 colors are used to display toolbars and other screen elements.

When a user with a computer that displays only 256 colors views your Web page, the user's Web browser will attempt to simulate colors that are not in the set of Web browser safe colors by dithering. Dithering is a process in which colors are combined to produce another color. This can cause an image to appear grainy. Converting an image to Web browser safe colors can help ensure that you will be satisfied with the way your image appears on a user's computer.

To convert an image to Web browser safe colors, you need an image editing program such as Jasc Paint Shop Pro or Adobe Photoshop.

CONVERT IMAGE TO WEB BROWSER SAFE COLORS

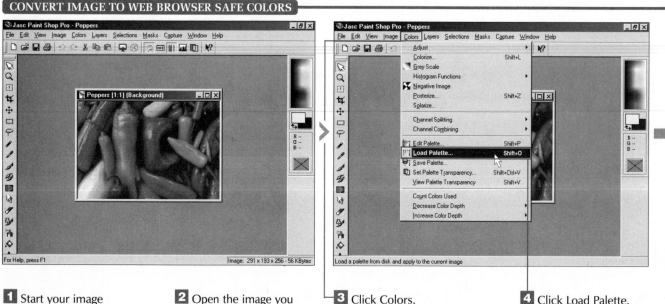

1 Start your image editing program. In this example, we started Paint Shop Pro.

2 Open the image you want to convert to Web browser safe colors.

Note: Do not convert a JPEG image to Web browser safe colors. For more information, see the top of page 73.

3 Click Colors.

4 Click Load Palette.

■ The Load Palette dialog box appears.

Extra

Do not convert a JPEG image to Web browser safe colors. JPEG images usually contain millions of colors. When you convert a JPEG image to Web browser safe colors, your image editing program has to simulate so many colors that the quality of the image is usually significantly reduced. By leaving the image the way it is, you can ensure that the image will at least appear properly on computers that display more than 256 colors.

If your image editing program does not include a file with Web browser safe colors, such as the Safety.pal file in Paint Shop Pro, try searching for a file on the program manufacturer's Web site. Refer to the documentation that came with your image editing program to find the Web site address.

Some image editing programs may not prevent dithering when you convert an image to Web browser safe colors. If areas of your image appear grainy after you convert the image to Web browser safe colors, consider leaving the image the way it is. You may want to refer to the documentation that came with your image editing program to determine if it is possible to turn off dithering for the program.

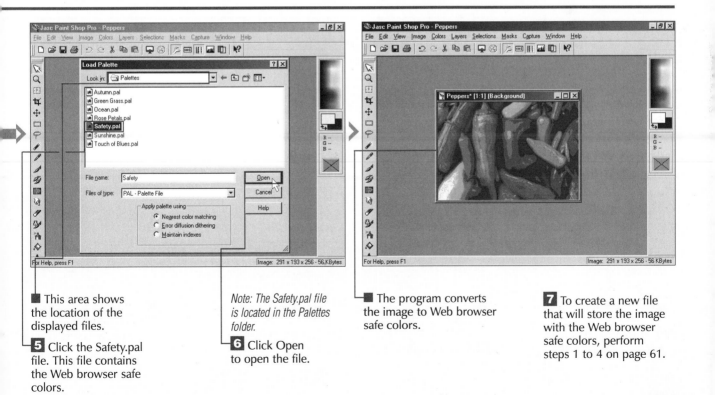

■ This area shows the location of the displayed files.

5 Click the Safety.pal file. This file contains the Web browser safe colors.

Note: The Safety.pal file is located in the Palettes folder.

6 Click Open to open the file.

■ The program converts the image to Web browser safe colors.

7 To create a new file that will store the image with the Web browser safe colors, perform steps 1 to 4 on page 61.

CREATE A LINK TO ANOTHER WEB PAGE

U se the <A> tag to link text or an image on your Web page to another page on the Web. When users select the link, the other Web page will appear. Make sure the text or image you use clearly indicates where the link will take users.

A link can take users to a Web page in your own Web site or to any page on the Web. When creating a link to a Web page you did not create, specify the absolute URL of the Web page. An absolute URL is the full address of the Web page,

such as http://www.maran.com. When creating a link to a Web page in your own Web site, you should use a *relative URL*. For more information, see the top of page 75.

Avoid placing two text links side by side on your Web page, since users may find it difficult to see that there are two separate links. When creating image links, keep in mind that some users do not see images. You may want to include corresponding text links for these users.

CREATE A TEXT LINK

1 Type the text you want users to select to display another Web page.

2 Type **<A HREF="?">** in front of the text, replacing **?** with the address of the Web page you want to display.

Note: To link the text to a Web page in your own Web site, see the top of page 75.

3 Type **</A>** after the text.

■ The Web browser displays the text link. The text link appears underlined and in color.

■ A user can click the text link to display the Web page you specified.

Extra

When creating a link to a Web page in your own Web site, specify the location of the Web page using a relative URL. If the Web page is stored in the same folder as the Web page that contains the link, the relative URL can specify just the name of the Web page (example: prices.html). If the Web page is stored in a subfolder, the relative URL must specify the name of the subfolder and the name of the Web page (example: products/prices.html).

Example:

```
<A HREF="products/prices.html">View our latest products!</A>
```

Include navigational links on your Web pages to help users move through your Web site. For example, each Web page in your Web site should include a link to your home page. Images for navigational links are available at the www.bycarel.com/buttons and www.station4.com/buttonfactory Web sites.

Example:

```
<A HREF="index.html"><IMG SRC="homebutton.gif"></A>
```

You may want to remove the border that automatically appears around an image link. In the <IMG> tag for the image you no longer want to display a border, type **BORDER="0"**.

Example:

```
<A HREF="http://www.maran.com"><IMG SRC="book.gif" BORDER="0"></A>
```

CREATE AN IMAGE LINK

1 Add the image you want users to select to display another Web page.

2 Type **<A HREF="?">** in front of the image, replacing ? with the address of the Web page you want to display.

Note: To link the image to a Web page in your own Web site, see the top of this page.

3 Type **</A>** after the image.

■ The Web browser displays the image link. A border appears around the image link.

■ A user can click the image link to display the Web page you specified.

CREATE A LINK
WITHIN A WEB PAGE

You may want to include a link on your Web page that will take users to another area of the same Web page. This lets users quickly display information of interest. For example, you may want to create a table of contents that contains links to different sections of a long Web page.

To create a link within a Web page, you must first name the Web page area you want users to be able to quickly display. This area is often referred to as an anchor. Use the <A> tag with the NAME attribute

to name the Web page area. The name you use should contain only letters and numbers.

After you have named the Web page area, create a link to the area. The <A> tag with the HREF attribute allows you to create a link to a Web page area. When a user selects the link, the Web page area you specified will appear on the screen.

When creating multiple links within the same Web page, make sure you give each linked Web page area a different name.

CREATE A LINK WITHIN A WEB PAGE

index - WordPad

File Edit View Insert Format Help

to build a birdhouse. On this page, I will introduce you to steps you can follow to construct a simple birdhouse.</P>

<P>STEP ONE: PREPARATION

STEP TWO: CUTTING, DRILLING AND ASSEMBLING</P>

<P>STEP ONE: PREPARATION

1) Decide what type of bird you want to attract. This decision will influence the dimensions of the house and the size of the entry hole you must drill.

2) Purchase wood. Pine is my favorite choice, but other types of wood are fine.

3) Make sure you have the necessary tools. You will need a saw, drill, hammer and nails.</P>

<P>STEP TWO: CUTTING, DRILLING AND ASSEMBLING

1) Cut the boards so they are the correct dimensions.

2) Select the board that will be the front of the house and drill an entry hole.

3) Carefully assemble the boards to complete the house.</P>

</BODY>
</HTML>

For Help, press F1

index - WordPad

File Edit View Insert Format Help

to build a birdhouse. On this page, I will introduce you to steps you can follow to construct a simple birdhouse.</P>

<P>STEP ONE: PREPARATION

STEP TWO: CUTTING, DRILLING AND ASSEMBLING</P>

<P>STEP ONE: PREPARATION

1) Decide what type of bird you want to attract. This decision will influence the dimensions of the house and the size of the entry hole you must drill.

2) Purchase wood. Pine is my favorite choice, but other types of wood are fine.

3) Make sure you have the necessary tools. You will need a saw, drill, hammer and nails.</P>

<P><A NAME="step2"></A>STEP TWO: CUTTING, DRILLING AND ASSEMBLING

1) Cut the boards so they are the correct dimensions.

2) Select the board that will be the front of the house and drill an entry hole.

3) Carefully assemble the boards to complete the house.</P>

</BODY>
</HTML>

For Help, press F1

NAME WEB PAGE AREA

1 Click in front of the Web page area you want users to be able to quickly display.

2 Type **<A NAME="?">** replacing **?** with a name that describes the Web page area. The name you use should contain only letters and numbers.

3 Type **</A>** to complete the naming of the Web page area.

Extra

It is also possible to create a link that will take users to a specific area on another Web page in your Web site. First, name the Web page area you want users to be able to quickly display. Then create a link to the area on a different Web page. When creating the link, specify the name and location of the Web page that contains the area before the number sign (#) and the name of the Web page area. For information on specifying the name and location of a Web page, see the top of page 75.

Example:

On the Web page that contains the area:
```
<A NAME="vacuumcleaners"></A>
```

On the Web page that contains the link:
```
<A HREF="products.html#vacuumcleaners">
Vacuum Cleaner Models</A>
```

Many people include links at the end of each section of a long Web page that users can select to return to the top of the page.

Example:
```
<A NAME="top"></A>Table of Contents
<A HREF="#top">Back to Top</A>
```

The ID attribute also lets you name the Web page area you want users to be able to quickly display. The ID attribute is not supported by some Web browsers.

Example:
```
<H1 ID="Introduction">Introduction to My
Web Page</H1>
```

---

index - WordPad

File Edit View Insert Format Help

```
construct a simple birdhouse.</P>

<P>STEP ONE: PREPARATION
<BR><A HREF="#step2">STEP TWO: CUTTING, DRILLING AND ASSEMBLING
</A></P>

<P>STEP ONE: PREPARATION
<BR>1) Decide what type of bird you want to attract. This decision will influence
the dimensions of the house and the size of the entry hole you must drill.
<BR>2) Purchase wood. Pine is my favorite choice, but other types of wood are
fine.
<BR>3) Make sure you have the necessary tools. You will need a saw, drill,
hammer and nails.</P>

<P> <A NAME="step2"> </A> STEP TWO: CUTTING, DRILLING AND
ASSEMBLING
<BR>1) Cut the boards so they are the correct dimensions.
<BR>2) Select the board that will be the front of the house and drill an entry
hole.
<BR>3) Carefully assemble the boards to complete the house.</P>

</BODY>
</HTML>
```

For Help, press F1   NUM

Bird Watchers Home Page - Microsoft Internet Explorer

File Edit View Favorites Tools Help

Back | Forward | Stop | Refresh | Home | Search | Favorites | History | Mail | Print | Edit

Address C:\My Documents\Web Pages\index.html   Go | Links

Bird Watchers' Home Page

The page dedicated to people who love to watch birds!

Bird watchers appreciate the beauty of birds and are always interested in ways to attract them. One of the best and easiest ways to draw birds to your backyard is to build a birdhouse. On this page, I will introduce you to steps you can follow to construct a simple birdhouse.

STEP ONE: PREPARATION
STEP TWO: CUTTING, DRILLING AND ASSEMBLING

STEP ONE: PREPARATION
1) Decide what type of bird you want to attract. This decision will influence the dimensions of the house and the size of the entry hole you must drill.
2) Purchase wood. Pine is my favorite choice, but other types of wood are fine.
3) Make sure you have the necessary tools. You will need a saw, drill, hammer and nails.

Done   My Computer

CREATE LINK TO WEB PAGE AREA

4 Click in front of the text or image you want users to select to display the Web page area you named on page 76.

5 Type **<A HREF="#?">** replacing **?** with the name you specified for the Web page area in step 2.

6 Type **</A>** after the text or image.

■ The Web browser displays the link.

■ A user can click the link to display the Web page area you specified.

CREATE A LINK TO AN IMAGE

If you plan to include a large image on your Web page, consider creating a link that will take users to the image. This will give users access to the image without increasing the time it takes for your Web page to transfer to a computer.

Creating a link to an image is useful when including a thumbnail image on your Web page. A thumbnail image is a small version of an image that users can select to display the larger image. This lets users decide if they want to wait for the larger image to transfer to their computer. For information on reducing an image size, see page 60.

Creating a link to an image is also useful when you want to include an image that some Web browsers cannot display, such as a Windows bitmap (BMP) image. When a user selects the link, the image will appear in a program on the user's computer.

When creating a link to an image, you should provide a description of the image, including the size of the linked image in kilobytes (K). This helps users estimate how long the linked image will take to transfer to their computer.

CREATE A LINK TO AN IMAGE

```
<HTML>
<HEAD>
<TITLE>My European Tour</TITLE>
</HEAD>
<BODY>

<H1><CENTER><I>My European Tour</I></CENTER></H1>

<P>After graduating from college, I spent the summer traveling across Europe. I visited popular tourist destinations such as the Eiffel Tower, and discovered parts of the continent that are not quite so well known, but equally spectacular. The photographs below chronicle my journey.</P>

<A HREF="bldglarge.jpg"><IMG SRC="bldgsmall.jpg"></A>
Greece (150K). Click the image to view a larger version.

<P><IMG SRC="landsmall.jpg"> Switzerland (150K). Click the image to view a larger version.</P>

</BODY>
</HTML>
```

My European Tour

After graduating from college, I spent the summer traveling across Europe. I visited popular tourist destinations such as the Eiffel Tower, and discovered parts of the continent that are not quite so well known, but equally spectacular. The photographs below chronicle my journey.

Greece (150K). Click the image to view a larger version.

Switzerland (150K). Click the image to view a larger version.

1 Type the text or add the image you want users to select to display the linked image.

2 Type **<A HREF="?">** in front of the text or image, replacing **?** with the location and name of the linked image on your computer.

Note: For information on specifying the location and name of an image, see the top of page 45.

3 Type **</A>** after the text or image.

■ The Web browser displays the link.

■ A user can click the link to display the linked image.

CREATE A LINK TO A FILE

Creating a link that users can select to transfer a file to their computers lets you make files such as documents and programs available to users.

When creating a link to a file, you must specify the location of the file on your computer. If the file is stored in the same folder as your Web page, specify just the name of the file (example: game.exe). If the file is stored in a subfolder, specify the name of the subfolder and the name of the file (example: programs/game.exe).

When a user selects a link to a file, the user's Web browser will attempt to display the file.

If the browser cannot display the file, it will attempt to open the file in a program on the user's computer. If the user does not have a program that can display or run the file, the Web browser will give the user the option to save the file on their computer.

Include a description beside a link to a file to help users decide if they want to transfer the file. The description should include the type and size of the file. You should also provide a link that will take users to a Web site where they can obtain a program that will display or run the file.

CREATE A LINK TO A FILE

```
<HTML>
<HEAD>
<TITLE>Game World</TITLE>
</HEAD>
<BODY>

<H1><CENTER><I>Game World</I></CENTER></H1>
<B>Welcome to Brian's Game World, where you can play some of the coolest
games on the Web!</B>
<BR>I am a computer programming student who loves to create games. This Web
site features my newest games as well as links to other gaming Web sites.

<P>My newest creation is a fantasy game called Dungeon Warrior. Strap on your
armor and prepare to rescue prisoners from a dungeon filled with creatures!</P>

<BR><A HREF="dungeonwarrior.exe">Dungeon Warrior</A>
<BR>Windows
<BR>3 MB

</BODY>
</HTML>
```

1 Type the text or add the image you want users to select to transfer a file.

2 Type **<A HREF="?">** in front of the text or image, replacing **?** with the location and name of the file on your computer.

3 Type **</A>** after the text or image.

■ The Web browser displays the link.

■ Users can click the link to transfer the file you specified to their computers.

CREATE AN E-MAIL LINK

Your Web page can include a link that will allow users to quickly send an e-mail message. Creating an e-mail link is useful when you want users to be able to send you questions and provide feedback that can help improve your Web pages.

When creating an e-mail link, you must specify the e-mail address of the person you want to receive the messages users send. For example, you may want to create an e-mail link that allows users to contact you or one of your employees.

When using text for an e-mail link, make sure that the text clearly indicates who will receive the e-mail messages. This helps users determine if they are contacting the correct person. For example, use informative text such as "E-mail a Technical Support Representative."

If you use an image for your e-mail link, you should include a corresponding text link for users who cannot view images. Some users turn off the display of images to browse the Web more quickly, while others use Web browsers that cannot display images.

CREATE AN E-MAIL LINK

```
<HTML>
<HEAD>
<TITLE>Beethoven Page</TITLE>
</HEAD>
<BODY>

<H1><CENTER><I>BEETHOVEN</I></CENTER></H1>

<P>Ludwig van Beethoven was born in Bonn, Germany in 1770. He spent most of
his life in Vienna, where he earned a living giving concerts, teaching piano and
selling his compositions. One of the most fascinating aspects of Beethoven's life
was his triumph over deafness, which struck him during adulthood. In fact, he
composed some of his most powerful works after losing his hearing.</P>

<P>Do you have interesting facts about Beethoven or a great Beethoven Web
page?</P>

E-mail me and let me know!

</BODY>
</HTML>
```

1 Type the text or add the image you want users to select to send an e-mail message.

```
<HTML>
<HEAD>
<TITLE>Beethoven Page</TITLE>
</HEAD>
<BODY>

<H1><CENTER><I>BEETHOVEN</I></CENTER></H1>

<P>Ludwig van Beethoven was born in Bonn, Germany in 1770. He spent most of
his life in Vienna, where he earned a living giving concerts, teaching piano and
selling his compositions. One of the most fascinating aspects of Beethoven's life
was his triumph over deafness, which struck him during adulthood. In fact, he
composed some of his most powerful works after losing his hearing.</P>

<P>Do you have interesting facts about Beethoven or a great Beethoven Web
page?</P>

<A HREF="mailto:webmaster@classicalmusic.com">E-mail me and let me know!
</A>

</BODY>
</HTML>
```

2 Type **<A HREF="mailto:?">** in front of the text or image, replacing **?** with the e-mail address of the person you want to receive the messages.

3 Type **</A>** after the text or image.

Extra

When creating an e-mail link, you can specify the e-mail address of a person you want to receive a copy of the e-mail messages users send. For example, you can have a supervisor automatically receive messages sent to your customer service department. When a user selects your e-mail link, the person's e-mail address will automatically appear in the Carbon Copy (Cc) area of the user's e-mail program. While many Web browsers support this feature, it is not part of the HTML standard.

Example:

```
<A HREF="mailto:customerservice@abc.com
?cc=bmartin@abc.com">Customer Service</A>
```

You may want to specify a subject for an e-mail link you create. When a user selects the link, the user's e-mail program will automatically display the subject you specified. This can help you identify messages sent using the link. While many Web browsers support this feature, it is not part of the HTML standard.

Example:

```
<A HREF="mailto:jsmith@abc.com
?subject=comments">Send me your comments!</A>
```

When specifying additional information for an e-mail link, such as an address for the Cc area and a subject, separate each new item you add with an ampersand (&).

Example:

```
<A HREF="mailto:jsmith@abc.com?
cc=bmartin@abc.com&subject=comments">Send me
your comments!</A>
```

■ The Web browser displays the e-mail link.

■ A user can click the e-mail link to send a message to the e-mail address you specified.

■ When a user selects an e-mail link, the user's e-mail program will start.

■ The e-mail program will automatically display the e-mail address you specified.

CREATE A LINK TO AN FTP SITE

Y our Web page can include a link that will take users to an FTP (File Transfer Protocol) site. FTP sites store files that users can download.

Many colleges, universities, government agencies and companies maintain FTP sites on the Internet. Some popular FTP sites include ftp.cdrom.com and ftp.winsite.com. You can find a list of FTP sites at the hoohoo.ncsa.uiuc.edu/ftp Web site.

When creating a link to an FTP site, you must specify the full address of the site, beginning the address with `ftp://`. For example, to create

a link to the ftp.cdrom.com site, you must type `ftp://ftp.cdrom.com`.

When a user selects a link to an FTP site, the main directory for the site usually appears on the screen. The user can then navigate through the site to find files of interest.

In most cases, users can visit FTP sites anonymously, which means they do not need a user name and password to visit the sites. If an FTP site requires a user name and password, include this information in the link. See the top of page 83 for more information.

CREATE A LINK TO AN FTP SITE

```
<HTML>
<HEAD>
<TITLE>Stan's History Home Page</TITLE>
</HEAD>
<BODY>

<H1>Stan's History Home Page</H1>
<P>Welcome to my history Web site, where you will find all kinds of interesting
information on major historical events. I am a History major at McDougall
Community College with a special interest in European history.</P>

<IMG SRC="venice.jpg" ALIGN="left">

<H3>Interesting History Exhibits</H3>
<BR>One of my favorite hobbies is visiting history exhibits at museums. Thanks to
the Internet, it is possible to visit many exhibits without even leaving home! To visit
some interesting exhibits from the Library of Congress, check out their FTP site!

<BR>Library of Congress

</BODY>
</HTML>
```

■1 Type the text or add the image you want users to select to display an FTP site.

```
<BR><A HREF="ftp://ftp.loc.gov">Library of Congress</A>
```

■2 Type **<A HREF="?">** in front of the text or image, replacing ? with the address of the FTP site.

■3 Type **</A>** after the text or image.

Extra

The information available at an FTP site is stored on an FTP server. The server communicates with Web browsers through a connection called a port. Most FTP servers use port 21. If an FTP server uses a different port, you must specify the number of the port in the link. Type a colon (:) after the address of the FTP site and then type the number of the port.

Example:

```
<A HREF="ftp://ftp.megaftp.com:9999">Mega FTP</A>
```

An FTP site you create a link to may require a user name and password. When specifying the address for the FTP site, type **ftp://** followed by the user name and password for the site. Separate the user name and password with a colon (:). Then type @ followed by the address of the FTP site.

Example:

```
<A HREF="ftp://username:password@ftp.megaftp.com">Mega FTP</A>
```

You may want to create a link to a specific file in an FTP site. This allows users to quickly find information without having to navigate through the site. After the address of the FTP site, type the path to the file.

Example:

```
<A HREF="ftp://ftp.megaftp.com/pub/newlist.txt">The Latest File</A>
```

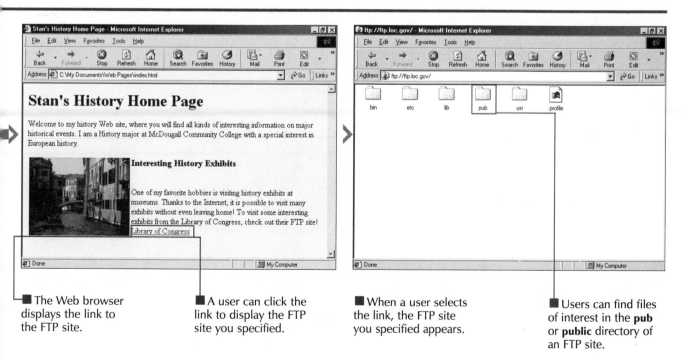

■ The Web browser displays the link to the FTP site.

■ A user can click the link to display the FTP site you specified.

■ When a user selects the link, the FTP site you specified appears.

■ Users can find files of interest in the **pub** or **public** directory of an FTP site.

OPEN A LINK IN A NEW WINDOW

The TARGET attribute allows you to open a link in a new window. The window containing the link will remain open, allowing users to quickly return to your Web page when they have finished viewing the linked information.

When opening a link in a new window, specify a name for the window using the TARGET attribute. The name you specify will identify the window to Web browsers but will not appear in the window. To have several links open in the same window, specify the same name for each link. Window names are case sensitive, so you must use the same uppercase and lowercase letters for each name.

To have a link open in a new, unnamed window, use the _blank value with the TARGET attribute. Each link that uses the _blank value will open in a different window.

Extra

To specify that you want all of the links on your Web page to open in the same new window, use the <BASE> tag with the TARGET attribute. This saves you from having to enter the information for each link individually. Between the <HEAD> and </HEAD> tags, type **<BASE TARGET="?">** replacing **?** with a name for the window.

Example:

<BASE TARGET="main">

OPEN A LINK IN A NEW WINDOW

```
index - WordPad

<HTML>
<HEAD>
<TITLE>Into the Wild</TITLE>
</HEAD>
<BODY>

<H1><I>Into the Wild!</I></H1>

<IMG SRC="cougar.jpg" WIDTH="150" HEIGHT="85" ALIGN="left">
<P><B>Would you like to venture beyond the beaten path? Do so with Into the Wild's
adventure tours.</B>
<BR>Whether you'd like to take a nature photography tour, camp in the rugged wilderness
of the Rocky Mountains or go on a canoeing adventure, we have the trip for you!
<BR>We provide once-in-a-lifetime adventures for groups or individuals. Call today for
information on our packages and sign up for an unforgettable experience!</P>

<IMG SRC="skier.jpg" WIDTH="150" HEIGHT="85" ALIGN="left">
<BR><H3><A HREF="skiing.html" TARGET="skiing" >Skiing</A></H3>
<P>Some of our most popular trips are alpine skiing excursions in the Rocky Mountains.
We will fly you to the top of the slopes by helicopter and provide comfortable
accommodations at the end of a fun-filled day! Cross-country ski packages are also
available!</P>

</BODY>
```

Into the Wild!

Would you like to venture beyond the beaten path? Do so with Into the Wild's adventure tours.

Whether you'd like to take a nature photography tour, camp in the rugged wilderness of the Rocky Mountains or go on a canoeing adventure, we have the trip for you!

We provide once-in-a-lifetime adventures for groups or individuals. Call today for information on our packages and sign up for an unforgettable experience!

Skiing

Some of our most popular trips are alpine skiing excursions in the Rocky Mountains. We will fly you to the top of the slopes by helicopter and provide comfortable accommodations at the end of a fun-filled day! Cross-country ski packages are also available!

1 In the <A> tag for a link you want to open in a new window, type **TARGET="?"** replacing **?** with a name for the window.

■ To have multiple links open in the same new window, repeat step 1 for each link, specifying the same name for the window.

Note: To have a link open in a new, unnamed window, type **TARGET="_blank"** *in step 1.*

■ The Web browser displays the link.

■ A user can click the link to open the linked information in a new window.

CHANGE LINK COLORS

The LINK, VLINK and ALINK attributes allow you to change the color of links on your Web page.

Use the LINK attribute to change the color of links that users have not yet selected and the VLINK attribute to change the color of links that users have previously selected. The ALINK attribute lets you change the color of active links. An active link is a link that a user is currently selecting.

When changing the color of links, make sure that you choose different colors for unvisited, visited

and active links. You should also make sure that the colors you choose work well with the background color of your Web page.

Keep in mind that the link colors you choose may not appear the way you expect on some computers since some users can set their Web browsers to override the colors you choose.

While the LINK, VLINK and ALINK attributes are still supported by Web browsers, the use of *style sheets* is now preferred. For information on style sheets, see page 196.

CHANGE LINK COLORS

```
<HTML>
<HEAD>
<TITLE>Cool Web Pages</TITLE>
</HEAD>
<BODY LINK="#FF0000">

<H1><CENTER>Wendy's Cool Web Pages</CENTER></H1>

<P>Welcome to my home page on the World Wide Web. My name is Wendy Oates.
I'm a third-year computer science student at City College in Sydney, Australia.</P>

<P>The purpose of this page is to introduce Web surfers to cool pages on the
Web. Visit here every day to learn about a page that has amazing graphics, funny
stories or other noteworthy things. Just click on the link below and you will instantly
go to today's cool page.</P>

<P><A HREF="funjokes.html">Today's Cool Page!</A></P>

<P>Do you know of other cool pages that should be featured here?</P>
<A HREF="mailto:wendy@xzy.com">Let me know!</A>

</BODY>
</HTML>
```

Wendy's Cool Web Pages

Welcome to my home page on the World Wide Web. My name is Wendy Oates. I'm a third-year computer science student at City College in Sydney, Australia.

The purpose of this page is to introduce Web surfers to cool pages on the Web. Visit here every day to learn about a page that has amazing graphics, funny stories or other noteworthy things. Just click on the link below and you will instantly go to today's cool page.

Today's Cool Page!

Do you know of other cool pages that should be featured here?

Let me know!

1 In the <BODY> tag, type the attribute for the type of link you want to change (**LINK**, **VLINK** or **ALINK**).

2 Type ="?" replacing ? with the name or hexadecimal value for the color you want to use (example: red or #FF0000).

Note: For a list of colors, see the color chart at the front of this book.

■ The Web browser displays the link colors you specified.

CREATE KEYBOARD SHORTCUTS

U se the ACCESSKEY attribute with the <A> tag to create keyboard shortcuts for links. Keyboard shortcuts allow users to select links without using a mouse.

When creating a keyboard shortcut for a link, specify the letter or number you want to use for the shortcut. You should also include a description that will let users know how to use the shortcut.

To select a link using a keyboard shortcut, a user will hold down the Alt key while pressing the letter or number you specified. The user can then press the Enter key to visit the link. Keyboard shortcuts you create for links do not yet work

on Macintosh computers, though Macintosh users will likely use the Command key rather than the Alt key when shortcuts are supported.

Keyboard shortcuts you create for links will override the keyboard shortcuts for a Web browser. For example, if you create an Alt+F keyboard shortcut, users will no longer be able to use Alt+F to display the File menu in Internet Explorer.

Although the ACCESSKEY attribute is part of the HTML standard, it is not yet supported by most Web browsers.

CREATE KEYBOARD SHORTCUTS

1 In the <A> tag for a link you want to use a keyboard shortcut, type **ACCESSKEY="?"** replacing **?** with a letter or number for the shortcut.

2 Add information about the keyboard shortcut to the text for the link.

■ The Web browser displays the link with the keyboard shortcut information you specified.

■ A user can press the keyboard shortcut you specified to select the link and then press Enter to visit the link.

CHANGE THE TAB ORDER

Users can navigate through the links on your Web page using the Tab key. By default, users tab through the links in the order the links appear in your HTML code. Changing the tab order for your links can help users select the links in a logical order.

Use the TABINDEX attribute to change the tab order for the links on your Web page. To include a link in the tab order, assign the link a TABINDEX value between 1 and 32,767. To exclude a link from the tab order, assign the link a negative TABINDEX value (example: TABINDEX="-1").

When users tab through your links, the tab order will start with the link you assigned the lowest value and will end with the link you assigned the highest value. If two links have the same value, the link that appears first in your HTML code will precede the other link in the tab order.

The TABINDEX attribute can also be used with other HTML elements, such as images and form elements.

While the TABINDEX attribute is part of the HTML standard, it is not yet fully supported by most Web browsers.

CHANGE THE TAB ORDER

1 In the <A> tag for a link on your Web page, type **TABINDEX="?"** replacing **?** with a number that specifies the position of the link in the tab order.

2 Repeat step 1 for each link you want to include in the tab order.

Note: To exclude a link from the tab order, specify a negative number in step 1.

■ Users can tab through the links on your Web page in the order you specified.

CREATE A TABLE

Create a table to neatly display information on your Web page, such as financial data or a price list.

When creating a table, you must use tags to create rows and cells in the table. The <TR> tag lets you create rows and the <TH> and <TD> tags let you create cells.

There are two types of cells you can create in a table. The <TH> tag lets you create header cells and the <TD> tag lets you create data cells. Header cells usually contain text that describes

the data in a row or column, while data cells usually contain the main information in the table. The text in header cells is bold and centered in the cells.

Many people use tables to organize the layout of a Web page. For example, adding paragraphs and images to the cells in a table can help you neatly position text and images on your Web page. Use the <IMG> tag to add an image to a cell. For information on the <IMG> tag, see page 44.

CREATE A TABLE

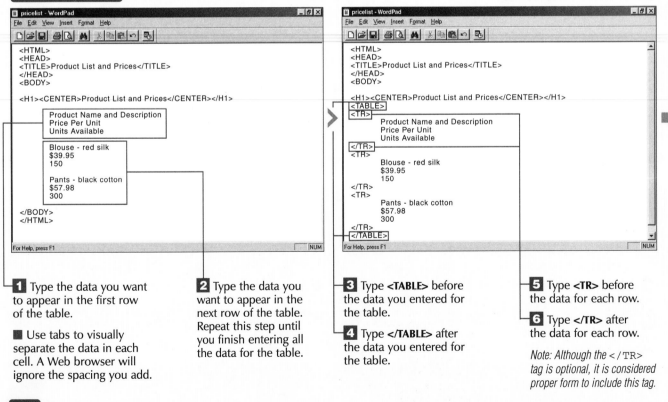

1 Type the data you want to appear in the first row of the table.

■ Use tabs to visually separate the data in each cell. A Web browser will ignore the spacing you add.

2 Type the data you want to appear in the next row of the table. Repeat this step until you finish entering all the data for the table.

3 Type **<TABLE>** before the data you entered for the table.

4 Type **</TABLE>** after the data you entered for the table.

5 Type **<TR>** before the data for each row.

6 Type **</TR>** after the data for each row.

Note: Although the </TR> tag is optional, it is considered proper form to include this tag.

Apply It

Use a table to present information on your Web page in columns like those found in a newspaper. For example, to display information in three columns, create a table that contains one row with three cells.

TYPE THIS:

```
<TABLE>
<TR>
    <TD>To use a table to display columns, create
    a table with one row that contains a cell for
    each column you want to display.</TD>
    <TD>Each cell should contain the information
    for one column. For example, you can display
    three columns of text or an image beside two
    columns of text.</TD>
    <TD>When you display your Web page in a Web
    browser, the information will appear in
    columns. The width of the columns will depend
    on the size of the Web browser window.</TD>
</TR>
</TABLE>
```

RESULT:

To use a table to display columns, create a table with one row that contains a cell for each column you want to display.

Each cell should contain the information for one column. For example, you can display three columns of text or an image beside two columns of text.

When you display your Web page in a Web browser, the information will appear in columns. The width of the columns will depend on the size of the Web browser window.

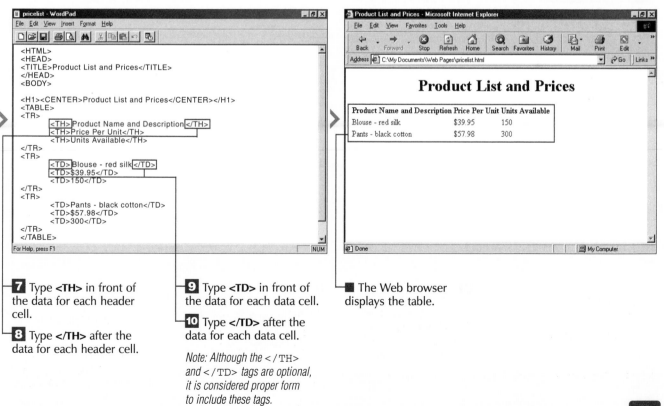

7 Type **<TH>** in front of the data for each header cell.

8 Type **</TH>** after the data for each header cell.

9 Type **<TD>** in front of the data for each data cell.

10 Type **</TD>** after the data for each data cell.

Note: Although the </TH> and </TD> tags are optional, it is considered proper form to include these tags.

■ The Web browser displays the table.

ADD A BORDER

The BORDER attribute allows you to add a border to a table. The border will separate each cell in the table, making the data in the table easier to read.

When adding a border to a table, specify the thickness you want the border to display in pixels. The thickness you specify will only affect the border around the outside of the table. To change the thickness of the border between the cells in the table, use the CELLSPACING attribute as shown on page 104.

A table border usually appears in gray on a Web page. If you have changed the background color of your Web page, Web browsers may display the border in the same color as the background. Use the BORDERCOLOR attribute to specify a different border color. Although the BORDERCOLOR attribute is supported by most Web browsers, it is not part of the HTML standard.

If you are using a table to organize the layout of your Web page, you may want to temporarily add a border to help you see where to place text, images and other elements. You can easily remove the border once your Web page is complete.

ADD A BORDER

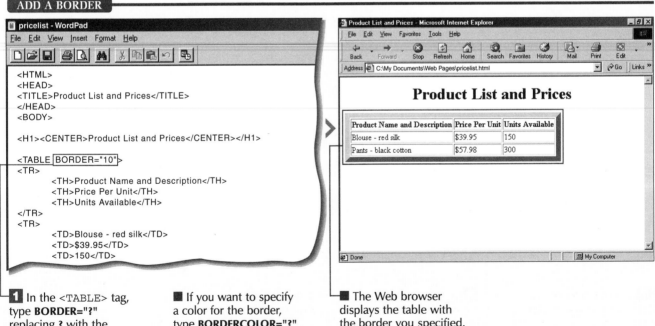

1 In the <TABLE> tag, type **BORDER="?"** replacing **?** with the thickness you want to use for the border in pixels.

■ If you want to specify a color for the border, type **BORDERCOLOR="?"** replacing **?** with the name or hexadecimal value for the color you want to use.

Note: For a list of colors, see the color chart at the front of this book.

■ The Web browser displays the table with the border you specified.

ADD A CAPTION

The `<CAPTION>` tag lets you add a caption to a table. Captions are useful for summarizing the information in a table.

By default, most Web browsers display captions centered above a table. This is useful for displaying a title for a table. Using the `ALIGN` attribute with the `bottom` value allows you to have a caption appear below your table. Displaying a caption below a table is useful when you want to provide additional information about a table or summarize the data in a table.

The HTML standard specifies that you should not add more than one caption to a table on your Web page. While some Web browsers support the use of multiple `<CAPTION>` tags with one `<TABLE>` tag, the results are inconsistent in different Web browsers. For example, Netscape Navigator may reverse the order of the captions you add.

While the `ALIGN` attribute is still supported by Web browsers, the use of *style sheets* is now preferred. For information on style sheets, see page 196.

ADD A CAPTION

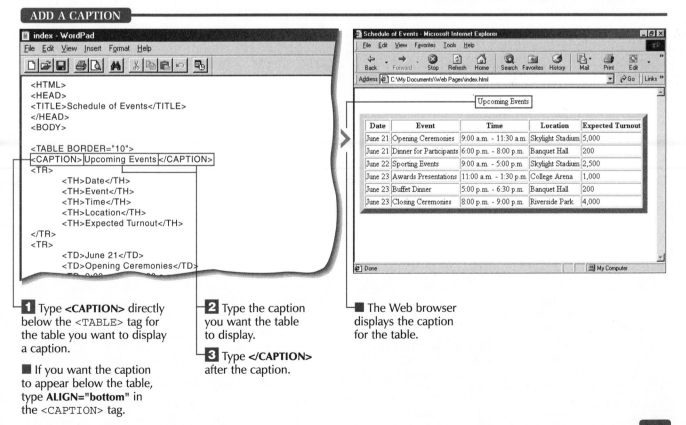

1 Type **<CAPTION>** directly below the `<TABLE>` tag for the table you want to display a caption.

■ If you want the caption to appear below the table, type **ALIGN="bottom"** in the `<CAPTION>` tag.

2 Type the caption you want the table to display.

3 Type **</CAPTION>** after the caption.

■ The Web browser displays the caption for the table.

CREATE COLUMN GROUPS

The <COLGROUP> and <COL> tags allow you to create column groups in a table. Column groups divide a table into vertical sections, allowing you to format one or more columns of cells at the same time.

Use the <COLGROUP> tag to create structural column groups that divide your table into logical sections. For example, you may want to use one structural column group for a column containing headings and another structural column group for the rest of the columns in your table.

The <COL> tag allows you to create non-structural column groups that divide your table into sections

without defining a structure for your table. This is useful when all of your columns contain the same type of information.

Once you have created column groups in a table, you can format the column groups. For example, use the BGCOLOR attribute with a <COLGROUP> or <COL> tag to add color to all the cells in a column group. For more information on adding color to cells, see page 96.

Although the <COLGROUP> and <COL> tags are part of the HTML standard, they are not currently supported by some Web browsers.

CREATE STRUCTURAL COLUMN GROUPS

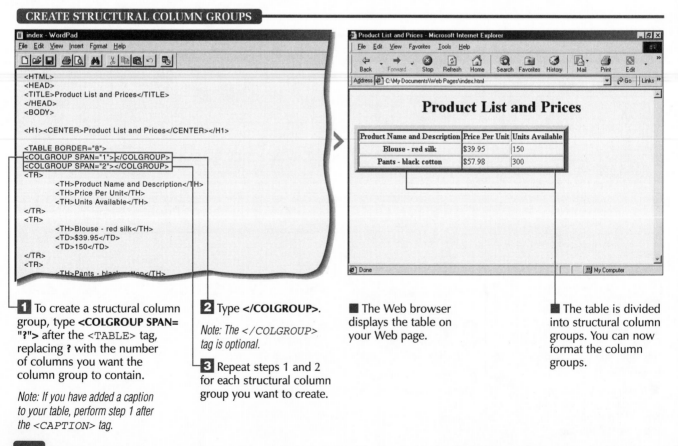

1 To create a structural column group, type **<COLGROUP SPAN= "?">** after the <TABLE> tag, replacing **?** with the number of columns you want the column group to contain.

Note: If you have added a caption to your table, perform step 1 after the <CAPTION> tag.

2 Type **</COLGROUP>**.

Note: The </COLGROUP> tag is optional.

3 Repeat steps 1 and 2 for each structural column group you want to create.

■ The Web browser displays the table on your Web page.

■ The table is divided into structural column groups. You can now format the column groups.

Apply It

A table can contain both structural and non-structural column groups. This allows you to divide structural column groups (`<COLGROUP>`) into sections using non-structural column groups (`<COL>`). You do not need to include the SPAN attribute in a `<COLGROUP>` tag that is divided into non-structural column groups, since the `<COL>` tags define the number of columns in the structural column group.

TYPE THIS:

```
<TABLE BORDER="2">
<COLGROUP>
<COL SPAN="1">
<COL SPAN="1">
<COL SPAN="1">
</COLGROUP>
<TR>    <TH>Score 1</TH>
        <TH>Score 2</TH>
        <TH>Average</TH> </TR>
<TR>    <TD>50</TD>
        <TD>75</TD>
        <TD>62.5</TD> </TR>
<TR>    <TD>45</TD>
        <TD>72</TD>
        <TD>58.5</TD> </TR>
</TABLE>
```

RESULT:

Score 1	Score 2	Average
50	75	62.5
45	72	58.5

- - - `<COLGROUP>`
(Structural column group)

——— `<COL>`
(non-structural column group)

CREATE NON-STRUCTURAL COLUMN GROUPS

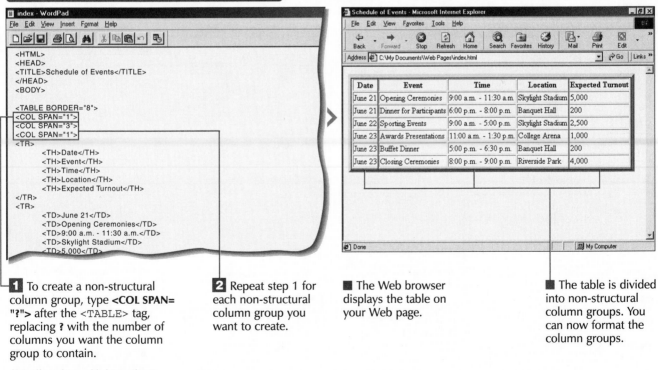

1 To create a non-structural column group, type **<COL SPAN="?">** after the `<TABLE>` tag, replacing ? with the number of columns you want the column group to contain.

Note: If you have added a caption to your table, perform step 1 after the `<CAPTION>` tag.

2 Repeat step 1 for each non-structural column group you want to create.

■ The Web browser displays the table on your Web page.

■ The table is divided into non-structural column groups. You can now format the column groups.

CREATE ROW GROUPS

Use the `<THEAD>`, `<TBODY>` and `<TFOOT>` tags to create row groups in a table. Row groups divide a table into horizontal sections, allowing you to quickly format multiple rows of cells at the same time.

The `<THEAD>` tag allows you to create a header row group in your table. This is useful for headings that you want to format differently than the main data in your table. The `<THEAD>` tag can only appear once in a table.

Use the `<TBODY>` tag to create one or more body row groups in your table. Body row groups usually contain the rows of data in your table.

The `<TFOOT>` tag allows you to create a footer row group in a table. This is useful for summary data or totals that appear at the bottom of your table. The `<TFOOT>` tag can only appear once in a table.

You do not need to include all three types of row groups in a table. For example, you may only want to create a body row group.

Although the `<THEAD>`, `<TBODY>` and `<TFOOT>` tags are part of the HTML standard, they are not yet supported by many Web browsers.

CREATE ROW GROUPS

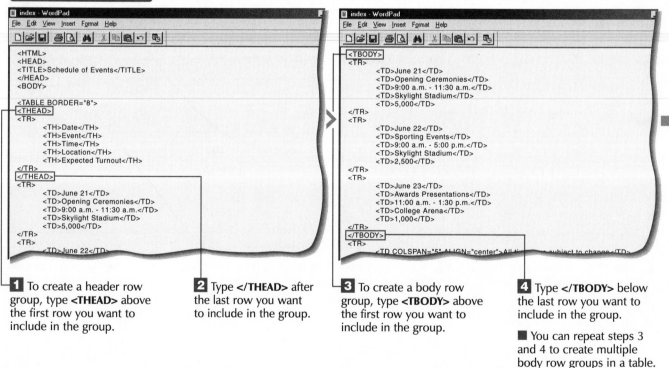

1 To create a header row group, type **<THEAD>** above the first row you want to include in the group.

2 Type **</THEAD>** after the last row you want to include in the group.

3 To create a body row group, type **<TBODY>** above the first row you want to include in the group.

4 Type **</TBODY>** below the last row you want to include in the group.

■ You can repeat steps 3 and 4 to create multiple body row groups in a table.

Extra

Once you have created row groups in a table, you can format the row groups. For example, use the ALIGN attribute with the <THEAD>, <TBODY> or <TFOOT> tag to change the alignment of data in every cell in the row group. For more information on changing the alignment of data in a table, see page 98.

Example:

`<TBODY ALIGN="left">`

The HTML standard specifies that when you print a long table containing header and footer row groups, Web browsers should print the header and footer information on every page. This will help make long tables easier to follow. Web browsers do not yet support this feature.

The HTML standard recommends entering the <TFOOT> information for your table above the <TBODY> information to have Web browsers display the footer row group while the data for the body row groups transfers to a user's computer. This will allow users to view the summary information for your table while waiting for the main data in the table to appear. Web browsers do not yet support this feature. As a result, some Web browsers may display the footer row group above the body row group if you use this method.

```
</TR>
<TR>
        <TD>June 22</TD>
        <TD>Sporting Events</TD>
        <TD>9:00 a.m. - 5:00 p.m.</TD>
        <TD>Skylight Stadium</TD>
        <TD>2,500</TD>
</TR>
<TR>
        <TD>June 23</TD>
        <TD>Awards Presentations</TD>
        <TD>11:00 a.m. - 1:30 p.m.</TD>
        <TD>College Arena</TD>
        <TD>1,000</TD>
</TR>
</TBODY>
<TFOOT>
<TR>
        <TD COLSPAN="5" ALIGN="center">All times are subject to change</TD>
</TR>
</TFOOT>
</TABLE>

</BODY>
</HTML>
```

Date	Event	Time	Location	Expected Turnout
June 21	Opening Ceremonies	9:00 a.m. - 11:30 a.m.	Skylight Stadium	5,000
June 22	Sporting Events	9:00 a.m. - 5:00 p.m.	Skylight Stadium	2,500
June 23	Awards Presentations	11:00 a.m. - 1:30 p.m.	College Arena	1,000
All times are subject to change				

5 To create a footer row group, type **<TFOOT>** above the first row you want to include in the group.

6 Type **</TFOOT>** after the last row you want to include in the group.

Note: Although the </THEAD>, </TBODY> *and* </TFOOT> *tags are optional, it is considered proper form to include these tags.*

■ The Web browser displays the table on your Web page.

■ The table is divided into row groups. You can now format the row groups.

ADD COLOR

The BGCOLOR attribute lets you add color to a table on your Web page. This can help emphasize important information in the table.

You can add color to a cell (<TH> or <TD>), a row (<TR>), a column group (<COLGROUP> or <COL>), a row group (<THEAD>, <TBODY> or <TFOOT>) or an entire table (<TABLE>). For information on column groups and row groups, see pages 92 to 95.

When adding color, specify the name or hexadecimal value for the color you want to use. A hexadecimal value is a code that tells Web browsers which color to display. The code is composed of a number sign (#)

followed by the red, green and blue (RGB) components of the color. For a list of the colors that you can specify by name, see the top of page 33. For a more complete list of colors, see the color chart at the front of this book.

Make sure the color you use does not affect the readability of your table. You may need to change the color of text to make the table easier to read.

While the BGCOLOR attribute is still supported by Web browsers, the use of *style sheets* is now preferred. For information on style sheets, see page 196.

ADD COLOR

1 Click in the tag for the cell (<TH> or <TD>), row (<TR>), column group (<COLGROUP> or <COL>), row group (<THEAD>, <TBODY> or <TFOOT>) or table (<TABLE>) you want to add color to.

Note: For more information on column groups and row groups, see pages 92 to 95.

2 Type **BGCOLOR="?"** replacing ? with the name or hexadecimal value for the color you want to use (example: red or #FF0000).

■ The Web browser displays the cell, row, column group, row group or entire table in the color you specified.

ADD A BACKGROUND IMAGE

Use the BACKGROUND attribute to add a background image to a single cell or an entire table. Adding a background image to a single cell can help make the information in the cell stand out. Adding a background image to an entire table can add an interesting design to the table.

Interesting background images are available at the www.nepthys.com/textures and imagine.metanet.com Web sites. Make sure the background image you choose does not affect the readability of your table. You should also make sure that the background image is an appropriate size. If you use a background that is larger than the cell or table you are adding the

image to, a Web browser will cut off the image to fit in the table.

When adding a background image to an entire table, consider that different Web browsers will display the background image in different ways. For example, Microsoft Internet Explorer will repeat the background image to fill the entire table, while Netscape Navigator will repeat the image in each cell in the table.

Although the BACKGROUND attribute is supported by most Web browsers, it is not part of the HTML standard for tables.

ADD A BACKGROUND IMAGE

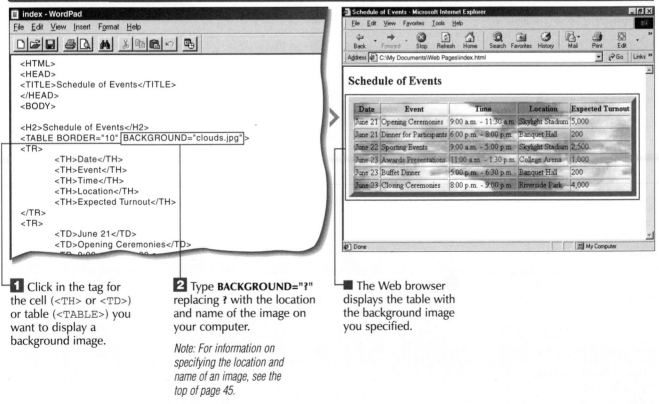

1 Click in the tag for the cell (<TH> or <TD>) or table (<TABLE>) you want to display a background image.

2 Type **BACKGROUND="?"** replacing **?** with the location and name of the image on your computer.

Note: For information on specifying the location and name of an image, see the top of page 45.

■ The Web browser displays the table with the background image you specified.

ALIGN DATA IN A TABLE

The ALIGN and VALIGN attributes allow you to change the horizontal and vertical alignment of data in a table.

Use the ALIGN attribute to change the horizontal alignment of data. By default, the data in header cells (<TH>) is centered and the data in data cells (<TD>) is left aligned.

The VALIGN attribute lets you change the vertical alignment of data. By default, data appears in the middle of each cell in a table.

You can change the alignment of data in a cell (<TH> or <TD>), a row (<TR>), a column group (<COLGROUP> or <COL>) or a row group (<THEAD>, <TBODY> or <TFOOT>). For information on column groups and row groups, see pages 92 to 95.

If you add *cell padding* to your table, the cell padding will affect the alignment of data. For example, if you specify a cell padding of 4 pixels and align data with the top of a cell, the data will appear 4 pixels below the top of the cell. For information on cell padding, see page 104.

ALIGN DATA HORIZONTALLY

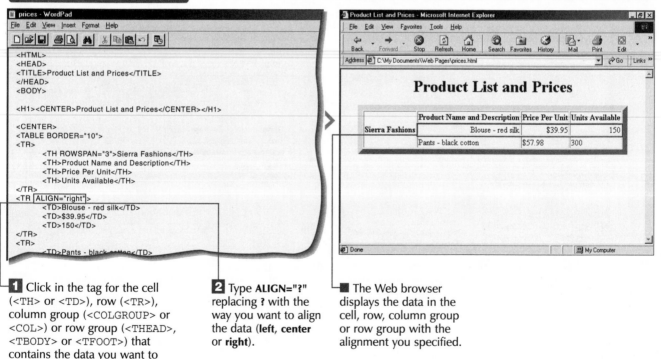

1 Click in the tag for the cell (<TH> or <TD>), row (<TR>), column group (<COLGROUP> or <COL>) or row group (<THEAD>, <TBODY> or <TFOOT>) that contains the data you want to align horizontally.

Note: For information on column groups and row groups, see pages 92 to 95.

2 Type **ALIGN="?"** replacing **?** with the way you want to align the data (**left**, **center** or **right**).

■ The Web browser displays the data in the cell, row, column group or row group with the alignment you specified.

98

Extra

When you specify an alignment for the data in a row, column group or row group, you can later specify a different alignment for the data in an individual cell. The alignment you specify for the cell will override the alignment you specified for the row, column group or row group.

Example:

```
<TR ALIGN="right">
    <TD>This text is right aligned.</TD>
    <TD ALIGN="center">This text is centered.</TD>
    <TD>This text is right aligned.</TD>
</TR>
```

The baseline value lets you vertically align data with the bottom of the first line of text in other cells. Only Netscape Navigator currently supports the baseline value.

Example:

```
<TD VALIGN="baseline">I want to align this data.</TD>
```

The HTML standard includes the justify value for aligning data with both the left and right edges of a cell. Web browsers do not currently support this value.

Example:

```
<TR ALIGN="justify">
```

The HTML standard specifies that the char value allows you to align the same character in cells. Type **ALIGN="char" CHAR="?"** in the tag for a cell, row, column group or row group, replacing **?** with the character you want to align. Web browsers do not currently support the char value.

Example:

```
<TR ALIGN="char" CHAR=".">
```

ALIGN DATA VERTICALLY

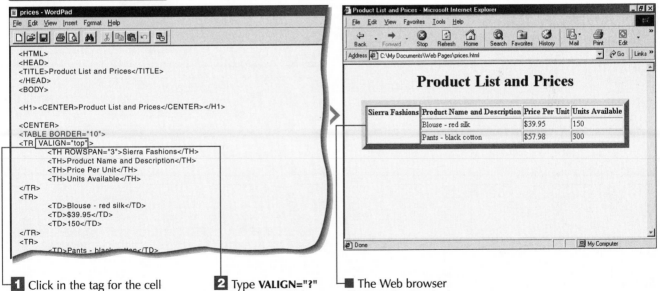

1 Click in the tag for the cell (<TH> or <TD>), row (<TR>), column group (<COLGROUP> or <COL>) or row group (<THEAD>, <TBODY> or <TFOOT>) that contains the data you want to align vertically.

Note: For information on column groups and row groups, see pages 92 to 95.

2 Type **VALIGN="?"** replacing **?** with the way you want to align the data (**top**, **middle** or **bottom**).

■ The Web browser displays the data in the cell, row, column group or row group with the alignment you specified.

CHANGE THE SIZE OF A TABLE

Changing the size of a table is useful when you want a table to take up a specific amount of space on your Web page.

The WIDTH attribute allows you to change the width of a table by specifying a new width in pixels or as a percentage of the Web browser window. When specifying a width in pixels, use a width of 600 pixels or less to ensure the entire table will fit on a user's screen. If you want the width of your table to vary according to the size of the Web browser window, specify the width as a percentage of the Web browser window.

Use the HEIGHT attribute to change the height of a table by specifying a new height in pixels or as a percentage of the Web browser window. The HEIGHT attribute is not part of the HTML standard for tables and some Web browsers do not fully support this attribute.

If you specify a width or height that is smaller than the contents of a table, a Web browser will display the table as small as the contents of the table allow.

CHANGE THE SIZE OF A TABLE

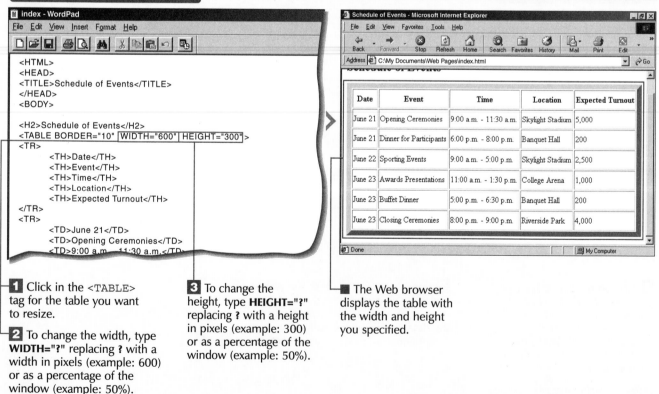

1 Click in the `<TABLE>` tag for the table you want to resize.

2 To change the width, type **WIDTH="?"** replacing ? with a width in pixels (example: 600) or as a percentage of the window (example: 50%).

3 To change the height, type **HEIGHT="?"** replacing ? with a height in pixels (example: 300) or as a percentage of the window (example: 50%).

■ The Web browser displays the table with the width and height you specified.

CHANGE THE SIZE OF A CELL

C hanging the size of a cell in a table can help improve the layout of the table. Use the WIDTH attribute to specify a new width for a cell in pixels or as a percentage of the table. The HEIGHT attribute lets you specify a new height for a cell in pixels.

You do not need to change the size of each individual cell in your table. When you change the width of a cell, all the cells in the same column will display the new width. When you change the height of a

cell, all the cells in the same row will display the new height.

If you specify a width or height that is smaller than the contents of a cell in the column or row, a Web browser will display the column or row as small as the contents of the cell allows.

While the WIDTH and HEIGHT attributes are still supported by Web browsers, the use of *style sheets* is now preferred. For information on style sheets, see page 196.

CHANGE THE SIZE OF A CELL

```
<HTML>
<HEAD>
<TITLE>Recipes</TITLE>
</HEAD>
<BODY>

<H2>Recipes</H2>
<TABLE BORDER="5">
<TR>
        <TH WIDTH="200"HEIGHT="100">Recipe</TH>
        <TH>Food Group</TH>
        <TH>Preparation Time</TH>
        <TH>Notes</TH>
</TR>
<TR>
        <TD>Vegetarian Lasagna</TD>
        <TD>Pasta</TD>
        <TD>45 minutes</TD>
        <TD>Good vegetarian dish</TD>
```

Recipes

Recipe	Food Group	Preparation Time	Notes
Vegetarian Lasagna	Pasta	45 minutes	Good vegetarian dish
Pepper Steak	Meat	1 hour	Delicious marinated
Onion Soup	Soups/ Salads	30 minutes	Filling side dish
Seafood Salad	Soups/ Salads	15 minutes	Tasty appetizer
Stuffed Pork Chops	Meat	1 hour and 30 minutes	Worth the effort!
Grilled Salmon	Fish	50 minutes	Delicious!

1 Click in the <TH> or <TD> tag for the cell you want to resize.

2 To change the width, type **WIDTH="?"** replacing **?** with a width in pixels (example: 200) or as a percentage of the table (example: 50%).

3 To change the height, type **HEIGHT="?"** replacing **?** with a height in pixels (example: 100).

■ The Web browser displays the cell with the size you specified. All the cells in the same column or row also display the new width or height.

SPAN CELLS

S panning cells allows you to combine two or more cells in a row or column into one large cell. This is useful when you want to display a title across the top or down the side of your table. Spanning cells is also useful when you want to display a heading across multiple rows or columns.

Use the COLSPAN attribute with the <TH> or <TD> tag to span a cell across columns. Use the ROWSPAN attribute with the <TH> or <TD> tag to span a cell down rows.

When spanning a cell across columns or down rows, you must specify the number of cells you want the cell to span across.

Some common errors people make when spanning cells include accidentally extending a row past the edge of a table or moving data to the wrong column or row. To avoid problems when spanning cells, you should sketch your table on a piece of paper before you begin. This allows you to clearly see the layout of your table.

SPAN CELLS

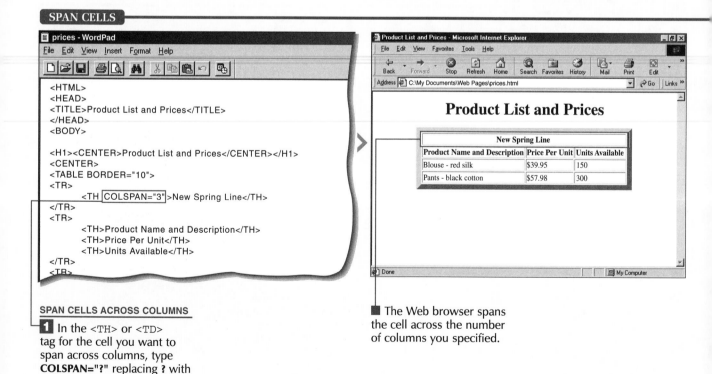

SPAN CELLS ACROSS COLUMNS

1 In the <TH> or <TD> tag for the cell you want to span across columns, type **COLSPAN="?"** replacing **?** with the number of columns you want the cell to span across.

■ The Web browser spans the cell across the number of columns you specified.

Apply It

Using the COLSPAN and ROWSPAN attributes in the same <TH> or <TD> tag allows you to span a cell across columns and down rows at the same time.

TYPE THIS:

```
<TABLE BORDER="10">
<TR>
    <TH>Schedule</TH>
    <TD>Othello</TD>
    <TD>Hamlet</TD>
    <TD>Julius Caesar</TD>
</TR>
<TR>
    <TD>Preview</TD>
    <TD COLSPAN="2" ROWSPAN="2">To Be
Announced</TD>
    <TD>Aug.28, 2000</TD>
</TR>
<TR>
    <TD>Opening Night</TD>
    <TD>Sep.30, 2000</TD>
</TR>
</TABLE>
```

RESULT:

Schedule	Othello	Hamlet	Julius Caesar
Preview	To Be Announced		Aug.28, 2000
Opening Night			Sep.30, 2000

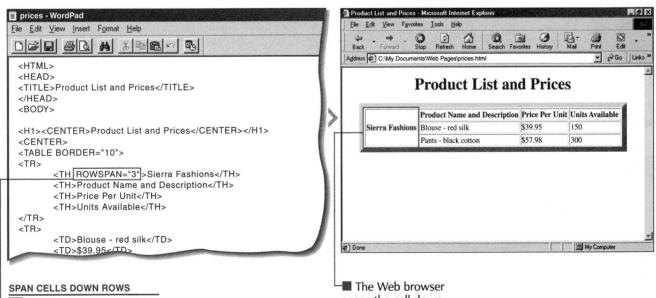

```
<HTML>
<HEAD>
<TITLE>Product List and Prices</TITLE>
</HEAD>
<BODY>

<H1><CENTER>Product List and Prices</CENTER></H1>
<CENTER>
<TABLE BORDER="10">
<TR>
        <TH ROWSPAN="3">Sierra Fashions</TH>
        <TH>Product Name and Description</TH>
        <TH>Price Per Unit</TH>
        <TH>Units Available</TH>
</TR>
<TR>
        <TD>Blouse - red silk</TD>
        <TD>$39.95</TD>
```

Product List and Prices

	Product Name and Description	Price Per Unit	Units Available
Sierra Fashions	Blouse - red silk	$39.95	150
	Pants - black cotton	$57.98	300

SPAN CELLS DOWN ROWS

1 In the <TH> or <TD> tag for the cell you want to span down rows, type **ROWSPAN="?"** replacing **?** with the number of rows you want the cell to span down.

■ The Web browser spans the cell down the number of rows you specified.

CHANGE CELL SPACING AND CELL PADDING

The CELLSPACING and CELLPADDING attributes are often used to improve the layout and readability of a table.

The CELLSPACING attribute lets you change the amount of space between each cell in a table. Changing the cell spacing will change the size of the border between cells. Specify the amount of space you want to use in pixels. By default, tables display a cell spacing of 2 pixels.

The CELLPADDING attribute lets you change the amount of space around the contents of each cell

in a table. Increasing the cell padding can make a table appear less cluttered. By default, the cell padding for a table is 1 pixel.

Changing the cell padding for a table will affect the alignment of data in the table. For example, if you align data with the top of a cell and then specify a cell padding of 4 pixels, the data will appear 4 pixels below the top of the cell. For information on changing the alignment of data in a table, see page 98.

CHANGE CELL SPACING AND CELL PADDING

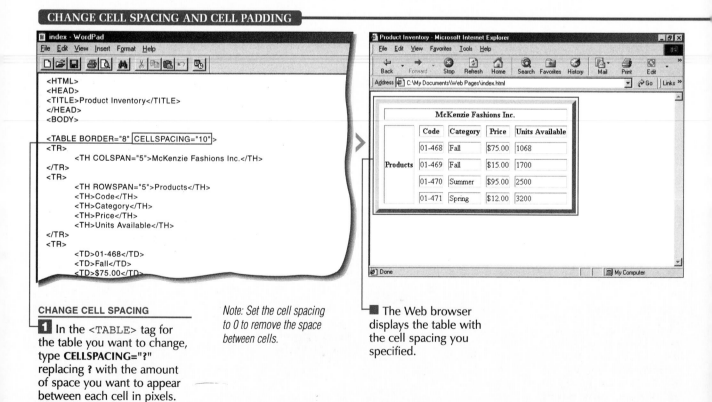

CHANGE CELL SPACING

1 In the <TABLE> tag for the table you want to change, type **CELLSPACING="?"** replacing ? with the amount of space you want to appear between each cell in pixels.

Note: Set the cell spacing to 0 to remove the space between cells.

■ The Web browser displays the table with the cell spacing you specified.

Apply It

Setting the CELLSPACING and CELLPADDING attributes to 0 can make two images in a table appear as one image. To completely remove the space between cells, you should also set the BORDER attribute to 0.

TYPE THIS:

```
<TABLE BORDER="0" CELLSPACING="0"
CELLPADDING="0">
<TR>
    <TD COLSPAN="2"><IMG SRC="banner.gif"></TD>
</TR>
<TR>
    <TD><IMG SRC="landscape.gif"></TD>
    <TD>This Web page includes information
    about my trip to Europe. I want to
    share with you all the interesting places
    and people I encountered. I have included
    some tips and tricks to help make your next
    trip to Europe enjoyable.</TD>
</TR>
</TABLE>
```

RESULT:

My European Trip

This Web page includes information about my trip to Europe. I want to share with you all the interesting places and people I encountered. I have included some tips and tricks to help make your next trip to Europe enjoyable.

---

index - WordPad

File Edit View Insert Format Help

```
<HTML>
<HEAD>
<TITLE>Product Inventory</TITLE>
</HEAD>
<BODY>

<TABLE BORDER="8" CELLPADDING="10">
<TR>
    <TH COLSPAN="5">McKenzie Fashions Inc.</TH>
</TR>
<TR>
    <TH ROWSPAN="5">Products</TH>
    <TH>Code</TH>
    <TH>Category</TH>
    <TH>Price</TH>
    <TH>Units Available</TH>
</TR>
<TR>
    <TD>01-468</TD>
    <TD>Fall</TD>
    <TD>$75.00</TD>
```

Product Inventory - Microsoft Internet Explorer

File Edit View Favorites Tools Help

Back Forward Stop Refresh Home Search Favorites History Mail Print Edit

Address C:\My Documents\Web Pages\index.html

	McKenzie Fashions Inc.			
	Code	Category	Price	Units Available
Products	01-468	Fall	$75.00	1068
	01-469	Fall	$15.00	1700
	01-470	Summer	$95.00	2500
	01-471	Spring	$12.00	3200

Done   My Computer

CHANGE CELL PADDING

1 In the <TABLE> tag for the table you want to change, type **CELLPADDING="?"** replacing **?** with the amount of space you want to appear around the contents of each cell in pixels.

Note: Set the cell padding to 0 to remove the space around the contents of each cell.

■ The Web browser displays the table with the cell padding you specified.

SPECIFY WHICH BORDERS TO DISPLAY

When you add a border to a table using the BORDER attribute, the border automatically appears around the outside of the table and between each cell. Use the FRAME and RULES attributes to display only some table borders.

The FRAME attribute lets you specify which external borders you want to display. For example, you may want to display borders above and below a table or on only the right side of the table.

The RULES attribute lets you specify which internal borders you want to display. For example, display borders between rows or columns or between

column groups and row groups. When displaying internal borders between column groups and row groups, keep in mind that only structural column groups will display the borders. For information on column groups and row groups, see pages 92 to 95.

Using the FRAME and RULES attributes in the same <TABLE> tag allows you to create interesting border designs for a table. For example, you can create a table that displays vertical borders on each side of columns, with no horizontal borders.

While the FRAME and RULES attributes are part of the HTML standard, these attributes are not yet supported by some Web browsers.

SPECIFY EXTERNAL BORDERS

```
index - WordPad
File  Edit  View  Insert  Format  Help

<HTML>
<HEAD>
<TITLE>Schedule of Events</TITLE>
</HEAD>
<BODY>

<H2>Schedule of Events</H2>
<TABLE BORDER="8" FRAME="hsides">
<TR>
        <TH>Date</TH>
        <TH>Event</TH>
        <TH>Time</TH>
        <TH>Location</TH>
        <TH>Expected Turnout</TH>
</TR>
<TR>
        <TD>June 21</TD>
        <TD>Opening Ceremonies</TD>
        <TD>9:00 a.m. - 11:30 a.m.</TD>
        <TD>Skylight Stadium</TD>
        <TD>5,000</TD>
```

Schedule of Events - Microsoft Internet Explorer

File Edit View Favorites Tools Help

Back Forward Stop Refresh Home Search Favorites History Mail Print Edit

Address C:\My Documents\Web Pages\index.html

Schedule of Events

Date	Event	Time	Location	Expected Turnout
June 21	Opening Ceremonies	9:00 a.m. - 11:30 a.m.	Skylight Stadium	5,000
June 21	Dinner for Participants	6:00 p.m. - 8:00 p.m.	Banquet Hall	200
June 22	Sporting Events	9:00 a.m. - 5:00 p.m.	Skylight Stadium	2,500
June 23	Awards Presentation	11:00 a.m. - 1:30 p.m.	College Arena	1,000
June 23	Closing Ceremonies	8:00 p.m. - 9:00 p.m.	Riverside Park	4,000

Done — My Computer

1 Add a border to your table as shown on page 90.

2 In the <TABLE> tag for the table, type **FRAME="?"** replacing **?** with the value for the external borders you want to display (**void**, **above**, **below**, **rhs**, **lhs**, **hsides**, **vsides** or **border**).

Note: For more information, see the top of page 107.

■ The Web browser displays the table with the external borders you specified.

External Borders

Use one of the following values for the FRAME attribute to specify the external borders you want your table to display.

SPECIFY THE VALUE	TO DISPLAY
void	No external borders.
above	A border above the table.
below	A border below the table.
rhs	A border on the right side of the table.
lhs	A border on the left side of the table.
hsides	Borders on the top and bottom of the table.
vsides	Borders on the left and right sides of the table.
border	All external borders (default).

Internal Borders

Use one of the following values for the RULES attribute to specify the internal borders you want your table to display.

SPECIFY THE VALUE	TO DISPLAY
none	No internal borders.
cols	Borders between columns.
rows	Borders between rows.
groups	Borders between column groups and row groups.
all	All internal borders (default).

SPECIFY INTERNAL BORDERS

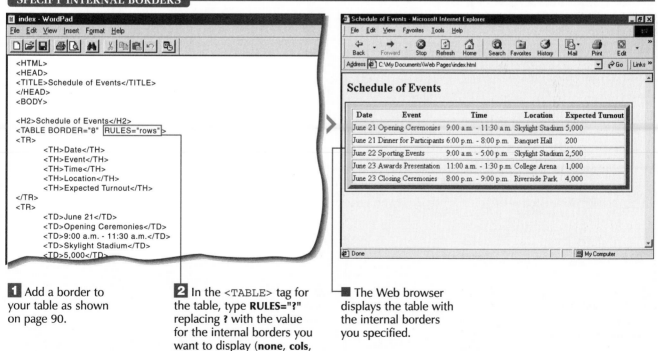

1 Add a border to your table as shown on page 90.

2 In the <TABLE> tag for the table, type **RULES="?"** replacing **?** with the value for the internal borders you want to display (**none**, **cols**, **rows**, **groups** or **all**).

Note: For more information, see the top of this page.

■ The Web browser displays the table with the internal borders you specified.

107

PREVENT TEXT WRAPPING IN CELLS

A Web browser will usually automatically wrap the text in a cell depending on the size of the table and the size of the Web browser window. Use the NOWRAP attribute to prevent the text in a cell from wrapping. This is useful when you want all the text in a cell to appear on one line.

Use the NOWRAP attribute only in cells that contain a small amount of text, such as cells containing a title or product name. Using the NOWRAP attribute in a cell that contains a large amount of text will create a very large cell that

may cause your table to extend past the edge of a Web browser window.

When using the NOWRAP attribute in a cell, keep in mind that the text in the cell will not appear on one line if the <P> or <BR> tags appear in the cell. For information on the <P> and <BR> tags, see pages 16 and 18.

While the NOWRAP attribute is still supported by Web browsers, the use of *style sheets* is now preferred. For information on style sheets, see page 196.

PREVENT TEXT WRAPPING IN CELLS

```
<HTML>
<HEAD>
<TITLE>Schedule of Events</TITLE>
</HEAD>
<BODY>

<H2>Schedule of Events</H2>
<TABLE BORDER="10">
<TR>
        <TH>Date</TH>
        <TH>Event</TH>
        <TH>Time</TH>
        <TH>Location</TH>
        <TH>Expected Turnout</TH>
</TR>
<TR>
        <TD NOWRAP >June 21, 2000</TD>
        <TD>Opening Ceremonies</TD>
        <TD>9:00 a.m. - 11:30 a.m.</TD>
        <TD>Skylight Stadium</TD>
        <TD>5,000</TD>
</TR>
<TR
```

Schedule of Events

Date	Event	Time	Location	Expected Turnout
June 21, 2000	Opening Ceremonies	9:00 a.m. - 11:30 a.m.	Skylight Stadium	5,000
June 21	Dinner for Participants	6:00 p.m. - 8:00 p.m.	Banquet Hall	200
June 22	Sporting Events	9:00 a.m. - 5:00 p.m.	Skylight Stadium	2,500
June 23	Awards Presentation	11:00 a.m. - 1:30 p.m.	College Arena	1,000
June 23	Closing Ceremonies	8:00 p.m. - 9:00 p.m.	Riverside Park	4,000

1 In the <TH> or <TD> tag for the cell that contains text you want to appear on one line, type **NOWRAP**.

Note: The text in the cell will not appear on one line if the <P> or <BR> tags appear in the cell.

■ The Web browser displays the text on one line.

CREATE NESTED TABLES

Nesting a table within another table allows you to create more complex table layouts.

To nest a table, you first create the main table, leaving the cell you want to contain the nested table empty. You can then nest a table by creating a new table in the empty cell.

When creating the tables, make sure you include all the end tags (</TH>, </TD>, </TR> and </TABLE>) for both the main table and the nested table. Forgetting to include an end tag may adversely affect the layout of the tables.

Some people prefer to create the main table and nested table separately. This can help you identify possible layout problems with the tables. Once you are satisfied with the appearance of both tables, copy the contents of the table you want to nest into the empty cell in the main table.

You can format nested tables as you would format any other table. For example, you may want to add color to a nested table as shown on page 96.

Avoid overusing nested tables on your Web page, since this can affect the performance of a user's Web browser.

CREATE NESTED TABLES

```
<H2>Product List and Prices</H2>

<TABLE BORDER="8">
<TR>
        <TH>Product Name and Description</TH>
        <TH>Price Per Unit</TH>
        <TH>Units Available</TH>
</TR>
<TR>
        <TD>
                <TABLE BORDER="1">
                <TR>
                <TD>White silk blouse - long sleeved</TD>
                </TR>
                <TR>
                <TD>Red silk blouse - long sleeved</TD>
                </TR>
                <TR>
                <TD>Black silk blouse - long sleeved</TD>
                </TR>
                </TABLE>
        </TD>
```

index - WordPad
File Edit View Insert Format Help

Product List and Prices - Microsoft Internet Explorer
File Edit View Favorites Tools Help
Back Forward Stop Refresh Home Search Favorites History Mail Print Edit
Address C:\My Documents\Web Pages\index.html

Product List and Prices

Product Name and Description	Price Per Unit	Units Available
White silk blouse - long sleeved		
Red silk blouse - long sleeved	$39.95	150
Black silk blouse - long sleeved		
Pants	$57.98	300

1 Create the table you want to contain a nested table, leaving the cell you want to contain the table empty.

2 Click in the cell you want to contain the nested table.

3 Create the nested table as you created the main table.

Note: You can use indents to visually separate the nested table from the main table. A Web browser will ignore the indents you add.

■ The Web browser displays the nested table within the main table.

WRAP TEXT AROUND A TABLE

The ALIGN attribute allows you to wrap text around a table. This can help give your Web page a professional look.

When wrapping text around a table, use the left or right value to specify how you want the text to wrap around the table. The left value places the table on the left side of the text, while the right value places the table on the right side of the text.

If you want only some of the text to wrap around a table, use the CLEAR attribute with the <BR> tag to mark where you want to

stop wrapping text around the table. Use the left, right or all value to have the text continue when the left margin, right margin or both margins are clear of tables.

You should only wrap text around small tables on your Web page. Wrapping text around large tables may produce unexpected results, such as text overlapping the table.

While the ALIGN and CLEAR attributes are still supported by Web browsers, the use of *style sheets* is now preferred. For information on style sheets, see page 196.

WRAP TEXT AROUND A TABLE

```
<HTML>
<HEAD>
<TITLE>Biography</TITLE>
</HEAD>
<BODY>

<H1><CENTER>The Jazz Kings' Biography</CENTER></H1>

<TABLE BORDER="8" ALIGN="left">
<TR>
        <TH>Record Name</TH>
        <TH>Year Produced</TH>
</TR>
<TR>
        <TD>Midnight Jazz</TD>
        <TD>1994</TD>
</TR>
<TR>
        <TD>Summer Songs</TD>
```

The Jazz Kings' Biography

Record Name	Year Produced
Midnight Jazz	1994
Summer Songs	1996
Live in Concert	1998
Best Hits	2000

The Jazz Kings burst onto the music scene in 1994 with their debut album entitled Midnight Jazz. Since then, the band has been gaining popularity throughout the United States.

The band consists of five talented musicians who met in New Orleans in 1991. Since then, they have produced four albums and have toured throughout the United States and Europe. Although their albums are great, the band really must be seen live to be truly appreciated! The Jazz Kings play with a great deal of energy, and the audience is always dancing in unison by the end of the first song! Whether they're playing a small club or a large stadium, the band is always at their best when on stage.

The Jazz Kings' newest album, Best Hits, is a collection of songs from their previous recordings. Be sure to pick it up at your local record store!

■1 To wrap text around the right side of a table, type **ALIGN="left"** in the <TABLE> tag for the table.

■ To wrap text around the left side of a table, type **ALIGN="right"** in the <TABLE> tag for the table.

■ The Web browser displays the text wrapped around the table.

Apply It

Use the `center` value with the `ALIGN` attribute to horizontally center a table on your Web page. Text will not wrap around a table you horizontally centered.

TYPE THIS:

```
<TABLE ALIGN="center" BORDER="1">
<TR>
     <TH>Product</TH>
     <TH>Price Per Unit</TH>
</TR>
<TR>
     <TD>Hammer</TD>
     <TD>$14.95</TD>
</TR>
<TR>
     <TD>Saw</TD>
     <TD>$29.99</TD>
</TR>
</TABLE>
```

RESULT:

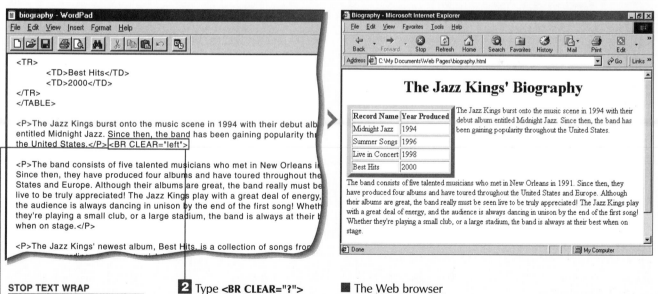

Product	Price Per Unit
Hammer	$14.95
Saw	$29.95

Welcome to Jacob & Sons Carpentry Supply Store! We've been a fixture in the Lincoln community for over eighty years, maintaining our commitment to tradition, honesty, and quality craftsmanship. But...

STOP TEXT WRAP

1 Click where you want to stop text from wrapping around a table.

2 Type **<BR CLEAR="?">** replacing **?** with the margin(s) you want to be clear of tables before the text continues (**left**, **right** or **all**).

■ The Web browser stops the text wrap where you specified.

CREATE A LINK TO A SOUND

Your Web page can contain a link that users can select to play a sound.

There are many places that offer sounds you can use on your Web pages, such as the www.wavcentral.com and www.soundamerica.com Web sites. You can also purchase sound collections at many computer stores or record your own sounds. To record sounds, your computer must have sound capabilities and a sound recording program. Popular sound recording programs include Microsoft Sound Recorder and QuickTime.

When creating a link to a sound, make sure the sound you use is a type of sound commonly used on the Web. For more information on sound types, see page 113. You should also make sure you have permission to use any sounds you did not create yourself.

When a user selects a sound link, the user's Web browser will attempt to play the sound. If the Web browser cannot play the sound, the browser will try to open the sound in a program on the user's computer. If the user does not have an appropriate program, the Web browser will allow the user to save the sound on their computer.

CREATE A LINK TO A SOUND

```
<HTML>
<HEAD>
<TITLE>Classical Music Composers</TITLE>
</HEAD>
<BODY>

<H1>Bach</H1>

<P>Johann Sebastian Bach was born into a family of musicians in 1685 in
Eisenach, Germany. Bach's works include church organ and choral music, music
for chamber orchestras and over 200 cantatas. Although he was more respected
as an organist during his lifetime, Bach's compositions influenced many later
composers, including Beethoven and Mozart. Bach is still considered one of the
greatest composers of the Baroque period (1600-1750).</P>

<P>Sound clips from some of Bach's most famous works:
<BR><A HREF="matthew.au">St. Matthew Passion</A>
<BR>Brandenburg Concertos</P>

</BODY>
</HTML>
```

Bach

Johann Sebastian Bach was born into a family of musicians in 1685 in Eisenach, Germany. Bach's works include church organ and choral music, music for chamber orchestras and over 200 cantatas. Although he was more respected as an organist during his lifetime, Bach's compositions influenced many later composers, including Beethoven and Mozart. Bach is still considered one of the greatest composers of the Baroque period (1600-1750).

Sound clips from some of Bach's most famous works:
St. Matthew Passion
Brandenburg Concertos

1 Type the text or add the image you want users to select to play the sound.

2 Type **<A HREF="?">** in front of the text or image, replacing **?** with the location and name of the sound on your computer.

Note: For information on specifying the location and name of a sound, see page 113.

3 Type **</A>** after the text or image.

■ The Web browser displays the sound link on your Web page.

■ When a user selects the sound link, the sound will transfer to their computer and play.

SOUND CONSIDERATIONS

Sound Type

There are several types of sound you can include on a Web page. The most popular type of sound is WAV. The file extension for a sound indicates the sound type.

The following chart displays sound types commonly used on the Web.

Type of Sound	Extension	Used For
MIDI	.mid	Instrumental music
MP3	.mp3	Songs
RealAudio	.ra	Live broadcasts
WAV	.wav	Short sound clips

Provide a Description

When creating a link to a sound, you should provide a short description of the sound to help users decide if they want to play the sound. The description should include the sound type, size and length of time the sound will play. Users may not want to play a sound with a large file size, since the sound may take a long time to transfer to their computer.

Provide Sound Alternatives

Some users may be hearing impaired or use computers that do not have sound capabilities. Consider including a description or text version of important sounds on your Web page. If the sound is a long clip from a movie, performance or speech, you may want to include a link to a text version of the sound.

Provide a Program Link

Some users may not have a program installed on their computers that will allow them to play a sound you added to your Web page. Consider including a link on your Web page that will take users to a Web site where they can obtain a program that will play the sound. For example, if your Web page contains RealAudio sounds, include a link to the www.real.com Web site where users can obtain the RealPlayer program. If you have included MP3 sounds on your Web page, you may want to include a link to the www.nullsoft.com Web site where users can obtain the Winamp program.

Specify Location of Sounds

You should store all of your Web pages and sounds in one folder on your computer. If the folder contains many files, you may want to store your sounds in a subfolder. If a sound you want to add to a Web page is stored in the same folder as the Web page, specify just the name of the sound (example: birdcall.wav). If a sound is stored in a subfolder, specify the name of the subfolder and the name of the sound (example: sounds/birdcall.wav).

ADD AN EMBEDDED SOUND

The <EMBED> tag allows you to add an embedded sound to your Web page. An embedded sound will play directly on your Web page.

When you add an embedded sound, your Web page will display sound controls that allow users to start and stop the sound. Use the WIDTH and HEIGHT attributes to specify a size for the sound controls.

By default, some Web browsers automatically play an embedded sound when users visit the Web page. Use the AUTOSTART attribute with

the false value to prevent a sound from playing automatically. If you want an embedded sound to play continuously, use the LOOP attribute with the true value.

To play an embedded sound, a Web browser must have the correct plug-in installed. A plug-in is software that adds features to a Web browser. If a user's Web browser does not have the correct plug-in, the browser may prompt the user to download the plug-in from the Web.

While the <EMBED> tag is supported by most Web browsers, it is not part of the HTML standard.

ADD AN EMBEDDED SOUND

index - WordPad
File Edit View Insert Format Help

```
<HTML>
<HEAD>
<TITLE>Classical Music Composers</TITLE>
</HEAD>
<BODY>

<H1>Beethoven</H1>
<P>Ludwig van Beethoven was born in Bonn, Germany in 1770. He spent most of his
Vienna, where he earned a living giving concerts, teaching piano and selling his comp
<BR>One of the most fascinating aspects of Beethoven's life was his triumph over dea
which struck him during adulthood. In fact, he composed some of his most powerful w
losing his hearing.</P>

<EMBED SRC="beethoven.wav">

</BODY>
</HTML>
```

index - WordPad
File Edit View Insert Format Help

```
<HTML>
<HEAD>
<TITLE>Classical Music Composers</TITLE>
</HEAD>
<BODY>

<H1>Beethoven</H1>
<P>Ludwig van Beethoven was born in Bonn, Germany in 1770. He spent most of his
Vienna, where he earned a living giving concerts, teaching piano and selling his comp
<BR>One of the most fascinating aspects of Beethoven's life was his triumph over dea
which struck him during adulthood. In fact, he composed some of his most powerful w
losing his hearing.</P>

<EMBED SRC="beethoven.wav" WIDTH="170" HEIGHT="25">

</BODY>
</HTML>
```

1 Type **<EMBED SRC="?">** where you want the controls for the sound to appear on your Web page. Replace **?** with the location and name of the sound on your computer.

Note: For information on specifying the location and name of a sound, see page 113.

2 In the <EMBED> tag, type **WIDTH="?" HEIGHT="?"** replacing **?** with the width and height of the sound controls in pixels.

Extra

The HIDDEN attribute lets you hide the controls for a sound. This is useful when you want to add a background sound to your Web page. When hiding the controls for a sound, you should use the AUTOSTART attribute with the true value to ensure the sound plays automatically when a user visits your Web page.

Example:

```
<EMBED SRC="backgroundmusic.wav"
HIDDEN AUTOSTART="true" LOOP="true">
```

Use the <NOEMBED> tag to provide alternative text that will appear if a Web browser does not support the <EMBED> tag. The alternative text you provide will not appear if a Web browser recognizes the <EMBED> tag.

Example:

```
<EMBED SRC="meow.wav"><NOEMBED>Sound
of my cat's meow.</NOEMBED>
```

The HTML standard recommends that you use the <OBJECT> tag to add objects such as embedded sounds to your Web page. Since Web browsers do not currently fully support the <OBJECT> tag, the <EMBED> tag is more commonly used.

To add an embedded sound using the <OBJECT> tag, use the DATA attribute to specify the location and name of the sound on your computer. Type text you want to appear if a Web browser does not support the <OBJECT> tag between the <OBJECT> and </OBJECT> tags.

Example:

```
<OBJECT DATA="firecracker.wav">
Firecracker Sounds Here</OBJECT>
```

```
<HTML>
<HEAD>
<TITLE>Classical Music Composers</TITLE>
</HEAD>
<BODY>

<H1>Beethoven</H1>
<P>Ludwig van Beethoven was born in Bonn, Germany in 1770. He spent most of his
Vienna, where he earned a living giving concerts, teaching piano and selling his comp
<BR>One of the most fascinating aspects of Beethoven's life was his triumph over dea
which struck him during adulthood. In fact, he composed some of his most powerful w
losing his hearing.</P>

<EMBED SRC="beethoven.wav" WIDTH="170" HEIGHT="25" AUTOSTART="false"
LOOP="true">

</BODY>
</HTML>
```

Beethoven

Ludwig van Beethoven was born in Bonn, Germany in 1770. He spent most of his life in Vienna, where he earned a living giving concerts, teaching piano and selling his compositions.
One of the most fascinating aspects of Beethoven's life was his triumph over deafness, which struck him during adulthood. In fact, he composed some of his most powerful works after losing his hearing.

Symphony No.9 (154KB)

3 If you do not want the sound to play automatically when a user visits your Web page, type **AUTOSTART="false"** in the <EMBED> tag.

4 If you want the sound to play continuously until a user clicks the Stop or Pause button or displays another Web page, type **LOOP="true"** in the <EMBED> tag.

■ The Web browser displays the sound controls on your Web page.

■ Users can use the sound controls to start or stop the sound at any time.

ADD AN EXTERNAL VIDEO

You may want to create a link on your Web page that users can select to play a video. A video that users play by selecting a link is called an external video.

There are many places where you can find videos for your Web pages, such as the www.picturesnow.com and www.jurassicpunk.com Web sites. You can also purchase collections of videos at computer stores or record videos. For information on recording videos, see page 117.

When creating a link to a video, provide a short description of the video that

includes the video type, size and length of time the video will play. This can help users decide if they want to play the video. You should also make sure the video is a type of video commonly used on the Web. For more information, see page 117.

When a user selects a video link, the user's Web browser will attempt to play the video. If the Web browser cannot play the video, the browser will try to open the video in a program on the user's computer. If the user does not have an appropriate program, the Web browser will allow the user to save the video on their computer.

ADD AN EXTERNAL VIDEO

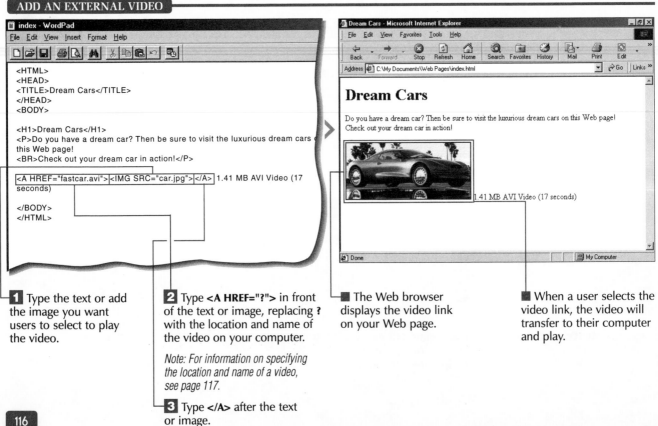

1 Type the text or add the image you want users to select to play the video.

2 Type **<A HREF="?">** in front of the text or image, replacing **?** with the location and name of the video on your computer.

Note: For information on specifying the location and name of a video, see page 117.

3 Type **</A>** after the text or image.

■ The Web browser displays the video link on your Web page.

■ When a user selects the video link, the video will transfer to their computer and play.

VIDEO CONSIDERATIONS

Video Types

There are several types of video you can include on a Web page. The file extension for a video indicates the video type.

The following chart displays video types commonly used on the Web.

Type of Video	Extension
AVI	.avi
MPEG	.mpg or .mpeg
QuickTime	.mov or .qt

File Size

Video files tend to be the largest files on the Web. The file size of a video depends on its resolution, sound quality and length. Videos with large file sizes can take a long time to transfer to a computer. For example, a video larger than 10 Megabytes (MB) can take more than an hour to download depending on the speed of your Internet connection. Whenever possible, you should use videos with small file sizes.

Provide a Program Link

Some users may not have a program installed on their computer that will allow them to play a video you added to your Web page. You should consider including a link on your Web page that will take users to a Web site where they can obtain a program that will play the video. For example, if you include QuickTime videos on your Web page, you may want to include a link to the www.apple.com/quicktime/download Web site where users can obtain the QuickTime Player program.

Record Videos

If your computer has a video capture card or built-in video capture capabilities, you can connect a VCR, video camera or DVD player to your computer to record videos. Video capture cards usually include all the necessary cables and software you need to record videos. Make sure you have permission to record videos that you did not create yourself. When recording videos, keep in mind that long videos will have large file sizes and will take a long time to transfer to a computer.

Specify Location of Videos

You should store all of your Web pages and videos in one folder on your computer. If the folder contains many files, you may want to store your videos in a subfolder. If a video you want to add to a Web page is stored in the same folder as the Web page, specify just the name of the video (example: airplane.avi). If a video is stored in a subfolder, specify the name of the subfolder and the name of the video (example: videos/airplane.avi).

ADD AN INTERNAL VIDEO

The <EMBED> tag allows you to add an internal video to your Web page. An internal video will play directly on your Web page.

When adding an internal video, you should specify the size of the video using the WIDTH and HEIGHT attributes. This ensures that the video will appear correctly in a Web browser. Use a video player program such as Windows Media Player or QuickTime Player to determine the correct width and height of a video.

The AUTOSTART and LOOP attributes allow you to specify the way you want a video to play. Use

the AUTOSTART attribute with the true value to have a video play automatically when a user visits your Web page. Using the LOOP attribute with the true value lets you have a video play continuously.

To play an internal video, a Web browser must have the correct plug-in installed. A plug-in is software that adds features to a Web browser. If a user's Web browser does not have the correct plug-in, the browser may prompt the user to download the plug-in from the Web.

While the <EMBED> tag is supported by most Web browsers, it is not part of the HTML standard.

ADD AN INTERNAL VIDEO

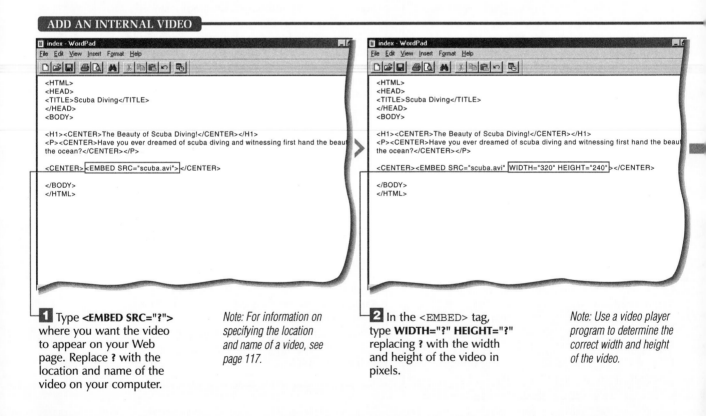

1 Type **<EMBED SRC="?">** where you want the video to appear on your Web page. Replace ? with the location and name of the video on your computer.

Note: For information on specifying the location and name of a video, see page 117.

2 In the <EMBED> tag, type **WIDTH="?" HEIGHT="?"** replacing ? with the width and height of the video in pixels.

Note: Use a video player program to determine the correct width and height of the video.

Extra

To wrap text around a video on your Web page, use the ALIGN attribute with the left or right value. The left value will place the video on the left side of the text and the right value will place the video on the right side of the text.

Example:

```
<EMBED SRC="race.avi" WIDTH="120"
HEIGHT="100" ALIGN="left">
```

Some people add internal AVI videos to their Web pages using the DYNSRC attribute with the <IMG> tag. Since only Internet Explorer currently supports the DYNSRC attribute, you should also use the SRC attribute to specify the location of an image on your computer that will appear if a Web browser cannot display the video.

Example:

```
<IMG DYNSRC="commercial.avi"
SRC="product.jpg">
```

The HTML standard recommends that you use the <OBJECT> tag to add objects such as internal videos to your Web page. Since Web browsers do not currently fully support the <OBJECT> tag, the <EMBED> tag is more commonly used.

When using the <OBJECT> tag, the DATA attribute allows you to specify the location and name of the video on your computer. Type the text you want to appear if a Web browser does not support the <OBJECT> tag between the <OBJECT> and </OBJECT> tags.

Example:

```
<OBJECT DATA="dance.avi" WIDTH="200"
HEIGHT="175">Dance video</OBJECT>
```

```
<HTML>
<HEAD>
<TITLE>Scuba Diving</TITLE>
</HEAD>
<BODY>

<H1><CENTER>The Beauty of Scuba Diving!</CENTER></H1>
<P><CENTER>Have you ever dreamed of scuba diving and witnessing first hand the beaut
the ocean?</CENTER></P>

<CENTER><EMBED SRC="scuba.avi" WIDTH="320" HEIGHT="240" AUTOSTART="true"
LOOP="true"></CENTER>

</BODY>
</HTML>
```

The Beauty of Scuba Diving!

Have you ever dreamed of scuba diving and witnessing first hand the beauty of the ocean?

3 If you want the video to play automatically when a user visits your Web page, type **AUTOSTART="true"** in the <EMBED> tag.

4 If you want the video to play continuously until a user clicks the video or displays another Web page, type **LOOP="true"** in the <EMBED> tag.

■ The Web browser displays the video on your Web page.

■ A user can click the video to start or stop the video at any time.

INTRODUCTION TO FORMS

Forms allow you to gather information from users who visit your Web pages. For example, forms allow users to send you questions and comments about your Web pages. Some forms allow users to purchase products and request services.

SET UP FORMS

Gather Information

Form elements such as text boxes, text areas, check boxes and menus allow users to enter information and select options on a form. Form elements are also known as controls.

When adding an element to a form, you must usually provide a name for the element. The name will identify the element in the form results and will not appear on your Web page. When a user enters information or selects an option using the element, a value is assigned to the element. The name of the element and its corresponding value will be sent to a Web server or to an e-mail address when the user clicks a submit button on the form. For example, if a user types "Cathy" in a text box you named "firstname," the name and value pair "firstname=Cathy" will appear in the form results.

Design Forms

Forms you design should be visually appealing and easy to use. To ensure an entire form will fit on a screen, the form should be a maximum of approximately 40 lines high and 75 characters wide.

When adding elements to your form, group related elements together and make sure the text you include beside each element clearly explains the information you want users to enter. When adding elements such as text boxes and large text areas, make sure the size you specify for each element is appropriate for the information users will enter. For example, a text box that requests a phone number should be 10 to 15 characters wide. You may also want to add sample text to a text box or large text area to help users enter the correct information.

Some forms use *JavaScript* to instruct a Web browser to perform a task when users fill out the form. For example, JavaScript can instruct a Web browser to verify that a user entered valid information in a form.

Process Information

When a Web server receives information from a form, the server runs a program called a Common Gateway Interface (CGI) script that processes the information. The CGI script you use determines how the information is processed. For example, a CGI script may send the form results in an e-mail message, save the results in a document or add the results to a database on your Web server. Most CGI scripts are written in the Perl programming language.

When a Web browser sends the information a user entered in a form, the browser encodes the information, causing the form results to contain additional characters that the user did not type. For example, each space is represented by a plus sign (+) and each name and value pair is separated by an ampersand (&). Characters that are not numbers or letters, such as a dollar sign ($), are represented by a percent sign and the hexadecimal equivalent for the character (example: %24).

Once a CGI script has processed the form results, the script usually displays a message in the user's Web browser window, indicating that the information was successfully sent.

Obtain CGI Scripts

Most Web servers contain CGI scripts for processing forms. These scripts are often stored in a directory named "cgi-bin." Contact your Web server administrator to determine the location of a CGI script on your Web server.

If your Web server does not offer CGI scripts, you can find CGI scripts on the Web or write your own CGI scripts. The www.cgi-resources.com, www.free-scripts.net and www.hotscripts.com Web sites offer CGI scripts. You may need to modify a CGI script you find on the Web.

Once you find a CGI script, you will need to transfer the CGI script to your Web server using a File Transfer Protocol (FTP) program such as WS_FTP Pro or Fetch.

Some Internet Service Providers (ISPs) do not allow CGI scripts on their Web servers for security reasons. If your ISP does not allow you to use CGI scripts on your Web server, you may want to use a form hosting service to process your form results. Form hosting services are available at the www.creative-dr.com and www.response-o-matic.com Web sites. If you prefer not to work with CGI scripts, you can set up your form to send information to an e-mail address. Some Web browsers do not support sending form information by e-mail.

SET UP A FORM

U se the <FORM> tag to set up a form on your Web page. You must set up a form before you can add information to the form. A Web page can contain more than one form.

The METHOD attribute lets you specify how the information a user enters in a form will transfer over the Internet. The most common transmission method is post.

Use the ACTION attribute to specify where a Web browser will send the information a user enters in your form. A Web browser can send the information to a CGI script on your Web server or to an e-mail address you specify.

A CGI (Common Gateway Interface) script is a program that a Web server runs to process the information from a form. Contact your Web server administrator to determine the location of a CGI script on your Web server.

If you choose to have your Web browser send form results to an e-mail address, use the ENCTYPE attribute with the text/plain value to ensure that the information users enter in the form will transfer in the proper format. Sending form results to an e-mail address is useful if your Web server does not allow you to use CGI scripts. Some Web browsers do not support sending form results to an e-mail address.

SET UP A FORM

```
survey - WordPad
File  Edit  View  Insert  Format  Help

<HTML>
<HEAD>
<TITLE>Customer Survey</TITLE>
</HEAD>
<BODY>

<H1><CENTER>Customer Survey</CENTER></H1>

<P>Please take a moment to fill out our customer survey:</P>

<FORM METHOD="post"  ACTION="/cgi-bin/survey.pl">


</BODY>
</HTML>
```

```
survey - WordPad
File  Edit  View  Insert  Format  Help

<HTML>
<HEAD>
<TITLE>Customer Survey</TITLE>
</HEAD>
<BODY>

<H1><CENTER>Customer Survey</CENTER></H1>

<P>Please take a moment to fill out our customer survey:</P>

<FORM METHOD="post" ACTION="/cgi-bin/survey.pl">
</FORM>

</BODY>
</HTML>
```

SEND FORM DATA TO A CGI SCRIPT

1 Type **<FORM METHOD="post"** where you want the form to appear on your Web page. Then add a blank space.

2 Type **ACTION="?">** replacing **?** with the location of the CGI script on your Web server that will process the information submitted by the form.

Note: To determine the location of the CGI script on your Web server, contact your Web server administrator.

3 Type **</FORM>** to complete the form.

■ You have now set up a form on your Web page. To add elements to the form, see pages 124 to 139.

Extra

A Web browser can send the information from a form using the `get` or `post` method. The `get` method contacts the Web server and sends the form information in one step, while the `post` method contacts the server and then sends the form information separately. The `post` method is more secure and is suitable for large forms.

Some Web servers can only receive form information that is transmitted using a specific method. Check with your Web server administrator to determine which method you should use.

Example:

```
<FORM METHOD="get" ACTION="/cgi-bin/order.pl">
```

Many CGI scripts instruct Web browsers to display a message once a user's information has been sent to the Web server. This message usually appears in the current Web browser window. Using the `TARGET` attribute allows you to specify the name of a new window or frame where you want the message to appear.

Example:

```
<FORM METHOD="post" ACTION="/cgi-bin/order.pl"
TARGET="new_window">
```

Use the `ACCEPT-CHARSET` attribute with the `<FORM>` tag to specify the character sets your Web server must support to interpret the information users send. For example, if users will enter Russian characters, your Web server may need to support the KO18-R character set. The `ACCEPT-CHARSET` attribute is not yet supported by Web browsers.

Example:

```
<FORM METHOD="post" ACTION="/cgi-bin/order.pl"
ACCEPT-CHARSET="KO18-R">
```

---

survey - WordPad

File Edit View Insert Format Help

```
<HTML>
<HEAD>
<TITLE>Customer Survey</TITLE>
</HEAD>
<BODY>

<H1><CENTER>Customer Survey</CENTER></H1>

<P>Please take a moment to fill out our customer survey:</P>

<FORM METHOD="post" ENCTYPE="text/plain"

</BODY>
</HTML>
```

survey - WordPad

File Edit View Insert Format Help

```
<HTML>
<HEAD>
<TITLE>Customer Survey</TITLE>
</HEAD>
<BODY>

<H1> <CENTER>Customer Survey</CENTER></H1>

<P>Please take a moment to fill out our customer survey:</P>

<FORM METHOD="post" ENCTYPE="text/plain" ACTION="mailto:jnelson@xyz.com">
</FORM>

</BODY>
</HTML>
```

SEND FORM DATA IN AN E-MAIL MESSAGE

1 Type **<FORM METHOD="post"** where you want the form to appear on your Web page. Then add a blank space.

2 Type **ENCTYPE="text/plain"** to ensure the information users enter in the form will transfer in the proper format. Then add a blank space.

3 Type **ACTION="mailto:?">** replacing **?** with the e-mail address where you want to send the results of the form.

4 Type **</FORM>** to complete the form.

■ You have now set up a form on your Web page. To add elements to the form, see pages 124 to 139.

CREATE A TEXT BOX

Text boxes allow users to enter a short line of text. Text boxes are commonly used for entering names, addresses and short responses.

When creating a text box, use the NAME attribute to provide a name for the text box. The name you specify will identify the text box in the form results. The name can contain letters and numbers, but should not contain spaces or punctuation. If you want to include spaces in a name, use an underscore character (_) instead.

Use the SIZE attribute to specify the width you want a text box to display. By default, the width

of a text box is approximately 20 typed characters. The width you specify will not affect the number of characters a user can enter in the text box.

To specify the maximum number of characters a user can enter in a text box, use the MAXLENGTH attribute. This can help ensure users enter the correct information in a text box. For example, if you want users to enter the abbreviation for their state, set the MAXLENGTH attribute to 2.

CREATE A TEXT BOX

```
beaches - WordPad
File  Edit  View  Insert  Format  Help

<HTML>
<HEAD>
<TITLE>Beaches</TITLE>
</HEAD>
<BODY>

<H1><CENTER>Beaches Around the World</CENTER></H1>
<H3><CENTER>Vote for your favorite beach!</CENTER></H3>
<CENTER><IMG SRC="beach.jpg"></CENTER>

<FORM METHOD="post" ACTION="/cgi-bin/survey.pl">
<BR>My favorite beach is:
</FORM>

</BODY>
</HTML>
```

```
beaches - WordPad
File  Edit  View  Insert  Format  Help

<HTML>
<HEAD>
<TITLE>Beaches</TITLE>
</HEAD>
<BODY>

<H1><CENTER>Beaches Around the World</CENTER></H1>
<H3><CENTER>Vote for your favorite beach!</CENTER></H3>
<CENTER><IMG SRC="beach.jpg"></CENTER>

<FORM METHOD="post" ACTION="/cgi-bin/survey.pl">
<BR>My favorite beach is: < INPUT TYPE="text"  NAME="beach"
</FORM>

</BODY>
</HTML>
```

1 Between the <FORM> and </FORM> tags, type the text you want to appear beside the text box. Then add a blank space.

Note: If you want the text box to appear on its own line, use the <P> or <BR> tag. For more information, see pages 16 and 18.

2 Type **<INPUT TYPE="text"** and then add a blank space.

3 Type **NAME="?"** replacing **?** with a word that describes the text box. Then add a blank space.

Note: The text you enter in step 3 will identify the text box in the form results and will not appear on your Web page.

Extra

Create a password box to prevent other people from viewing confidential information a user types, such as a credit card number. When a user types information in a password box, an asterisk (*) appears for each character. A password box will not protect the information as it transfers over the Internet.

Example:

```
Enter your password:<INPUT TYPE="password"
NAME="pwd" SIZE="8" MAXLENGTH="7">
```

Use the VALUE attribute to specify text that you want to appear in a text box. Users can edit or delete this text to enter their own information. This lets you provide instructions about the information you want users to enter in a text box.

Example:

```
Your Birth Date:<INPUT TYPE="text" NAME="bdate"
VALUE="mmddyy">
```

Many people use *JavaScript* to make sure users enter the correct information in a form. For example, use JavaScript to verify that a user typed numbers rather than letters in a text box that requests a Zip Code. Use the ONSUBMIT event attribute in the <FORM> tag to activate the JavaScript when a user clicks the Submit button. For more information on JavaScript, see page 158.

Example:

```
<FORM NAME="form1" METHOD="post" ACTION="/cgi-bin/survey.pl"
ONSUBMIT="return verifyZip()">
```

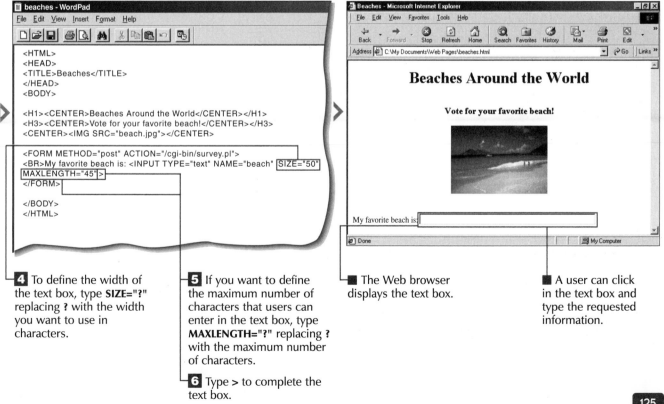

4 To define the width of the text box, type **SIZE="?"** replacing **?** with the width you want to use in characters.

5 If you want to define the maximum number of characters that users can enter in the text box, type **MAXLENGTH="?"** replacing **?** with the maximum number of characters.

6 Type **>** to complete the text box.

■ The Web browser displays the text box.

■ A user can click in the text box and type the requested information.

CREATE A LARGE TEXT AREA

U se the <TEXTAREA> tag to create a large text area on your form where users can enter several lines or paragraphs of text. This is useful for gathering comments or questions.

The NAME attribute allows you to provide a name for a large text area you create. The name will identify the text area in the form results.

The ROWS and COLS attributes allow you to specify a height and width for a large text area. Since users will not be able to resize a large text area on your Web page, make sure that

the text area you create will fit on a computer screen and will be wide enough to clearly display the text a user types.

Use the WRAP attribute to specify how you want the text a user enters in a large text area to wrap. The soft value wraps text within a large text area but will not wrap text in the form results. The hard value wraps text in both the text area and the form results. Use the off value when you do not want the text a user types to wrap automatically. Although the WRAP attribute is supported by most Web browsers, it is not part of the HTML standard.

CREATE A LARGE TEXT AREA

```
index - WordPad                                          _ 8 X
File  Edit  View  Insert  Format  Help

<HTML>
<HEAD>
<TITLE>Customer Survey</TITLE>
</HEAD>
<BODY>

<CENTER><FONT SIZE="5">Customer Survey</FONT></CENTER>
<P>Please take a moment to rate this Web site:
<FORM METHOD="post" ACTION="/cgi-bin/survey.pl">
<INPUT TYPE="radio" NAME="rating" VALUE="excellent" CHECKED>Excellent
<BR><INPUT TYPE="radio" NAME="rating" VALUE="verygood">Very Good
<BR><INPUT TYPE="radio" NAME="rating" VALUE="good">Good
<BR><INPUT TYPE="radio" NAME="rating" VALUE="poor">Poor</P>

<P>Suggestions/Comments:
<BR><TEXTAREA

<P><INPUT TYPE="submit" VALUE="Send">
<INPUT TYPE="reset" VALUE="Clear"></P>
</FORM>

</BODY>
</HTML>

For Help, press F1                                        NUM
```

```
index - WordPad                                          _ 8 X
File  Edit  View  Insert  Format  Help

<HTML>
<HEAD>
<TITLE>Customer Survey</TITLE>
</HEAD>
<BODY>

<CENTER><FONT SIZE="5">Customer Survey</FONT></CENTER>
<P>Please take a moment to rate this Web site:
<FORM METHOD="post" ACTION="/cgi-bin/survey.pl">
<INPUT TYPE="radio" NAME="rating" VALUE="excellent" CHECKED>Excellent
<BR><INPUT TYPE="radio" NAME="rating" VALUE="verygood">Very Good
<BR><INPUT TYPE="radio" NAME="rating" VALUE="good">Good
<BR><INPUT TYPE="radio" NAME="rating" VALUE="poor">Poor</P>

<P>Suggestions/Comments:
<BR><TEXTAREA NAME="commentbox" ROWS="5"

<P><INPUT TYPE="submit" VALUE="Send">
<INPUT TYPE="reset" VALUE="Clear"></P>
</FORM>

</BODY>
</HTML>

For Help, press F1                                        NUM
```

1 Between the <FORM> and </FORM> tags, type the text you want to appear beside the large text area.

2 Type **<TEXTAREA** and then add a blank space.

Note: If you want the text area to appear on its own line, use the <P> or <BR> tag. For more information, see pages 16 and 18.

3 Type **NAME="?"** replacing **?** with a word that describes the text area. Then add a blank space.

Note: The text you enter in step 3 will identify the text area in the form results. The text will not appear on the Web page.

4 Type **ROWS="?"** replacing **?** with a height for the text area in rows. Then add a blank space.

Extra

Any text you type between the <TEXTAREA> and </TEXTAREA> tags will appear in the large text area on your Web page. Users can then edit or delete the text to enter their own information. This is useful when you want to provide instructions or examples for users.

Example:

```
<TEXTAREA NAME="comments" ROWS="10"
COLS="25" WRAP="soft">Please enter your
comments here.</TEXTAREA>
```

Use the READONLY attribute to prevent users from editing the information in a form element. For example, making a large text area read-only is useful when the text area contains information you want a user to verify. Netscape Navigator does not currently support the READONLY attribute.

Example:

```
<TEXTAREA NAME="message" ROWS="10"
COLS="30" READONLY></TEXTAREA>
```

Use the DISABLED attribute to prevent people from using a form element. A disabled element will usually appear grayed-out on your form. For example, disabling a large text area that is only needed if users select a particular option will prevent users from entering unnecessary information. You can then add a *JavaScript* that will enable the large text area if the appropriate option is selected. Netscape Navigator does not currently support the DISABLED attribute.

Example:

```
<TEXTAREA NAME="other" ROWS="5" COLS="20"
WRAP="soft" DISABLED>If "other," please
specify.</TEXTAREA>
```

```
<HTML>
<HEAD>
<TITLE>Customer Survey</TITLE>
</HEAD>
<BODY>

<CENTER><FONT SIZE="5">Customer Survey</FONT></CENTER>
<P>Please take a moment to rate this Web site:
<FORM METHOD="post" ACTION="/cgi-bin/survey.pl">
<INPUT TYPE="radio" NAME="rating" VALUE="excellent" CHECKED>Excellent
<BR><INPUT TYPE="radio" NAME="rating" VALUE="verygood">Very Good
<BR><INPUT TYPE="radio" NAME="rating" VALUE="good">Good
<BR><INPUT TYPE="radio" NAME="rating" VALUE="poor">Poor</P>

<P>Suggestions/Comments:
<BR><TEXTAREA NAME="commentbox" ROWS="5" COLS="65" WRAP="hard">
</TEXTAREA>

<P><INPUT TYPE="submit" VALUE="Send">
<INPUT TYPE="reset" VALUE="Clear"></P>
</FORM>

</BODY>
</HTML>
```

5 Type **COLS="?"** replacing **?** with a width for the text area in characters. Then add a blank space.

6 Type **WRAP="?">** replacing **?** with the way you want the text a user types in the text area to wrap (**soft**, **hard** or **off**).

7 Type **</TEXTAREA>** to complete the text area.

■ The Web browser displays the text area.

■ A user can click in the text area and type the requested information.

■ If the text a user types does not fit in the text area, the user can scroll through the text using the scroll bar.

CREATE CHECK BOXES

nclude check boxes on your form if you want users to be able to select one or more options.

The NAME attribute allows you to provide a name for each group of check boxes you create. The names you specify will identify each group of check boxes in the form results.

The VALUE attribute allows you to specify a name for each check box in a group. The name you specify for a check box will appear in the form results if a user selects the check box. Use a name that you can easily identify, such as the text that appears beside the check box on your Web page. If you do not use the VALUE attribute, the form results will display

the name "on" for each selected check box, making it impossible to determine which options a user selected.

The names you specify using the NAME and VALUE attributes can contain letters and numbers, but should not contain spaces or punctuation. If you want to include spaces in a name, use an underscore character (_) instead.

You may want to use the CHECKED attribute to have one or more check boxes automatically appear selected on your form. This is useful when you expect that most users will select a particular check box on your form.

CREATE CHECK BOXES

```
<HTML>
<HEAD>
<TITLE>Music Survey</TITLE>
</HEAD>
<BODY>

<H1><CENTER>Music Survey</CENTER></H1>

<FORM METHOD="post" ACTION="/cgi-bin/survey.pl">
<P>We'd like to serve you better! Please tell us about your listening interests:</P>
<BR><INPUT TYPE="checkbox" NAME="music"
</FORM>

</BODY>
</HTML>
```

```
<HTML>
<HEAD>
<TITLE>Music Survey</TITLE>
</HEAD>
<BODY>

<H1><CENTER>Music Survey</CENTER></H1>

<FORM METHOD="post" ACTION="/cgi-bin/survey.pl">
<P>We'd like to serve you better! Please tell us about your listening interests:</P>
<BR><INPUT TYPE="checkbox" NAME="music" VALUE="classical" CHECKED
</FORM>

</BODY>
</HTML>
```

1 Between the <FORM> and </FORM> tags, type **<INPUT TYPE="checkbox"** and then add a blank space.

2 Type **NAME="?"** replacing **?** with a word that describes the group of check boxes you want to create. Then add a blank space.

Note: The text you enter in step 2 will identify the group of check boxes in the form results and will not appear on your Web page.

3 To specify the information for one check box, type **VALUE="?"** replacing **?** with a word that describes the check box.

Note: The text you enter in step 3 will identify the check box in the form results and will not appear on your Web page.

4 If you want the check box to be selected automatically, add a blank space and then type **CHECKED**.

128

Apply It

If your form contains only one group of check boxes, you may want to use the NAME attribute to name each check box rather than the group of check boxes. The VALUE attribute can then be set to a value you want to appear beside the check box name in the form results, such as on or yes.

TYPE THIS:

```
<FORM METHOD="post" ACTION="/cgi-bin/questionnaire.pl">
<P>Please tell us which types of media you have purchased in
the last year:</P>
<INPUT TYPE="checkbox" NAME="books" VALUE="on">Books
<BR><INPUT TYPE="checkbox" NAME="audiocds" VALUE="on">Audio CDs
<BR><INPUT TYPE="checkbox" NAME="tapes" VALUE="on">Cassettes
<BR><INPUT TYPE="checkbox" NAME="datacds" VALUE="on">CD-ROMs
</FORM>
```

RESULT:

Please tell us which types of media you have purchased in the last year:

☐ Books
☐ Audio CDs
☐ Cassettes
☐ CD-ROMs

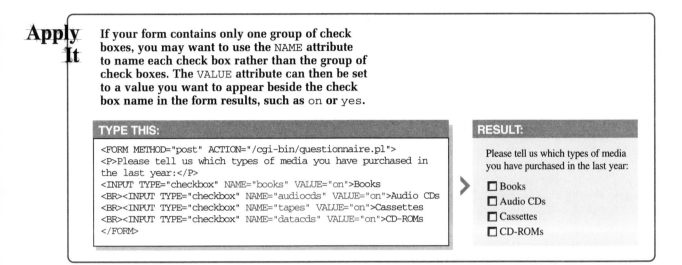

5 Type > to complete the check box.

6 Type the text you want to appear beside the check box on your Web page.

7 Repeat steps 1 to 6 for each check box you want to create.

Note: If you want each check box to appear on its own line, use the <P> or <BR> tag. For more information, see pages 16 and 18.

■ The Web browser displays the check boxes.

■ Users can click the check box for each option they want to select (☐ changes to ☑).

CREATE RADIO BUTTONS

I nclude radio buttons on your form when you want users to select only one of several options.

Use the NAME attribute to provide a name for each group of radio buttons you create. The names you specify will identify each group of radio buttons in the form results.

The VALUE attribute allows you to specify a name for each radio button in a group. The name you specify for a radio button will appear in the form results if a user selects the radio button. Use a name that you can easily identify, such as the text that appears beside the radio button on your Web page. If you do not use the VALUE attribute, the form results will

display the name "on" for the selected radio button, making it impossible to determine which option a user selected.

The names you specify using the NAME and VALUE attributes can contain letters and numbers, but should not contain spaces or punctuation. If you want to include spaces in a name, use an underscore character (_) instead.

To have one of the radio buttons in a group automatically appear selected on your form, use the CHECKED attribute. Pre-selecting the most popular options can help users save time when entering information.

CREATE RADIO BUTTONS

```
<HTML>
<HEAD>
<TITLE>Customer Survey</TITLE>
</HEAD>
<BODY>

<H1> <CENTER>Customer Survey</CENTER></H1>

<FORM METHOD="post" ACTION="/cgi-bin/survey.pl">
<P ALIGN="center">Please take a moment to rate this Web site:</P>
<INPUT TYPE="radio"  NAME="rating"
</FORM>

</BODY>
</HTML>
```

```
<HTML>
<HEAD>
<TITLE>Customer Survey</TITLE>
</HEAD>
<BODY>

<H1><CENTER>Customer Survey</CENTER></H1>

<FORM METHOD="post" ACTION="/cgi-bin/survey.pl">
<P ALIGN="center">Please take a moment to rate this Web site:</P>
<INPUT TYPE="radio" NAME="rating" VALUE="excellent">Excellent
</FORM>

</BODY>
</HTML>
```

1 Between the <FORM> and </FORM> tags, type **<INPUT TYPE="radio"** and then add a blank space.

2 Type **NAME="?"** replacing **?** with a word that describes the group of radio buttons you want to create. Then add a blank space.

Note: The text you enter in step 2 will identify the group of radio buttons in the form results and will not appear on your Web page.

3 To specify the information for one radio button, type **VALUE="?">** replacing **?** with a word that describes the radio button.

Note: The text you enter in step 3 will identify the radio button in the form results and will not appear on your Web page.

4 Type the text you want to appear beside the radio button on your Web page.

Apply It

The ACCESSKEY attribute allows you to add keyboard shortcuts to form elements such as radio buttons. Type **ACCESSKEY="?"** in the tag for the element, replacing **?** with a letter or number. Users can hold down the Alt key and press the letter or number to select the form element. While the ACCESSKEY attribute is part of the HTML standard, it is not currently supported by all Web browsers.

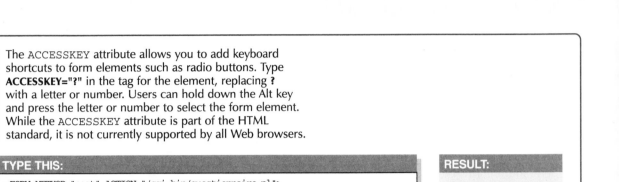

TYPE THIS:

```
<FORM METHOD="post" ACTION="/cgi-bin/questionnaire.pl">
<P>Please select your age:</P>
<INPUT TYPE="radio" NAME="age" VALUE="under_21" ACCESSKEY="1">Under 21 (Alt-1)
<BR><INPUT TYPE="radio" NAME="age" VALUE="21_29" ACCESSKEY="2">21-29 (Alt-2)
<BR><INPUT TYPE="radio" NAME="age" VALUE="30_40" ACCESSKEY="3">30-40 (Alt-3)
<BR><INPUT TYPE="radio" NAME="age" VALUE="over_40" ACCESSKEY="4">Over 40 (Alt-4)
</FORM>
```

RESULT:

Please select your age:

- ○ Under 21 (Alt-1)
- ○ 21-29 (Alt-2)
- ○ 30-40 (Alt-3)
- ○ Over 40 (Alt-4)

---

survey - WordPad

File Edit View Insert Format Help

```
<HTML>
<HEAD>
<TITLE>Customer Survey</TITLE>
</HEAD>
<BODY>

<H1><CENTER>Customer Survey</CENTER></H1>

<FORM METHOD="post" ACTION="/cgi-bin/survey.pl">
<P ALIGN="center">Please take a moment to rate this Web site:</P>
<INPUT TYPE="radio" NAME="rating" VALUE="excellent" CHECKED>Excellent
<BR><INPUT TYPE="radio" NAME="rating" VALUE="verygood">Very Good
<BR><INPUT TYPE="radio" NAME="rating" VALUE="good">Good
<BR><INPUT TYPE="radio" NAME="rating" VALUE="poor">Poor
</FORM>

</BODY>
</HTML>
```

Customer Survey - Microsoft Internet Explorer

File Edit View Favorites Tools Help

Back Forward Stop Refresh Home Search Favorites History Mail Print Edit

Address C:\My Documents\Web Pages\survey.html

Customer Survey

Please take a moment to rate this Web site:

- ⊙ Excellent
- ○ Very Good
- ○ Good
- ○ Poor

Done   My Computer

5 Repeat steps 1 to 4 for each radio button you want to create.

Note: If you want each radio button to appear on its own line, use the <P> or <BR> tag. For more information, see pages 16 and 18.

6 If you want a radio button to be selected automatically, type **CHECKED** after the VALUE attribute for the radio button.

Note: You can have only one radio button in a group selected automatically.

■ The Web browser displays the radio buttons.

■ A user can click a radio button to select one of several options (○ changes to ⊙).

CREATE A MENU

I f you want to provide users with a list of options to choose from, add a menu to your form. Menus are commonly used for displaying lists of age groups, states and products.

Use the NAME attribute to specify a name for a menu you create. The name will identify the menu in the form results.

By default, a menu appears on a form as a drop-down menu with only the first option visible. If you want more than one option to be visible, use the SIZE attribute to specify the number of options you want users to see without having to use a scroll bar.

The <OPTION> tag allows you to specify information for one menu option. Use the VALUE attribute to specify a name for the option. The name will appear in the form results if a user selects the option. Use a name that you can easily identify, such as the text that appears in the menu on your Web page.

You may want to use the SELECTED attribute to have an option in the menu automatically appear selected on your form. This is useful when you expect most users will select an option.

CREATE A MENU

```
survey - WordPad
File  Edit  View  Insert  Format  Help

<HTML>
<HEAD>
<TITLE>Customer Survey</TITLE>
</HEAD>
<BODY>

<H1><CENTER>Customer Survey</CENTER></H1>

<P>Please select your age:</P>

<FORM METHOD="post" ACTION="/cgi-bin/survey.pl">
<SELECT NAME="age" SIZE="4">
</FORM>

</BODY>
</HTML>
```

```
survey - WordPad
File  Edit  View  Insert  Format  Help

<HTML>
<HEAD>
<TITLE>Customer Survey</TITLE>
</HEAD>
<BODY>

<H1><CENTER>Customer Survey</CENTER></H1>

<P>Please select your age:</P>

<FORM METHOD="post" ACTION="/cgi-bin/survey.pl">
<SELECT NAME="age" SIZE="4">
<OPTION VALUE="child">Under 12
</FORM>

</BODY>
</HTML>
```

1 Between the <FORM> and </FORM> tags, type **<SELECT NAME="?"** replacing **?** with a word that describes the menu. Then add a blank space.

Note: The text you enter in step 1 will identify the menu in the form results and will not appear on your Web page.

2 Type **SIZE="?"** replacing **?** with the number of options you want users to see in the menu without having to use the scroll bar.

3 To specify the information for one menu option, type **<OPTION VALUE="?">** replacing **?** with a word that describes the menu option.

Note: The text you enter in step 3 will identify the menu option in the form results and will not appear on your Web page.

4 Type the text you want to appear in the menu on your Web page.

Extra

The <OPTGROUP> tag lets you divide your menu into submenus. This is useful if you want to organize a large menu into categories. Use the LABEL attribute to give each submenu a title. While the <OPTGROUP> tag is part of the HTML standard, it is not currently supported by Web browsers.

Example:

```
<P>What is your favorite snack food?</P>
<SELECT NAME="snackfood">
<OPTGROUP LABEL="Healthy">
<OPTION VALUE="apple">Apple
<OPTION VALUE="banana">Banana
</OPTGROUP>
<OPTGROUP LABEL="Junk Food">
<OPTION VALUE="chips">Chips
<OPTION VALUE="cookie">Cookie
<OPTION VALUE="chocolate">Chocolate Bar
</OPTGROUP>
</SELECT>
```

Use the MULTIPLE attribute with the <SELECT> tag to allow users to select multiple menu options. Users can hold down the Ctrl key and then click each option they want to select. When you use the MULTIPLE attribute, the menu will appear as a list rather than as a drop-down menu.

Example:

```
<P>Which of the following states have you visited?</P>
<SELECT NAME="states" MULTIPLE>
<OPTION VALUE="NY">NY
<OPTION VALUE="CA">CA
<OPTION VALUE="OH">OH
</SELECT>
```

```
survey - WordPad
File  Edit  View  Insert  Format  Help

<HTML>
<HEAD>
<TITLE>Customer Survey</TITLE>
</HEAD>
<BODY>

<H1><CENTER>Customer Survey</CENTER></H1>

<P>Please select your age:</P>

<FORM METHOD="post" ACTION="/cgi-bin/survey.pl">
<SELECT NAME="age" SIZE="4">
<OPTION VALUE="child">Under 12
<OPTION VALUE="teen">13-19
<OPTION VALUE="adult" SELECTED >20-64
<OPTION VALUE="senior">65 or Older
</SELECT>
</FORM>
```

Customer Survey - Microsoft Internet Explorer
File Edit View Favorites Tools Help

Back | Forward | Stop | Refresh | Home | Search | Favorites | History | Mail | Print | Edit

Address C:\My Documents\Web Pages\survey.html

Customer Survey

Please select your age:

```
Under 12
13-19
20-64
65 or Older
```

Done   My Computer

5 Repeat steps 3 and 4 for each menu option you want to appear in the menu.

6 If you want a menu option to be selected automatically, type **SELECTED** after the VALUE attribute for the menu option.

7 Type **</SELECT>** to complete the menu.

■ The Web browser displays the menu.

■ A user can click a menu option to select the option. A selected menu option appears highlighted.

ALLOW USERS TO UPLOAD FILES

A form can include an area that allows users to send you files. Allowing users to upload files is useful for collecting information that is best displayed in a separate file, such as a résumé or an order form. The files users send are usually stored on your Web server.

In the <FORM> tag, use the ENCTYPE attribute with the multipart/form-data value to ensure that the files users send will transfer in the proper format.

Use the NAME attribute with the <INPUT> tag to provide a name for the files users send.

The name will identify the files to the Web server.

When you allow users to upload files, your Web page will display a box where users can enter the location and name of the file they want to send. The SIZE attribute allows you to specify a width for the box. Increasing the width of the box can help ensure that users will be able to see the entire path to the file. Your Web page will also display a Browse button to help users locate the files they want to send.

ALLOW USERS TO UPLOAD FILES

```
employment - WordPad                                    _ |8|X
File  Edit  View  Insert  Format  Help

<HTML>
<HEAD>
<TITLE>Employment Opportunities</TITLE>
</HEAD>
<BODY>

<P><B>Interested in working for our company? Please fill out the information below:</B></P>

<FORM METHOD="post" ACTION="/cgi-bin/info.pl" ENCTYPE="multipart/form-data">
<BR><INPUT TYPE="radio" NAME="sex" VALUE="male" CHECKED>Mr.
<BR><INPUT TYPE="radio" NAME="sex" VALUE="female">Ms.
<P>First Name: <INPUT TYPE="text" NAME="name" SIZE="25">
<BR>Last Name: <INPUT TYPE="text" NAME="name" SIZE="25"></P>

<P><INPUT TYPE="submit" VALUE="Send"></P>
</FORM>

</BODY>
</HTML>

For Help, press F1                                           NUM
```

```
employment - WordPad                                    _ |8|X
File  Edit  View  Insert  Format  Help

<HTML>
<HEAD>
<TITLE>Employment Opportunities</TITLE>
</HEAD>
<BODY>

<P><B>Interested in working for our company? Please fill out the information below:</B></P>

<FORM METHOD="post" ACTION="/cgi-bin/info.pl" ENCTYPE="multipart/form-data">
<BR><INPUT TYPE="radio" NAME="sex" VALUE="male" CHECKED>Mr.
<BR><INPUT TYPE="radio" NAME="sex" VALUE="female">Ms.
<P>First Name: <INPUT TYPE="text" NAME="name" SIZE="25">
<BR>Last Name: <INPUT TYPE="text" NAME="name" SIZE="25"></P>

<BR>Files:<INPUT TYPE="file"

<P><INPUT TYPE="submit" VALUE="Send"></P>
</FORM>

</BODY>
</HTML>

For Help, press F1                                           NUM
```

■ To allow users to upload files, make sure the METHOD attribute is set to post in the <FORM> tag. For more information on the METHOD attribute, see page 122.

1 In the <FORM> tag, type **ENCTYPE="multipart/form-data"** to ensure the files users send will transfer in the proper format.

2 Between the <FORM> and </FORM> tags, type the text you want to appear beside the area that will allow users to send you files.

Note: If you want the area to appear on its own line, use the <P> or <BR> tag. For more information, see pages 16 and 18.

3 Type **<INPUT TYPE="file"** and then add a blank space.

Extra

When a user uploads a file, your Web server must run a CGI script to process the file. Most regular CGI scripts cannot process uploaded files. To find CGI scripts for uploaded files, visit the script collections at the www.cgi-resources.com and www.hotscripts.com Web sites.

If the CGI script on your Web server can only process certain types of files, use the ACCEPT attribute with the <INPUT> tag to specify the types of files users can send. List the MIME (Multi-purpose Internet Mail Extensions) types, separating each type with a comma (,). MIME types are part of the MIME standard that specifies how files will be formatted when transferred over the Internet. Although the ACCEPT attribute is part of the HTML standard, it is not yet supported by Web browsers.

Example:

```
<INPUT TYPE="file" NAME="usersimage"
ACCEPT="image/gif, image/jpeg, image/png">
```

If your form is set up to send form results to an e-mail address, the files users upload will usually appear as e-mail attachments. Sending form results in an e-mail message is useful if your Web server does not contain a CGI script that can process form results.

Example:

```
<FORM METHOD="post" ENCTYPE="multipart/form-data"
ACTION="mailto:bmartin@xyz.com">
```

---

employment - WordPad

File Edit View Insert Format Help

```
<HTML>
<HEAD>
<TITLE>Employment Opportunities</TITLE>
</HEAD>
<BODY>

<P><B>Interested in working for our company? Please fill out the information below:</B></P>

<FORM METHOD="post" ACTION="/cgi-bin/info.pl" ENCTYPE="multipart/form-data">
<BR><INPUT TYPE="radio" NAME="sex" VALUE="male" CHECKED>Mr.
<BR><INPUT TYPE="radio" NAME="sex" VALUE="female">Ms.
<P>First Name: <INPUT TYPE="text" NAME="name" SIZE="25">
<BR>Last Name: <INPUT TYPE="text" NAME="name" SIZE="25"></P>

<BR>Files:<INPUT TYPE="file" NAME="resume" SIZE="45" >

<P><INPUT TYPE="submit" VALUE="Send"></P>
</FORM>

</BODY>
</HTML>
```

For Help, press F1 — NUM

Employment Opportunities - Microsoft Internet Explorer

File Edit View Favorites Tools Help

Back | Forward | Stop | Refresh | Home | Search | Favorites | History | Mail | Print | Edit

Address C:\My Documents\Web Pages\employment.html   Go Links »

Interested in working for our company? Please fill out the information below:

⊙ Mr.
○ Ms.

First Name: [   ]
Last Name: [   ]

Files [   ] Browse...

[Send]

Done — My Computer

4 Type **NAME="?"** replacing **?** with a word that describes the files users will send. Then add a blank space.

Note: The text you enter in step 4 will identify the files to the Web server and will not appear on your Web page.

5 To define the width of the box where users will enter the location and name of the file they want to send, type **SIZE="?">** replacing **?** with a width in characters.

■ The Web browser displays an area that allows users to send you files.

■ A user can click in the box and type the location and name of the file they want to send.

■ A user can also click the Browse button to open a dialog box that will help them locate the file they want to send.

CREATE A SUBMIT AND RESET BUTTON

Including a submit button on your form allows users to send the information they entered in your form.

Use the VALUE attribute to specify the text you want to appear on a submit button. If you do not use the VALUE attribute, the submit button will automatically display the text "Submit Query" or "Submit."

Creating a reset button on your form allows users to clear the information they entered in your form. When a user clicks the reset button, the user's Web browser will reset the form

elements so the form displays its original settings. This lets users start over if they have made a mistake while filling out your form.

The VALUE attribute lets you specify the text you want to appear on a reset button. If you do not use the VALUE attribute, the reset button will automatically display the text "Reset."

When a user clicks a submit or reset button, their Web browser will send or clear the information in all the form elements. The user will not be able to reverse submitting or resetting the form.

CREATE A SUBMIT BUTTON

```
<HTML>
<HEAD>
<TITLE>Customer Survey</TITLE>
</HEAD>
<BODY>

<H1><CENTER>Customer Survey</CENTER></H1>

<FORM METHOD="post" ACTION="/cgi-bin/survey.pl">
<P>Please take a moment to rate this Web site:</P>
<INPUT TYPE="radio" NAME="rating" VALUE="excellent" CHECKED>Excel
<BR><INPUT TYPE="radio" NAME="rating" VALUE="verygood">Very Good
<BR><INPUT TYPE="radio" NAME="rating" VALUE="good">Good
<BR><INPUT TYPE="radio" NAME="rating" VALUE="poor">Poor

<P><INPUT TYPE="submit" VALUE="Send"></P>

</FORM>
```

Customer Survey

Please take a moment to rate this Web site:

- ⦿ Excellent
- ○ Very Good
- ○ Good
- ○ Poor

[Send]

1 Between the <FORM> and </FORM> tags, type **<INPUT TYPE="submit"** and then add a blank space.

2 Type **VALUE="?">** replacing **?** with the text you want to appear on the submit button.

Note: If you want the submit button to appear on its own line, use the <P> or <BR> tag. For more information, see pages 16 and 18.

■ The Web browser displays the submit button.

■ When a user clicks the submit button, the information they entered in the form will transfer to the Web server.

Extra

The `<BUTTON>` tag lets you create a submit or reset button that displays an image. Between the `<BUTTON>` and `</BUTTON>` tags, use the `<IMG>` tag to specify the image you want to use. Then type the text you want to appear on the button. Although the `<BUTTON>` tag is part of the HTML standard, it is currently only supported by Internet Explorer.

Example:

```
<BUTTON TYPE="submit"><IMG SRC="dollarsign.gif>
Order Now</BUTTON>
```

You may want to provide a user with multiple submit buttons. This is useful if your CGI script will process the form differently depending on the button a user clicks. Use the `NAME` attribute with the `<INPUT>` tag to provide a different name for each button. This will help you identify which button a user clicked in the form results.

Example:

```
<INPUT TYPE="submit" NAME="personal"
VALUE="Send Personal Information">
<INPUT TYPE="submit" NAME="order"
VALUE="Send Order">
```

Using *JavaScript* allows you to have a user's Web browser perform a task when a user clicks a submit or reset button. Use the `ONCLICK` event attribute with the `<INPUT>` tag to activate the JavaScript. For example, you may want to have a dialog box appear asking users to confirm that they want to submit the form.

Example:

```
<INPUT TYPE="submit" ONCLICK="return confirm('Do
you wish to send information?')">
```

CREATE A RESET BUTTON

```
<HTML>
<HEAD>
<TITLE>Customer Survey</TITLE>
</HEAD>
<BODY>

<H1><CENTER>Customer Survey</CENTER></H1>

<FORM METHOD="post" ACTION="/cgi-bin/survey.pl">
<P>Please take a moment to rate this Web site:</P>
<INPUT TYPE="radio" NAME="rating" VALUE="excellent" CHECKED>Excell
<BR><INPUT TYPE="radio" NAME="rating" VALUE="verygood">Very Good
<BR><INPUT TYPE="radio" NAME="rating" VALUE="good">Good
<BR><INPUT TYPE="radio" NAME="rating" VALUE="poor">Poor

<P><INPUT TYPE="submit" VALUE="Send">
<INPUT TYPE="reset"  VALUE="Clear"></P>

</FORM>
```

Customer Survey

Please take a moment to rate this Web site:

- ⦿ Excellent
- ○ Very Good
- ○ Good
- ○ Poor

[Send] [Clear]

1 Between the `<FORM>` and `</FORM>` tags, type **<INPUT TYPE="reset"** and then add a blank space.

2 Type **VALUE="?">** replacing **?** with the text you want to appear on the reset button.

Note: If you want the reset button to appear on its own line, use the `<P>` or `<BR>` tag. For more information, see pages 16 and 18.

■ The Web browser displays the reset button.

■ When a user clicks the reset button, the form clears and once again displays its original settings.

CREATE A GRAPHICAL SUBMIT BUTTON

A graphical submit button is an image that allows users to enter information and submit the results of their form at the same time.

When a user clicks a graphical submit button, the horizontal and vertical coordinates of the user's mouse pointer are submitted along with the rest of the information in the form. This is useful when the areas of an image represent different options, such as the locations on a map or floor plan. You should provide text that warns users that clicking the image will submit all their information.

Use the SRC attribute with the <INPUT> tag to specify the location and name of the GIF or JPEG image you want to use. To specify the location and name of an image, see the top of page 45.

The NAME attribute allows you to provide a name for a graphical submit button. The name will identify the horizontal (x) and vertical (y) coordinates of a user's mouse pointer in the form results. The coordinates will be measured in pixels from the top left corner of the image.

You may want to use a custom CGI script to process the results of a graphical submit button. For example, a script can instruct a Web browser to display a magnified version of the area a user clicks.

CREATE A GRAPHICAL SUBMIT BUTTON

```
<HTML>
<HEAD>
<TITLE>Feedback Form</TITLE>
</HEAD>
<BODY>

<H1><CENTER>Feedback Form</CENTER></H1>

<P>Please take a moment to provide us with your feedback:</P>

<FORM METHOD="post" ACTION="/cgi-bin/survey.pl">
Comments:<TEXTAREA NAME="commentbox" ROWS="5" COLS="50" WRAP></
<P>Click your region below to submit your comments:

<BR><INPUT TYPE="image" SRC="map.gif" NAME="location">

</FORM>

</BODY>
</HTML>
```

1 Between the <FORM> and </FORM> tags, type **<INPUT TYPE="image"** and then add a blank space.

2 Type **SRC="?"** replacing **?** with the location and name of the image on your computer. Then add a blank space.

3 Type **NAME="?">** replacing **?** with a word that describes the image.

Note: The text you enter in step 3 will identify the image in the form results and will not appear on your Web page.

■ The Web browser displays the image.

■ When a user clicks the image, the horizontal (x) and vertical (y) coordinates of the mouse pointer will be sent to the Web server along with the rest of the information in the form.

CREATE A HIDDEN FIELD

A hidden field is a form element that will not appear on your Web page, but will appear in the form results. Hidden fields are useful for including information such as the date and time you created a form.

When creating a hidden field, use the NAME attribute to provide a name for the hidden field and the VALUE attribute to specify the information you want the hidden field to contain.

If your Web pages contain multiple forms, hidden fields can help you identify the information users submit. For example, use a hidden field to assign each form a different name or number. When you

view the form results, the name or number will identify the form a user filled out.

Some people use hidden fields to provide information that their *CGI Script* will use when processing their form. For example, a hidden field may specify a subject for e-mail messages containing form results.

Some CGI scripts can add hidden fields to a form for you. For example, once a user has entered personal information in a form, your CGI script may be able to add the information to hidden fields in another form so the user will not have to enter the information again.

CREATE A HIDDEN FIELD

```
<HTML>
<HEAD>
<TITLE>Feedback Form</TITLE>
</HEAD>
<BODY>

<H1><CENTER>Feedback Form</CENTER></H1>

<P>Please take a moment to provide us with your feedback:</P>

<FORM METHOD="post" ACTION="/cgi-bin/survey.pl">

<INPUT TYPE="hidden" NAME="feedback" VALUE="Form1">

<BR>First Name:<INPUT TYPE="text" NAME="firstname" SIZE="20">
Password:<INPUT TYPE="password" NAME="pass" SIZE="20">
<BR>Last Name:<INPUT TYPE="text" NAME="lastname" SIZE="20">
<BR>Comments:<TEXTAREA NAME="commentbox" ROWS="5" COLS="50" WRA
</TEXTAREA>
</FORM>
```

1 Between the <FORM> and </FORM> tags, type **<INPUT TYPE="hidden"** and then add a blank space.

2 Type **NAME="?"** replacing ? with a word that describes the hidden field. Then add a blank space.

3 Type **VALUE="?">** replacing ? with the information you want the hidden field to contain.

■ The Web browser does not display the hidden field.

ORGANIZE FORM ELEMENTS

I f your form contains many elements, you may want to use the `<FIELDSET>` tag to organize the elements into groups. A Web browser that supports the `<FIELDSET>` tag will visually separate the elements you include in a group. For example, Internet Explorer displays a thin, solid border around the elements.

Organizing form elements can help users understand your form by dividing the form into logical sections. For example, you may want to create one group for required information and another group for optional information.

The `<LEGEND>` tag allows you to add a title to your grouped elements. If you choose to include a title, use the `ALIGN` attribute to specify if you want the title to appear at the left, right, top or bottom of the group of elements. Only the `left` and `right` values are currently supported. While the `ALIGN` attribute is still supported by Web browsers, the use of *style sheets* is now preferred. For information on style sheets, see page 196.

Although the `<FIELDSET>` and `<LEGEND>` tags are part of the HTML standard, only Internet Explorer currently supports these tags.

ORGANIZE FORM ELEMENTS

customers - WordPad

File Edit View Insert Format Help

```
<HTML>
<HEAD>
<TITLE>Customer Information</TITLE>
</HEAD>
<BODY>

<H4><CENTER>Please fill out the following information so we can serve you better:
</CENTER></H4>

<FORM METHOD="post" ACTION="/cgi-bin/customers.pl">
<FIELDSET>
<BR>Name: <INPUT TYPE="text" NAME="name" SIZE="30" MAXLENGTH="15">
<BR>E-mail: <INPUT TYPE="text" NAME="email" SIZE="30" MAXLENGTH="15">
<BR>Credit Card: <INPUT TYPE="password" NAME="credit" SIZE="30" MAXLENGTH=
<BR>Address: <TEXTAREA NAME="address" ROWS="3" COLS="30" WRAP></TEXTAF
</FIELDSET>

<P>What is your salary range?
<BR><INPUT TYPE="radio" NAME="salary" VALUE="over50">Over $50,000
<BR><INPUT TYPE="radio" NAME="salary" VALUE="35to50">$35,000 to $50,000
<BR><INPUT TYPE="radio" NAME="salary" VALUE="20to34">$20,000 to $34,000
<BR><INPUT TYPE="radio" NAME="salary" VALUE="under20">Under $20,000</P>
</FORM>
```

customers - WordPad

File Edit View Insert Format Help

```
<HTML>
<HEAD>
<TITLE>Customer Information</TITLE>
</HEAD>
<BODY>

<H4><CENTER>Please fill out the following information so we can serve you better:
</CENTER></H4>

<FORM METHOD="post" ACTION="/cgi-bin/customers.pl">
<FIELDSET>
<LEGEND ALIGN="left">
<BR>Name: <INPUT TYPE="text" NAME="name" SIZE="30" MAXLENGTH="15">
<BR>E-mail: <INPUT TYPE="text" NAME="email" SIZE="30" MAXLENGTH="15">
<BR>Credit Card: <INPUT TYPE="password" NAME="credit" SIZE="30" MAXLENGTH=
<BR>Address: <TEXTAREA NAME="address" ROWS="3" COLS="30" WRAP></TEXTAF
</FIELDSET>

<P>What is your salary range?
<BR><INPUT TYPE="radio" NAME="salary" VALUE="over50">Over $50,000
<BR><INPUT TYPE="radio" NAME="salary" VALUE="35to50">$35,000 to $50,000
<BR><INPUT TYPE="radio" NAME="salary" VALUE="20to34">$20,000 to $34,000
<BR><INPUT TYPE="radio" NAME="salary" VA
```

1 Type **<FIELDSET>** directly above the first element you want include in the group.

2 Type **</FIELDSET>** after the last element you want to include in the group.

3 Directly below the `<FIELDSET>` tag, type **<LEGEND** to specify a title for the group of elements. Then add a blank space.

4 Type **ALIGN="?">** replacing **?** with the location where you want to place the title in relation to the group of elements on the form (**left**, **right**, **top** or **bottom**).

Apply It

Since most Web browsers do not yet support the `<FIELDSET>` tag, you may want to use tables to organize form elements on your Web page.

TYPE THIS:

```
<FORM METHOD="post" ACTION="/cgi-bin/signup.pl">
<TABLE BORDER="3">
<TR>
    <TD><INPUT TYPE="checkbox" NAME="ads" VALUE="yes">
    Would like to receive our advertisements by e-mail?
    <BR><INPUT TYPE="checkbox" NAME="public" VALUE="yes">
    Do you want your name to be in our public directory?</TD>
    <TD><INPUT TYPE="submit" VALUE="Submit"></TD>
</TR>
</TABLE>
</FORM>
```

RESULT:

☐ Would like to receive our advertisements by e-mail?
☐ Do you want your name to be in our public directory?   [Submit]

---

customers - WordPad

File Edit View Insert Format Help

```
<HTML>
<HEAD>
<TITLE>Customer Information</TITLE>
</HEAD>
<BODY>

<H4><CENTER>Please fill out the following information so we can serve you better:
</CENTER></H4>

<FORM METHOD="post" ACTION="/cgi-bin/customers.pl">
<FIELDSET>
<LEGEND ALIGN="left">Required Information</LEGEND>
<BR>Name: <INPUT TYPE="text" NAME="name" SIZE="30" MAXLENGTH="15">
<BR>E-mail: <INPUT TYPE="text" NAME="email" SIZE="30" MAXLENGTH="15">
<BR>Credit Card: <INPUT TYPE="password" NAME="credit" SIZE="30" MAXLENGTH=
<BR>Address: <TEXTAREA NAME="address" ROWS="3" COLS="30" WRAP></TEXTAR
</FIELDSET>

<P>What is your salary range?
<BR><INPUT TYPE="radio" NAME="salary" VALUE="over50">Over $50,000
<BR><INPUT TYPE="radio" NAME="salary" VALUE="35to50">$35,000 to $50,000
<BR><INPUT TYPE="radio" NAME="salary" VALUE="20to34">$20,000 to $34,000
<BR><INPUT TYPE="radio" NAME="salary" VALUE="und20">Under $20,000</
```

Customer Information - Microsoft Internet Explorer

File Edit View Favorites Tools Help

Back Forward Stop Refresh Home Search Favorites History Mail Print Edit

Address C:\My Documents\Web Pages\customers.html

Please fill out the following information so we can serve you better:

Required Information

Name:
E-mail:
Credit Card:

Address:

What is your salary range?
○ Over $50,000
○ $35,000 to $50,000
○ $20,000 to $34,000
○ Under $20,000

Done   My Computer

---

5 Type the text for the title.

6 Type **</LEGEND>** to complete the title.

7 Repeat steps 1 to 6 for each set of elements you want to group together on the form.

■ The Web browser groups the form elements together.

■ The title for the group of elements appears in the location you specified.

LABEL FORM ELEMENTS

U se the `<LABEL>` tag to identify the text beside a form element as a label for the element. This instructs Web browsers to interpret the text as part of the form element.

To label a form element, use the `ID` attribute to identify the element you want to label. Then use the `FOR` attribute with the `<LABEL>` tag to identify the text for the label.

Labeling form elements can help users quickly enter information in a form. For example, when a user clicks the label beside a check box on your Web page, the check box will be selected.

Similarly, users can click a label for a text box to place the cursor in the text box.

You may want to label a form element to have Web browsers apply specialized settings to the label. For example, Web browsers configured for the hearing impaired may read labels using a speech-synthesizer.

While the `<LABEL>` tag is part of the HTML standard, it is not currently supported by many Web browsers.

LABEL FORM ELEMENTS

```
<HTML>
<HEAD>
<TITLE>Music Survey</TITLE>
</HEAD>
<BODY>

<H1><CENTER>Music Survey</CENTER></H1>

<FORM METHOD="post" ACTION="/cgi-bin/survey.pl">
<P>We'd like to serve you better! Please tell us about your listening interests:</P>
<INPUT TYPE="checkbox" NAME="music" VALUE="jazz" ID="jazz"><LABEL FOR="jazz">
Jazz</LABEL>
<BR><INPUT TYPE="checkbox" NAME="music" VALUE="r&b">R&B
<BR><INPUT TYPE="checkbox" NAME="music" VALUE="rock">Rock
</FORM>

</BODY>
</HTML>
```

Music Survey

We'd like to serve you better! Please tell us about your listening interests:

☐ Jazz
☐ R&B
☐ Rock

1 In the tag for the form element that you want to use a label, type **ID="?"** replacing **?** with a word that describes the element.

2 Before the text you want to use as the label for the form element, type **<LABEL FOR="?">** replacing **?** with the word you typed in step 1.

3 After the text you want to use as the label for the form element, type **</LABEL>**.

■ The Web browser displays the form element and its label.

■ In this example, users can select the check box or the text "Jazz" to select the item.

142

CHANGE THE TAB ORDER

Users can navigate through the elements on your form using the Tab key. By default, users tab through the elements in the order the elements appear in your HTML code. Changing the tab order for your form can help users fill out your form in a logical order.

To change the tab order, use the TABINDEX attribute with the tags for every element on your form. To include an element in the tab order, assign the element a TABINDEX value between 1 and 32,767. To exclude an element from the tab order, assign the element a negative TABINDEX value (example: TABINDEX="-1").

When users tab through your form, the tab order will start with the element you assigned the lowest value and will end with the element you assigned the highest value. If two elements have the same value, the element that appears first in your HTML code will precede the other element in the tab order.

The TABINDEX attribute can also be used with elements outside of your form, such as images (<IMG>), links (<A>) and image map areas (<AREA>).

While the TABINDEX attribute is part of the HTML standard, it is not yet fully supported by most Web browsers.

CHANGE THE TAB ORDER

1 In the tag for an element on your form, type **TABINDEX="?"** replacing **?** with a number that specifies the position of the element in the tab order.

2 Repeat step 1 for each element on the form.

Note: To exclude an element from the tab order, specify a negative number in step 1.

■ Users can tab through the elements on your form in the order you specified.

CREATE FRAMES

F rames allow you to divide a Web browser window into sections. Each section will display a different Web page in your Web site.

Frames are useful when you want to keep information on the screen at all times. For example, place a table of contents or navigational links in a frame to help users move through your Web pages and find information of interest.

To create frames, set up a Web page that defines the structure of the frames using the <FRAMESET> and <FRAME> tags.

The <FRAMESET> tag allows you to create a set of frames, called a frameset, that divides a Web browser window into rows or columns. You must specify a height or width for each row or column using a percentage of the Web browser window, a number of pixels or an asterisk (*). When you use an asterisk, the size of the frame will depend on the size of your other frames. For example, if one frame uses 70% of the window, the frame with the asterisk will use 30% of the window.

Use the <FRAME> tag to specify information for each frame, such as the name of the frame and the Web page you want to appear in the frame.

CREATE FRAMES

```
<HTML>
<HEAD>
<TITLE>Oceanography.com</TITLE>
</HEAD>
<FRAMESET

</HTML>
```

```
<HTML>
<HEAD>
<TITLE>Oceanography.com</TITLE>
</HEAD>
<FRAMESET ROWS="50,*">

</HTML>
```

1 Set up a Web page as shown on pages 10 to 13. Do not type any text for the Web page or include the <BODY> tags.

2 Type **<FRAMESET** directly below the </HEAD> tag. Then add a blank space.

3 To create frames in rows, type **ROWS="a,b..."** replacing **a, b** and so on with the height of each row you want to create.

■ To create frames in columns, type **COLS="a,b..."** replacing **a, b** and so on with the width of each column you want to create.

Apply It

Combining framesets allows you to create complex frame layouts that contain both rows and columns. To combine framesets, use the `<FRAMESET>` tag to divide a frame in your original frameset into rows or columns.

TYPE THIS:

```
<HTML>
<HEAD>
<TITLE>My Home Page</TITLE>
</HEAD>
<FRAMESET ROWS="110,*">
    <FRAME NAME="banner" SRC="banner.html">
    <FRAMESET COLS="150,*">
        <FRAME NAME="contents" SRC="contents.html">
        <FRAME NAME="main" SRC="startpage.html">
    </FRAMESET>
</FRAMESET>
</HTML>
```

RESULT:

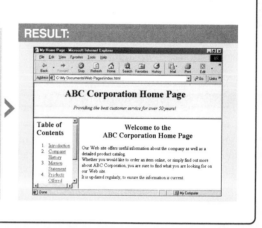

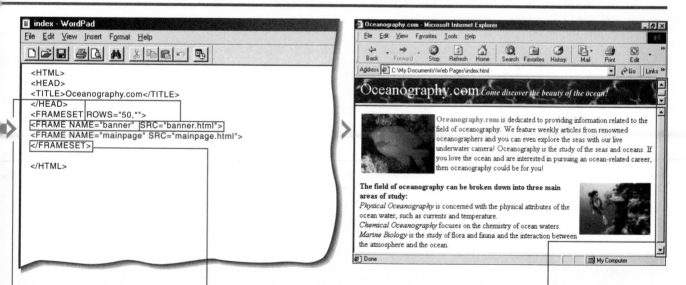

■ **4** To specify the information for one frame, type **<FRAME NAME="?"** replacing **?** with a name for the frame. Then add a blank space.

■ **5** Type **SRC="?">** replacing **?** with the location and name of the Web page you want to appear in the frame.

Note: To specify the location and name of a Web page in your Web site, see the top of page 75.

■ **6** Repeat steps 4 and 5 for each frame you created in step 3.

■ **7** Type **</FRAMESET>**.

■ The Web browser displays the frames.

■ Scroll bars appear automatically when a frame is too small to display the contents of an entire Web page.

FRAME CONSIDERATIONS

While frames are useful for effectively presenting your Web site in an easy-to-navigate format, there are several factors you should take into consideration before using frames. Consider the following advantages and disadvantages of frames to determine if frames are appropriate for your Web site.

ADVANTAGES OF USING FRAMES

If your Web site is large and complex, frames offer many advantages that can help users better understand your Web site structure and navigate through your Web pages.

Frames display multiple Web pages in one Web browser window. This allows you to display a variety of information on the screen at once. For example, you can display a table of contents for your Web site, copyright information and the current Web page on the screen at the same time.

Using frames also allows you to keep information, such as your company logo or a disclaimer, on the screen at all times without having to add the information to every Web page in your Web site.

Many Web page authors find frames useful for displaying a navigation bar that contains links to the Web pages in their Web site. This lets users see the structure of the Web site at all times and allows them to easily access information of interest.

DISADVANTAGES OF USING FRAMES

Designing a frames-based Web site requires careful organization and planning. There are several disadvantages you should consider before using frames.

Since frames divide a Web browser window into sections, the viewing area for each Web page is reduced. Web pages designed to be displayed in an entire Web browser window may not fit well in frames.

When creating frames, it can be difficult to determine the best size for each frame. Although users can scroll through the information in a frame, they may become annoyed if they have to continually scroll to view important information.

It is difficult to predict how your frames will appear on a user's computer, since the resolution of a user's monitor determines the amount of information that appears in the frames. People using lower screen resolutions will not see as much information in each frame.

You should also keep in mind that not all Web browsers support frames. If you want to ensure that all users will be able to view your Web pages, you will need to design a non-frames version of your Web site.

PROVIDE ALTERNATIVE INFORMATION

S ome Web browsers cannot display frames, while others allow users to turn off the display of frames. You should use the <NOFRAMES> tag to provide alternative information that will appear if a user's Web browser does not display frames. If you do not provide alternative information, users with Web browsers that do not display frames will see a blank screen.

The alternative information you provide can include information from your Web pages. The <NOFRAMES> tag supports the use of HTML tags, allowing you to include elements such as images and tables in your alternative information.

Some people prefer to provide only a short explanation of why users cannot see their Web pages. If you include only a short explanation, you may also want to provide a link that will take users to a version of your Web site that does not use frames. For information on creating a link to another Web page, see page 74.

The information you provide using the <NOFRAMES> tag will not appear if a user's Web browser can display frames.

PROVIDE ALTERNATIVE INFORMATION

```
index - WordPad
File  Edit  View  Insert  Format  Help

<HTML>
<HEAD>
<TITLE>Oceanography.com</TITLE>
</HEAD>

<FRAMESET ROWS="50,*">
<FRAME NAME="banner" SRC="banner.html">
<FRAME NAME="mainpage" SRC="oceanography.html">

<NOFRAMES>
This Web page uses frames. Your current Web browser does not display frames or
frame viewing has been turned off.
</NOFRAMES>
</FRAMESET>

</HTML>

For Help, press F1                                                    NUM
```

```
index - WordPad
File  Edit  View  Insert  Format  Help

<HTML>
<HEAD>
<TITLE>Oceanography.com</TITLE>
</HEAD>

<FRAMESET ROWS="50,*">
<FRAME NAME="banner" SRC="banner.html">
<FRAME NAME="mainpage" SRC="oceanography.html">

<NOFRAMES>
<BODY>
This Web page uses frames. Your current Web browser does not display frames or
frame viewing has been turned off.
</BODY>
</NOFRAMES>
</FRAMESET>

</HTML>

For Help, press F1                                                    NUM
```

1 Type **<NOFRAMES>** directly above the last </FRAMESET> tag on your Web page.

2 Type the information you want to appear if a Web browser does not display frames.

3 Type **</NOFRAMES>**.

4 Type **<BODY>** directly above the information you typed in step 2.

5 Type **</BODY>** directly below the information you typed in step 2.

Note: The <BODY> and </BODY> tags are optional.

■ If a user views your Web page in a Web browser that does not display frames, the information you specified will appear.

CREATE A LINK TO A FRAME

U se the TARGET attribute with the <A> tag to create a link that users can select to display a Web page in another frame.

Creating links to frames can help users move through your Web site. For example, create navigation links in one frame that will open in another frame. This lets you keep the navigation links on the screen while users browse through your Web pages.

When creating a link to a frame, specify the name of the frame using the TARGET attribute.

You assigned names to your frames when you created the frames on page 144. If you do not use the TARGET attribute to specify the name of a frame, the link will open in the frame that contains the link.

If you plan to have all the links on a Web page open in the same frame, set the default target for the links using the <BASE> tag with the TARGET attribute. This will save you time since you will not need to specify a target for each link you create.

CREATE A LINK TO A FRAME

```
contents - WordPad
File  Edit  View  Insert  Format  Help

<HTML>
<HEAD>
<TITLE>Table of Contents</TITLE>
</HEAD>
<BODY>

<H2>Table of Contents</H2>

<A HREF="intro.html">Introduction

</BODY>
</HTML>
```

```
contents - WordPad
File  Edit  View  Insert  Format  Help

<HTML>
<HEAD>
<TITLE>Table of Contents</TITLE>
</HEAD>
<BODY>

<H2>Table of Contents</H2>

<A HREF="intro.html" TARGET="main">Introduction</A>

</BODY>
</HTML>
```

1 On the Web page you want to display the link, type the text or add the image you want users to select to display a Web page in another frame.

2 Type **<A HREF="?"** in front of the text or image, replacing **?** with the location and name of the Web page you want to appear in another frame.

Note: To specify the location and name of a Web page in your own Web site, see the top of page 75.

3 Add a blank space and then type **TARGET="?">** replacing **?** with the name of the frame where you want the Web page to appear.

Note: You assigned names to your frames in step 4 on page 144.

4 Type **</A>** after the text or image.

Extra

If a Web page does not display well in a frame, use the TARGET attribute with the _blank or _top value to open the Web page in a window. The _blank value opens a linked Web page in a new, unnamed window. The _top value opens a linked Web page in the current window, replacing the frames.

Example:

<A HREF="survey.html" TARGET="_top">Take the Survey</A>

If you have set the default target for the links on a Web page, you can still have some links open in a different frame. Use the TARGET attribute in the <A> tag for each link you want to open in a different frame. The target you specify for an individual link will override the default target for the links on the Web page.

The HTML standard also includes the _self and _parent values for the TARGET attribute. The _self value opens a linked Web page in the frame containing the link. The _parent value opens a linked Web page in the frameset containing the link. Use the _parent value to specify the target for a link in a nested frameset. For information on nested framesets, see page 155.

Example:

<A HREF="comingsoon.html" TARGET="_self">Upcoming Movies</A>

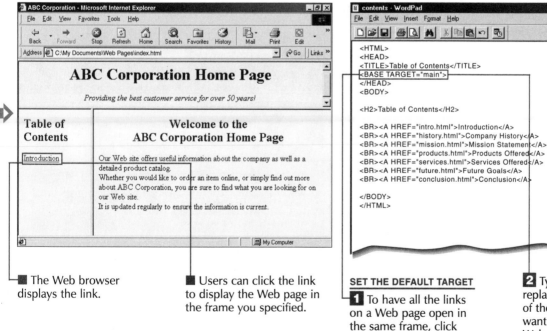

■ The Web browser displays the link.

■ Users can click the link to display the Web page in the frame you specified.

SET THE DEFAULT TARGET

1 To have all the links on a Web page open in the same frame, click between the <HEAD> and </HEAD> tags.

2 Type **<BASE TARGET="?">** replacing **?** with the name of the frame where you want all the links on the Web page to open.

Note: You assigned names to your frames in step 4 on page 144.

HIDE OR DISPLAY SCROLL BARS

B y default, Web browsers will only display scroll bars for a frame when a Web page contains too much information to fit in the frame. Use the SCROLLING attribute with the no or yes value to hide or display the scroll bars for a frame at all times.

If you never want a frame to display scroll bars, specify the no value. Hiding the scroll bars for a frame is useful for reducing clutter in a small frame. If you always want a frame to display scroll bars, specify the yes value. This is useful when the scroll bars improve the layout of a frame.

When hiding the scroll bars for a frame, keep in mind that the scroll bars will be hidden even if some information does not fit in the frame. If a user displays your Web page using a small Web browser window or a low screen resolution, your information may no longer fit in the frame. After hiding the scroll bars for a frame, you should view the frame at a lower screen resolution to make sure users will not need the scroll bars to display all the information in the frame.

HIDE OR DISPLAY SCROLL BARS

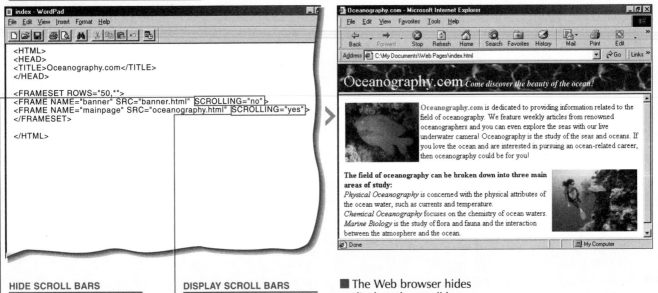

HIDE SCROLL BARS

1 Type **SCROLLING="no"** in the <FRAME> tag for the frame you never want to display scroll bars.

DISPLAY SCROLL BARS

1 Type **SCROLLING="yes"** in the <FRAME> tag for the frame you always want to display scroll bars.

■ The Web browser hides or displays the scroll bars for the frame.

PREVENT USERS FROM RESIZING FRAMES

Use the NORESIZE attribute to prevent users from resizing your frames. This is useful when you do not want the layout of your frames to change.

If you do not prevent users from resizing frames, users can drag a frame border to a new location to resize a frame. Users may want to change the size of a frame to display more information in the frame.

When you prevent users from resizing a frame, users will also be unable to resize frames that share the same frame border. This saves you from having to use the NORESIZE attribute for all of your frames.

Make sure that the frames you have prevented users from resizing are large enough to attractively display the information they contain. Keep in mind that users who view your Web pages at lower resolutions will see less information in each frame.

If you have hidden the borders around your frames, users will automatically be unable to resize the frames. You will only need to use the NORESIZE attribute if you later redisplay the frame borders. For information on hiding frame borders, see page 152.

PREVENT USERS FROM RESIZING FRAMES

```
<HTML>
<HEAD>
<TITLE>Oceanography.com</TITLE>
</HEAD>

<FRAMESET ROWS="50,*">
<FRAME NAME="banner" SRC="banner.html" NORESIZE>
<FRAME NAME="mainpage" SRC="oceanography.html">
</FRAMESET>

</HTML>
```

1 Type **NORESIZE** in the <FRAME> tag for a frame you do not want users to resize.

2 Repeat step 1 for each frame you do not want users to resize.

Note: When you prevent users from resizing a frame, users will automatically be unable to resize frames that share the same frame border.

■ The Web browser will not allow users to resize the frames you specified.

151

CHANGE FRAME BORDERS

There are several options available for changing the appearance of the borders between your frames.

Use the BORDER attribute with the <FRAMESET> tag to change the thickness of your frame borders. By default, most Web browsers display frame borders with a thickness of 6 pixels.

Web browsers usually display frame borders in gray. Using the BORDERCOLOR attribute with the <FRAMESET> tag allows you to change the color of your frame borders. This is useful when you want to coordinate the color of the borders with the background color of the Web pages in your frames.

Although the BORDER and BORDERCOLOR attributes are supported by most Web browsers, they are not part of the HTML standard for frames.

To hide all the borders between your frames, use the FRAMEBORDER attribute with the <FRAMESET> tag. This is useful when you want to make the contents of your frames appear as one Web page. After you hide the frame borders, a space may remain between the frames. To completely remove the space, set the BORDER attribute to 0 pixels.

While the FRAMEBORDER attribute with the <FRAMESET> tag is supported by most Web browsers, it is not part of the HTML standard.

CHANGE FRAME BORDERS

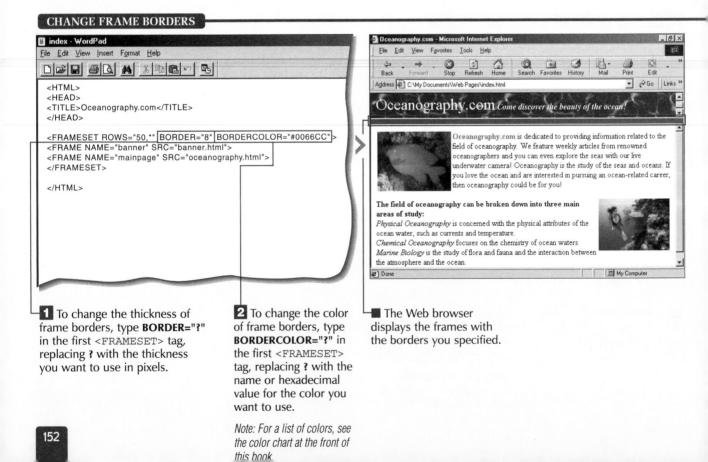

1 To change the thickness of frame borders, type **BORDER="?"** in the first <FRAMESET> tag, replacing ? with the thickness you want to use in pixels.

2 To change the color of frame borders, type **BORDERCOLOR="?"** in the first <FRAMESET> tag, replacing ? with the name or hexadecimal value for the color you want to use.

Note: For a list of colors, see the color chart at the front of this book.

■ The Web browser displays the frames with the borders you specified.

Extra

The FRAMESPACING attribute also allows you to change the thickness of your frame borders. Type **FRAMESPACING="?"** in the first <FRAMESET> tag, replacing **?** with the thickness you want to use in pixels. The FRAMESPACING attribute is not part of the HTML standard and is currently supported only by Internet Explorer.

Example:

```
<FRAMESET ROWS="35%,*" FRAMESPACING="10">
```

The HTML standard specifies that you can use the FRAMEBORDER attribute with the <FRAME> tag to hide the borders for an individual frame. Specify a value of 0 to hide the borders. Most Web browsers do not yet fully support the FRAMEBORDER attribute with the <FRAME> tag.

Example:

```
<FRAME NAME="mainpage" SRC="index.html" FRAMEBORDER="0">
```

Use the BORDERCOLOR attribute with the <FRAME> tag to change the color of the border for an individual frame. This can help draw attention to the frame. When changing the color of an individual frame, keep in mind that many Web browsers do not yet fully support the BORDERCOLOR attribute with the <FRAME> tag. Web browsers may produce inconsistent results depending on the layout of your frames.

Example:

```
<FRAME NAME="navigation" SRC="navigation.html"
BORDERCOLOR="red">
```

```
<HTML>
<HEAD>
<TITLE>Oceanography.com</TITLE>
</HEAD>

<FRAMESET ROWS="50,*" FRAMEBORDER="0">
<FRAME NAME="banner" SRC="banner.html">
<FRAME NAME="mainpage" SRC="oceanography.html">
</FRAMESET>

</HTML>
```

HIDE FRAME BORDERS

1 To hide all frame borders, type **FRAMEBORDER="0"** in the first <FRAMESET> tag.

Note: To completely remove the space between frames, type **BORDER="0"** *in the first* <FRAMESET> *tag.*

■ The Web browser hides the borders around your frames.

CHANGE FRAME MARGINS

Changing the margins of a frame allows you to adjust the amount of space between the contents of the frame and the edges of the frame. This can help improve the layout of a frame.

By default, most Web browsers display frame margins of approximately 10 pixels. Use the MARGINWIDTH and MARGINHEIGHT attributes to change the size of the margins for a frame. The MARGINWIDTH attribute lets you specify a new size in pixels for the left and right margins. The MARGINHEIGHT attribute lets you specify a new size in pixels for the top and bottom margins.

If you want the contents of a frame to appear directly beside the edges of the frame, set the margins of the frame to 0 pixels. Only some Web browsers can display margins set to 0 pixels.

When changing the frame margins, make sure you specify both a margin width and margin height. If you only specify one margin size, your Web browser may automatically change the other margin to the smallest size the browser supports.

CHANGE FRAME MARGINS

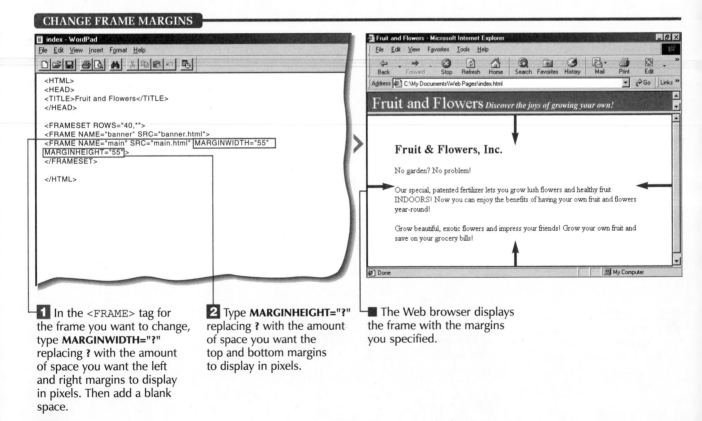

1 In the <FRAME> tag for the frame you want to change, type **MARGINWIDTH="?"** replacing **?** with the amount of space you want the left and right margins to display in pixels. Then add a blank space.

2 Type **MARGINHEIGHT="?"** replacing **?** with the amount of space you want the top and bottom margins to display in pixels.

■ The Web browser displays the frame with the margins you specified.

CREATE NESTED FRAMESETS

N esting a frameset within another frameset allows you to create more elaborate frame layouts. A frameset is a set of frames that divide a Web browser window into sections. For information on creating framesets, see page 144.

Nested framesets consist of two separate frameset documents–an inner frameset and an outer frameset. You can create an inner frameset as you would create any frameset document. The inner frameset should have a simple design, since it will appear in a frame rather than in an entire window.

When creating an outer frameset, you must determine which frame you want to contain

the nested frameset. When entering the information for this frame, specify the location and name of the inner frameset rather than the location and name of a Web page.

Combining framesets can produce results similar to nesting framesets, though you may find nested framesets easier to work with, since the framesets are stored in separate files. For information on combining framesets, see the top of page 145.

You should not create nested framesets that contain more than two framesets, since this can affect the performance of a user's Web browser.

CREATE NESTED FRAMESETS

```
<HTML>
<HEAD>
<TITLE>ABC Corporation Home Page</TITLE>
</HEAD>
<FRAMESET ROWS="90,*">
        <FRAME NAME="banner" SRC="banner.html">
        <FRAMESET COLS="150,*">
                <FRAME NAME="contents" SRC="contents.html">
                <FRAME NAME="innerframeset" SRC="inner.html">
        </FRAMESET>
</FRAMESET>

</HTML>
```

1 Create the frames for the inner frameset as shown on page 144.

2 Create the frames for the outer frameset. When creating the frame that you want to contain the inner frameset, enter the location and name of the inner frameset you created in step 1 rather than the location and name of a Web page.

■ The Web browser displays the inner frameset nested within the outer frameset.

CREATE AN INLINE FRAME

U se the <IFRAME> tag to create an inline frame on your Web page. An inline frame, or floating frame, is a frame that appears within the content of a Web page. Unlike conventional frames, inline frames do not require you to create a frameset on a separate Web page.

Use the NAME attribute to provide a name for an inline frame. Naming an inline frame allows you to later create links that will open another Web page in the inline frame. To create a link to a frame, see page 148.

Use the WIDTH and HEIGHT attributes to specify a width and height for an inline frame.

Make sure the size you specify is large enough to properly display the contents of the frame. Users will not be able to resize an inline frame on your Web page.

Although the <IFRAME> tag is part of the HTML standard, it is currently only supported by Internet Explorer. To specify text that will appear for users with other Web browsers, type the text between the <IFRAME> and </IFRAME> tags. You may want to include a link in the alternative text that will allow these users to access the Web page in the inline frame.

CREATE AN INLINE FRAME

```
index - WordPad
File  Edit  View  Insert  Format  Help

<HTML>
<HEAD>
<TITLE>Oceanography</TITLE>
</HEAD>
<BODY>

<IMG SRC="banner.jpg">

<IFRAME SRC="introduction.html"

<IMG SRC="scuba.jpg" ALIGN="right">
<P><B>The field of oceanography can be broken down into three main areas of study:<
<BR><I>Physical Oceanography</I> is concerned with the physical attributes of the oce
water, such as currents and temperature.
<BR><I>Chemical Oceanography</I> focuses on the chemistry of ocean waters.
<BR><I>Marine Biology</I> is the study of flora and fauna and the interaction between th
atmosphere and the ocean.</P>

</BODY>
</HTML>
```

```
index - WordPad
File  Edit  View  Insert  Format  Help

<HTML>
<HEAD>
<TITLE>Oceanography</TITLE>
</HEAD>
<BODY>

<IMG SRC="banner.jpg">

<IFRAME SRC="introduction.html"  NAME="intro"  WIDTH="600px" HEIGHT="150px">

<IMG SRC="scuba.jpg" ALIGN="right">
<P><B>The field of oceanography can be broken down into three main areas of study:<
<BR><I>Physical Oceanography</I> is concerned with the physical attributes of the oce
water, such as currents and temperature.
<BR><I>Chemical Oceanography</I> focuses on the chemistry of ocean waters.
<BR><I>Marine Biology</I> is the study of flora and fauna and the interaction between th
atmosphere and the ocean.</P>

</BODY>
</HTML>
```

1 On the Web page that you want to contain an inline frame, type **<IFRAME SRC="?"** replacing **?** with the location and name of the Web page you want to appear in the inline frame. Then add a blank space.

Note: To specify the location and name of a Web page in your own Web site, see the top of page 75.

2 Type **NAME="?"** replacing **?** with a name for the inline frame. Then add a blank space.

3 Type **WIDTH="?"** **HEIGHT="?">** replacing **?** with a width and height for the inline frame in pixels or as a percentage of the Web browser window.

Extra

Use the ALIGN attribute with the left or right value to wrap text around an inline frame. The left value places the inline frame on the left side of the text and the right value places the inline frame on the right side of the text.

Example:

```
<IFRAME SRC="products.html" NAME="products"
WIDTH="400" HEIGHT="300" ALIGN="left"></IFRAME>
```

Use the MARGINWIDTH and MARGINHEIGHT attributes to change the size of the margins for an inline frame. The MARGINWIDTH attribute lets you specify a new size in pixels for the left and right margins. The MARGINHEIGHT attribute lets you specify a new size in pixels for the top and bottom margins.

Example:

```
<IFRAME SRC="advertising.html" NAME="advertising"
WIDTH="300" HEIGHT="300" MARGINWIDTH="10"
MARGINHEIGHT="5"></IFRAME>
```

Use the SCROLLING attribute to hide or display the scroll bars for an inline frame. If you never want an inline frame to display scroll bars, specify the no value. Hiding the scroll bars is useful for reducing clutter in a small frame. If you always want an inline frame to display scroll bars, specify the yes value. This is useful when the scroll bars will improve the layout of a frame.

Example:

```
<IFRAME SRC="sales.html" NAME="sales" WIDTH="400"
HEIGHT="300" SCROLLING="no"></IFRAME>
```

4 Type the text you want to appear if a Web browser does not support inline frames.

5 Type **</IFRAME>** to complete the inline frame.

■ The Web browser displays the inline frame on your Web page.

■ Scroll bars automatically appear when a Web page contains too much information to fit in the frame.

157

ADD JAVASCRIPT TO A WEB PAGE

Adding JavaScript to a Web page can help make the page interactive and entertaining. For example, JavaScript can perform tasks such as displaying alert messages, validating information in forms and changing images in response to mouse movements.

JavaScripts are small programs written using the JavaScript scripting language. Although the names are similar, JavaScript and Java have very little in common.

The <SCRIPT> tag allows you to add JavaScript to your Web page. Enter the code for the JavaScript between the <SCRIPT> and </SCRIPT> tags.

Do not enter any HTML tags or plain text between the <SCRIPT> tags, since Web browsers will attempt to interpret the information as JavaScript.

The <SCRIPT> tags are often placed in the head section of a Web page, though JavaScript can also be included in the body of a Web page. A JavaScript you obtain on the Internet usually includes instructions that indicate where you should place the JavaScript on your Web page.

Although JavaScript is the most common scripting language on the Web, many Web browsers also recognize other scripting languages, such as VBScript.

ADD JAVASCRIPT TO A WEB PAGE

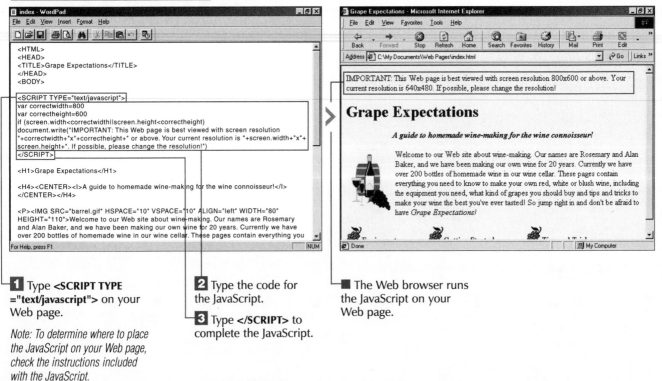

1 Type **<SCRIPT TYPE ="text/javascript">** on your Web page.

Note: To determine where to place the JavaScript on your Web page, check the instructions included with the JavaScript.

2 Type the code for the JavaScript.

3 Type **</SCRIPT>** to complete the JavaScript.

■ The Web browser runs the JavaScript on your Web page.

Extra

There are many places on the Internet that offer JavaScripts. For example, JavaScripts are available at the javascript.internet.com, www.javascripts.com and www.javascripts-galore.com Web sites. Make sure you have permission to use any JavaScripts you find on the Internet. Most JavaScripts come with instructions on how to properly add the JavaScript to your Web page.

If you know the JavaScript scripting language, you can create your own JavaScripts. To learn more about creating JavaScripts, visit the www.htmlgoodies.com/primers/jsp Web site.

According to the HTML standard, you should use the `<META>` tag to specify the default scripting language used on your Web page. Between the `<HEAD>` and `</HEAD>` tags, type **<META HTTP-EQUIV="Content-Script-Type" CONTENT="?">** replacing **?** with the scripting language you are using. For example, type **text/javascript** for JavaScript or **text/vbscript** for VBScript.

Example:

```
<META HTTP-EQUIV="Content-Script-Type"
CONTENT="text/javascript">
```

Although the `TYPE` attribute is still supported by Web browsers, the `LANGUAGE` attribute is now preferred for specifying the scripting language you are using. The value of the `LANGUAGE` attribute is the name of the language, such as `JavaScript` or `VBScript`. You may want to use both the `LANGUAGE` and `TYPE` attributes to help ensure that Web browsers will know which scripting language you are using.

Example:

```
<SCRIPT LANGUAGE="JavaScript"
TYPE="text/javascript">
```

Some JavaScript functions, such as `document.write()`, instruct your Web browser to add information to your Web page. If the JavaScript you are using does not add information to your Web page, you may want to use the `DEFER` attribute with the `<SCRIPT>` tag to help your Web page appear on a user's screen more quickly. The `DEFER` attribute informs Web browsers that they do not need to create any Web page content.

Example:

```
<SCRIPT TYPE="text/javascript"
DEFER>alert('Welcome to my Web Page!');
</SCRIPT>
```

JavaScript can perform actions on a user's computer and therefore presents security risks. For example, some Web browsers allow JavaScript to read files that may contain sensitive information, such as files that store passwords. When adding JavaScript to your Web page, keep in mind that some users turn off JavaScript in their Web browsers because of the security risks.

Dynamic HTML (DHTML) is a combination of technologies, including JavaScript, HTML, Cascading Style Sheets and others. DHTML allows you to create complex animated and interactive Web pages that do not need to be processed by a Web server.

HIDE JAVASCRIPT

Use the <!-- and --> delimiters to hide JavaScript from older Web browsers that cannot run JavaScript. This will prevent the Web browsers from displaying the code for the JavaScript on your Web page.

When hiding JavaScript, type two slashes (//) in front of the final delimiter (-->) to prevent Web browsers that recognize JavaScript from interpreting the delimiter as part of the JavaScript code.

If you have stored JavaScript code in a separate file, you do not need to hide the JavaScript. For information on storing JavaScript code in a separate file, see page 161.

The <NOSCRIPT> tag allows you to provide alternative text that will be displayed in Web browsers that do not run JavaScript. This lets you provide users with information about the missing JavaScript.

Using the <NOSCRIPT> tag does not guarantee that the alternative text you provide will appear. For example, the alternative text may not appear if there is an error in the JavaScript code.

Some older Web browsers that support JavaScript may both run the JavaScript and display the alternative text you provide.

HIDE JAVASCRIPT

```
index - WordPad
File  Edit  View  Insert  Format  Help

<HTML>
<HEAD>
<TITLE>Grape Expectations</TITLE>
</HEAD>
<BODY>

<SCRIPT TYPE="text/javascript">
<!--
var correctwidth=800
var correctheight=600
if (screen.width<correctwidth||screen.height<correctheight)
document.write("IMPORTANT: This Web page is best viewed with screen resolution
"+correctwidth+"x"+correctheight+" or above. Your current resolution is "+screen.width
screen.height+". If possible, please change the resolution!")
//-->
</SCRIPT>

<H1>Grape Expectations</H1>

<H4><CENTER><I>A guide to homemade wine-making for the wine connoisseur!</
</CENTER></H4>
```

1 Type **<!--** directly below the <SCRIPT> tag.

2 Type **//-->** directly above the </SCRIPT> tag.

■ If a user displays your Web page in an older Web browser that cannot run JavaScript, the JavaScript code will not appear.

PROVIDE ALTERNATIVE TEXT

```
index - WordPad
File  Edit  View  Insert  Format  Help

<HTML>
<HEAD>
<TITLE>Grape Expectations</TITLE>
</HEAD>
<BODY>

<SCRIPT TYPE="text/javascript">
<!--
var correctwidth=800
var correctheight=600
if (screen.width<correctwidth||screen.height<correctheight)
document.write("IMPORTANT: This Web page is best viewed with screen resolution
correctwidth+"x"+correctheight+" or above. Your current resolution is "+screen.width
screen.height+". If possible, please change the resolution!")
//-->
</SCRIPT>
<NOSCRIPT>This site is best viewed at a resolution of 800x600.</NOSCRIPT>

<H1>Grape Expectations</H1>

<H4><CENTER><I>A guide to homemade wine-making for the wine connoisseur!<
</CENTER></H4>
```

1 Type **<NOSCRIPT>** directly below the </SCRIPT> tag.

2 Type the text you want to display if a Web browser does not run JavaScript.

3 Type **</NOSCRIPT>**.

■ If JavaScript does not run, the Web browser will display the text you specified.

STORE JAVASCRIPT IN A SEPARATE FILE

f you want to use the same JavaScript on several Web pages, consider storing the JavaScript code in a separate file. Then include a reference to the file on each Web page that you want to use the JavaScript. This prevents you from having to type the JavaScript code on each Web page.

Storing JavaScript in a separate file is also useful for JavaScript code you plan to use on only one Web page. For example, if the JavaScript code is long, saving the code in a separate file will make your Web page less cluttered and easier to read.

To store a JavaScript in a separate file, you must type the JavaScript code into a new file in a word processor or text editor and save the file in the text-only format. Use the .js extension when naming the file.

On each Web page you want to use the JavaScript, use the <SCRIPT> tag with the SRC attribute to specify the location and name of the JavaScript file on your computer. You can specify the location and name of a JavaScript file as you would specify the location and name of an image. For more information, see the top of page 45.

STORE JAVASCRIPT IN A SEPARATE FILE

Document - WordPad

File Edit View Insert Format Help

```
var correctwidth=800
var correctheight=600
if (screen.width<correctwidth||screen.height<correctheight)
document.write("IMPORTANT: This Web page is best viewed with screen resolution "+
correctwidth+"x"+correctheight+" or above. Your current resolution is "+screen.width+"x"+
screen.height+". If possible, please change the resolution!")
```

Save As

Save in: Web Pages

File name: myscript.js   Save

Save as type: Text Document   Cancel

For Help, press F1   NUM

index - WordPad

File Edit View Insert Format Help

```
<HTML>
<HEAD>
<TITLE>Grape Expectations</TITLE>
</HEAD>
<BODY>

<SCRIPT TYPE="text/javascript"  SRC="myscript.js"> </SCRIPT>

<H1>Grape Expectations</H1>

<H4><CENTER><I>A guide to homemade wine-making for the wine connoisseur!</
</CENTER></H4>

<P><IMG SRC="barrel.gif" HSPACE="10" VSPACE="10" ALIGN="left" WIDTH="80"
HEIGHT="110">Welcome to our Web site about wine-making. Our names are Rosema
Alan Baker, and we have been making our own wine for 20 years. Currently we have
bottles of homemade wine in our wine cellar. These pages contain everything you nee
to make your own red, white or blush wine, including the equipment you need, what k
grapes you should buy and tips and tricks to make your wine the best you've ever tas
jump right in and don't be afraid to have <I>Grape Expectations!</I></P>

<P><IMG SRC="grapes.gif"><B><A HREF="equipment.html">Equipment</A>&nb
```

1 Create a new file in a word processor or text editor.

2 Type the code for the JavaScript.

3 Save the file in the text-only format. Use the .js extension to name the file (example: myscript.js).

4 On a Web page you want to use the JavaScript, type **<SCRIPT TYPE="text/javascript"** and then add a blank space.

5 Type **SRC="?">** replacing **?** with the location and name of the JavaScript file on your computer.

6 Type **</SCRIPT>** to complete the JavaScript.

7 Repeat steps 4 to 6 on each Web page you want to use the JavaScript.

ADD AN EVENT THAT RUNS A JAVASCRIPT

I f you do not want a JavaScript on your Web page to run as soon as the Web page appears on a user's screen, add an event to control when the JavaScript will run. For example, use the ONCLICK event to have a JavaScript run when a user clicks an element.

The HTML standard defines a collection of events that you can use. These events are often called "intrinsic events," since they are commonly included as attributes in HTML tags. Intrinsic events can be used with most HTML tags.

The value of an event you add to a tag is the JavaScript you want to run. In most cases, you

will type the JavaScript code directly in the tag. Some JavaScripts you find on the Internet may recommend that you type the JavaScript in the head section of your Web page and then add a reference to the JavaScript in the tag. Check the instructions provided with a JavaScript to determine where to place the JavaScript.

The HTML standard recommends that you specify the default scripting language when you add an event that runs a JavaScript to a Web page. To specify the default scripting language, see page 159.

ADD AN EVENT THAT RUNS A JAVASCRIPT

1 In the tag for the element you want to associate with a JavaScript, type the event that you want to run the JavaScript.

2 Type ="?" replacing **?** with the JavaScript that you want to run when the event occurs.

Note: If your JavaScript contains quotation marks, use single quotation marks (') to differentiate them from the quotation marks (") that enclose the entire JavaScript.

■ The Web browser runs the JavaScript when a user performs the event you specified.

INTRINSIC EVENTS

MOUSE EVENTS

A mouse event runs a JavaScript when a user performs an action with the mouse. For example, a mouse event can run a JavaScript when a user clicks an element, presses the mouse button, releases the mouse button or moves the mouse.

EVENT	EVENT OCCURS WHEN	USED WITH
ONCLICK	A user clicks an element.	Most tags.
ONDBLCLICK	A user double-clicks an element.	Most tags.
ONMOUSEDOWN	A user presses the mouse button.	Most tags.
ONMOUSEUP	A user releases the mouse button.	Most tags.
ONMOUSEOVER	A user positions the mouse over an element.	Most tags.
ONMOUSEMOVE	A user moves the mouse while the mouse is over an element.	Most tags.
ONMOUSEOUT	A user moves the mouse away from an element.	Most tags.
ONFOCUS	A user selects or tabs to an element.	<A>, <AREA>, <LABEL>, <INPUT>, <SELECT>, <BUTTON>, <TEXTAREA>
ONBLUR	A user deselects or tabs away from an element.	<A>, <AREA>, <LABEL>, <INPUT>, <SELECT>, <BUTTON>, <TEXTAREA>

KEYBOARD EVENTS

A keyboard event runs a JavaScript when a user presses a key on the keyboard. Some Web browsers only support using keyboard events with form elements that allow you to enter text, such as text boxes and large text areas.

EVENT	EVENT OCCURS WHEN	USED WITH
ONKEYPRESS	A user presses and releases a key on the keyboard.	Most tags.
ONKEYDOWN	A user presses a key on the keyboard.	Most tags.
ONKEYUP	A user releases a key on the keyboard.	Most tags.

DOCUMENT EVENTS

A document event runs a JavaScript when a user changes or enters information in a form or when a Web browser processes an element, such as a frame.

EVENT	EVENT OCCURS WHEN	USED WITH
ONSELECT	A user selects text in a form element.	<INPUT>, <TEXTAREA>
ONCHANGE	A user changes a form element's value and then leaves the element.	<INPUT>, <SELECT>, <TEXTAREA>
ONSUBMIT	A user clicks the submit button on a form.	<FORM>
ONRESET	A user clicks the reset button on a form.	<FORM>
ONLOAD	A Web page appears in a frame or window.	<BODY>, <FRAMESET>
ONUNLOAD	A Web page disappears from a frame or window.	<BODY>, <FRAMESET>

CREATE A BUTTON THAT RUNS A JAVASCRIPT

U se the `<BUTTON>` tag to create a button that users can click to run a JavaScript. This lets you give users control over when a JavaScript will run. For example, users can click a button to run a JavaScript that performs a calculation or displays the current date and time.

To create a button that runs a JavaScript, use the `TYPE` attribute with the `button` value to specify that you want to create a button. Then use the `ONCLICK` event attribute to specify the JavaScript that you want to run when a user clicks the button. The value of the `ONCLICK` event attribute

is usually the code for the JavaScript you want to use.

The text you type between the `<BUTTON>` and `</BUTTON>` tags will appear on the button. You may also want to use the `<IMG>` tag between the `<BUTTON>` and `</BUTTON>` tags to specify an image you want to appear on the button. This can help you enhance the appearance of the button.

Although the `<BUTTON>` tag is part of the HTML standard, it is not yet supported by some Web browsers.

CREATE A BUTTON THAT RUNS A JAVASCRIPT

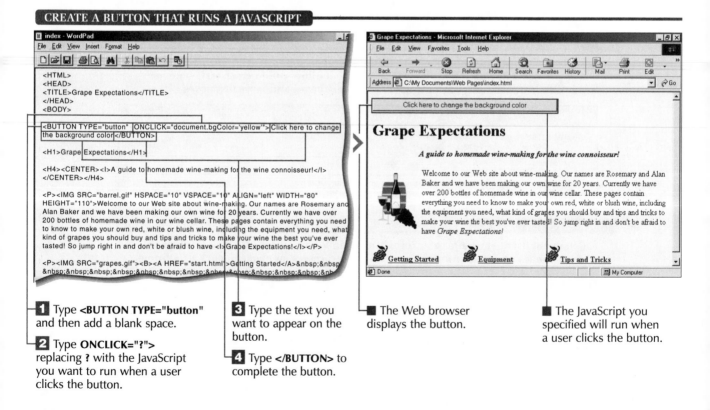

1 Type **<BUTTON TYPE="button"** and then add a blank space.

2 Type **ONCLICK="?">** replacing **?** with the JavaScript you want to run when a user clicks the button.

3 Type the text you want to appear on the button.

4 Type **</BUTTON>** to complete the button.

■ The Web browser displays the button.

■ The JavaScript you specified will run when a user clicks the button.

CREATE A LINK THAT RUNS A JAVASCRIPT

U se the <A> tag to create a link that users can select to run a JavaScript. This lets you give users control over when a JavaScript will run.

Unlike a link to another Web page, a link that runs a JavaScript contains JavaScript code rather than the URL of a Web page. When users select the link, their Web browser will run the JavaScript and display the results in the Web browser window. For example, users can select a link that runs a JavaScript that asks them for information and then generates a new Web page based on their answers.

When specifying the text you want to use for a link, make sure the text clearly indicates what will happen when users select the link. This can help prevent users who have Web browsers that do not run JavaScript from trying to use the link.

A link that runs a JavaScript can be an image link. When using an image link, keep in mind that some users do not see images. You may want to include corresponding text links for these users.

CREATE A LINK THAT RUNS A JAVASCRIPT

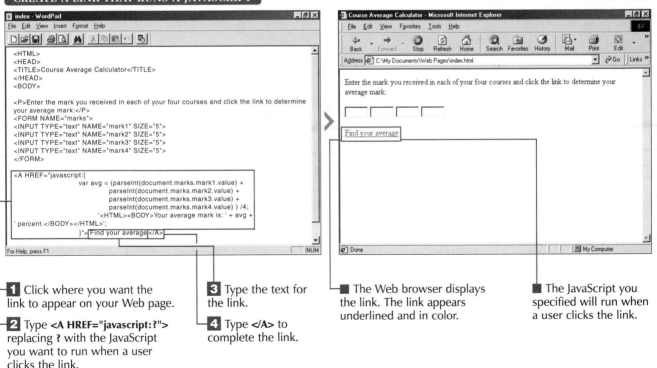

1 Click where you want the link to appear on your Web page.

2 Type **<A HREF="javascript:?">** replacing **?** with the JavaScript you want to run when a user clicks the link.

3 Type the text for the link.

4 Type **</A>** to complete the link.

■ The Web browser displays the link. The link appears underlined and in color.

■ The JavaScript you specified will run when a user clicks the link.

ADD THE DATE AND TIME

Use the `Date()` function to add the current date and time to your Web page. This instructs a Web browser to display the date and time whenever a user displays or refreshes the Web page.

Adding the current date and time to your Web page will make the Web page appear up-to-date. This is useful for Web pages that are regularly updated, such as pages displaying news items.

A Web browser will use the built-in clock in a user's computer to determine the date and time. If a user has the wrong date and

time set in their computer, the incorrect date and time will appear on your Web page.

When you use the JavaScript shown below, most Web browsers will display the day, month, year and time on a Web page. Some Web browsers may also include time zone information. There are other JavaScripts available that allow you to display more elaborate date and time information. For example, a JavaScript can format the date and time or display a real-time clock on your Web page. Date and time JavaScripts are available at the javascript.internet.com Web site.

ADD THE DATE AND TIME

```
<HTML>
<HEAD>
<TITLE>ABC Corporation</TITLE>
</HEAD>
<BODY>
<H2><CENTER>Welcome to the <BR>ABC Corporation Home Page</CENTER

<P>Our Web site offers useful information about the company as well as a det
catalog.</P>
<P>Whether you would like to order an item online, or simply find out more ab
Corporation, you are sure to find what you are looking for on our Web site.</P>
<P>The site is updated regularly, to ensure the information is up-to-date.</P>

<SCRIPT TYPE="text/javascript">document.write(Date())</SCRIPT>

</BODY>
</HTML>
```

index - WordPad

ABC Corporation - Microsoft Internet Explorer

Address C:\My Documents\Web Pages\index.html

Welcome to the
ABC Corporation Home Page

Our Web site offers useful information about the company as well as a detailed product catalog.

Whether you would like to order an item online, or simply find out more about ABC Corporation, you are sure to find what you are looking for on our Web site.

The site is updated regularly, to ensure the information is up-to-date.

Mon Apr 24 11:39:02 2000

1 Click where you want the date and time to appear on your Web page.

2 Type **<SCRIPT TYPE= "text/javascript">** to begin the JavaScript.

3 Type **document.write(Date( ))** to add the date and time.

4 Type **</SCRIPT>** to complete the JavaScript.

■ The Web browser displays the current date and time on your Web page.

DISPLAY AN ALERT MESSAGE

U se JavaScript to add an alert message that will appear when a user visits your Web page.

Alert messages are useful for providing users with information. For example, use an alert message to provide instructions about an element on your Web page, such as a form.

If you want to guarantee that users read important information about your Web page, such as a disclaimer or a copyright statement, include the information in an alert message.

The alert message will help ensure that users who visit your Web page read the information since they will have to click an OK button before they can browse through your Web page.

You may want to add an alert message that will appear when a user performs an action. For example, you can add an alert message that will appear when a user clicks a submit button on a form. For information on adding JavaScript that will run when a user performs an action, see page 162.

DISPLAY AN ALERT MESSAGE

```
<HTML>
<HEAD>
<TITLE>Sports Pools</TITLE>
</HEAD>
<BODY>

<H1><I><CENTER>Sports Pools</CENTER></I></H1>
<H3><CENTER>Enter our weekly pools and compete against thousands of sports fans! Weekly
prizes are awarded to the winners!</CENTER></H3>

<SCRIPT TYPE="text/javascript">
alert('Congratulations to last week\'s winner John Huggins of New Jersey! Good luck in this
week\'s pool!')
</SCRIPT>

</BODY>
</HTML>
```

1 Type **<SCRIPT TYPE= "text/javascript">** to begin the JavaScript.

2 Type **alert('?')** replacing **?** with the message you want to appear when a user first displays your Web page.

3 Type **</SCRIPT>** to complete the JavaScript.

■ The Web browser displays the message in a dialog box when a user first visits your Web page.

■ A user can click the OK button to remove the dialog box.

DISPLAY A POP-UP WINDOW

U se JavaScript to display a pop-up window that will appear when a user visits your Web page. Pop-up windows are useful for providing users with information. For example, use a pop-up window to announce a sale or upcoming event.

When creating a pop-up window, specify the location and name of the Web page you want to appear in the window. For information on specifying the location and name of a Web page in your own Web site, see the top of page 75.

You should also specify the width and height you want the pop-up window to display. Pop-up windows are usually large enough to display the Web page in the pop-up window but small enough to avoid blocking your Web page in the Web browser window.

There are many JavaScripts available that let you display different types of pop-up windows. For example, you may want to use a pop-up window that will automatically close after a period of time. JavaScripts are available at the javascript.internet.com Web site.

Extra

To add scroll bars to a pop-up window, type **,scrollbars=yes** directly after the width for the window. Make sure you do not add any blank spaces to the code.

Example:

```
<BODY ONLOAD="javascript:window.open('index.html',
'homepage','HEIGHT=200,WIDTH=150,scrollbars=yes')">
```

DISPLAY A POP-UP WINDOW

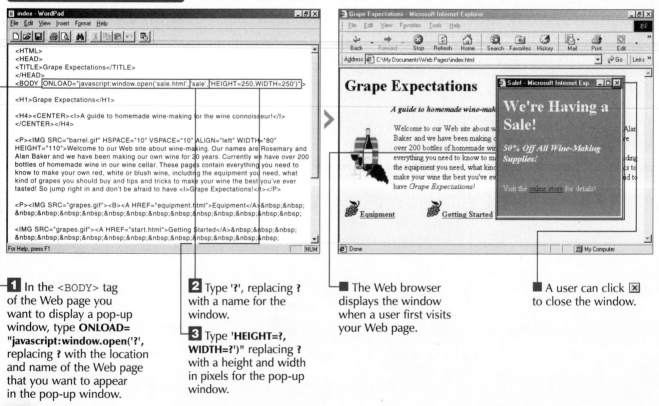

1 In the `<BODY>` tag of the Web page you want to display a pop-up window, type **ONLOAD= "javascript:window.open('?',** replacing **?** with the location and name of the Web page that you want to appear in the pop-up window.

2 Type **'?'**, replacing **?** with a name for the window.

3 Type **'HEIGHT=?, WIDTH=?')"** replacing **?** with a height and width in pixels for the pop-up window.

■ The Web browser displays the window when a user first visits your Web page.

■ A user can click ☒ to close the window.

CHANGE STATUS BAR FOR A LINK

B y default, when a user positions the mouse over a link on a Web page, the address of the linked Web page appears in the status bar of the Web browser window. Use JavaScript to customize the text that will appear in the status bar for a link.

Specifying your own text for the status bar allows you to give users extra information about a link. This is particularly useful for links that have complex URLs.

The ONMOUSEOVER event attribute with the <A> tag lets you add a JavaScript that will run when a user positions the mouse over a link.

In this case, the value of the ONMOUSEOVER event attribute is a JavaScript that contains text you want to appear in the status bar of a Web browser window. When specifying the text, type a backslash (\) before any quotation marks or apostrophes you want to include (example: Mike\'s Home Page).

Some Web browsers also support using the ONMOUSEOVER event attribute with the <IMG> tag to have text appear in the status bar when a user positions the mouse over an image. This is useful for images that do not have accompanying text.

CHANGE STATUS BAR FOR A LINK

```
<HTML>
<HEAD>
<TITLE>Foster City Zoo</TITLE>
</HEAD>
<BODY>

<H1><CENTER>Foster City Zoo</CENTER></H1>
<CENTER><IMG SRC="tiger.jpg"></CENTER>
<P>The spacious grounds of Foster City Zoo were established in 1960 on 350 acres of forest
and farmland located five miles west of Foster City, NY. Our primary commitment is to educate
the public about the animal kingdom.</P>
<P>Foster City Zoo is proud to announce the completion of our newest exhibit, The World of
Cats. This week, in keeping with The World of Cats exhibit, the featured site of the week is all
about tigers!

<BR><A HREF="http://www.tigerkingdom.com" ONMOUSEOVER="window.status='More About
Tigers!';return true">Click here</A> to find out more about tigers!</P>

</BODY>
</HTML>
```

Foster City Zoo

The spacious grounds of Foster City Zoo were established in 1960 on 350 acres of forest and farmland located five miles west of Foster City, NY. Our primary commitment is to educate the public about the animal kingdom.

Foster City Zoo is proud to announce the completion of our newest exhibit, The World of Cats. This week, in keeping with The World of Cats exhibit, the featured site of the week is all about tigers!
Click here to find out more about tigers!

More About Tigers!

1 In the <A> tag for the link you want to display descriptive text in the status bar, type **ONMOUSEOVER="window.status='**.

2 Type the text you want to appear in the status bar.

3 Type **';return true"** to complete the JavaScript.

Note: Make sure you type the double quotes (") and single quotes (') correctly in steps 1 and 3.

■ The Web browser displays the link.

■ The text you specified appears in the status bar when a user positions the mouse over the link.

CREATE AN IMAGE ROLLOVER

U se JavaScript to create an image rollover, which is an image link that changes to another image when a user positions the mouse over the link.

Image rollovers are often used to enhance menus on a Web page. For example, creating an image rollover for each item in a menu can help users determine which menu item they are selecting. When a user positions the mouse over an item, the item will change.

To create an image rollover, add the image you want to originally appear on your Web page and make the image a link using the <A> tag.

Then use the ONMOUSEOVER event attribute to specify the image you want to appear when a user positions the mouse over the link. Use the ONMOUSEOUT event attribute to specify the image you want to appear when a user moves the mouse away from the link. Most people specify the original image for the ONMOUSEOUT event attribute so that the original image will reappear when a user moves their mouse away from the link.

When creating an image rollover, use images that are the same size to prevent Web browsers from resizing one of the images to match the other.

CREATE AN IMAGE ROLLOVER

```
<HTML>
<HEAD>
<TITLE>In Focus</TITLE>
</HEAD>
<BODY>

<H1><CENTER><FONT COLOR="#FF0000">IN FOCUS</FONT><I> Wildlife Photography
</I></CENTER></H1>

<CENTER><IMG SRC="cougar.jpg" NAME="rollover"></CENTER>

<P><B><CENTER>Click the image above to view a selection of wildlife photographs taken
our professional photographers.</CENTER></B></P>

</BODY>
</HTML>
```

```
<HTML>
<HEAD>
<TITLE>In Focus</TITLE>
</HEAD>
<BODY>

<H1><CENTER><FONT COLOR="#FF0000">IN FOCUS</FONT><I> Wildlife Photography
</I></CENTER></H1>

<CENTER><A HREF="photos.html"><IMG SRC="cougar.jpg" NAME="rollover"></A>
</CENTER>

<P><B><CENTER>Click the image above to view a selection of wildlife photographs taken
our professional photographers.</CENTER></B></P>

</BODY>
</HTML>
```

1 Type **<IMG SRC="?"** replacing ? with the location and name of the image you want to originally appear on your Web page. Then add a blank space.

Note: For information on specifying the location and name of an image, see the top of page 45.

2 Type **NAME="rollover">** to specify a name for the image.

3 Before the <IMG> tag, type **<A HREF="?">** replacing ? with the address of the Web page you want to appear when a user clicks the image.

Note: To link the image to a Web page in your own Web site, see the top of page 75.

4 After the <IMG> tag, type **</A>** to complete the link.

Extra

Use the WIDTH and HEIGHT attributes with the <IMG> tag to specify the dimensions for an image rollover. This ensures that both images will display the same size on your Web page.

Example:

```
<IMG SRC="logo.gif" NAME="rollover"
WIDTH="100" HEIGHT="50">
```

The name you specify for your original image using the NAME attribute does not need to be "rollover" as shown in step 2 below. If you use a different name, make sure you adjust the values of the ONMOUSEOVER and ONMOUSEOUT event attributes to use the name you choose. If your Web page contains more than one image rollover, each image rollover must use a different name.

Example:

```
<A HREF="family.html"
ONMOUSEOVER="document.picture.src='parents.jpg'"
ONMOUSEOUT="document.picture.src='kids.jpg'">
<IMG SRC="kids.jpg" NAME="picture"></A>
```

If you want to create an image rollover that is not a link, create a text link that will activate the image rollover. When a user positions the mouse over the text link, the image rollover will change. When creating the image rollover, place the text for the link and the </A> tag before the <IMG> tag for the image rollover.

Example:

```
<A HREF="zoo.html"
ONMOUSEOVER="document.rollover.src='giraffe.gif'"
ONMOUSEOUT="document.rollover.src='lion.gif'">
Come see the animals!</A><IMG SRC="lion.gif"
NAME="rollover">
```

5 In the <A> tag, type **ONMOUSEOVER="document.rollover.src='?'"** replacing **?** with the location and name of the image you want to appear when a user positions the mouse over the original image. Then add a blank space.

6 Type **ONMOUSEOUT="document.rollover.src='?'"** replacing **?** with the location and name of the image you added in step 1.

Note: Make sure you include both the single (') and double (") quotation marks in steps 5 and 6.

■ The Web browser displays the image you specified in step 1.

■ When a user positions the mouse over the image, the image will change to the image you specified in step 5.

■ A user can click the image to display the Web page you specified.

171

VALIDATE FORM INFORMATION

U se JavaScript to validate the information that users enter in a form on your Web page. This helps ensure that users enter the correct information.

There are many ways to validate form information using JavaScript. For example, use JavaScript to ensure that a user does not enter specific characters in a text box or large text area. This is useful for detecting errors that users may make, such as accidentally entering a name in a text box that requests a telephone number.

JavaScript is also useful for verifying that users enter the minimum number of characters in a

form element. This can help ensure that users enter all the information you require. For example, specify a minimum of 10 characters for a text box that requests a telephone number to ensure that users include the area code.

When using JavaScript to validate form information, you can create an error message that you want to appear when users enter incorrect information. The error message you create should help users determine how to enter the correct information. For example, a message such as "Please enter a valid Zip Code" is more helpful than a message that reads "Invalid Entry."

VALIDATE CHARACTERS

1 In the `<INPUT>` or `<TEXTAREA>` tag for the text box or large text area you want to validate, type **ONCHANGE= "var pattern=/[?]/;** replacing **?** with the characters you do not want users to enter.

Note: See the top of page 173 for more information.

2 Type **if (pattern.test (this.value)) alert('?')"** replacing **?** with the error message you want to display if a user enters the characters you specified in step 1.

■ The Web browser displays the text box or large text area on your form.

■ If a user enters any of the characters you specified in step 1, the error message you created will appear.

Extra

When specifying the characters that you do not want users to enter in step 1 on page 172, type each character without adding spaces between the characters. When entering letters, keep in mind that you must enter uppercase and lowercase letters separately. To specify a range of characters that you do not want users to enter, see the following chart.

SPECIFY	USERS CANNOT ENTER
A-Z	Uppercase letters.
a-z	Lowercase letters.
0-9	Any number.
\d	Any number.
\s	Any spacing.
\w	Any letters, numbers or the underscore character (_).

JavaScript can be used to validate almost any type of form information. For example, there are JavaScripts available that will verify whether users have filled in all the required information in a form, whether they have entered a valid e-mail address or whether they have entered information in the proper format. If you know the JavaScript scripting language, you can create your own form validation JavaScripts. To find JavaScripts on the Internet that will validate information in your forms, visit the javascript.internet.com and www.javascripts.com Web sites.

VALIDATE MINIMUM LENGTH

```
<HTML>
<HEAD>
<TITLE>Customer Information</TITLE>
</HEAD>
<BODY>

<H1><CENTER>Customer Information</CENTER></H1>

<P>Please enter the following information:</P>

<FORM METHOD="post" ACTION="/cgi-bin/address.pl">

<BR>First Name:<INPUT TYPE="text" NAME="firstname" SIZE="20">
<BR>Last Name:<INPUT TYPE="text" NAME="lastname" SIZE="20">
<BR>Street Address:<INPUT TYPE="text" NAME="street" SIZE="30">
<BR>Zip Code:<INPUT TYPE="text" NAME="zip" SIZE="5">
<BR>Phone Number:<INPUT TYPE="text" NAME="phone" SIZE="10" ONCHANGE="
if (this.value.length < 10)  alert('Please include your area code.')">
</FORM>

</BODY>
</HTML>
```

1 In the <INPUT> or <TEXTAREA> tag for the text box or large text area you want to validate, type **ONCHANGE=" if (this.value.length < ?)** replacing **?** with the minimum number of characters you want users to enter.

2 Type **alert('?')"** replacing **?** with the error message you want to display if a user enters too few characters.

■ The Web browser displays the text box or large text area on your form.

■ If a user enters fewer characters than you specified in step 1, the error message you created will appear.

INDENT TEXT USING LISTS

The HTML standard does not provide a tag for indenting text. Using the <UL> tag allows you to trick Web browsers into indenting text.

The <UL> tag is designed for creating unordered lists, which are indented from the left edge of a Web page. When creating an unordered list, you use the <LI> tag to have each list item display a bullet. Using the <UL> tag without the <LI> tag allows you to indent text without displaying a bullet beside the text. For more information on unordered lists, see page 40.

When you use the <UL> tag to indent text, Web browsers will indent every line in the section of text. To indent only the first line of text, use the <DD> tag. The <DD> tag is designed to mark the beginning of a definition when creating a definition list. For more information on definition lists, see page 43.

Although most Web browsers support using the <UL> and <DD> tags to indent text, the HTML standard recommends that you use *style sheets* to indent text. For more information on style sheets, see page 196.

INDENT TEXT USING LISTS

```
index - WordPad
File  Edit  View  Insert  Format  Help

<HTML>
<HEAD>
<TITLE>Classical Music Composers</TITLE>
</HEAD>
<BODY>

<H2>Beethoven</H2>
<P><UL>Ludwig van Beethoven was born in Bonn, Germany in 1770. He spent most
in Vienna, where he earned a living giving concerts, teaching piano and selling his
compositions.
<BR>One of the most fascinating aspects of Beethoven's life was his triumph over dea
which struck him during adulthood. In fact, he composed some of his most powerful w
losing his hearing.</UL></P>

<H2>Bach</H2>
<P>Johann Sebastian Bach was born into a family of musicians in 1685 in Eisenach, G
Bach's works include church organ and choral music, music for chamber orchestras and
200 cantatas. Although he was more respected as an organist during his lifetime, Bach
compositions influenced many later composers, including Beethoven and Mozart.</P>

</BODY>
</HTML>
```

Classical Music Composers - Microsoft Internet Explorer

File Edit View Favorites Tools Help

Back Forward Stop Refresh Home Search Favorites History Mail Print Edit

Address C:\My Documents\Web Pages\index.html

Beethoven

Ludwig van Beethoven was born in Bonn, Germany in 1770. He spent most of his life in Vienna, where he earned a living giving concerts, teaching piano and selling his compositions. One of the most fascinating aspects of Beethoven's life was his triumph over deafness, which struck him during adulthood. In fact, he composed some of his most powerful works after losing his hearing.

Bach

Johann Sebastian Bach was born into a family of musicians in 1685 in Eisenach, Germany. Bach's works include church organ and choral music, music for chamber orchestras and over 200 cantatas. Although he was more respected as an organist during his lifetime, Bach's compositions influenced many later composers, including Beethoven and Mozart.

Done   My Computer

1 Type **<UL>** in front of the text you want to indent.

2 Type **</UL>** after the text you want to indent.

■ The Web browser indents the text.

*Note: To indent only the first line of text in a paragraph, type **<DD>** in front of the paragraph and type **</DD>** after the paragraph.*

CREATE A DROP CAP

A drop cap is a large capital letter you can use at the beginning of a paragraph to enhance the appearance of the paragraph.

To add a drop cap to your Web page, create a GIF image of the drop cap and then add the image to your page.

To create a drop cap image, you will need an image editing program such as Jasc Paint Shop Pro or Adobe Photoshop. Consult the documentation that came with your image editing program to determine how to create an image.

The drop cap image you create should have a transparent background to ensure that it will blend into the background of your Web page. For information on making an image background transparent, see page 68.

Use the <IMG> tag to add a drop cap image to your Web page. Add the image beside the paragraph you want to contain the drop cap and use the ALIGN attribute with the left value to wrap the text in the paragraph around the image.

CREATE A DROP CAP

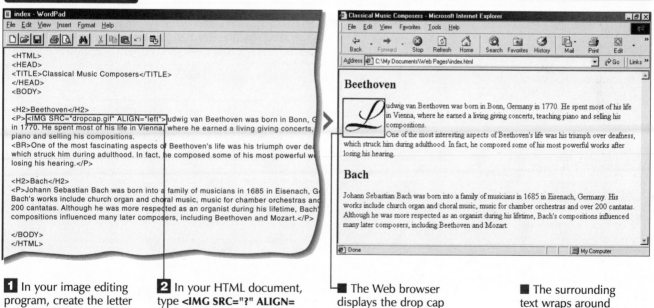

1 In your image editing program, create the letter for your drop cap, making the background of the image transparent as shown on page 68.

2 In your HTML document, type **<IMG SRC="?" ALIGN="left">** where you want the drop cap to appear, replacing **?** with the location and name of the drop cap image on your computer.

Note: To specify the location and name of an image, see the top of page 45.

■ The Web browser displays the drop cap on your Web page.

■ The surrounding text wraps around the drop cap.

CREATE A MARQUEE

U se the <MARQUEE> tag when you want to have text scroll across a user's screen.

The BEHAVIOR attribute allows you to specify the way you want text for a marquee to scroll. Use the scroll value to have text enter on one side of the screen and exit on the opposite side. The slide value has text enter on one side of the screen and stop when it reaches the opposite side. Use the alternate value to have text move back and forth across the screen.

The DIRECTION attribute allows you to specify the direction you want text to scroll. Use the LOOP attribute to specify the number of times you want scrolling text to move across the screen.

Use the SCROLLAMOUNT attribute to specify the number of pixels you want text to move at a time. The SCROLLDELAY attribute lets you specify the number of milliseconds you want to elapse between each movement.

When creating a marquee, enter the text you want the marquee to display between the <MARQUEE> and </MARQUEE> tags. You can format text for a marquee as you would format any text on your Web page. Only Internet Explorer supports the <MARQUEE> tag, though other Web browsers will display the text you specify for a marquee as non-scrolling text.

CREATE A MARQUEE

index - WordPad

File Edit View Insert Format Help

```
<HTML>
<HEAD>
<TITLE>Grape Expectations</TITLE>
</HEAD>
<BODY>

<MARQUEE BEHAVIOR="scroll" DIRECTION="left"

<H1>Grape Expectations</H1>

<H4><CENTER><I>A guide to homemade wine-making for the wine connoisseur!</I>
</CENTER></H4>

<P><IMG SRC="barrel.gif" HSPACE="10" VSPACE="10" ALIGN="left" WIDTH="80"
HEIGHT="110">Welcome to our Web site about wine-making. Our names are Rosemary and
Alan Baker and we have been making our own wine for 20 years. Currently we have over 20
bottles of homemade wine in our wine cellar. These pages contain everything you need to
know to make your own red, white or blush wine, including the equipment you need, what
kind of grapes you should buy and tips and tricks to make your wine the best you've ever
tasted! So jump right in and don't be afraid to have <I>Grape Expectations!</I></P>

<P><IMG SRC="grapes.gif"><B><A HREF="equipment.html">Equipment</A>  
            
```

```
<HTML>
<HEAD>
<TITLE>Grape Expectations</TITLE>
</HEAD>
<BODY>

<MARQUEE BEHAVIOR="scroll" DIRECTION="left" LOOP="25" SCROLLAMOUNT="6"

<H1>Grape Expectations</H1>

<H4><CENTER><I>A guide to homemade wine-making for the wine connoisseur!</I>
</CENTER></H4>

<P><IMG SRC="barrel.gif" HSPACE="10" VSPACE="10" ALIGN="left" WIDTH="80"
HEIGHT="110">Welcome to our Web site about wine-making. Our names are Rosemary and
Alan Baker and we have been making our own wine for 20 years. Currently we have over 20
bottles of homemade wine in our wine cellar. These pages contain everything you need to
know to make your own red, white or blush wine, including the equipment you need, what
kind of grapes you should buy and tips and tricks to make your wine the best you've ever
tasted! So jump right in and don't be afraid to have <I>Grape Expectations!</I></P>

<P><IMG SRC="grapes.gif"><B><A HREF="equipment.html">Equipment</A>  
            
```

1 Type **<MARQUEE** where you want the marquee to appear on your Web page.

2 Type **BEHAVIOR="?"** replacing **?** with the way you want the text for the marquee to scroll (**scroll**, **slide** or **alternate**).

3 To specify which direction you want the text to scroll, type **DIRECTION="left"** or **DIRECTION="right"**.

4 To specify the number of times you want text to scroll across the screen, type **LOOP="?"** replacing **?** with the number of times.

Note: To have the text scroll continuously, type ***LOOP="infinite"*** *in step 4.*

5 Type **SCROLLAMOUNT="?"** replacing **?** with the number of pixels you want the text to move at a time.

Extra

Use the BGCOLOR attribute to change the background color of a marquee. Specify the name or hexadecimal value for the color you want to use. For a list of colors, see the color chart at the front of this book.

Example:

```
<MARQUEE BEHAVIOR="scroll" DIRECTION="left"
SCROLLAMOUNT="2" SCROLLDELAY="60"
BGCOLOR="red">Breaking News!</MARQUEE>
```

By default, Internet Explorer uses a minimum SCROLLDELAY value of 60 milliseconds, even if you specify a smaller value. Use the TRUESPEED attribute to override the minimum value. This is useful when you want text to scroll more quickly across the screen.

Example:

```
<MARQUEE BEHAVIOR="scroll" DIRECTION="left"
SCROLLAMOUNT="2" SCROLLDELAY="10" TRUESPEED>Visit
our Web site!</MARQUEE>
```

To change the size of a marquee, use the WIDTH and HEIGHT attributes to specify a new size in pixels or as a percentage of the Web browser window. Changing the width or height of a marquee will not change the size of the text in the marquee.

Example:

```
<MARQUEE BEHAVIOR="alternate" DIRECTION="right"
SCROLLAMOUNT="5" SCROLLDELAY="80" WIDTH="600"
HEIGHT="30">SALE! Two days only!</MARQUEE>
```

Use the HSPACE and VSPACE attributes to add space around a marquee on your Web page. The HSPACE attribute adds space to the left and right sides of a marquee and the VSPACE attribute adds space to the top and bottom of a marquee. Specify the amount of space in pixels.

Example:

```
<MARQUEE BEHAVIOR="scroll" DIRECTION="right"
SCROLLAMOUNT="5" SCROLLDELAY="60" HSPACE="10"
VSPACE="10">Visit the new, updated photo
gallery.</MARQUEE>
```

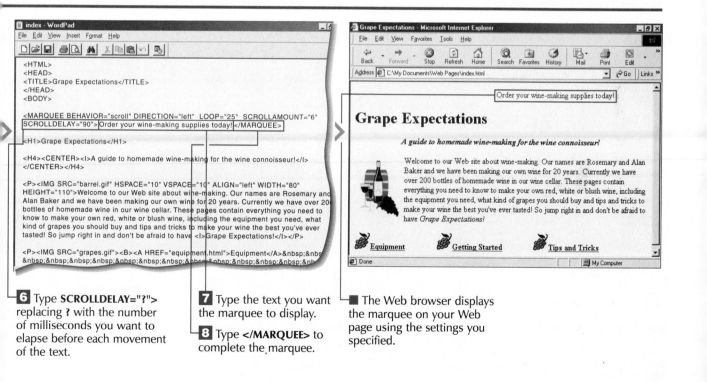

6 Type **SCROLLDELAY="?">** replacing ? with the number of milliseconds you want to elapse before each movement of the text.

7 Type the text you want the marquee to display.

8 Type **</MARQUEE>** to complete the marquee.

■ The Web browser displays the marquee on your Web page using the settings you specified.

PLACE TEXT OVER AN IMAGE

If you want text to appear on top of an image on your Web page, you can use a table to position the text and the image.

To place text over an image using a table, create a table with one row that contains one cell. Set the BORDER, CELLPADDING and CELLSPACING attributes to a value of 0 pixels to remove the borders and spacing from the cell. This helps ensure that the text and image will line up properly.

Use the WIDTH and HEIGHT attributes to specify a size for the cell in pixels. To ensure the entire image will appear in the cell, make the cell the

same size as the image you want to add to the cell. To determine the size of an image, see page 58. Use the BACKGROUND attribute to add the image to the background of the cell.

The VALIGN attribute allows you to specify the way you want to vertically align the text over the image. The text you type between the <TD> and </TD> tags will appear over the image.

Text can also be placed over an image by *absolutely positioning* the text using style sheets. For information on absolute positioning, see page 236.

PLACE TEXT OVER AN IMAGE

index - WordPad

File Edit View Insert Format Help

```
<H1><I>Into the Wild!</I></H1>

<P><B>Would you like to venture beyond the beaten path? Do so with Into the Wild's
adventure tours.</B>
<BR>Whether you'd like to take a nature photography tour, camp in the rugged wilderness of
the Rocky Mountains or go on a canoeing adventure, we have the trip for you!
<BR>We provide once-in-a-lifetime adventures for groups or individuals. Call today for
information on our packages and sign up for an unforgettable experience!</P>

<TABLE BORDER="0" CELLPADDING="0" CELLSPACING="0">
<TR>
<TD WIDTH="150" HEIGHT="100"

<P>Some of our most popular trips are alpine skiing excursions in the Rocky Mountains.
We will fly you to the top of the slopes by helicopter and provide comfortable
accommodations at the end of a fun-filled day! Cross-country ski packages are also
available!</P>

</BODY>
</HTML>
```

index - WordPad

File Edit View Insert Format Help

```
<H1><I>Into the Wild!</I></H1>

<P><B>Would you like to venture beyond the beaten path? Do so with Into the Wild's
adventure tours.</B>
<BR>Whether you'd like to take a nature photography tour, camp in the rugged wilderness of
the Rocky Mountains or go on a canoeing adventure, we have the trip for you!
<BR>We provide once-in-a-lifetime adventures for groups or individuals. Call today for
information on our packages and sign up for an unforgettable experience!</P>

<TABLE BORDER="0" CELLPADDING="0" CELLSPACING="0">
<TR>
<TD WIDTH="150" HEIGHT="100" BACKGROUND="skier.jpg" VALIGN="bottom">

<P>Some of our most popular trips are alpine skiing excursions in the Rocky Mountains.
We will fly you to the top of the slopes by helicopter and provide comfortable
accommodations at the end of a fun-filled day! Cross-country ski packages are also
available!</P>

</BODY>
</HTML>
```

1 Type **<TABLE BORDER="0" CELLPADDING="0" CELLSPACING="0">** to create a table that will not display any borders or extra spacing.

2 Type **<TR>** to create a row in the table.

3 To create a cell the same size as the image you want to use, type **<TD WIDTH="?" HEIGHT="?"** replacing ? with the width and height of the image in pixels.

Note: To determine the size of an image, see page 58.

4 To add the image to the background of the cell, type **BACKGROUND="?"** replacing ? with the location and name of the image you want to use.

Note: To specify the location and name of an image, see the top of page 45.

5 Type **VALIGN="?">** replacing ? with the way you want to vertically align the text over the image (**top**, **middle** or **bottom**).

Extra

If you want a border to appear around the image, add a border to the table containing the image. Set the BORDER attribute to a value greater than 0 pixels to specify a width for the border.

Example:
`<TABLE BORDER="10" CELLPADDING="0" CELLSPACING="0">`

Placing text over an image is useful for creating navigation buttons on your Web page. To create a navigation button, make the text that appears over the image a link. Text you make a link will appear underlined.

Example:
```
<TABLE BORDER="0" CELLPADDING="0" CELLSPACING="0">
<TR>
<TD WIDTH="70" HEIGHT="72" BACKGROUND="button.gif"
VALIGN="middle"><A HREF="index.html">Home</A></TD>
</TR>
</TABLE>
```

When you add an image to a table, the image is displayed as a block-level element, meaning that a blank line appears above and below the image. If you want the image to appear on the same line as the surrounding elements, use style sheets to change the table containing the image to an inline element. For information on changing the display of elements, see page 229.

Example:
```
<TABLE BORDER="0" CELLPADDING="0" CELLSPACING="0"
STYLE="display: inline">
```

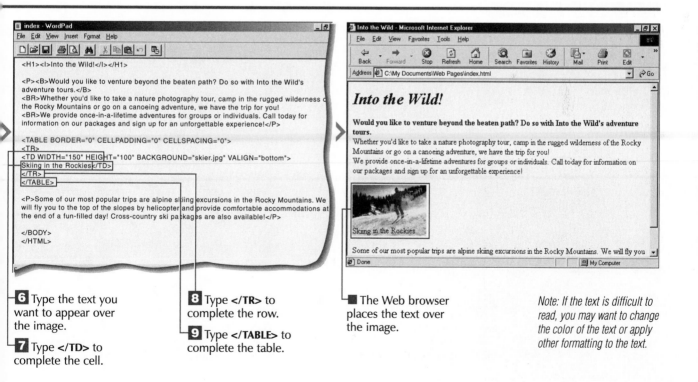

6 Type the text you want to appear over the image.

7 Type **</TD>** to complete the cell.

8 Type **</TR>** to complete the row.

9 Type **</TABLE>** to complete the table.

■ The Web browser places the text over the image.

Note: If the text is difficult to read, you may want to change the color of the text or apply other formatting to the text.

USE ANIMATED GIF IMAGES

U se animated GIF images to add interest to your Web pages. Adding an animated GIF image is similar to adding a regular image to a Web page.

Animated GIF image files consist of a series of images that Web browsers display one after another. Since the animation is a collection of images, users do not need a special program to view the animation. Anyone who uses a Web browser that displays images will be able to see animated GIF images.

Interesting animated GIF images are available at the www.animfactory.com and www.artie.com Web sites. Make sure you have permission to use animated GIF images you obtain on the Internet.

Some image editing programs offer tools for creating your own animated GIF images. For example, Jasc Paint Shop Pro comes with the Animation Shop program. You can also obtain programs on the Internet, such as the GIF Construction Set program, which is available at the www.mindworkshop.com/alchemy/gifcon.html Web site.

When adding animated GIF images to your Web pages, keep in mind that animated images often have large file sizes and may take a long time to appear on a user's screen. Overusing animated GIF images may adversely affect the transfer speed of your Web pages.

USE ANIMATED GIF IMAGES

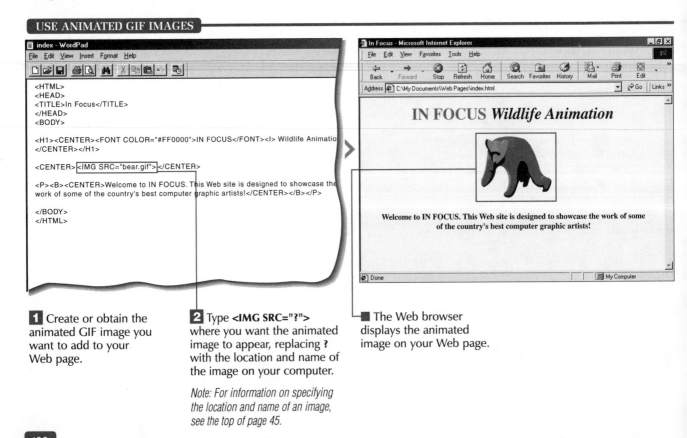

1 Create or obtain the animated GIF image you want to add to your Web page.

2 Type **<IMG SRC="?">** where you want the animated image to appear, replacing **?** with the location and name of the image on your computer.

Note: For information on specifying the location and name of an image, see the top of page 45.

■ The Web browser displays the animated image on your Web page.

CREATE TOOL TIPS FOR ELEMENTS

The TITLE attribute allows you to provide additional information about an element on your Web page. When a user positions the mouse over the element, Web browsers will display the information as a tool tip, which is a small box containing text.

The TITLE attribute can be used with most HTML tags. For example, use the TITLE attribute with the <A> tag to add a tool tip to a link. This can help users determine where the link will take them. Tool tips are also useful for adding brief instructions or examples to form elements to help users determine the type of information they should enter.

You do not need to create tool tips for images if you have used the ALT attribute to provide alternative text for the images. Images you have provided alternative text for will automatically display the alternative text as a tool tip. For information on adding alternative text to images, see page 44.

Although the TITLE attribute is part of the HTML standard, it is currently only supported by Internet Explorer.

CREATE TOOL TIPS FOR ELEMENTS

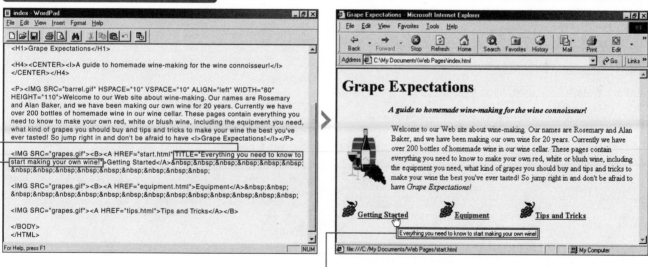

1 In the tag for the element you want to display a tool tip, type **TITLE="?"** replacing **?** with the text you want to appear when a user positions the mouse over the element.

Note: The TITLE attribute cannot be used with the <BASE>, <BASEFONT>, <HEAD>, <HTML>, <META>, <PARAM>, <SCRIPT> or <TITLE> tag.

■ When a user positions the mouse over the element, the Web browser displays the information you specified as a tool tip.

CREATE A WATERMARK

U se a watermark to add an interesting visual effect to your Web page. A watermark is a background image that remains stationary while a user scrolls through the contents of a Web page.

To create a watermark, use the BACKGROUND attribute with the <BODY> tag to add a background image to your Web page. To prevent the background image from moving when a user scrolls through your Web page, use the BGPROPERTIES attribute with the fixed value.

When selecting a background image for a watermark, keep in mind that the text on your Web page will

move over the image. If the image affects the readability of the text, you may need to change the color of the text. To change the color of text, see page 32.

The background image you use for a watermark can be a small image that repeats to fill the background area or a large image that takes up the entire background of the Web page.

Using the BACKGROUND and BGPROPERTIES attributes to create a watermark is currently only supported by Internet Explorer.

CREATE A WATERMARK

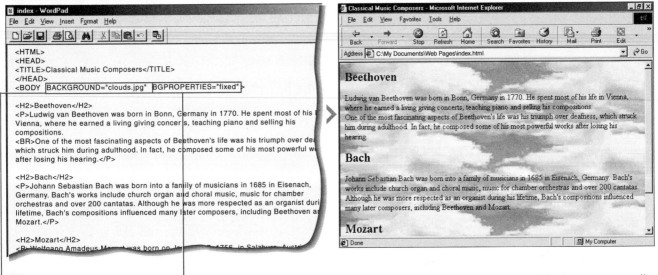

1 In the <BODY> tag, type **BACKGROUND="?"** replacing **?** with the location and name of the background image on your computer that you want to use as a watermark. Then add a blank space.

Note: To specify the location and name of an image, see the top of page 45.

2 Type **BGPROPERTIES= "fixed"** to make the image a watermark.

■ The Web browser displays the background image on your Web page.

■ When a user scrolls through the Web page, the background image will not move.

USE A HIT COUNTER

A dding a hit counter, or access counter, to your Web page allows you to keep track of the number of times people have visited your Web page.

A hit counter displays the number of times a Web page has been loaded. For example, a hit counter will display "50" if one person loads the Web page 50 times or if 50 people load the page once.

There are a wide variety of hit counters available, including hit counters that can perform advanced tasks, such as determining where users are from, the time of day the users visited your Web page and the average length of time users displayed your page.

OBTAIN A HIT COUNTER

Before obtaining a hit counter, you should contact your Web presence provider to make sure that they allow hit counters on their Web server. Some Web presence providers offer hit counters you can use. Your Web presence provider may also offer a Web page that helps you add a hit counter to your Web page.

If your Web presence provider does not offer a hit counter, you can find hit counters on the Internet.

Some companies offer hit counters for a fee. There are also free hit counters available. Companies that offer free hit counters may require your Web site to be non-profit and display an advertisement for the company on your Web page. Free hit counters are available at the counter.bloke.com, www.pagecount.com and www.sitemeter.com Web sites.

ADD A HIT COUNTER

A hit counter can be added to any page in your Web site. Most people add a hit counter to their home page, since this is the first page people will see when they visit the Web site. If you want to determine which of your pages are the most popular, add hit counters to multiple Web pages in your Web site.

The method you use to add a hit counter to your Web page depends on the type of hit counter you are adding. Some hit counters use CGI (Common

Gateway Interface) scripts, which are programs that a Web server runs to process information. If your Web server does not allow you to use CGI scripts, you may want to use a different type of hit counter, such as a Java applet hit counter. A Java applet is a program written using the Java programming language. For information on Java applets, see page 190.

USE PIXEL SHIMS

A pixel shim is a small GIF image that you can add to your Web page to help adjust the spacing between elements on the page. Pixel shims transfer quickly over the Internet and are supported by most Web browsers.

To create a pixel shim image, you will need an image editing program such as Jasc Paint Shop Pro or Adobe Photoshop. The pixel shim image you create should be one pixel wide and one pixel high. Consult the documentation that came with your image editing program to determine how to create an image.

If you want to add a block of colored space to your Web page, create a pixel shim in the color

you want to use. To create an invisible pixel shim, make the pixel shim image transparent as shown on page 68.

Once you have created a pixel shim, use the <IMG> tag to add the pixel shim to your Web page. Use the WIDTH and HEIGHT attributes to specify the dimensions for the amount of space you want the pixel shim to occupy.

If you want the pixel shim to appear beside a block of text, use the ALIGN attribute with the left or right value to wrap the text around the pixel shim.

USE PIXEL SHIMS

```
index - WordPad
File  Edit  View  Insert  Format  Help

<HTML>
<HEAD>
<TITLE>Into the Wild</TITLE>
</HEAD>
<BODY>

<H1><I>Into the Wild!</I></H1>
<P><IMG SRC="cougar.jpg" ALIGN="left">

<IMG SRC="myshim.gif"

<B>Would you like to venture beyond the beaten path? Do so with Into the Wild's
tours.</B>
<BR>Whether you'd like to take a nature photography tour, camp in the rugged w
the Rocky Mountains or go on a canoeing adventure, we have the trip for you!
<BR>We provide once-in-a-lifetime adventures for groups or individuals. Call toda
information on our packages and sign up for an unforgettable experience!</P>

<P><IMG SRC="skier.jpg" ALIGN="right">
<H3>Skiing</H3>
Some of our most popular trips are alpine skiing excursions in the Rocky Mo
```

```
index - WordPad
File  Edit  View  Insert  Format  Help

<HTML>
<HEAD>
<TITLE>Into the Wild</TITLE>
</HEAD>
<BODY>

<H1><I>Into the Wild!</I></H1>
<P><IMG SRC="cougar.jpg" ALIGN="left">

<IMG SRC="myshim.gif"  WIDTH="50" HEIGHT="35">

<B>Would you like to venture beyond the beaten path? Do so with Into the Wild's
tours.</B>
<BR>Whether you'd like to take a nature photography tour, camp in the rugged w
the Rocky Mountains or go on a canoeing adventure, we have the trip for you!
<BR>We provide once-in-a-lifetime adventures for groups or individuals. Call toda
information on our packages and sign up for an unforgettable experience!</P>

<P><IMG SRC="skier.jpg" ALIGN="right">
<H3>Skiing</H3>
Some of our most popular trips are alpine skiing excursions in the Rocky Mo
```

1 In your image editing program, create a GIF image that measures 1 pixel by 1 pixel.

Note: To create an invisible pixel shim, make the image transparent as shown on page 68.

2 In your HTML document, type **<IMG SRC="?"** where you want to add the pixel shim, replacing **?** with the location and name of the pixel shim image on your computer.

Note: To specify the location and name of an image, see the top of page 45.

3 Type **WIDTH="?" HEIGHT="?">** replacing **?** with a width and height in pixels for the amount of space you want the pixel shim to occupy.

■ You can also specify a WIDTH or HEIGHT value as a percentage of the Web browser window (example: 30%).

If you use a colored pixel shim, you may want to add space around the pixel shim to prevent elements from appearing directly beside the pixel shim. This can help enhance the appearance of your Web page. Use the HSPACE attribute to add space to both the left and right sides of a pixel shim. The VSPACE attribute allows you to add space to both the top and bottom of a pixel shim. Specify the amount of space you want to add in pixels.

Example:

```
<IMG SRC="myshim.gif" WIDTH="100"
HEIGHT="400" ALIGN="left" HSPACE="10"
VSPACE="10">
```

The <SPACER> tag also lets you add a block of space to a Web page. Use the block value with the TYPE attribute to create the block of space. The WIDTH and HEIGHT attributes allow you to specify a width and height for the block of space. To wrap text around the block of space, use the ALIGN attribute with the left or right value. The <SPACER> tag is not part of the HTML standard and is only supported by Netscape Navigator.

Example:

```
<SPACER TYPE="block" WIDTH="100" HEIGHT="350"
ALIGN="left">
```

4 To wrap text around the pixel shim, type **ALIGN="left"** or **ALIGN="right"** after the HEIGHT attribute.

Note: Specifying the left value will wrap text around the right side of the pixel shim, while specifying the right value will wrap text around the left side of the pixel shim.

■ The Web browser displays the pixel shim as a space on your Web page.

DISPLAY ANOTHER WEB PAGE AUTOMATICALLY

The `<META>` tag allows you to have a Web page automatically display another Web page after a certain period of time. This is useful for creating interesting title pages for your Web site and for redirecting Web browsers when a Web page has moved.

A Web page that automatically displays another Web page is a client-pull document. Client-pull documents instruct Web browsers to retrieve information from a Web server.

When a user displays a Web page, the Web server that stores the page sends HTTP header fields containing information about the page to the user's Web browser. Use the `HTTP-EQUIV` attribute with the `Refresh` property to specify that you want a Web server to include instructions in the HTTP header fields that will have Web browsers automatically display a new page.

Use the `CONTENT` attribute to specify the number of seconds you want to elapse before the Web browser automatically displays another Web page. The `URL` attribute lets you specify the location and name of the Web page you want to automatically appear. Make sure you give users enough time to read the contents of your Web page.

DISPLAY ANOTHER WEB PAGE AUTOMATICALLY

```
index - WordPad
File  Edit  View  Insert  Format  Help

<HTML>
<HEAD>
<TITLE>This Page Has Moved</TITLE>
<META HTTP-EQUIV="Refresh"
</HEAD>
<BODY>

<H1>This Page Has Moved!</H1>
<B>Please update your bookmarks! The new ABC Corporation Home Page is located at:
<A HREF="http://www.abccorporation.com"><I>www.abccorporation.com</I></A></B>

<P><B>You will automatically be taken to the new Web site in 10 seconds.</B></P>

</BODY>
</HTML>
```

```
index - WordPad
File  Edit  View  Insert  Format  Help

<HTML>
<HEAD>
<TITLE>This Page Has Moved</TITLE>
<META HTTP-EQUIV="Refresh"  CONTENT="10;
</HEAD>
<BODY>

<H1>This Page Has Moved!</H1>
<B>Please update your bookmarks! The new ABC Corporation Home Page is located at:
<A HREF="http://www.abccorporation.com"><I>www.abccorporation.com</I></A></B>

<P><B>You will automatically be taken to the new Web site in 10 seconds.</B></P>

</BODY>
</HTML>
```

1 Between the `<HEAD>` and `</HEAD>` tags on the Web page you want to automatically display another Web page, type **<META HTTP-EQUIV="Refresh"** and then add a blank space.

2 Type **CONTENT="?;** replacing **?** with the number of seconds you want to elapse before another Web page appears on the screen. Then add a blank space.

Extra

To create a slide show that automatically displays a series of Web pages, perform the steps below for each Web page you want to include in the slide show. If you want the slide show to run continuously, make sure the last Web page specifies the location of the first Web page in the slide show. If you do not want the slide show to run continuously, do not perform the steps below for the last Web page in the slide show.

If you want Web browsers to automatically redisplay the same Web page, do not include the URL attribute when performing the steps below. This allows you to repeatedly refresh your Web page and is useful for updating Web pages that contain information that is constantly changing, such as the weather or news.

Example:

`<META HTTP-EQUIV="Refresh" CONTENT="30">`

Some Web servers can automatically refresh embedded files on a Web page, such as images and videos. This is useful for updating information such as a weather map or a traffic video. Contact your Web presence provider to determine if your Web server will allow you to automatically refresh embedded files.

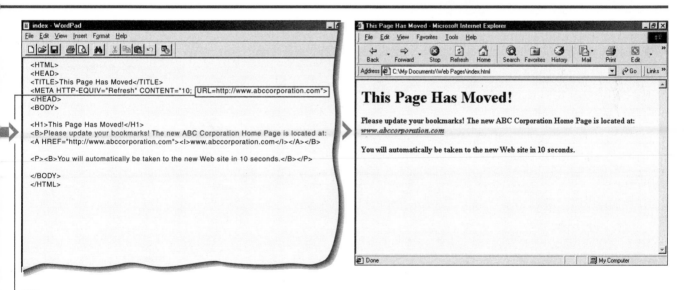

3 Type **URL=?">** replacing **?** with the location and name of the Web page you want to automatically appear.

Note: To specify the location and name of a Web page in your own Web site, see the top of page 75.

■ The Web browser displays the first Web page.

■ After the time period you specified, the other Web page will automatically appear.

ADD PAGE TRANSITIONS

Use the <META> tag to add page transitions to your Web pages. Page transitions are interesting visual effects that appear when a user displays or leaves your Web page. Page transitions are supported only by Internet Explorer.

To have a transition appear when a user displays your Web page, add a Page-Enter transition. To have a transition appear when a user leaves your Web page, add a Page-Exit transition.

There are many different page transitions you can use, such as Box In and Checkerboard Across. Each page transition is represented

by a number. For a list of the available page transitions, see the top of page 189.

When adding a page transition to your Web page, specify the amount of time you want the transition to last in seconds. Keep in mind that some users may become impatient with page transitions that last more than a few seconds.

Avoid overusing page transitions on your Web pages. Users may become annoyed with a Web site that displays page transitions for every Web page.

ADD A PAGE-ENTER TRANSITION

1 Between the <HEAD> and </HEAD> tags, type **<META HTTP-EQUIV= "Page-Enter" CONTENT= "RevealTrans(Duration=?,** replacing **?** with the number of seconds you want the transition to last.

2 Type **Transition=?)">** replacing **?** with the number for the transition you want to use.

Note: For a list of transitions, see the top of page 189.

■ When a user visits your Web page, the page will appear on the screen using the page transition you specified.

Extra Use one of the following numbers to specify the page transition you want to appear when a user enters or exits your Web page. Specifying transition number 23 will have a Web browser randomly select the transition that will appear.

TRANSITION NUMBER	TRANSITION	TRANSITION NUMBER	TRANSITION
0	Box In	12	Random Dissolve
1	Box Out	13	Split Vertical In
2	Circle In	14	Split Vertical Out
3	Circle Out	15	Split Horizontal In
4	Wipe Up	16	Split Horizontal Out
5	Wipe Down	17	Strips Left Down
6	Wipe Right	18	Strips Left Up
7	Wipe Left	19	Strips Right Down
8	Vertical Blinds	20	Strips Right Up
9	Horizontal Blinds	21	Random Bars Horizontal
10	Checkerboard Across	22	Random Bars Vertical
11	Checkerboard Down	23	Random Transition

ADD A PAGE-EXIT TRANSITION

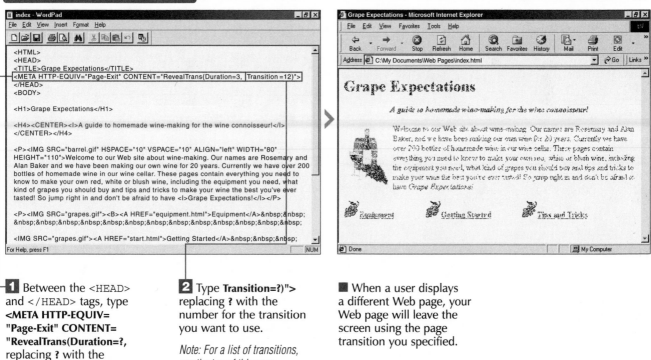

1 Between the `<HEAD>` and `</HEAD>` tags, type **<META HTTP-EQUIV= "Page-Exit" CONTENT= "RevealTrans(Duration=?,** replacing **?** with the number of seconds you want the transition to last.

2 Type **Transition=?)">** replacing **?** with the number for the transition you want to use.

Note: For a list of transitions, see the top of this page.

■ When a user displays a different Web page, your Web page will leave the screen using the page transition you specified.

ADD A JAVA APPLET

A Java applet is a program written using the Java programming language. Java applets are useful for adding animated and interactive information to your Web pages.

There are many places on the Internet that offer Java applets. For example, Java applets are available at the javaboutique.internet.com and www.javashareware.com Web sites. If you know the Java programming language, you can create your own Java applets. To learn more about Java, visit the java.sun.com Web site.

When adding a Java applet, use the CODE attribute to specify the location and name of the Java applet on your computer. Remember to include the

proper extension in the name. Most Java applets have the .class extension.

Use the WIDTH and HEIGHT attributes to specify the width and height of a Java applet in pixels. If you do not specify the correct dimensions, all or part of the applet may not appear on your Web page.

Some users may have older Web browsers that cannot run Java applets, while others may turn off Java applets in their Web browsers. To specify text that will appear for users with Web browsers that do not run Java applets, type the text between the <APPLET> and </APPLET> tags.

ADD A JAVA APPLET

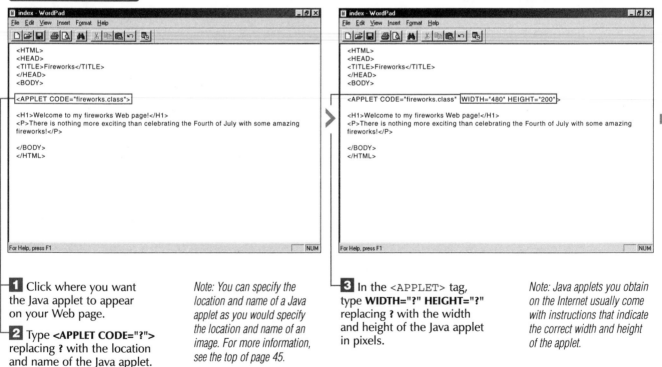

1 Click where you want the Java applet to appear on your Web page.

2 Type **<APPLET CODE="?">** replacing ? with the location and name of the Java applet.

Note: You can specify the location and name of a Java applet as you would specify the location and name of an image. For more information, see the top of page 45.

3 In the <APPLET> tag, type **WIDTH="?" HEIGHT="?"** replacing ? with the width and height of the Java applet in pixels.

Note: Java applets you obtain on the Internet usually come with instructions that indicate the correct width and height of the applet.

Extra

The HTML standard recommends that you use the <OBJECT> tag to add objects such as Java applets to your Web pages. Since Web browsers do not yet fully support the <OBJECT> tag, the <APPLET> tag is more commonly used.

In the <OBJECT> tag, type **CLASSID="java: ?"** replacing ? with the location and name of the Java applet on your computer. The text you type between the <OBJECT> and </OBJECT> tags will appear if a Web browser does not support the <OBJECT> tag.

Example:

```
<OBJECT CLASSID="java:applets/lightshow.class"
WIDTH="320" HEIGHT="240">Flashing
lights</OBJECT>
```

Some Java applets are part of a compressed file called a Java archive, or JAR file. To use a Java applet stored in a Java archive, use the CODE attribute to specify the name of the Java applet in the Java archive. Then use the ARCHIVE attribute to specify the location and name of the Java archive file on your computer.

Example:

```
<APPLET CODE="lightshow.class" WIDTH="320"
HEIGHT="240" ARCHIVE="applets/visualfx.jar">
</APPLET>
```

ActiveX is another programming technology that allows you to create applets. Applets created with ActiveX, called ActiveX controls, are commonly used to create drop-down menus and dialog boxes. Many Web browsers do not support ActiveX controls. To learn more about ActiveX, visit the vb-world.net/activex Web site.

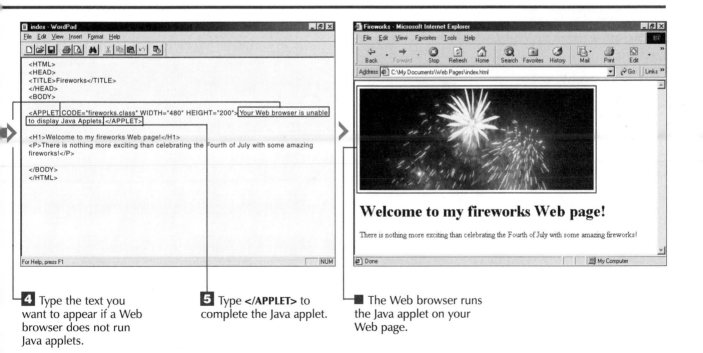

4 Type the text you want to appear if a Web browser does not run Java applets.

5 Type **</APPLET>** to complete the Java applet.

■ The Web browser runs the Java applet on your Web page.

CREATE AN IMAGE MAP

A n image map divides an image into different areas that each link to a different Web page. When a user clicks an area of the image, the linked Web page will appear.

The image you use for an image map should have several distinct areas that users can select. For this reason, photographs do not usually make good image maps.

Most image maps are client-side image maps. Client-side image maps are interpreted by a user's Web browser and are simpler to create than server-side image maps, which are interpreted by a CGI script. For more information on server-side image maps, see the top of page 195.

Before creating an image map, use an image editing program such as Jasc Paint Shop Pro or Adobe Photoshop to determine the coordinates of each image area you want the image map to contain.

To create an image map, add the image you want to use to your Web page and give the image map a name using the USEMAP attribute. Then use the <MAP> tag with the NAME attribute to begin defining the information for the image map. The information for an image map can appear anywhere on your Web page.

CREATE AN IMAGE MAP

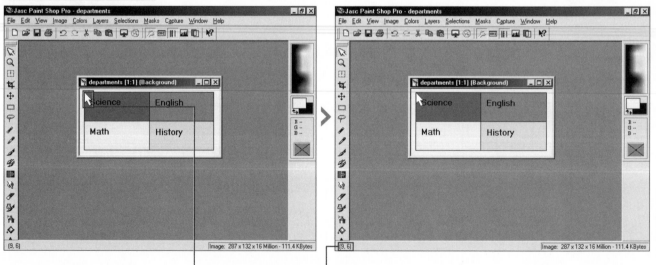

DETERMINE COORDINATES OF IMAGE AREAS

1 Start your image editing program. In this example, we started Paint Shop Pro.

2 Open the image you want to use as an image map.

3 Position the mouse over a point on the image for the coordinates you need.

Note: For information on the coordinates you need, see the top of page 193.

4 Write down the coordinates displayed in this area.

5 Repeat steps 3 and 4 until you have all the coordinates you need for the image area.

6 Repeat steps 3 to 5 until you have all the coordinates for each image area you want to create.

Extra

The coordinates you need for an image area depend on the shape of the image area.

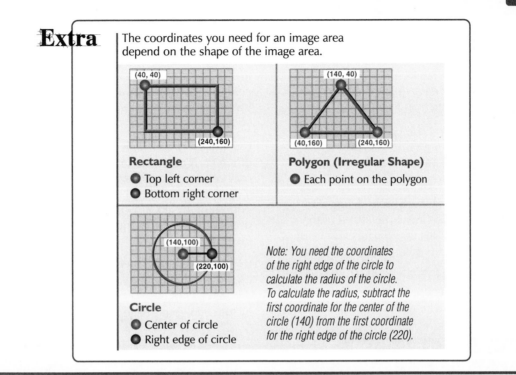

Rectangle
● Top left corner
● Bottom right corner

Polygon (Irregular Shape)
● Each point on the polygon

Circle
● Center of circle
● Right edge of circle

Note: You need the coordinates of the right edge of the circle to calculate the radius of the circle. To calculate the radius, subtract the first coordinate for the center of the circle (140) from the first coordinate for the right edge of the circle (220).

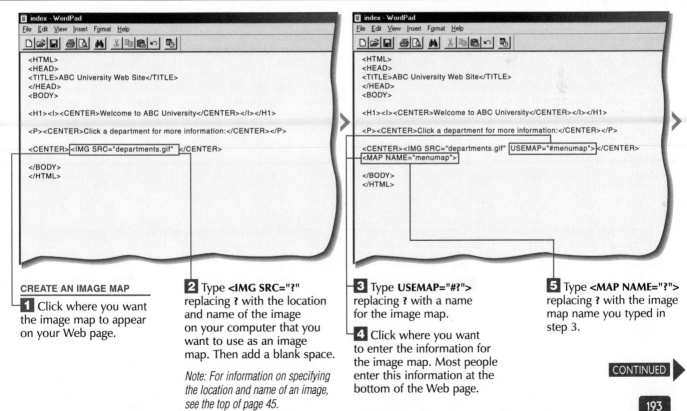

CREATE AN IMAGE MAP

1 Click where you want the image map to appear on your Web page.

2 Type **<IMG SRC="?"** replacing **?** with the location and name of the image on your computer that you want to use as an image map. Then add a blank space.

Note: For information on specifying the location and name of an image, see the top of page 45.

3 Type **USEMAP="#?">** replacing **?** with a name for the image map.

4 Click where you want to enter the information for the image map. Most people enter this information at the bottom of the Web page.

5 Type **<MAP NAME="?">** replacing **?** with the image map name you typed in step 3.

CONTINUED ▶

CREATE AN IMAGE MAP (CONTINUED)

Use the `<AREA>` tag to specify the information for each image area you want your image map to include.

The SHAPE attribute lets you specify the shape of an image area. Use the `rect` value for a rectangle, the `circle` value for a circle and the `poly` value for a polygon.

The COORDS attribute allows you to define the coordinates for an image area. The shape of the image area determines the coordinates you need to define.

If you accidentally enter coordinates that cause two image areas to overlap, most Web browsers will interpret the overlapping area as part of the first image area you defined. If you accidentally enter coordinates that are outside of the image, Web browsers will ignore these coordinates.

Use the HREF attribute to specify the address of the Web page you want to appear when users click an image area. This address, called a destination URL, will usually appear at the bottom of a Web browser window when a user positions the mouse pointer over the image area.

You should provide text links below your image map so users who do not see images will still be able to access the links you included in your image map.

CREATE AN IMAGE MAP (CONTINUED)

```
index - WordPad
File  Edit  View  Insert  Format  Help

<HTML>
<HEAD>
<TITLE>ABC University Web Site</TITLE>
</HEAD>
<BODY>

<H1><I><CENTER>Welcome to ABC University</CENTER></I></H1>

<P><CENTER>Click a department for more information:</CENTER></P>

<CENTER><IMG SRC="departments.gif" USEMAP="#menumap"></CENTER>
<MAP NAME="menumap">
<AREA SHAPE="rect"

</BODY>
</HTML>
```

```
index - WordPad
File  Edit  View  Insert  Format  Help

<HTML>
<HEAD>
<TITLE>ABC University Web Site</TITLE>
</HEAD>
<BODY>

<H1><I><CENTER>Welcome to ABC University</CENTER></I></H1>

<P><CENTER>Click a department for more information:</CENTER></P>

<CENTER><IMG SRC="departments.gif" USEMAP="#menumap"></CENTER>
<MAP NAME="menumap">
<AREA SHAPE="rect" COORDS="9,6,142,63"

</BODY>
</HTML>
```

6 Type **<AREA** to specify the information for one image area of the image map. Then add a blank space.

7 Type **SHAPE="?"** replacing **?** with the shape of the area (**rect** for rectangle, **circle** for circle or **poly** for an irregular shape). Then add a blank space.

8 For a rectangle, type **COORDS="a,b,c,d"** where **a,b** are the coordinates of the top left corner and **c,d** are the coordinates of the bottom right corner.

■ For a circle, type **COORDS="a,b,r"** where **a,b** are the coordinates for the center of the circle and **r** is the radius.

■ For a polygon, type **COORDS="a,b,c,d..."** where **a,b,c,d** and so on are the coordinates of each point on the polygon.

Extra

Image map editors are programs that can help you create image maps. These programs determine the necessary coordinates and define image areas for you. Mapedit is a popular image map editor that is available at the www.boutell.com/mapedit Web site.

Use the `ALT` attribute with each `<AREA>` tag to provide text labels for the image areas in your image map. When a user positions the mouse pointer over an image area, most Web browsers will display a box containing the text you provided. This can help users determine where clicking an image area will take them.

Example:

```
<AREA SHAPE="rect" COORDS="9,6,142,63"
HREF="abcscience.html" ALT="Visit the
Science Department!">
```

If your Web server has a CGI script that supports image maps, you can create a server-side image map. When a user clicks a server-side image map, the coordinates of the mouse pointer are sent to the Web server and are interpreted by a CGI script. The CGI script then instructs the Web browser to perform an action, such as displaying another Web page. When creating a server-side image map, you must specify the location of the CGI script on your Web server. Then use the `ISMAP` attribute with the `<IMG>` tag to create the image map.

Example:

```
<A HREF="cgi-bin/imap"><IMG SRC="sitemap.gif"
ISMAP></A>
```

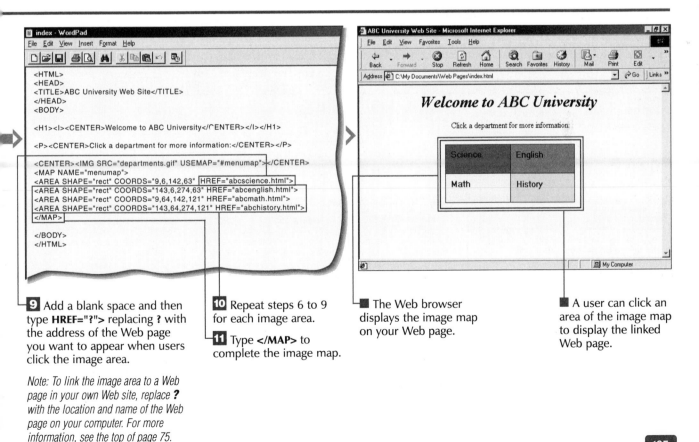

9 Add a blank space and then type **HREF="?">** replacing **?** with the address of the Web page you want to appear when users click the image area.

Note: To link the image area to a Web page in your own Web site, replace ? with the location and name of the Web page on your computer. For more information, see the top of page 75.

10 Repeat steps 6 to 9 for each image area.

11 Type **</MAP>** to complete the image map.

■ The Web browser displays the image map on your Web page.

■ A user can click an area of the image map to display the linked Web page.

CREATE AN INTERNAL STYLE SHEET

Using an internal style sheet allows you to define in one centralized location the formatting and layout for a Web page. This saves you from having to type information in each individual tag. Style sheets are also known as Cascading Style Sheets (CSS).

Use the <STYLE> tag to create an internal style sheet. When creating a style sheet, specify the name of the tag you want to define properties for, such as H1 or P, and then list the properties you want the tag to use. The properties you define for a tag will affect all the elements on your Web page that use the tag.

Style sheets allow you to format and lay out Web pages in ways you cannot accomplish with HTML tags alone. Style sheets are also easy to update and can help keep your Web page consistent, since you can change the appearance of all the elements that use a particular tag at once.

If a user displays your Web page in an older Web browser that cannot understand style sheets, the style sheet information may appear on your Web page. To prevent this information from appearing, you should hide your internal style sheet.

CREATE AN INTERNAL STYLE SHEET

```
index - WordPad
File  Edit  View  Insert  Format  Help

<HTML>
<HEAD>
<TITLE>Classical Music Composers</TITLE>
<STYLE>
H1
</HEAD>
<BODY>

<H1>Beethoven</H1>
<P>Ludwig van Beethoven was born in Bonn, Germany in 1770. He spe
Vienna, where he earned a living giving concerts, teaching piano and se
compositions.
<BR>One of the most fascinating aspects of Beethoven's life was his triu
which struck him during adulthood. In fact, he composed some of his mos
after losing his hearing.</P>

<H1>Bach</H1>
<P>Johann Sebastian Bach was born into a family of musicians in 168
```

```
index - WordPad
File  Edit  View  Insert  Format  Help

<HTML>
<HEAD>
<TITLE>Classical Music Composers</TITLE>
<STYLE>
H1 {text-align: center; font-style: italic}
</HEAD>
<BODY>

<H1>Beethoven</H1>
<P>Ludwig van Beethoven was born in Bonn, Germany in 1770. He spe
Vienna, where he earned a living giving concerts, teaching piano and se
compositions.
<BR>One of the most fascinating aspects of Beethoven's life was his triu
which struck him during adulthood. In fact, he composed some of his mos
after losing his hearing.</P>

<H1>Bach</H1>
<P>Johann Sebastian Bach was born into a family of musicians in 168
```

1 On the Web page you want to use a style sheet, type **<STYLE>** between the <HEAD> and </HEAD> tags.

2 Type a tag you want to define properties for.

3 Type { to begin the properties for the tag.

4 Enter properties for the tag. A semi-colon (;) must separate each property. To add properties, see pages 206 to 237.

5 Type } to end the properties for the tag.

Extra

Many HTML tags perform tasks that can also be performed with style sheets. These tags are called deprecated tags. The HTML standard recommends that you use style sheets instead of deprecated tags, though Web browsers still support these tags. When using style sheets, keep in mind that Web browsers do not currently support all the features of style sheets.

To define the properties for several tags at the same time, type each tag separated by a comma (,). Web browsers will apply the properties you define to each tag you specify.

Example:

```
H1, H2, H3 {font-family: "Arial"}
```

To define properties that will apply to elements that use more than one tag, type each tag separated by a space. For example, type **H1 CENTER** to define properties for elements that use both the <H1> and <CENTER> tags. Make sure you type the tags in the order they appear on your Web page. For example, type **H1 CENTER** rather than **CENTER H1**. If you type the tags in the incorrect order, Web browsers will not apply the properties.

Example:

```
H1 CENTER {color: red}
```

■ index - WordPad

File   Edit   View   Insert   Format   Help

```
<HTML>
<HEAD>
<TITLE>Classical Music Composers</TITLE>
<STYLE>
H1 {text-align: center; font-style: italic}
P {color: #FF0000}
</STYLE>
</HEAD>
<BODY>

<H1>Beethoven</H1>
<P>Ludwig van Beethoven was born in Bonn, Germany in 1770. He spen
Vienna, where he earned a living giving concerts, teaching piano and sel
compositions.
<BR>One of the most fascinating aspects of Beethoven's life was his triu
which struck him during adulthood. In fact, he composed some of his mo
after losing his hearing.</P>
```

6 Repeat steps 2 to 5 for each tag you want to define properties for.

7 Type **</STYLE>** to complete the style sheet.

■ index - WordPad

File   Edit   View   Insert   Format   Help

```
<HTML>
<HEAD>
<TITLE>Classical Music Composers</TITLE>
<STYLE>
<!--
H1 {text-align: center; font-style: italic}
P {color: #FF0000}
-->
</STYLE>
</HEAD>
<BODY>

<H1>Beethoven</H1>
<P>Ludwig van Beethoven was born in Bonn, Germany in 1770. He spen
Vienna, where he earned a living giving concerts, teaching piano and se
compositions.
<BR>One of the most fascinating aspects of Beethoven's life was his tri
which struck him during adulthood. In fact, he composed some of his
```

HIDE AN INTERNAL STYLE SHEET

1 Type **<!--** directly below the <STYLE> tag.

2 Type **-->** directly above the </STYLE> tag.

■ If a user displays your Web page in an older Web browser that cannot understand style sheets, the Web browser will ignore the style sheet information.

CREATE AN EXTERNAL STYLE SHEET

Using an external style sheet allows you to define in one centralized location the formatting and layout for multiple Web pages.

Unlike internal style sheets, which appear at the top of a Web page, external style sheets are stored in a separate file. This allows you to update the styles for multiple Web pages by changing information in a single file rather than on each Web page. For information on internal style sheets, see page 196.

When creating an external style sheet, specify the name of a tag you want to define properties

for, such as H1 or P, and then list the properties you want the tag to use. The properties you define for a tag will affect all the elements that use the tag on your Web pages.

After you create an external style sheet, link the style sheet to each Web page in your Web site that you want to use the properties you defined. If you want all the Web pages in your Web site to use the same styles, create a link on each Web page. This can help give your Web site a consistent appearance.

CREATE AN EXTERNAL STYLE SHEET

1 Create a new document in a word processor or text editor.

2 Type a tag you want to define properties for.

3 Type { to begin the properties for the tag.

4 Enter properties for the tag. A semi-colon (;) must separate each property. To add properties, see pages 206 to 237.

5 Type } to end the properties for the tag.

Extra

To use more than one external style sheet on the same Web page, import the style sheets using the `@import` command. Add the `<STYLE>` and `</STYLE>` tags to the HEAD section of the Web page you want to use the style sheets. For each style sheet you want to import, type **@import url ("?");** between the `<STYLE>` and `</STYLE>` tags replacing **?** with the location and name of the style sheet. Some Web browsers, such as Netscape Navigator, do not currently support the `@import` command.

Example:

```
<STYLE>
@import url("styles/newssheet.css");
@import url("styles/mystyles.css");
</STYLE>
```

Use the /* and */ delimiters to add a comment to a style sheet. Comments are useful for adding reminders to your style sheets. The comments you add will not appear when users view your Web page. Since Web browsers will ignore the information between the /* and */ delimiters, you can use the delimiters to temporarily hide style sheet information you are revising. The hidden style sheet information will not be applied until you remove the delimiters.

Example:

```
P {color: black} /*Might look better blue*/
```

---

mystyles - WordPad

File Edit View Insert Format Help

```
H1 {text-align: center; font-style: italic}
P {color: #FF0000}
```

index - WordPad

File Edit View Insert Format Help

```
<HTML>
<HEAD>
<TITLE>Classical Music Composers</TITLE>
<LINK REL="stylesheet" TYPE="text/css"  HREF="styles/mystyles.css">
</HEAD>
<BODY>

<H1>Beethoven</H1>
<P>Ludwig van Beethoven was born in Bonn, Germany in 1770. He spen
Vienna, where he earned a living giving concerts, teaching piano and sel
<BR>One of the most fascinating aspects of Beethoven's life was his triun
which struck him during adulthood. In fact, he composed some of his most
losing his hearing.</P>

<H1>Bach</H1>
<P>Johann Sebastian Bach was born into a family of musicians in 1685 in
Bach's works include church organ and choral music, music for chamber
200 cantatas. Although he was more respected as an organist during his
compositions influenced many later com         including Beethoven a
```

6 Repeat steps 2 to 5 for each tag you want to define properties for.

7 Save the document in the text-only format. Use the .css extension to name the document (example: mystyles.css).

Perform the following steps on each Web page you want to link the style sheet to.

8 Type **<LINK REL="stylesheet" TYPE="text/css"** between the `<HEAD>` and `</HEAD>` tags. Then add a blank space.

9 Type **HREF="?">** replacing **?** with the location and name of the style sheet on your computer.

APPLY STYLES LOCALLY

Use the STYLE attribute when you want to apply a style to a single instance of a tag without changing the appearance of other elements that use the tag. For example, use the STYLE attribute in the <P> tag to change the appearance of a single paragraph.

Applying a style locally allows you to take advantage of the formatting and layout features offered by styles without having to create a style sheet. This is useful when you want to perform a task that cannot be accomplished with HTML tags alone, such as changing the margins for your Web page.

Applying a style locally is useful even if your Web page already contains an internal or external style sheet. The local style you use will override any styles defined for the same tag in the internal or external style sheet. For information on internal and external style sheets, see pages 196 to 199.

When you apply styles locally, your Web pages will be more difficult to update since the styles are not located in one centralized location. You should use internal or external style sheets if you plan to update the style of your Web pages regularly.

APPLY STYLES LOCALLY

index - WordPad

File Edit View Insert Format Help

```
<HTML>
<HEAD>
<TITLE>Grape Expectations</TITLE>
</HEAD>
<BODY>

<H1 STYLE="font-style: italic; color: #9900CC">Grape Expectations</

<H4><CENTER><I>A guide to homemade wine-making for the wine co
</I></CENTER></H4>

<P><IMG SRC="barrel.gif" HSPACE="10" VSPACE="10" ALIGN="left" WI
HEIGHT="110">Welcome to our Web site about wine-making. Our names
Alan Baker, and we have been making our own wine for 20 years. Curren
200 bottles of homemade wine in our wine cellar. These pages contain e
to know to make your own red, white or blush wine, including the equipm
kind of grapes you should buy and tips and tricks to make your wine the
tasted! So jump right in and don't be afraid to have <I>Grape Expecta
```

Grape Expectations - Microsoft Internet Explorer

File Edit View Favorites Tools Help

Back Forward Stop Refresh Home Search Favorites History Mail Print Edit

Address C:\My Documents\Web Pages\index.html

Grape Expectations

A guide to homemade wine-making for the wine connoisseur!

Welcome to our Web site about wine-making. Our names are Rosemary and Alan Baker, and we have been making our own wine for 20 years. Currently we have over 200 bottles of homemade wine in our wine cellar. These pages contain everything you need to know to make your own red, white or blush wine, including the equipment you need, what kind of grapes you should buy and tips and tricks to make your wine the best you've ever tasted! So jump right in and don't be afraid to have *Grape Expectations!*

Equipment   Getting Started   Tips and Tricks

Done   My Computer

1 In the tag for the element you want to change, type **STYLE=""**.

2 Enter properties for the element between the quotation marks. A semi-colon (;) must separate each property. To add properties, see pages 206 to 237.

■ The Web browser displays the element with the properties you specified.

APPLY STYLES USING ID

The ID attribute allows you to apply a style to an individual element on your Web page using a style sheet.

To apply a style using the ID attribute, you must assign a unique name, or identifier, to the tag for the element you want to apply the style to. According to the HTML standard, you must not use the same identifier with more than one tag on your Web page.

Once you have identified the tag you want to apply a style to, you can set up a style for the tag in your internal or external style sheet. The

properties you use to define the formatting for the style will only apply to the element you identified using the ID attribute.

Applying styles using the ID attribute rather than applying styles locally makes your Web pages easy to update since the styles are located in one centralized location. For information on applying styles locally, see page 200.

If you want to apply styles to more than one element that uses a specific tag, you should create a *class* for the tag rather than using the ID attribute. To create a class, see page 202.

APPLY STYLES USING ID

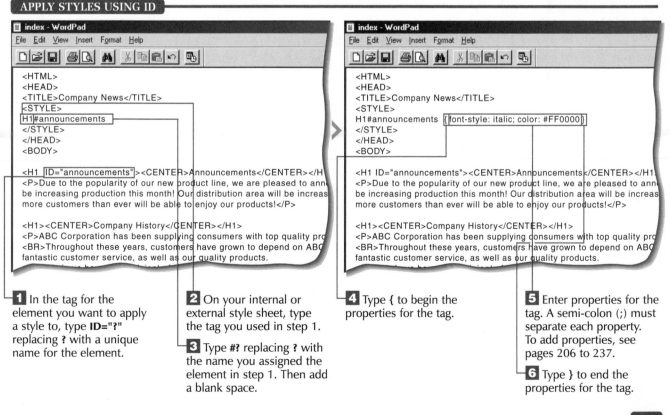

1 In the tag for the element you want to apply a style to, type **ID="?"** replacing ? with a unique name for the element.

2 On your internal or external style sheet, type the tag you used in step 1.

3 Type **#?** replacing ? with the name you assigned the element in step 1. Then add a blank space.

4 Type { to begin the properties for the tag.

5 Enter properties for the tag. A semi-colon (;) must separate each property. To add properties, see pages 206 to 237.

6 Type } to end the properties for the tag.

CREATE A CLASS

If you want to apply a style to only some of the elements on your Web page that use a specific tag, create a class for the tag. For example, create a class of introductory paragraphs (P.intro) that you want to format differently than regular paragraphs (P).

To create a class for a tag, you must first set up the class in your internal or external style sheet. When setting up a class, specify the tag you want to create the class for and provide a name for the class. Then add properties to define the formatting you want the class to use.

Once you have set up a class, use the CLASS attribute to specify the elements on your Web page you want to include in the class. The elements you include must use the tag you created the class for.

The elements that you include in a class will display the properties you define for the class as well as any properties you have defined for the original tag in your style sheet. For example, if you have formatted a class of introductory paragraphs (P.intro) in red and regular paragraphs (P) with italics, the introductory paragraphs will display both the red and italic formatting.

CREATE A CLASS

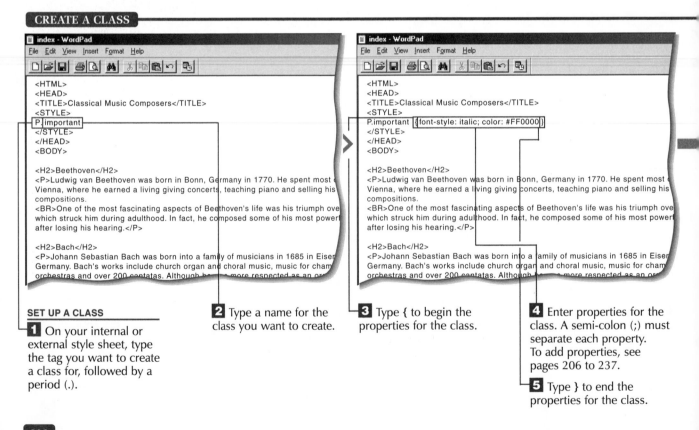

SET UP A CLASS

1 On your internal or external style sheet, type the tag you want to create a class for, followed by a period (.).

2 Type a name for the class you want to create.

3 Type { to begin the properties for the class.

4 Enter properties for the class. A semi-colon (;) must separate each property. To add properties, see pages 206 to 237.

5 Type } to end the properties for the class.

Apply It

A generic class is a class that you can use with different tags. For example, a generic class can format both elements that use the `<H2>` tag and elements that use the `<P>` tag. When setting up a generic class in your style sheet, type a period (.) followed by a name for the class.

TYPE THIS:

```
<HTML>
<HEAD>
<TITLE>Create a Generic Class</TITLE>
<STYLE>
.definition {font-style: italic; text-align: center}
</STYLE>
</HEAD>
<BODY>
<H2 CLASS="definition">Generic Classes</H2>
<P CLASS="definition">A generic class allows you to
apply the style you define for the class to elements
that use different tags. For example, you can format
both a heading and a paragraph using the same class.</P>
</BODY>
</HTML>
```

RESULT:

Generic Classes

A generic class allows you to apply the style you define for the class to elements that use different tags. For example, you can format both a heading and a paragraph using the same class.

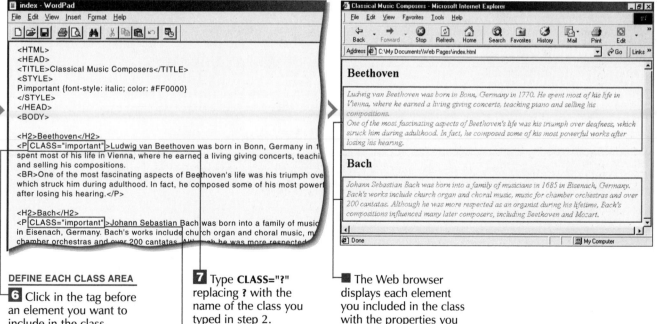

DEFINE EACH CLASS AREA

6 Click in the tag before an element you want to include in the class.

Note: The element must use the tag you typed in step 1.

7 Type **CLASS="?"** replacing **?** with the name of the class you typed in step 2.

8 Repeat steps 6 and 7 for each element you want to include in the class.

■ The Web browser displays each element you included in the class with the properties you specified.

APPLY STYLES USING DIV

The `<DIV>` tag allows you to apply a style to an area of your Web page. All the elements in the area will display the formatting for the style, regardless of the tags they use. This lets you quickly format an area without having to define styles for each tag individually.

To apply styles using the `<DIV>` tag, you must first set up a DIV style in your internal or external style sheet. To set up a DIV style, provide a name for the style and then add properties to define the formatting you want the style to use.

Once you have set up a DIV style, use the `<DIV>` tag to indicate each Web page area you want to use the style. The `<DIV>` tag is a block-level tag, which means that a blank line will appear before and after elements that use the tag on your Web page. For this reason, the `<DIV>` tag should surround other block-level tags such as `<P>` or `<H1>` rather than interrupting them. For example, interrupting a paragraph with the `<DIV>` tag will make the paragraph appear as two paragraphs.

APPLY STYLES USING DIV

```
<HTML>
<HEAD>
<TITLE>Classical Music Composers</TITLE>
<STYLE>
DIV.beethoven
</STYLE>
</HEAD>
<BODY>

<H2>Beethoven</H2>
<P>Ludwig van Beethoven was born in Bonn, Germany in 1770. He spent most
Vienna, where he earned a living giving concerts, teaching piano and selling his
compositions.
<BR>One of the most fascinating aspects of Beethoven's life was his triumph ove
which struck him during adulthood. In fact, he composed some of his most power
after losing his hearing.</P>

<H2>Bach</H2>
<P>Johann Sebastian Bach was born into a family of musicians in 1685 in Eiser
Germany. Bach's works include church organ and choral music, music for cham
orchestras and over 200 cantatas. Although be more respected as an or
```

SET UP A DIV STYLE

1 On your internal or external style sheet, type **DIV.?** replacing ? with a name for the DIV style you want to create.

```
<HTML>
<HEAD>
<TITLE>Classical Music Composers</TITLE>
<STYLE>
DIV.beethoven  {background: #FFFF10; font-style: italic}
</STYLE>
</HEAD>
<BODY>

<H2>Beethoven</H2>
<P>Ludwig van Beethoven was born in Bonn, Germany in 1770. He spent most
Vienna, where he earned a living giving concerts, teaching piano and selling his
compositions.
<BR>One of the most fascinating aspects of Beethoven's life was his triumph ove
which struck him during adulthood. In fact, he composed some of his most power
after losing his hearing.</P>

<H2>Bach</H2>
<P>Johann Sebastian Bach was born into a family of musicians in 1685 in Eiser
Germany. Bach's works include church organ and choral music, music for cham
orchestras and over 200 cantatas. Although be more respected as an or
```

2 Type { to begin the properties for the DIV style.

3 Enter properties for the DIV style. A semi-colon (;) must separate each property. To add properties, see pages 206 to 237.

4 Type } to end the properties for the DIV style.

Apply It

The <SPAN> tag allows you to apply a style to a section of text on your Web page. For example, use the <SPAN> tag to format only part of a paragraph or heading on your Web page. The <SPAN> tag is an inline tag, which means that it will not add blank lines to your Web page like the <DIV> tag.

TYPE THIS:

```
<HTML>
<HEAD>
<TITLE>Learn HTML</TITLE>
<STYLE>
SPAN.newterm {font-weight: bold; font-style: italic}
</STYLE>
</HEAD>
<BODY>

<H4>Style Sheets</H4>
<P><SPAN CLASS="newterm">Internal style
sheets</SPAN> are part of a Web page and affect
only the information on that Web page.
<SPAN CLASS="newterm">External style sheets</SPAN>
are stored in a separate file and can be applied
to multiple Web pages.</P>

</BODY>
</HTML>
```

RESULT:

Style Sheets

Internal style sheets are part of a Web page and affect only the information on that Web page. ***External style sheets*** are stored in a separate file and can be applied to multiple Web pages.

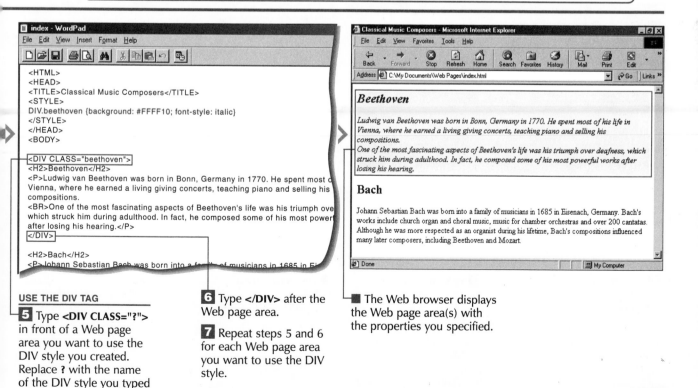

USE THE DIV TAG

5 Type **<DIV CLASS="?">** in front of a Web page area you want to use the DIV style you created. Replace **?** with the name of the DIV style you typed in step 1.

6 Type **</DIV>** after the Web page area.

7 Repeat steps 5 and 6 for each Web page area you want to use the DIV style.

■ The Web browser displays the Web page area(s) with the properties you specified.

BOLD TEXT

U sing the `font-weight` property with the `bold` value lets you bold all of the text on your Web page that uses a specific tag. Bolding text is useful for emphasizing information on your Web page.

The `bolder` and `lighter` values also allow you to change the boldness of text. The `bolder` value increases the boldness of text relative to the surrounding text, while the `lighter` value decreases the boldness of text relative to the surrounding text.

The boldness of text can also be specified as a multiple of 100, with `100` the lightest and

900 the boldest. A value of `400` is equivalent to the normal font weight, while `700` is the font weight that appears when you use the `bold` value. Web browsers may display some values with the same boldness, since most fonts do not have nine font weights available. For example, a Web browser may display a value of `200` with the same boldness as `300`.

The `normal` value removes bold formatting from text. This is useful for tags that automatically bold text, such as heading tags (`H1` to `H6`) or the tag for a header cell in a table (`TH`).

BOLD TEXT

```
<HTML>
<HEAD>
<TITLE>Classical Music Composers</TITLE>
<STYLE>
P {font-weight: bold}
</STYLE>
</HEAD>
<BODY>

<H2>Beethoven</H2>
<P>Ludwig van Beethoven was born in Bonn, Germany in 1770. He spen
Vienna, where he earned a living giving concerts, teaching piano and sel
compositions.
<BR>One of the most fascinating aspects of Beethoven's life was his triu
which struck him during adulthood. In fact, he composed some of his mo
after losing his hearing.</P>

<H2>Bach</H2>
```

Beethoven

Ludwig van Beethoven was born in Bonn, Germany in 1770. He spent most of his life in Vienna, where he earned a living giving concerts, teaching piano and selling his compositions.
One of the most fascinating aspects of Beethoven's life was his triumph over deafness, which struck him during adulthood. In fact, he composed some of his most powerful works after losing his hearing.

Bach

Johann Sebastian Bach was born into a family of musicians in 1685 in Eisenach, Germany. Bach's works include church organ and choral music, music for chamber orchestras and over 200 cantatas. Although he was more respected as an organist during his lifetime, Bach's compositions influenced many later composers, including Beethoven and Mozart.

1 To bold all the text that uses a specific tag, click between the brackets { } for the tag.

2 Type **font-weight:** and then add a blank space.

3 Type **bold** to bold the text.

■ You can also specify a boldness for the text relative to the surrounding text (**bolder** or **lighter**) or by using a multiple of 100, with 100 the lightest and 900 the boldest.

■ The Web browser bolds all the text that uses the tag.

*Note: To remove the bolding from text, type **normal** in step 3.*

ITALICIZE TEXT

The `font-style` property allows you to italicize all the text on your Web page that uses a specific tag.

Fonts usually offer italic versions and may also have oblique versions. The italic and oblique versions of a font are often similar, though they may display a different slant. Use the `italic` value to display text using an italic version of the current font and the `oblique` value to display text using an oblique version of the font. Some Web browsers do not yet support the `oblique` value.

If you specify the `italic` value and no italic version of the font is available on a user's

computer, a Web browser may display the font using an oblique version. When you specify the `oblique` value, a user's computer may be able to display the text as oblique even if an oblique version is not available.

Using the `normal` value allows you to remove italic formatting from all the text on your Web page that uses a specific tag. This is useful when text has inherited italic formatting from a parent element. For example, use the `normal` value to remove italic formatting from bold text (B) that has inherited italic formatting from a parent paragraph element (P).

ITALICIZE TEXT

```
<HTML>
<HEAD>
<TITLE>Classical Music Composers</TITLE>
<STYLE>
H2 {font-style: italic}
</STYLE>
</HEAD>
<BODY>

<H2>Beethoven</H2>
<P>Ludwig van Beethoven was born in Bonn, Germany in 1770. He spen
Vienna, where he earned a living giving concerts, teaching piano and sel
compositions.
<BR>One of the most fascinating aspects of Beethoven's life was his triu
which struck him during adulthood. In fact, he composed some of his mo
after losing his hearing.</P>

<H2>Bach</H2>
```

Beethoven

Ludwig van Beethoven was born in Bonn, Germany in 1770. He spent most of his life in Vienna, where he earned a living giving concerts, teaching piano and selling his compositions.
One of the most fascinating aspects of Beethoven's life was his triumph over deafness, which struck him during adulthood. In fact, he composed some of his most powerful works after losing his hearing.

Bach

Johann Sebastian Bach was born into a family of musicians in 1685 in Eisenach, Germany. Bach's works include church organ and choral music, music for chamber orchestras and over 200 cantatas. Although he was more respected as an organist during his lifetime, Bach's compositions influenced many later composers, including Beethoven and Mozart.

1 To italicize all the text that uses a specific tag, click between the brackets { } for the tag.

2 Type **font-style:** and then add a blank space.

3 Type the way you want to italicize the text (**italic**, **oblique** or **normal**).

■ The Web browser italicizes all the text that uses the tag.

ADD A LINE TO TEXT

U se the text-decoration property to add a line to all the text on your Web page that uses a specific tag. There are three different types of lines you can add to text.

The underline value lets you place a line below text. Be careful when underlining text, since users may mistake the text for a *link*. For information on links, see page 74.

Use the line-through value to place a line through text. People often use this value to strike out information they are revising.

The overline value allows you to place a line above text. The overline value is not yet supported by some Web browsers.

Using the none value removes line formatting from text. This is useful for removing the underlines that automatically appear for text links. When removing underlines from text links, keep in mind that many users expect links to be underlined. You may want to add formatting, such as a background color, to emphasize the links.

ADD A LINE TO TEXT

index - WordPad

File Edit View Insert Format Help

```
<HTML>
<HEAD>
<TITLE>Classical Music Composers</TITLE>
<STYLE>
H2 {text-decoration: underline}
</STYLE>
</HEAD>
<BODY>

<H2>Beethoven</H2>
<P>Ludwig van Beethoven was born in Bonn, Germany in 1770. He spen
Vienna, where he earned a living giving concerts, teaching piano and se
compositions.
<BR>One of the most fascinating aspects of Beethoven's life was his triu
which struck him during adulthood. In fact, he composed some of his mo
after losing his hearing.</P>

<H2>Bach</H2>
```

Classical Music Composers - Microsoft Internet Explorer

File Edit View Favorites Tools Help

Back Forward Stop Refresh Home Search Favorites History Mail Print Edit

Address C:\My Documents\Web Pages\index.html

Beethoven

Ludwig van Beethoven was born in Bonn, Germany in 1770. He spent most of his life in Vienna, where he earned a living giving concerts, teaching piano and selling his compositions.
One of the most fascinating aspects of Beethoven's life was his triumph over deafness, which struck him during adulthood. In fact, he composed some of his most powerful works after losing his hearing.

Bach

Johann Sebastian Bach was born into a family of musicians in 1685 in Eisenach, Germany. Bach's works include church organ and choral music, music for chamber orchestras and over 200 cantatas. Although he was more respected as an organist during his lifetime, Bach's compositions influenced many later composers, including Beethoven and Mozart.

Done My Computer

1 To add a line to all the text that uses a specific tag, click between the brackets { } for the tag.

2 Type **text-decoration:** and then add a blank space.

3 Type the kind of line you want to add (**underline**, **line-through**, **overline** or **none**).

■ The Web browser displays all the text that uses the tag with the kind of line you specified.

INDENT TEXT

U se the `text-indent` property to indent the first line of all the text on your Web page that uses a specific tag.

When indenting text, specify a size for the indent in pixels, millimeters, centimeters, inches, points, picas, x-height, em or as a percentage of the text block width. Using x-height specifies an indent size based on the height of the lowercase letter "x" for the current font (example: 5ex), while using em changes the indent size based on the height of the current font (example: 5em).

Specifying a negative indent size lets you create a hanging indent. For example, specify

a size of -40px to shift the first line of text 40 pixels to the left, making the rest of the text appear indented. Hanging indents are commonly used for creating a bibliography or glossary.

Before creating a hanging indent, use the `margin-left` property to increase the size of the left margin. This will help ensure that when the first line of text shifts to the left it will not extend past the left edge of a Web browser window. Specify a left margin size that is equal to or greater than the indent size you want to use. To use the `margin-left` property, see page 225.

INDENT TEXT

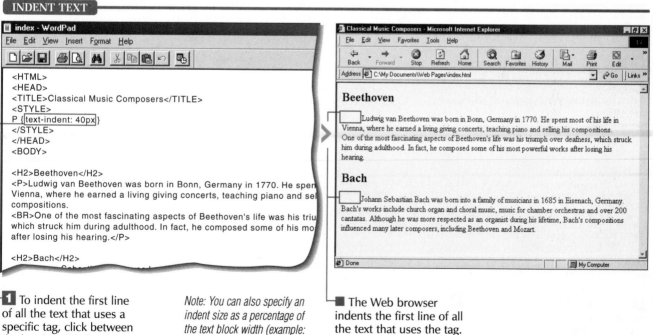

1 To indent the first line of all the text that uses a specific tag, click between the brackets { } for the tag.

2 Type **text-indent: ?** replacing **?** with the amount of space you want to use in pixels (example: 40px).

Note: You can also specify an indent size as a percentage of the text block width (example: 10%) or in millimeters (mm), centimeters (cm), inches (in), points (pt), picas (pc), x-height (ex) or em.

■ The Web browser indents the first line of all the text that uses the tag.

CHANGE THE FONT

Use the `font-family` property to change the font of all of the text on your Web page that uses a specific tag. You can specify a new font by name, such as Courier, or by type, such as monospace.

If you specify a font by name, you should specify more than one font in case your first choice is not available on a user's computer. One of the fonts you specify should be a common font, such as Arial, to increase the probability that a computer will display one of your font choices. Web browsers will use the first font that matches a font installed on a user's computer.

The available font types include serif, sans-serif, cursive, fantasy and monospace. Netscape Navigator does not currently support the fantasy or cursive types.

When you specify a font by type, a user's Web browser will look for a font installed on the user's computer that matches the requested type. Many people include a font type after a list of font names to ensure that they will have control over the font a Web browser displays if the fonts they specified by name are not available.

CHANGE THE FONT

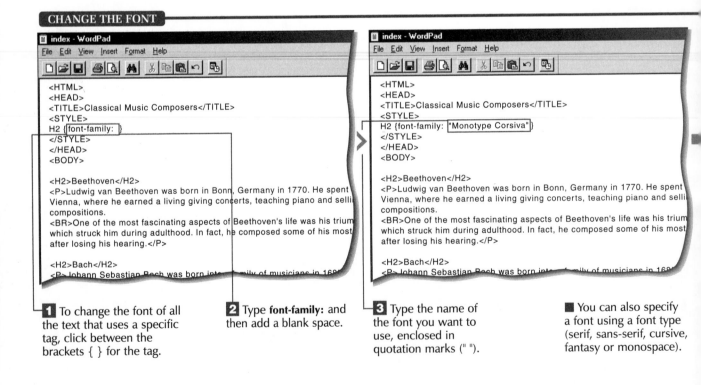

1 To change the font of all the text that uses a specific tag, click between the brackets { } for the tag.

2 Type **font-family:** and then add a blank space.

3 Type the name of the font you want to use, enclosed in quotation marks (" ").

■ You can also specify a font using a font type (serif, sans-serif, cursive, fantasy or monospace).

Extra

Use the `font` property to change multiple font settings at the same time, such as the style, size and font of text. Some Web browsers require you to enter the font settings in a particular order. For example, you may need to enter a font style before a font size.

Example:

`P {font: italic 14pt "Arial", "Verdana"}`

The `@font-face` command embeds a font in your Web page so that Web browsers will display the font even if a user does not have the font installed on their computer. Embedded fonts must currently be in the Embedded OpenType (EOT) format, though other formats may be supported in the future. The `@font-face` command is currently only supported by Internet Explorer.

Example:

```
@font-face {font-family: "Chess Utrecht"; src:
url("fonts/chessut.eot")}
P {font-family: "Chess Utrecht"}
```

When applying styles locally, enclose font names in single quotation marks (' ') rather than double quotation marks (" "). For information on applying styles locally, see page 200.

Example:

`<P STYLE="font-family: 'Arial'">`

To make all the text on your Web page that uses a specific tag blink, use the `text-decoration` property with the `blink` value. Blinking text is useful for drawing attention to information on your Web page. The `blink` value is currently only supported by Netscape Navigator.

Example:

`H1 {text-decoration: blink}`

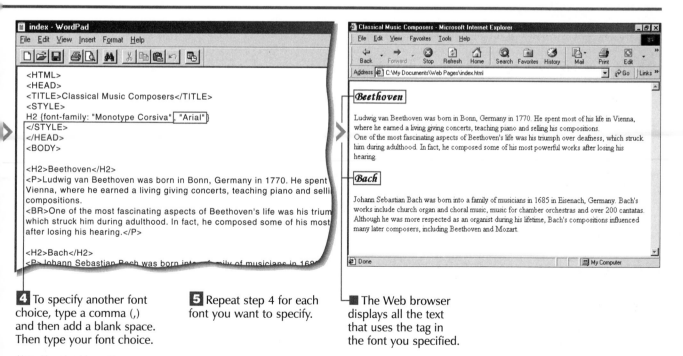

4 To specify another font choice, type a comma (,) and then add a blank space. Then type your font choice.

Note: You should specify more than one font in case your first font choice is not available on a user's computer.

5 Repeat step 4 for each font you want to specify.

■ The Web browser displays all the text that uses the tag in the font you specified.

CHANGE THE FONT SIZE

se the `font-size` property to change the size of all the text on your Web page that uses a specific tag. Increasing the size of text can make the text easier to read, while decreasing the size of text allows you to fit more information on a screen.

There are many ways to specify a new size for text. For example, specify a size in points, pixels, millimeters, centimeters, inches, picas, x-height or em. Use x-height to specify a font size based on the height of the lowercase letter "x" for the current font (example: 2ex). Use em to change the font size based on the height of the current font (example: 2em).

You can also specify a font size as a descriptive or relative size. Specify a descriptive font size using a value such as `small`, `medium` or `large`. Specify a relative font size using a value such as `larger` or `smaller` or by using a percentage (example: 150%). When you specify a relative font size for text, the size of the text will depend on the size of the surrounding text.

Keep in mind that the font size you use may not appear the way you expect on some computers, since some users can set their Web browsers to display the font size they prefer.

CHANGE THE FONT SIZE

```
<HTML>
<HEAD>
<TITLE>Classical Music Composers</TITLE>
<STYLE>
P {font-size: 14pt}
</STYLE>
</HEAD>
<BODY>

<H2>Beethoven</H2>
<P>Ludwig van Beethoven was born in Bonn, Germany in 1770. He spent most of
Vienna, where he earned a living giving concerts, teaching piano and selling his
compositions.
<BR>One of the most fascinating aspects of Beethoven's life was his triumph over
which struck him during adulthood. In fact, he composed some of his most powerfu
after losing his hearing.</P>

<H2>Bach</H2>
<P>Johann Sebastian Bach was born into a family of musicians in 1685 in Eisen
Germany. Bach's works include church organ and choral music, music for cham
```

Beethoven

Ludwig van Beethoven was born in Bonn, Germany in 1770. He spent most of his life in Vienna, where he earned a living giving concerts, teaching piano and selling his compositions.
One of the most fascinating aspects of Beethoven's life was his triumph over deafness, which struck him during adulthood. In fact, he composed some of his most powerful works after losing his hearing.

Bach

Johann Sebastian Bach was born into a family of musicians in 1685 in Eisenach, Germany. Bach's works include church organ and choral music, music for chamber orchestras and over 200 cantatas. Although he was more respected as an organist during his lifetime, Bach's compositions influenced many later composers, including Beethoven and Mozart.

■1 To change the font size of all the text that uses a specific tag, click between the brackets { } for the tag.

■2 Type **font-size:** and then add a blank space.

■3 Type a font size in points (pt), pixels (px), millimeters (mm), centimeters (cm), inches (in), picas (pc), x-height (ex) or em.

■ You can also type a descriptive font size (**xx-small**, **x-small**, **small**, **medium**, **large**, **x-large** or **xx-large**).

■ The Web browser displays all the text that uses the tag in the font size you specified.

*Note: You can also specify a font size relative to the font size of the surrounding text (**smaller** or **larger**) or as a percentage of the font size of the surrounding text (example: 150%).*

CHANGE THE CASE OF TEXT

U se the `text-transform` property to change the case of all the text on your Web page that uses a specific tag.

The `capitalize` value allows you to change the first letter of each word to an uppercase letter. This is useful for formatting all the titles and headings on your Web page at once.

The `uppercase` value lets you change all the letters in each word to uppercase letters, while the `lowercase` value lets you change all the letters to lowercase letters.

Using the `none` value allows you to remove case formatting from all the text on your Web page that uses a specific tag. This is useful when text has

inherited case formatting from a parent element. For example, use the `none` value to remove lowercase formatting from bold text (`B`) that has inherited the formatting from a parent paragraph element (`P`).

 Extra

Use the `font-variant` property with the `small-caps` value to display all the text on your Web page that uses a specific tag in small caps. This changes lowercase letters to small uppercase letters. The `font-variant` property is not yet supported by most Web browsers.

Example:

`H1 {font-variant: small-caps}`

CHANGE THE CASE OF TEXT

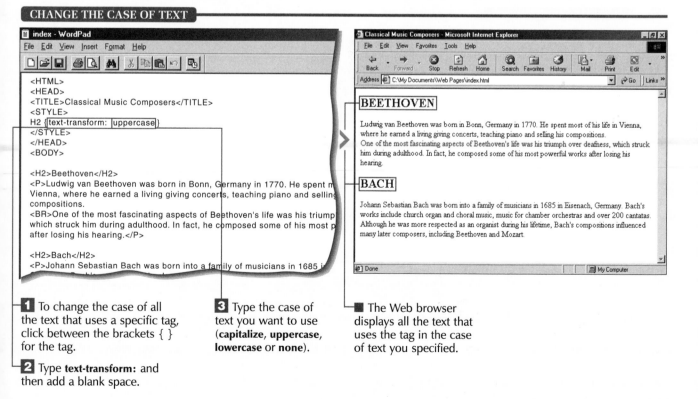

1 To change the case of all the text that uses a specific tag, click between the brackets { } for the tag.

2 Type **text-transform:** and then add a blank space.

3 Type the case of text you want to use (**capitalize**, **uppercase**, **lowercase** or **none**).

■ The Web browser displays all the text that uses the tag in the case of text you specified.

CHANGE ALIGNMENT OF TEXT

By default, most Web browsers left align text. Use the `text-align` property to change the alignment of all the text on your Web page that uses a specific tag. This is useful for emphasizing text on your Web page.

The text you align with the `text-align` property must use a block-level tag. A block-level tag, such as `<P>` or `<TABLE>`, displays a blank line before and after elements that use the tag.

The `text-align` property supports the `left`, `center`, `right` and `justify` values. The `justify` value aligns text with both the left

and right margins by adding space between the words in each line of text. This may negatively affect the word spacing of the text.

When you use the `text-align` property for a table, Web browsers will align the text in the table and will not change the alignment of the table on your Web page. Some Web browsers, such as Netscape Navigator, do not support using the `text-align` property to change the alignment of text in a table.

CHANGE ALIGNMENT OF TEXT

index - WordPad

File Edit View Insert Format Help

```
<HTML>
<HEAD>
<TITLE>Classical Music Composers</TITLE>
<STYLE>
H2 {text-align: center}
</STYLE>
</HEAD>
<BODY>

<H2>Beethoven</H2>
<P>Ludwig van Beethoven was born in Bonn, Germany in 1770. He spent
Vienna, where he earned a living giving concerts, teaching piano and selli
compositions.
<BR>One of the most fascinating aspects of Beethoven's life was his trium
which struck him during adulthood. In fact, he composed some of his mos
after losing his hearing.</P>

<H2>Bach</H2>
```

Classical Music Composers - Microsoft Internet Explorer

File Edit View Favorites Tools Help

Back Forward Stop Refresh Home Search Favorites History Mail Print Edit

Address C:\My Documents\Web Pages\index.html

Beethoven

Ludwig van Beethoven was born in Bonn, Germany in 1770. He spent most of his life in Vienna, where he earned a living giving concerts, teaching piano and selling his compositions.
One of the most fascinating aspects of Beethoven's life was his triumph over deafness, which struck him during adulthood. In fact, he composed some of his most powerful works after losing his hearing.

Bach

Johann Sebastian Bach was born into a family of musicians in 1685 in Eisenach, Germany. Bach's works include church organ and choral music, music for chamber orchestras and over 200 cantatas. Although he was more respected as an organist during his lifetime, Bach's compositions influenced many later composers, including Beethoven and Mozart.

Done My Computer

1 To change the alignment of all the text that uses a specific tag, click between the brackets { } for the tag.

2 Type **text-align:** and then add a blank space.

3 Type the way you want to align the text (**left**, **center**, **right** or **justify**).

■ The Web browser displays all the text that uses the tag with the alignment you specified.

CHANGE THE TEXT COLOR

U se the `color` property to change the color of all of the text on your Web page that uses a specific tag.

When changing the color of text, specify the name or hexadecimal value for the color you want to use. A hexadecimal value is a code that tells Web browsers which color to display. The code is composed of a number sign (#) followed by the red, green and blue (RGB) components of the color. For a list of the colors that you can specify by name, see the top of page 33.

The `color` property also supports specifying a color by the amount of red, green and blue (r,g,b) in the color. Specify the amounts as values from 0 to 255 or as percentages.

The `color` property is also useful for changing the color of other elements on your Web page, such as horizontal rules, form elements and tables. The `color` property cannot be used to change the color of images on your Web page.

CHANGE THE TEXT COLOR

```
index - WordPad
File  Edit  View  Insert  Format  Help

<HTML>
<HEAD>
<TITLE>Classical Music Composers</TITLE>
<STYLE>
H2 {color: #FF0000}
</STYLE>
</HEAD>
<BODY>

<H2>Beethoven</H2>
<P>Ludwig van Beethoven was born in Bonn, Germany in 1770. He spent m
Vienna, where he earned a living giving concerts, teaching piano and sellin
<BR>One of the most fascinating aspects of Beethoven's life was his triump
which struck him during adulthood. In fact, he composed some of his most p
after losing his hearing.</P>

<H2>Bach</H2>
<P>Johann Sebastian Bach was born into a family of musicians in 1685 in
Germany. Bach's works include church organ and choral music, music for
```

```
Classical Music Composers - Microsoft Internet Explorer
File  Edit  View  Favorites  Tools  Help

Back  Forward  Stop  Refresh  Home  Search  Favorites  History  Mail  Print  Edit
Address  C:\My Documents\Web Pages\index.html

Beethoven

Ludwig van Beethoven was born in Bonn, Germany in 1770. He spent most of his life in Vienna,
where he earned a living giving concerts, teaching piano and selling his compositions.
One of the most fascinating aspects of Beethoven's life was his triumph over deafness, which struck
him during adulthood. In fact, he composed some of his most powerful works after losing his
hearing.

Bach

Johann Sebastian Bach was born into a family of musicians in 1685 in Eisenach, Germany. Bach's
works include church organ and choral music, music for chamber orchestras and over 200 cantatas.
Although he was more respected as an organist during his lifetime, Bach's compositions influenced
many later composers, including Beethoven and Mozart.

Done                                                          My Computer
```

■1 To change the color of all the text that uses a specific tag, click between the brackets { } for the tag.

■2 Type **color:** and then add a blank space.

■3 Type the name or hexadecimal value for the color you want to use (example: red or #FF0000).

Note: For a list of colors, see the color chart at the front of this book.

■ The Web browser displays all the text that uses the tag in the color you specified.

*Note: You can also specify a color by providing the amount of red, green and blue (r,g,b) in the color as values or as percentages. For example, type **rgb(255,0,0)** or **rgb(100%,0%,0%)** to display the text in red.*

CHANGE THE LINE SPACING

Use the `line-height` property to change the line spacing, or leading, of all the text on your Web page that uses a specific tag. Increasing the line spacing can make text on your Web page easier to read.

When changing the line spacing, people commonly specify a number that will be multiplied by the current font size to determine the new line spacing. For example, specifying a value of `2.0` will make the line spacing twice the size of the text.

When you change the line spacing by specifying a number, the line spacing will depend on the current font size. If you later change the font size, the line spacing will also change.

Line spacing can also be specified as a percentage of the text size (example: 150%) or in millimeters, centimeters, inches, pixels, points, picas, x-height or em. Use x-height to specify a new line spacing based on the height of the lowercase letter "x" for the current font (example: 2ex). Use em to change the line spacing based on the height of the current font (example: 2em).

CHANGE THE LINE SPACING

```
<HTML>
<HEAD>
<TITLE>Classical Music Composers</TITLE>
<STYLE>
P {line-height: 2.0}
</STYLE>
</HEAD>
<BODY>

<H2>Beethoven</H2>
<P>Ludwig van Beethoven was born in Bonn, Germany in 1770. He spen
Vienna, where he earned a living giving concerts, teaching piano and se
compositions.
<BR>One of the most fascinating aspects of Beethoven's life was his tri
which struck him during adulthood. In fact, he composed some of his mo
after losing his hearing.</P>

<H2>Bach</H2>
```

Beethoven

Ludwig van Beethoven was born in Bonn, Germany in 1770. He spent most of his life in Vienna, where he earned a living giving concerts, teaching piano and selling his compositions.

One of the most fascinating aspects of Beethoven's life was his triumph over deafness, which struck him during adulthood. In fact, he composed some of his most powerful works after losing his hearing.

Bach

Johann Sebastian Bach was born into a family of musicians in 1685 in Eisenach, Germany. Bach's works include church organ and choral music, music for chamber orchestras and over 200 cantatas.

1 To change the line spacing of all the text that uses a specific tag, click between the brackets { } for the tag.

2 Type **line-height:** and then add a blank space.

3 Type the number that you want to multiply by the current font size to determine the line spacing (example: 2.0).

■ The Web browser displays all the text that uses the tag with the line spacing you specified.

Note: You can also specify the line spacing as a percentage of the text size (example: 150%) or in millimeters (mm), centimeters (cm), inches (in), pixels (px), points (pt), picas (pc), x-height (ex) or em.

CHANGE THE LETTER SPACING

The letter-spacing property lets you change the letter spacing, or kerning, of all the text on your Web page that uses a specific tag.

When changing the letter spacing, people commonly specify a new size in points or pixels. You can also specify a letter spacing in millimeters, centimeters, inches, picas, x-height or em. Use x-height to specify a letter spacing based on the height of the lowercase letter "x" for the current font (example: 2ex). Use em to change the letter spacing based on the height of the current font (example: 2em).

The letter-spacing property also supports negative values (example: -1px). Specifying a negative value decreases the amount of space between letters.

While the letter-spacing property is part of the HTML standard, it is not currently supported by some Web browsers.

To change the spacing between words rather than letters, use the word-spacing property. Changing the word spacing can help make text easier to read. The word-spacing property is not currently supported by most Web browsers.

CHANGE THE LETTER SPACING

```
<HTML>
<HEAD>
<TITLE>Classical Music Composers</TITLE>
<STYLE>
H2 {letter-spacing: 2pt}
</STYLE>
</HEAD>
<BODY>

<H2>Beethoven</H2>
<P>Ludwig van Beethoven was born in Bonn, Germany in 1770. He spen
Vienna, where he earned a living giving concerts, teaching piano and se
compositions.
<BR>One of the most fascinating aspects of Beethoven's life was his tri
which struck him during adulthood. In fact, he composed some of his mo
after losing his hearing.</P>

<H2>Bach</H2>
```

Beethoven

Ludwig van Beethoven was born in Bonn, Germany in 1770. He spent most of his life in Vienna, where he earned a living giving concerts, teaching piano and selling his compositions.
One of the most fascinating aspects of Beethoven's life was his triumph over deafness, which struck him during adulthood. In fact, he composed some of his most powerful works after losing his hearing.

Bach

Johann Sebastian Bach was born into a family of musicians in 1685 in Eisenach, Germany. Bach's works include church organ and choral music, music for chamber orchestras and over 200 cantatas. Although he was more respected as an organist during his lifetime, Bach's compositions influenced many later composers, including Beethoven and Mozart.

■1 To change the letter spacing of all the text that uses a specific tag, click between the brackets { } for the tag.

■2 Type **letter-spacing: ?** replacing ? with the amount of space you want to use in points or pixels (example: 2pt or 2px).

Note: You can also specify the amount of space in millimeters (mm), centimeters (cm), inches (in), picas (pc), x-height (ex) or em.

■ The Web browser displays all the text that uses the tag with the letter spacing you specified.

*Note: To change the spacing between words rather than letters, type **word-spacing** instead of **letter-spacing** in step 2.*

217

CHANGE APPEARANCE OF LINKS

U se the :link, :visited and :active pseudo-classes to change the appearance of all the unvisited, visited and active links (A) on your Web page. An active link is a link that a user is currently selecting.

Pseudo-classes are similar to *classes*, but have predetermined names rather than names you assign. For information on classes, see page 202.

The color property allows you to change the color of links by specifying the name or *hexadecimal value* for the color you want to use. You can also specify a color by providing

the amount of red, green and blue (r,g,b) in the color as values from 0 to 255 or as percentages.

When changing the color of links, make sure you specify a different color for each type of link. The colors you choose should work well with the background color of your Web page.

Using the text-decoration property with the none value allows you to remove the underline from links. When you remove the underline from one type of link, Netscape Navigator automatically removes the underline from other types of links.

CHANGE APPEARANCE OF LINKS

```
index - WordPad
File  Edit  View  Insert  Format  Help

<HTML>
<HEAD>
<TITLE>Grape Expectations</TITLE>
<STYLE>
A:link {}
</STYLE>
</HEAD>
<BODY>

<H1>Grape Expectations</H1>

<H4><CENTER><I>A guide to homemade wine-making for the wine connoiss
</CENTER></H4>

<P><IMG SRC="barrel.gif" HSPACE="10" VSPACE="10" ALIGN="left" WIDTH=
HEIGHT="110">Welcome to our Web site about wine-making. Our names are
and Alan Baker and we have been making our own wine for 20 years. Current
over 200 bottles of homemade wine in our wine cellar. These pages contain
you need to know to make your own red, white or blush wine, including the
you need, what kind of grapes you should b    tips and tricks to mak
```

```
index - WordPad
File  Edit  View  Insert  Format  Help

<HTML>
<HEAD>
<TITLE>Grape Expectations</TITLE>
<STYLE>
A:link {color: #FF0000}
</STYLE>
</HEAD>
<BODY>

<H1>Grape Expectations</H1>

<H4><CENTER><I>A guide to homemade wine-making for the wine connoiss
</CENTER></H4>

<P><IMG SRC="barrel.gif" HSPACE="10" VSPACE="10" ALIGN="left" WIDTH=
HEIGHT="110">Welcome to our Web site about wine-making. Our names are
and Alan Baker and we have been making our own wine for 20 years. Current
over 200 bottles of homemade wine in our wine cellar. These pages contain
you need to know to make your own red, white or blush wine, including the
you need, what kind of grapes you should b    tips and tricks to mak
```

1 Click between the <STYLE> and </STYLE> tags.

2 Type **A:?** { } replacing **?** with the type of link you want to change (**link**, **visited** or **active**).

3 Click between the brackets { }.

4 To specify a color for the links, type **color:** and then add a blank space.

5 Type the name or hexadecimal value for the color you want to use (example: red or #FF0000).

Note: For a list of colors, see the color chart at the front of this book.

Extra

Many other style sheet properties, such as the `background` and `font-family` properties, can be used to change the appearance of links. When using multiple properties, make sure you separate each property with a semi-colon (;). In Netscape Navigator, when you change the appearance of one type of link, the other types of links will automatically display the same style.

Example:

`A:link {background: red; font-family: "Courier"}`

Use the `:hover` pseudo-class to specify how you want links to appear when users position the mouse over the links. This can help users see which link they are selecting. For example, you can have the color of a link change when a user positions the mouse over the link. The `:hover` pseudo-class is currently only supported by Internet Explorer.

Example:

`A:hover {color: green}`

If you change the appearance of links (A) without using a pseudo-class, every type of link on your Web page will use the same style. This can be confusing to users, since they will not be able to see the difference between visited and unvisited links.

Example:

`A {color: green}`

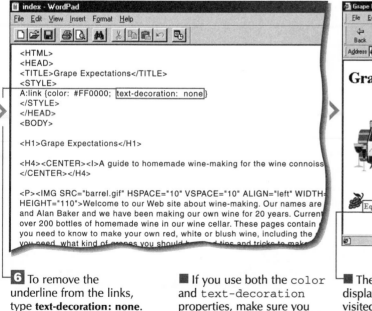

6 To remove the underline from the links, type **text-decoration: none.**

■ If you use both the `color` and `text-decoration` properties, make sure you separate the properties with a semi-colon (;).

■ The Web browser displays the unvisited, visited or active links in the color you specified, without an underline.

*Note: You can also specify a color for links by providing the amount of red, green and blue (r,g,b) in the color as values or as percentages. For example, type **rgb(255,0,0)** or **rgb(100%,0%,0%)** to display the links in red.*

ADD A BACKGROUND IMAGE

U se the background property to add a background image to every element on your Web page that uses a specific tag. Interesting background images are available at the www.nepthys.com/textures and imagine.metanet.com Web sites.

When adding a background image, you must specify the location and name of the image on your computer. Make sure that the background image you use works well with the elements on your Web page.

By default, a Web browser will repeat the background image you add until it fills the background area for an element. Use the

repeat-x value to make the background image repeat horizontally. To have the background image repeat vertically, use the repeat-y value. The no-repeat value prevents a background image from repeating.

Specify a background image for the body of your Web page (BODY) to add the background image to your entire Web page. By default, the background image you add will move when a user scrolls through the Web page. If you want the background image to remain stationary when a user scrolls through the Web page, use the fixed value. The fixed value is not currently supported by some Web browsers.

ADD A BACKGROUND IMAGE

```
index - WordPad
File  Edit  View  Insert  Format  Help

<HTML>
<HEAD>
<TITLE>Classical Music Composers</TITLE>
<STYLE>
P {background: }
</STYLE>
</HEAD>
<BODY>

<H2>Beethoven</H2>
<P>Ludwig van Beethoven was born in Bonn, Germany in 1770. He spent most
Vienna, where he earned a living giving concerts, teaching piano and selling his
compositions.
<BR>One of the most fascinating aspects of Beethoven's life was his triumph ove
which struck him during adulthood. In fact, he composed some of his most powerf
after losing his hearing.</P>

<H2>Bach</H2>
<P>Johann Sebastian Bach was born into a family of musicians in 1685 in Eise
Germany. Bach's works include church organ and choral music, music for cham
orchestras and over 200 cantatas. Although he more respected as an or
```

```
index - WordPad
File  Edit  View  Insert  Format  Help

<HTML>
<HEAD>
<TITLE>Classical Music Composers</TITLE>
<STYLE>
P {background: url("background.jpg") }
</STYLE>
</HEAD>
<BODY>

<H2>Beethoven</H2>
<P>Ludwig van Beethoven was born in Bonn, Germany in 1770. He spent most
Vienna, where he earned a living giving concerts, teaching piano and selling his
compositions.
<BR>One of the most fascinating aspects of Beethoven's life was his triumph ove
which struck him during adulthood. In fact, he composed some of his most powerf
after losing his hearing.</P>

<H2>Bach</H2>
<P>Johann Sebastian Bach was born into a family of musicians in 1685 in Eise
Germany. Bach's works include church organ and choral music, music for cham
orchestras and over 200 cantatas. Although he more respected as an or
```

1 To add a background to every element that uses a specific tag, click between the brackets { } for the tag.

2 Type **background:** and then add a blank space.

3 Type **url("?")** replacing **?** with the location and name of the background image on your computer.

Note: For information on specifying the location and name of an image, see the top of page 45.

Extra

You may want to specify both a background image and a background color for elements on your Web page. The color you specify will appear on a user's screen as the background image transfers. Users who do not see images will see the background color instead of the background image.

Example:

```
H1 {background: red url("images/fruit.gif")}
```

The HTML standard also includes properties that let you specify the information for a background image separately. Use the `background-image` property to specify the image you want to use, the `background-repeat` property to specify how you want the image to repeat and the `background-attachment` property to specify if you want the image to remain stationary. A semi-colon (;) must separate each property you use.

Example:

```
BODY {background-image: url("images/trees.gif");
background-repeat: repeat-y;
background-attachment: fixed}
```

The `background-position` property allows you to specify a starting position for a background image. The image will repeat to fill the background area from this starting position. When specifying a starting position, enter the horizontal and vertical coordinates for the new position as percentages (example: 40% 30%), lengths (example: 10px 30px) or by using descriptive values (example: top left).

Example:

```
P {background: url("images/splash.gif");
background-position: 10px 30px}
```

```
index - WordPad
File  Edit  View  Insert  Format  Help

<HTML>
<HEAD>
<TITLE>Classical Music Composers</TITLE>
<STYLE>
P {background: url("background.jpg") repeat }
</STYLE>
</HEAD>
<BODY>

<H2>Beethoven</H2>
<P>Ludwig van Beethoven was born in Bonn, Germany in 1770. He spent most
Vienna, where he earned a living giving concerts, teaching piano and selling his
compositions.
<BR>One of the most fascinating aspects of Beethoven's life was his triumph ove
which struck him during adulthood. In fact, he composed some of his most powerf
after losing his hearing.</P>

<H2>Bach</H2>
<P>Johann Sebastian Bach was born into a family of musicians in 1685 in Eiser
Germany. Bach's works include church organ and choral music, music for cham
orchestras and over 200 cantatas. Although he was more respected as an or
```

```
Classical Music Composers - Microsoft Internet Explorer
File  Edit  View  Favorites  Tools  Help
Back  Forward  Stop  Refresh  Home  Search  Favorites  History  Mail  Print  Edit
Address  C:\My Documents\Web Pages\index.html

Beethoven

Ludwig van Beethoven was born in Bonn, Germany in 1770. He spent most of his life in Vienna,
where he earned a living giving concerts, teaching piano and selling his compositions.
One of the most fascinating aspects of Beethoven's life was his triumph over deafness, which struck
him during adulthood. In fact, he composed some of his most powerful works after losing his
hearing.

Bach

Johann Sebastian Bach was born into a family of musicians in 1685 in Eisenach, Germany. Bach's
works include church organ and choral music, music for chamber orchestras and over 200 cantatas.
Although he was more respected as an organist during his lifetime, Bach's compositions influenced
many later composers, including Beethoven and Mozart.
```

4 Type the way you want the background image to repeat behind each element (**repeat**, **repeat-x**, **repeat-y** or **no-repeat**).

Note: When adding a background image to the body of a Web page (BODY), *type an option to specify if you want the image to move (**scroll**) or remain stationary (**fixed**) when a user scrolls through the Web page.*

■ The Web browser displays every element that uses the tag with the background image you specified.

ADD A BACKGROUND COLOR

The background property allows you to add a background color to every element on your Web page that uses a specific tag.

When adding a background color, specify the name or hexadecimal value for the color you want to use. A hexadecimal value is a code that tells Web browsers which color to display. The code is composed of a number sign (#) followed by the red, green and blue (RGB) components of the color. For a list of colors you can specify by name, see the top of page 33.

The background property also supports specifying a color by the amount of red, green

and blue (r,g,b) in the color. Specify the amounts as values from 0 to 255 or as percentages.

To add a background color to your entire Web page, use the background property to specify a color for the body of your Web page (BODY).

After adding a background color to the elements that use a specific tag, make sure that the color you selected works well with the color of the elements. For example, adding a blue background to red text can make the text difficult to read.

ADD A BACKGROUND COLOR

index - WordPad

```
<HTML>
<HEAD>
<TITLE>Classical Music Composers</TITLE>
<STYLE>
H2 {background: #FF0000}
</STYLE>
</HEAD>
<BODY>

<H2>Beethoven</H2>
<P>Ludwig van Beethoven was born in Bonn, Germany in 1770. He spent mo
Vienna, where he earned a living giving concerts, teaching piano and selling
compositions.
<BR>One of the most fascinating aspects of Beethoven's life was his triumph
which struck him during adulthood. In fact, he composed some of his most po
after losing his hearing.</P>

<H2>Bach</H2>
<P>Johann Sebastian Bach was born into a family of musicians in 1685 in
Germany. Bach's works include church org...     choral music, music fo
```

Classical Music Composers - Microsoft Internet Explorer

Address: C:\My Documents\Web Pages\index.html

Beethoven

Ludwig van Beethoven was born in Bonn, Germany in 1770. He spent most of his life in Vienna, where he earned a living giving concerts, teaching piano and selling his compositions.
One of the most fascinating aspects of Beethoven's life was his triumph over deafness, which struck him during adulthood. In fact, he composed some of his most powerful works after losing his hearing.

Bach

Johann Sebastian Bach was born into a family of musicians in 1685 in Eisenach, Germany. Bach's works include church organ and choral music, music for chamber orchestras and over 200 cantatas. Although he was more respected as an organist during his lifetime, Bach's compositions influenced many later composers, including Beethoven and Mozart.

1 To add a background color to every element that uses a specific tag, click between the brackets { } for the tag.

2 Type **background:** and then add a blank space.

3 Type the name or hexadecimal value for the color you want to use (example: red or #FF0000).

Note: For a list of colors, see the color chart at the front of this book.

■ The Web browser displays every element that uses the tag with the background color you specified.

Note: You can also specify a background color by providing the amount of red, green and blue (r,g,b) in the color as values or as percentages. For example, type **rgb(255,0,0)** *or* **rgb(100%,0%,0%)** *to display a red background.*

SET THE WIDTH AND HEIGHT

The width and height properties allow you to specify a width and height for every element on your Web page that uses a specific tag. This is useful when you want the elements to all display the same size.

Specify a width or height for elements in pixels or as a percentage of their parent element's width or height. You can also specify a width or height in millimeters, centimeters, inches, points, picas, x-height or em. Use x-height to specify a width or height based on the height of the lowercase letter "x" for the current font (example: 2ex). Use em to specify a width or height based on the height of the current font (example: 2em).

If the dimensions you specify for text elements are too small to properly display their contents, Web browsers will usually display the elements with the width you specified, but ignore the height.

When specifying both a width and height for images (IMG), you may want to use the auto value for either the width or height. Web browsers will calculate a size for the auto value based on the size you specified for the other dimension. This can help prevent your image from becoming distorted due to resizing. The auto value is not supported by some Web browsers.

SET THE WIDTH AND HEIGHT

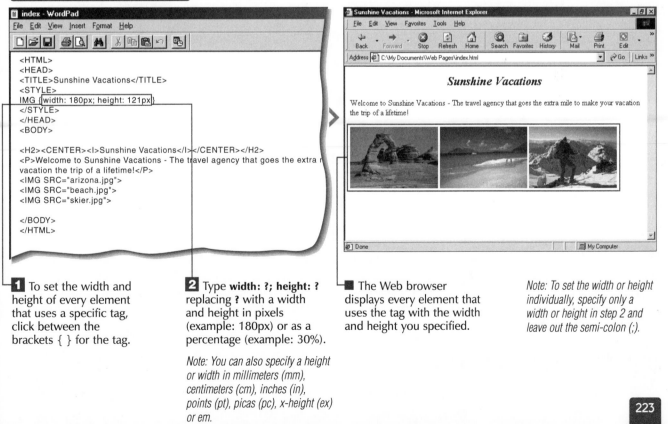

1 To set the width and height of every element that uses a specific tag, click between the brackets { } for the tag.

2 Type **width: ?; height: ?** replacing **?** with a width and height in pixels (example: 180px) or as a percentage (example: 30%).

Note: You can also specify a height or width in millimeters (mm), centimeters (cm), inches (in), points (pt), picas (pc), x-height (ex) or em.

■ The Web browser displays every element that uses the tag with the width and height you specified.

Note: To set the width or height individually, specify only a width or height in step 2 and leave out the semi-colon (;).

ADD PADDING

Use the `padding` property to add space, or padding, around every element on your Web page that uses a specific tag.

Specify the amount of padding you want to use for elements in pixels or as a percentage of their parent element's width. You can also specify padding in millimeters, centimeters, inches, points, picas, x-height or em. Use x-height to specify padding based on the height of the lowercase letter "x" for the current font (example: 2ex). Use em to specify padding based on the height of the current font (example: 2em).

Think of the elements on your Web page as appearing in invisible boxes, with each element in the center of a box, surrounded by padding, borders and margins.

The padding you specify for elements will appear between each element and its border. For information on margins and borders, see pages 225 and 226.

Although the `padding` property is part of the HTML standard, it is not currently supported by some Web browsers.

Extra

The `padding-left`, `padding-right`, `padding-top` and `padding-bottom` properties allow you to specify a different padding for each side of elements that use a specific tag. Separate each property you use with a semi-colon (;).

Example:

P {padding-left: 10px; padding-right: 20px}

ADD PADDING

```
<HTML>
<HEAD>
<TITLE>Classical Music Composers</TITLE>
<STYLE>
P {padding: 60px}
</STYLE>
</HEAD>
<BODY>

<H2>Beethoven</H2>
<P>Ludwig van Beethoven was born in Bonn, Germany in 1770. He spent mo
Vienna, where he earned a living giving concerts, teaching piano and selling
compositions.
<BR>One of the most fascinating aspects of Beethoven's life was his triumph
which struck him during adulthood. In fact, he composed some of his most po
after losing his hearing.</P>

<H2>Bach</H2>
<P>Johann Sebastian Bach was born into a family of musicians in 1685 in
Germany. Bach's works include church org      choral music music fo
```

Beethoven

Ludwig van Beethoven was born in Bonn, Germany in 1770. He spent most of his life in Vienna, where he earned a living giving concerts, teaching piano and selling his compositions.
One of the most fascinating aspects of Beethoven's life was his triumph over deafness, which struck him during adulthood. In fact, he composed some of his most powerful works after losing his hearing.

Bach

1 To change the padding for every element that uses a specific tag, click between the brackets { } for the tag.

2 Type **padding:** and then add a blank space.

3 Type the amount of space for the padding in pixels (example: 60px).

■ The Web browser displays every element that uses the tag with the padding you specified.

Note: You can also specify the padding as a percentage of the parent element's width (example: 10%) or in millimeters (mm), centimeters (cm), inches (in), points (pt), picas (pc), x-height (ex) or em.

224

CHANGE THE MARGINS

U se the `margin-top`, `margin-bottom`, `margin-left` and `margin-right` properties to change the margins for every element on your Web page that uses a specific tag.

Changing the margins adjusts the amount of transparent space around elements. The margin size you specify will be added to any padding or borders you have added to the elements. For more information on adding padding and borders, see pages 224 and 226.

Specify a new margin size as a percentage of an element's width or in pixels, millimeters, centimeters, inches, points, picas, x-height or em. Use x-height to specify a margin size based on the height of the lowercase letter "x" for the current font

(example: 2ex). Use em to change the margin size based on the height of the current font (example: 2em).

You can specify a negative value for a margin to reduce the amount of space around elements (example: -1px).

Extra

Use the `margin` property to change all the margins at once for elements that use a specific tag. Specifying one value will change all the margins to the same size. Specifying four values will change the margins in the following order: top, right, bottom, left.

Example:

P {margin: 15px 30px 20px 10px}

CHANGE THE MARGINS

```
<HTML>
<HEAD>
<TITLE>Classical Music Composers</TITLE>
<STYLE>
P {margin-left: 60px}
</STYLE>
</HEAD>
<BODY>

<H2>Beethoven</H2>
<P>Ludwig van Beethoven was born in Bonn, Germany in 1770. He spent
Vienna, where he earned a living giving concerts, teaching piano and selli
compositions.
<BR>One of the most fascinating aspects of Beethoven's life was his triu
which struck him during adulthood. In fact, he composed some of his mos
after losing his hearing.</P>

<H2>Bach</H2>
```

Beethoven

Ludwig van Beethoven was born in Bonn, Germany in 1770. He spent most of his life in Vienna, where he earned a living giving concerts, teaching piano and selling his compositions.
One of the most fascinating aspects of Beethoven's life was his triumph over deafness, which struck him during adulthood. In fact, he composed some of his most powerful works after losing his hearing.

Bach

Johann Sebastian Bach was born into a family of musicians in 1685 in Eisenach, Germany. Bach's works include church organ and choral music, music for chamber orchestras and over 200 cantatas. Although he was more respected as an organist during his lifetime, Bach's compositions influenced many later composers, including Beethoven and Mozart.

■1 To change a margin for every element that uses a specific tag, click between the brackets { } for the tag.

■2 Type **margin-?:** replacing **?** with the margin you want to change (**top**, **bottom**, **left** or **right**). Then add a blank space.

■3 Type the amount of space for the margin in pixels (example: 60px).

■4 Repeat steps 1 to 3 for each margin you want to change, separating each margin setting with a semi-colon (;).

■ The Web browser displays every element that uses the tag with the margin you specified.

Note: You can also specify the margin size as a percentage of the element's width (example: 10%) or in millimeters (mm), centimeters (cm), inches (in), points (pt), picas (pc), x-height (ex) or em.

ADD A BORDER

The `border` property allows you to place a border around every element on your Web page that uses a specific tag. Adding borders to elements is useful for making the elements stand out.

To specify a thickness for a border, use a descriptive value (`thin`, `medium` or `thick`) or specify a value in pixels, millimeters, centimeters, inches, points, picas, x-height or em. Use x-height to specify a thickness based on the height of the lowercase letter "x" for the current font (example: 2ex). Use em to specify a thickness based on the height of the current font (example: 2em).

When adding a border, you must specify a border style or the border will not appear on your Web page. The available styles include `solid`, `double`, `groove`, `ridge`, `inset`, `outset`, `dotted`, and `dashed`. Some Web browsers do not yet support the `dotted` and `dashed` border styles.

You can specify a color for a border using the name of the color, the *hexadecimal value* of the color or the amount of red, green and blue in the color (r,g,b).

Netscape Navigator does not currently support using the `border` property for images (`IMG`), tables (`TABLE`) or embedded elements (`EMBED`), such as sounds.

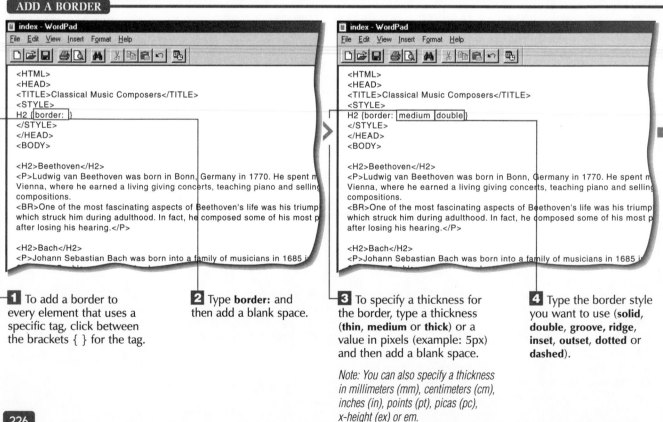

1 To add a border to every element that uses a specific tag, click between the brackets { } for the tag.

2 Type **border:** and then add a blank space.

3 To specify a thickness for the border, type a thickness (**thin**, **medium** or **thick**) or a value in pixels (example: 5px) and then add a blank space.

Note: You can also specify a thickness in millimeters (mm), centimeters (cm), inches (in), points (pt), picas (pc), x-height (ex) or em.

4 Type the border style you want to use (**solid**, **double**, **groove**, **ridge**, **inset**, **outset**, **dotted** or **dashed**).

Extra

Use the `none` value with the `border` property to remove borders from elements. This is useful for removing the borders that automatically appear around images you have used as links. Some Web browsers do not yet support the `none` value.

Example:

`IMG {border: none}`

Use the `border-left`, `border-right`, `border-top` and `border-bottom` properties to specify the information for each side of your borders separately. Separate each property you use with a semi-colon (;). Some Web browsers do not yet support these properties.

Example:

`H1 {border-left: solid 3px; border-right: solid 3px; border-top: double 6px; border-bottom: double 6px}`

Some Web browsers support using the `border-width`, `border-style` and `border-color` properties to specify the thickness, style and color for borders separately. Separate each property you use with a semi-colon (;). If you specify one value for a property, the value will affect all four sides of your borders. If you specify two values, the first value will affect the top and bottom borders and the second value will affect the left and right borders. Specifying four values will affect the sides of your borders in the following order: top, right, bottom, left.

Example:

`H1 {border-width: 14px; border-style: double solid; border-color: red green blue yellow}`

```
index - WordPad
File  Edit  View  Insert  Format  Help

<HTML>
<HEAD>
<TITLE>Classical Music Composers</TITLE>
<STYLE>
H2 {border: medium double #FF0000}
</STYLE>
</HEAD>
<BODY>

<H2>Beethoven</H2>
<P>Ludwig van Beethoven was born in Bonn, Germany in 1770. He spent m
Vienna, where he earned a living giving concerts, teaching piano and selling
compositions.
<BR>One of the most fascinating aspects of Beethoven's life was his triump
which struck him during adulthood. In fact, he composed some of his most p
after losing his hearing.</P>

<H2>Bach</H2>
<P>Johann Sebastian Bach was born into a family of musicians in 1685 i
```

```
Classical Music Composers - Microsoft Internet Explorer
File  Edit  View  Favorites  Tools  Help
Back   Forward   Stop   Refresh   Home   Search   Favorites   History   Mail   Print   Edit
Address  C:\My Documents\Web Pages\index.html

Beethoven

Ludwig van Beethoven was born in Bonn, Germany in 1770. He spent most of his life in Vienna,
where he earned a living giving concerts, teaching piano and selling his compositions.
One of the most fascinating aspects of Beethoven's life was his triumph over deafness, which struck
him during adulthood. In fact, he composed some of his most powerful works after losing his
hearing.

Bach

Johann Sebastian Bach was born into a family of musicians in 1685 in Eisenach, Germany. Bach's
works include church organ and choral music, music for chamber orchestras and over 200 cantatas.
Although he was more respected as an organist during his lifetime, Bach's compositions influenced
many later composers, including Beethoven and Mozart.

Done                                                          My Computer
```

5 To specify a color for the border, add a blank space and then type the name or hexadecimal value for the color you want to use (example: red or #FF0000). For a list of colors, see the color chart at the front of this book.

*Note: You can also specify a color by providing the amount of red, green and blue (r,g,b) in the color as values or percentages. For example, type **rgb(255, 0, 0)** or **rgb(100%, 0%, 0%)** to display the text in red.*

■ The Web browser displays every element that uses the tag with the border you specified.

WRAP TEXT AROUND ELEMENTS

The `float` property allows you to wrap text around every element on your Web page that uses a specific tag. For example, you may want to wrap text around images (`IMG`), tables (`TABLE`) or H1 headings (`H1`).

When wrapping text around elements, use the `left` value to wrap text around the right side of each element. The `right` value allows you to wrap text around the left side of each element.

To ensure text wraps correctly around elements, each element in your HTML document should appear directly before the text you want to wrap around the element.

You cannot use the `float` property to wrap text around elements that you have absolutely positioned. For information on absolute positioning, see page 236.

Extra

Use the `clear` property with the `left`, `right` or `both` value to stop text that uses a specific tag from wrapping around elements. The `left` value stops text from wrapping around elements that use the `float: left` style. The `right` value stops text from wrapping around elements that use the `float: right` style. Use the `both` value to stop text from wrapping around elements that use either style.

Example:

`H1 {clear: left}`

WRAP TEXT AROUND ELEMENTS

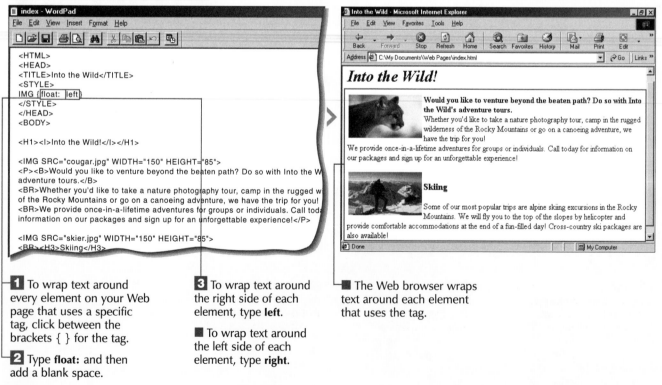

1 To wrap text around every element on your Web page that uses a specific tag, click between the brackets { } for the tag.

2 Type **float:** and then add a blank space.

3 To wrap text around the right side of each element, type **left**.

■ To wrap text around the left side of each element, type **right**.

■ The Web browser wraps text around each element that uses the tag.

CHANGE DISPLAY OF ELEMENTS

The `display` property allows you to specify how you want to display all the elements on your Web page that use a specific tag.

Use the `block` value to display elements as block-level elements. A block-level element is offset from the rest of your Web page with a blank line above and below the element. The `block` value is useful for displaying elements such as images (`IMG`) and links (`A`) on their own lines.

The `inline` value lets you display elements as inline elements. An inline element appears on the same line as the surrounding elements. The `inline` value is useful for displaying

block-level elements, such as headings (`H1` to `H6`), within the flow of text.

Use the `list-item` value to display elements as list items. List-item elements will appear as block-level elements that display bullets. The `list-item` value is not yet supported by many Web browsers.

Using the `none` value allows you to hide every element on your Web page that uses a specific tag. When you hide elements, the surrounding elements will shift to fill the space previously occupied by the hidden elements. You may want to temporarily hide elements that you have not yet completed.

CHANGE DISPLAY OF ELEMENTS

```
<HTML>
<HEAD>
<TITLE>Classical Music Composers</TITLE>
<STYLE>
H2 {display: inline}
</STYLE>
</HEAD>
<BODY>

<P><H2>Beethoven: </H2>
Ludwig van Beethoven was born in Bonn, Germany in 1770. He spent most of hi
Vienna, where he earned a living giving concerts, teaching piano and selling his
compositions.
<BR>One of the most fascinating aspects of Beethoven's life was his triumph ove
which struck him during adulthood. In fact, he composed some of his most power
after losing his hearing.</P>

<P><H2>Bach: </H2>
Johann Sebastian Bach was born into a family of musicians in 1685 in Eisenach
Bach's works include church organ and choral music, music for chamber orche
200 cantatas. Although he was more respected
```

Beethoven: Ludwig van Beethoven was born in Bonn, Germany in 1770. He spent most of his life in Vienna, where he earned a living giving concerts, teaching piano and selling his compositions.
One of the most fascinating aspects of Beethoven's life was his triumph over deafness, which struck him during adulthood. In fact, he composed some of his most powerful works after losing his hearing.

Bach: Johann Sebastian Bach was born into a family of musicians in 1685 in Eisenach, Germany. Bach's works include church organ and choral music, music for chamber orchestras and over 200 cantatas. Although he was more respected as an organist during his lifetime, Bach's compositions influenced many later composers, including Beethoven and Mozart.

1 To change the display of all the elements that use a specific tag, click between the brackets { } for the tag.

2 Type **display:** and then add a blank space.

3 Type the way you want to display the elements (**block**, **inline**, **list-item** or **none**).

■ The Web browser displays all the elements that use the tag with the display style you specified.

Note: If you specified the none value, the elements will not appear on your Web page.

CHANGE BULLET OR
NUMBER STYLE OF LISTS

The list-style property allows you to change the bullet style of all the unordered lists (UL) or the number style of all the ordered lists (OL) on your Web page. For information on creating unordered and ordered lists, see pages 40 and 38.

Use the circle (o), disc (●) or square (■) value to specify a new bullet style for unordered lists. The default bullet style is disc.

If you want to use an image as a bullet, use the url value to specify the location and name of the image on your computer. Interesting bullet images are available at the www.grapholina.com/Graphics and www.theshockzone.com Web sites. Some

Web browsers do not yet fully support the url value.

To specify a new number style for ordered lists, use the decimal (1,2,3), lower-alpha (a,b,c), upper-alpha (A,B,C), lower-roman (i,ii,iii) or upper-roman (I,II,III) value. The default number style is decimal.

If your Web page contains lists with more than 26 items, you may want to avoid using the lower-alpha or upper-alpha number styles. The HTML standard does not define how Web browsers should display these styles once the end of the alphabet is reached.

CHANGE BULLET OR NUMBER STYLE OF LISTS

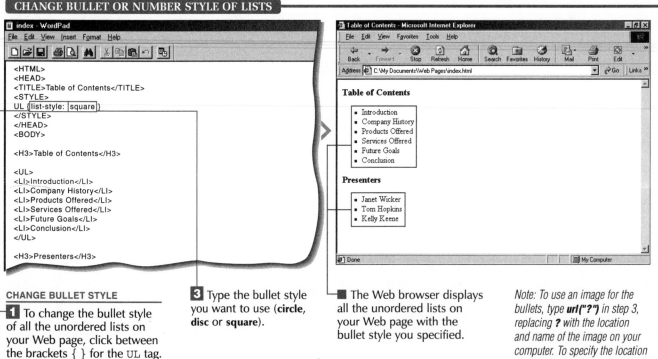

CHANGE BULLET STYLE

1 To change the bullet style of all the unordered lists on your Web page, click between the brackets { } for the UL tag.

2 Type **list-style:** and then add a blank space.

3 Type the bullet style you want to use (**circle**, **disc** or **square**).

■ The Web browser displays all the unordered lists on your Web page with the bullet style you specified.

Note: To use an image for the bullets, type **url("?")** in step 3, replacing **?** with the location and name of the image on your computer. To specify the location and name of an image, see the top of page 45.

230

Extra

If you have specified an image for the bullets in your unordered lists, you may also want to specify a bullet style that will appear if a user's Web browser does not display images. Some users have Web browsers that cannot display images, while others turn off the display of images to browse the Web more quickly.

Example:

```
UL {list-style: url("goldring.gif") circle}
```

If you want to change the bullet or number style of only some items in your lists, apply styles locally to the <LI> tags for the list items or create a class for the list items. For information on applying styles locally, see page 200. To create a class, see page 202.

Example:

```
<LI STYLE="list-style: circle">24-Hour Tech
Support</LI>
```

Use the inside or outside value to specify a position for the bullets or numbers in your lists. The inside value positions bullets or numbers within lists, wrapping the text for long list items below the bullets or numbers. The outside value positions bullets or numbers outside of lists, preventing text from wrapping below the bullets or numbers. Some Web browsers do not yet fully support the inside value.

Example:

```
OL {list-style: lower-roman inside}
```

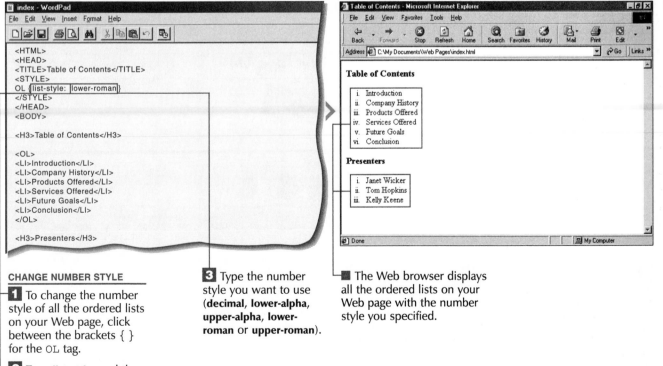

CHANGE NUMBER STYLE

1 To change the number style of all the ordered lists on your Web page, click between the brackets { } for the OL tag.

2 Type **list-style:** and then add a blank space.

3 Type the number style you want to use (**decimal**, **lower-alpha**, **upper-alpha**, **lower-roman** or **upper-roman**).

■ The Web browser displays all the ordered lists on your Web page with the number style you specified.

ALIGN ELEMENTS VERTICALLY

Use the `vertical-align` property to specify a vertical alignment for all the inline elements on your Web page that use a specific tag. Inline elements, such as images, are elements that do not automatically appear on a new line.

When vertically aligning elements with text, use the `baseline` value to align the elements with the baseline of text. The baseline of text is the bottom of letters such as "a" rather than letters such as "g." Use the `text-top` value to align elements with the top edge of the surrounding text. The `text-bottom` value lets you align elements with the bottom edge of the surrounding text.

Use the `middle` value to align elements with the middle of the surrounding elements. For example, using the `middle` value for images (`IMG`) that appear in a paragraph will align the middle of the images with the middle of a line of text.

Use the `top` value to align elements with the top of the highest element on the current line. The `bottom` value lets you align elements with the bottom of the lowest element on the current line.

ALIGN ELEMENTS VERTICALLY

```
<HTML>
<HEAD>
<TITLE>Into the Wild</TITLE>
<STYLE>
IMG {vertical-align: baseline}
</STYLE>
</HEAD>
<BODY>

<H1><I>Into the Wild!</I></H1>

<P><IMG SRC="cougar.jpg" WIDTH="150" HEIGHT="85" ALIGN="left">
Whether you'd like to take a nature photography tour, camp in the rugged wilderness o
Rocky Mountains or go on a canoeing adventure, we have the trip for you!
<BR>We provide once-in-a-lifetime adventures for groups or individuals. Call today for
information on our packages and sign up for an unforgettable experience!</P>

<P><IMG SRC="skier.jpg" WIDTH="150" HEIGHT="85" ALIGN="left">
Some of our most popular trips are alpine skiing excursions in the Rocky Mountains. W
fly you to the top of the slopes by helicopter and provide comfortable accommodations
end of a fun-filled day! Cross-country ski packages are also available!</P>

</BODY>
</HTML>
```

1 To vertically align all the inline elements on your Web page that use a specific tag, click between the brackets { } for the tag.

2 Type **vertical-align: ?** replacing **?** with the way you want to align the elements (**baseline**, **text-top**, **text-bottom**, **middle**, **top** or **bottom**).

■ The Web browser displays all the elements that use the tag with the vertical alignment you specified.

ADD PAGE BREAKS

Style sheets allow you to control where page breaks will occur when a user prints your Web page.

Use the `page-break-before` property with the `always` value to have a page break occur before every element that uses a specific tag. For example, add a page break before H1 headings (`H1`) to have every H1 heading begin on a new printed page.

Use the `page-break-after` property with the `always` value to have a page break occur after every element that uses a specific tag. For example, you may want a page break to occur after every table

(`TABLE`) to ensure that information will never follow your tables on a printed page.

To prevent a page break from occurring before or after every element that uses a specific tag, use the `avoid` value instead of the `always` value. This is useful when you do not want a page break to occur immediately before or after certain elements on your Web page. The `avoid` value is not yet supported by most Web browsers.

Although the `page-break-before` and `page-break-after` properties are part of the HTML standard, they are not yet supported by some Web browsers.

ADD PAGE BREAKS

```
<HTML>
<HEAD>
<TITLE>Classical Music Composers</TITLE>
<STYLE>
H1 {page-break-before: always}
</STYLE>
</HEAD>
<BODY>

<H1>Beethoven</H1>
<P>Ludwig van Beethoven was born in Bonn, Germany in 1770. He spent most of his
Vienna, where he earned a living giving concerts, teaching piano and selling his
compositions.
<BR>One of the most fascinating aspects of Beethoven's life was his triumph over dea
which struck him during adulthood. In fact, he composed some of his most powerful wo
after losing his hearing.</P>

<H1>Bach</H1>
<P>Johann Sebastian Bach was born into a family of musicians in 1685 in Eisenach,
Germany. Bach's works include church organ and choral music, music for chamber
orchestras and over 200 cantatas. Although he was more respected as an organist du
his lifetime, Bach's compositions influenced many later composers, including Beetho
and Mozart.</P>
```

ADD PAGE BREAKS BEFORE ELEMENTS

1 To add a page break before every element on your Web page that uses a specific tag, type **page-break-before: always** between the brackets { } for the tag.

*Note: To prevent a page break from occurring before every element that uses a specific tag, type **avoid** instead of **always** in step 1.*

```
<HTML>
<HEAD>
<TITLE>Classical Music Composers</TITLE>
<STYLE>
TABLE {page-break-after: always}
</STYLE>
</HEAD>
<BODY>

<H1>Beethoven</H1>
<P>Ludwig van Beethoven was born in Bonn, Germany in 1770. He spent most of his
Vienna, where he earned a living giving concerts, teaching piano and selling his
compositions.
<BR>One of the most fascinating aspects of Beethoven's life was his triumph over dea
which struck him during adulthood. In fact, he composed some of his most powerful wo
after losing his hearing.</P>

<TABLE BORDER="8">
<TR>
        <TH>Composer</TH>
        <TH>Year of Birth</TH>
</TR>
<TR
```

ADD PAGE BREAKS AFTER ELEMENTS

1 To add a page break after every element on your Web page that uses a specific tag, type **page-break-after: always** between the brackets { } for the tag.

*Note: To prevent a page break from occurring after every element that uses a specific tag, type **avoid** instead of **always** in step 1.*

POSITION ELEMENTS RELATIVELY

se the `position` property with the `relative` value to move every element that uses a specific tag from its original location on your Web page. This is useful if you want to move elements, such as images, without changing the position of the surrounding elements. Positioning elements relatively may cause elements on your Web page to overlap.

The `top`, `bottom`, `right` and `left` properties allow you to move elements relative to their original locations. For example, specify the `top` value to move elements away from the top edge of their original locations. Using more than one property allows you to move elements in more than one direction at a time. This is useful for moving elements on a diagonal.

Specify the distance you want to move the elements in pixels or as a percentage of the parent elements' height or width. You can also specify the distance in millimeters, centimeters, inches, points, picas, x-height or em. Use x-height to specify the distance based on the height of the lowercase letter "x" for the current font (example: 2ex). Use em to specify the distance based on the height of the current font (example: 2em).

Some Web browsers do not yet fully support relative positioning.

POSITION ELEMENTS RELATIVELY

```
index - WordPad
File  Edit  View  Insert  Format  Help

<HTML>
<HEAD>
<TITLE>Into the Wild</TITLE>
<STYLE>
IMG {position: relative;}
</STYLE>
</HEAD>
<BODY>

<H1><I>Into the Wild!</I></H1>

<P><B>Join Into the Wild for the adventure of a lifetime!</B>
<BR>Whether you'd like to take a nature photography tour, camp in the rugged wildern
the Rocky Mountains or go on a canoeing adventure, we have the trip for you!</P>
<P><IMG SRC="cougar.jpg" WIDTH="170" HEIGHT="105">
</BODY>
</HTML>
```

```
index - WordPad
File  Edit  View  Insert  Format  Help

<HTML>
<HEAD>
<TITLE>Into the Wild</TITLE>
<STYLE>
IMG {position: relative; top: 70px}
</STYLE>
</HEAD>
<BODY>

<H1><I>Into the Wild!</I></H1>

<P><B>Join Into the Wild for the adventure of a lifetime!</B>
<BR>Whether you'd like to take a nature photography tour, camp in the rugged wildern
the Rocky Mountains or go on a canoeing adventure, we have the trip for you!</P>
<P><IMG SRC="cougar.jpg" WIDTH="170" HEIGHT="105">
</BODY>
</HTML>
```

1 To change the relative position of every element that uses a specific tag, click between the brackets { } for the tag.

2 Type **position: relative** and then type a semi-colon (;).

3 To move the elements from their original locations, type the edge you want to move the elements away from (**top**, **bottom**, **right** or **left**).

4 Type **: ?** replacing **?** with the distance you want to move the elements in pixels (example: 70px).

Note: You can also specify a distance as a percentage of the parent elements' height or width or in millimeters (mm), centimeters (cm), inches (in), points (pt), picas (pc), x-height (ex) or em.

Apply
It

Relative positoning allows you to create interesting visual effects by overlapping elements. For example, overlap text to create a shadow effect.

TYPE THIS:

```
<HTML>
<HEAD>
<TITLE>XYZ Corporation</TITLE>
<STYLE>
H1.ontop {position: relative; bottom: 57px; left: 5px; color: blue}
</STYLE>
</HEAD>
<BODY>
<H1>XYZ Products</H1>
<H1 CLASS="ontop">XYZ Products</H1>
```

RESULT:

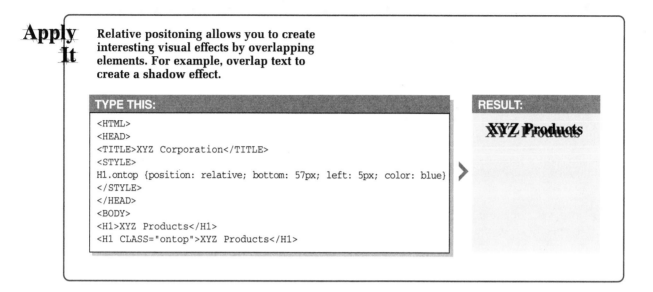

XYZ Products

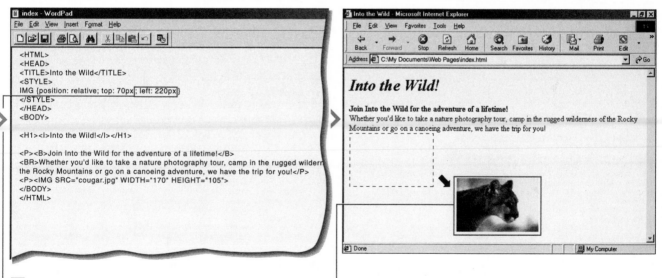

5 To move the elements in more than one direction at a time, type a semicolon (;) and then repeat steps 3 and 4.

Note: Moving elements in more than one direction allows you to move the elements on a diagonal.

■ The Web browser displays all the elements that use the tag with the positioning you specified.

Note: If elements overlap, you can change the way they overlap as shown on the top of page 237.

POSITION ELEMENTS ABSOLUTELY

U se the `position` property with the `absolute` value to specify an absolute position for every element on your Web page that uses a specific tag.

Absolutely positioning elements removes the elements from the natural flow of your Web page. Other elements on your page will shift to fill in the space previously occupied by the elements you positioned. This may cause elements to overlap.

The `top`, `bottom`, `left` and `right` properties allow you to specify an absolute position for elements in relation to their parent elements. For example, use the `left` property to position elements in relation to the left edge of their parent elements. Use two properties to position the elements in relation to two edges of the parent elements, such as the top and left edges.

Specify the distance you want to position elements away from a parent element edge in pixels or as a percentage of the parent elements' height or width. You can also specify the distance in millimeters, centimeters, inches, points, picas, x-height or em. Use x-height to specify the distance based on the height of the lowercase letter "x" for the current font. Use em to change the distance based on the height of the current font.

Some Web browsers do not yet fully support absolute positioning.

POSITION ELEMENTS ABSOLUTELY

```
index - WordPad
File  Edit  View  Insert  Format  Help

<HTML>
<HEAD>
<TITLE>Into the Wild</TITLE>
<STYLE>
IMG {position: absolute;}
</STYLE>
</HEAD>
<BODY>

<H1><I><CENTER>Into the Wild!</CENTER></I></H1>

<IMG SRC="cougar.jpg" WIDTH="185" HEIGHT="130">
<P ALIGN="right"><B>Are you interested in venturing beyond the beaten path?
<BR>Try an exciting trip with Into the Wild's adventure tours!</B></P>
<P>Whether you'd like to take a nature photography tour, camp in the rugged wilderness
the Rocky Mountains or go on a canoeing adventure, we have the trip for you!
We provide once-in-a-lifetime adventures for groups or individuals. Call us today for
information on our packages and sign up for an unforgettable experience!</P>

<IMG SRC="skier.jpg" WIDTH="100" HEIGHT="50">
<H3>Skiing</H3>
<P>Some of our most popular trips are alpine skiing excursions in the Rocky Mounta
will fly you to the top of the slopes by helicopter
```

```
index - WordPad
File  Edit  View  Insert  Format  Help

<HTML>
<HEAD>
<TITLE>Into the Wild</TITLE>
<STYLE>
IMG {position: absolute;  bottom: 185px}
</STYLE>
</HEAD>
<BODY>

<H1><I><CENTER>Into the Wild!</CENTER></I></H1>

<IMG SRC="cougar.jpg" WIDTH="185" HEIGHT="130">
<P ALIGN="right"><B>Are you interested in venturing beyond the beaten path?
<BR>Try an exciting trip with Into the Wild's adventure tours!</B></P>
<P>Whether you'd like to take a nature photography tour, camp in the rugged wilderness
the Rocky Mountains or go on a canoeing adventure, we have the trip for you!
We provide once-in-a-lifetime adventures for groups or individuals. Call us today for
information on our packages and sign up for an unforgettable experience!</P>

<IMG SRC="skier.jpg" WIDTH="100" HEIGHT="50">
<H3>Skiing</H3>
<P>Some of our most popular trips are alpine skiing excursions in the Rocky Mounta
will fly you to the top of the slopes by helicopter
```

1 To specify an absolute position for every element that uses a specific tag, click between the brackets { } for the tag.

2 Type **position: absolute** and then type a semi-colon (;).

3 Type the parent element edge you want to use to position the elements (**top**, **bottom**, **left** or **right**).

4 Type **: ?** replacing **?** with the distance in pixels you want the elements to appear from the edge you specified (example: 185px).

Note: You can specify a distance as a percentage of the parent elements' height or width or in millimeters (mm), centimeters (cm), inches (in), points (pt), picas (pc), x-height (ex) or em.

Extra

After you position elements on your Web page, the elements may overlap other elements. Use the `z-index` property in the tag for each element you positioned to control how the elements will overlap. You can specify a negative or positive value. The higher the `z-index` value you assign, the closer to the top an overlapping element will appear. The `z-index` property can be used with elements that have been absolutely or relatively positioned. For information on relative positioning, see page 234.

Example:

```
<IMG SRC="backdrop.gif" STYLE="z-index: -1">
```

Netscape Navigator's `<LAYER>` tag also allows you to absolutely position elements. Use the `<LAYER>` tag to divide the elements on your Web page into layers, with the elements between each `<LAYER>` and `</LAYER>` tag making up one layer. To absolutely position a layer, use the `TOP` and `LEFT` attributes to specify a distance in pixels from the top and left edges of a Web browser window. The `WIDTH` and `HEIGHT` attributes allow you to specify the dimensions for a layer in pixels. If layers overlap, use the `Z-INDEX` attribute to specify the order you want the layers to overlap.

Example:

```
<LAYER TOP="40" LEFT="100" WIDTH="250" HEIGHT="100"
Z-INDEX="1">Latest Stories<IMG SRC="newspaper.gif">
</LAYER>
```

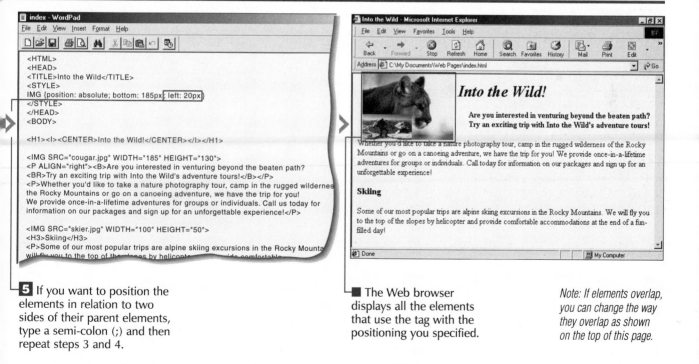

5 If you want to position the elements in relation to two sides of their parent elements, type a semi-colon (;) and then repeat steps 3 and 4.

■ The Web browser displays all the elements that use the tag with the positioning you specified.

Note: If elements overlap, you can change the way they overlap as shown on the top of this page.

SPECIFY KEYWORDS

The <META> tag allows you to specify keywords to help search tools catalog your Web page.

Search tools are Web sites that help users find information of interest on the Web. Popular search tools include Yahoo! (www.yahoo.com) and Lycos (www.lycos.com). When users enter words in a search tool that match your keywords, your Web page will be more likely to appear in the search results.

The best keywords are simple, common words that accurately describe your Web page. Using both general and specific keywords can help increase the probability that the words users enter in a search tool will match your keywords. For example, if your Web page contains information about corvettes, use the keywords "car" and "corvette." You may also want to include misspelled words that users may type, such as "corvete."

Including many keywords will not necessarily increase the probability that your Web page will appear in the search results. It is more important to carefully select the keywords that you predict users will enter.

SPECIFY KEYWORDS

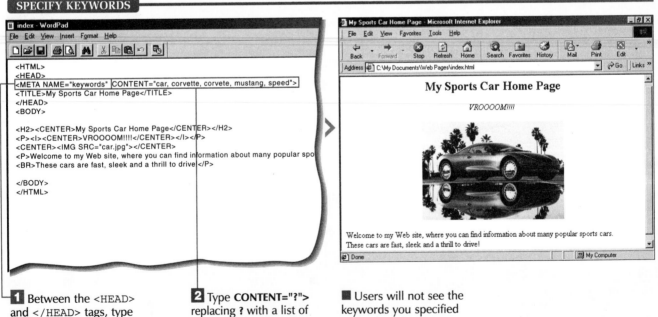

1 Between the <HEAD> and </HEAD> tags, type **<META NAME="keywords"** and then add a blank space.

2 Type **CONTENT="?">** replacing **?** with a list of keywords that describe your Web page. Separate each keyword with a comma and a blank space.

■ Users will not see the keywords you specified when they view your Web page.

SPECIFY A WEB PAGE SUMMARY

The <META> tag allows you to specify a summary that you want search tools to display when they find your Web page. A search tool is a Web site that helps users quickly find information on the Web. Popular search tools include Yahoo! (www.yahoo.com) and Lycos (www.lycos.com).

If you do not specify a summary for your Web page, search tools will use text from the top of your Web page for the summary. This may be confusing for users, particularly if the top

of your Web page contains a banner or a list of links rather than a summary.

When specifying a summary for your Web page, limit the summary to one or two sentences. Most search tools will not display more than three lines for a summary. A concise, descriptive summary can help convince users to visit your Web pages.

The summary you specify using the <META> tag will not appear on your Web page.

SPECIFY A WEB PAGE SUMMARY

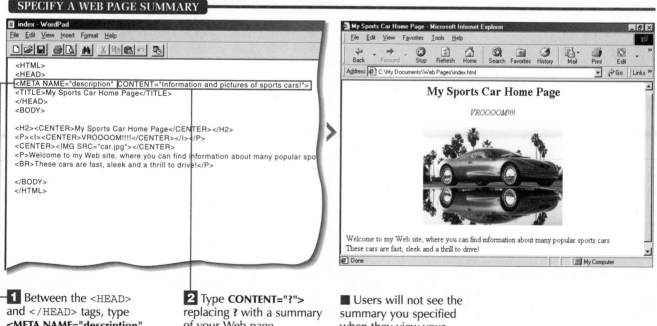

1 Between the <HEAD> and </HEAD> tags, type **<META NAME="description"** and then add a blank space.

2 Type **CONTENT="?">** replacing **?** with a summary of your Web page.

■ Users will not see the summary you specified when they view your Web page.

SPECIFY AUTHOR AND COPYRIGHT INFORMATION

The `<META>` tag lets you specify information about your Web page, including the name of the author and a copyright statement.

When specifying the name of the author, you may also want to include the names of any people who helped create the Web page.

When specifying copyright information, you should include the year of the copyright and the name of the person or company that holds the copyright. Specifying copyright information lets you indicate that you do not want people to copy the contents of your Web page without your permission.

The author and copyright information you specify will not appear on your Web page. Only users who view the HTML code for your Web page will see the information. For information on viewing the HTML code for a Web page, see page 9.

Extra

Some people use the `<META>` tag to provide information about the program they used to create a Web page. Type **<META NAME= "generator" CONTENT="?">** replacing **?** with information about the program, such as the name of the program.

Example:

`<META NAME="generator" CONTENT="WordPad">`

SPECIFY AUTHOR

```
index - WordPad
File  Edit  View  Insert  Format  Help

<HTML>
<HEAD>
<TITLE>Grape Expectations</TITLE>
<META NAME="author"  CONTENT="Rosemary Baker">
</HEAD>
<BODY>

<H1>Grape Expectations</H1>

<H4><CENTER><I>A guide to homemade wine-making for the wine connoisseur!</
</CENTER></H4>

<P><IMG SRC="barrel.gif" HSPACE="10" VSPACE="10" ALIGN="left" WIDTH="80"
HEIGHT="110">Welcome to our Web site about wine-making. Our names are Rosema
and Alan Baker, and we have been making our own wine for 20 years. Currently we
have over 200 bottles of homemade wine in our wine cellar. These pages contain
everything you need to know to make your own red, white or blush wine, including the
equipment you need, what kind of grapes you should buy and tips and tricks to make
your wine the best you've ever tasted! So jump right in and don't be afraid to have <
Grape Expectations!</I></P>

<P><IMG SRC="grapes.gif"><B><A HREF="equipment.html">Equipment</A>&nb
```

1 Between the `<HEAD>` and `</HEAD>` tags, type **<META NAME="author"** and then add a blank space.

2 Type **CONTENT="?">** replacing **?** with the name of the person who created the Web page.

SPECIFY COPYRIGHT INFORMATION

```
index - WordPad
File  Edit  View  Insert  Format  Help

<HTML>
<HEAD>
<TITLE>Grape Expectations</TITLE>
<META NAME="author" CONTENT="Rosemary Baker">
<META NAME="copyright"  CONTENT="2000 Grape Expectations">
</HEAD>
<BODY>

<H1>Grape Expectations</H1>

<H4><CENTER><I>A guide to homemade wine-making for the wine connoisseur!</
</CENTER></H4>

<P><IMG SRC="barrel.gif" HSPACE="10" VSPACE="10" ALIGN="left" WIDTH="80"
HEIGHT="110">Welcome to our Web site about wine-making. Our names are Rosema
and Alan Baker, and we have been making our own wine for 20 years. Currently we
have over 200 bottles of homemade wine in our wine cellar. These pages contain
everything you need to know to make your own red, white or blush wine, including the
equipment you need, what kind of grapes you should buy and tips and tricks to make
your wine the best you've ever tasted! So jump right in and don't be afraid to have <
Grape Expectations!</I></P>
```

1 Between the `<HEAD>` and `</HEAD>` tags, type **<META NAME="copyright"** and then add a blank space.

2 Type **CONTENT="?">** replacing **?** with the year of the copyright and the name of the person or company who holds the copyright.

SPECIFY AN EXPIRY DATE

The <META> tag allows you to specify an expiry date for your Web page to help ensure that users will see the latest version of the page. This is useful if your Web page contains information that is regularly updated, such as news articles.

When a user displays a Web page, a copy of the page is stored in the temporary memory, or cache, on their computer. The next time the user displays the Web page, the user's Web browser may redisplay the stored copy rather than retrieving a new copy from the Web server. Providing an expiry date allows you to specify

when you want a Web browser to retrieve a new copy of your Web page from the Web server.

The format for expiry dates is standardized to ensure that Web browsers will be able to recognize the date (example: Tues, 6 Jun 2001 21:59:59 GMT). Some parts of the date, such as the weekday or time, may be omitted.

Search tools may also use the expiry date you specify. When search tools find your Web page, they create a record of the page in their index. After the expiry date passes, search tools may remove your Web page from their index.

SPECIFY AN EXPIRY DATE

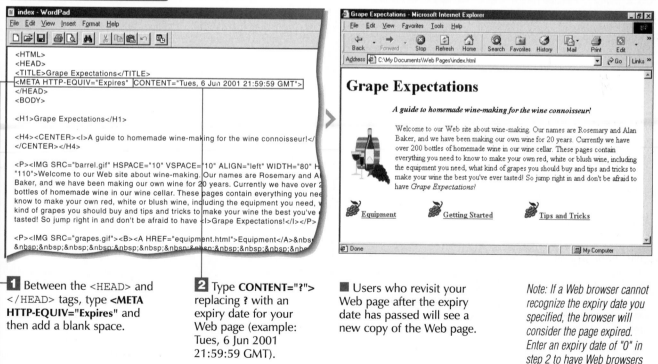

1 Between the <HEAD> and </HEAD> tags, type **<META HTTP-EQUIV="Expires"** and then add a blank space.

2 Type **CONTENT="?">** replacing **?** with an expiry date for your Web page (example: Tues, 6 Jun 2001 21:59:59 GMT).

■ Users who revisit your Web page after the expiry date has passed will see a new copy of the Web page.

Note: If a Web browser cannot recognize the expiry date you specified, the browser will consider the page expired. Enter an expiry date of "0" in step 2 to have Web browsers always retrieve the latest copy of your Web page.

PREVENT ROBOTS FROM INDEXING A WEB PAGE

Many search tools use programs, called *robots* or *spiders*, to find new and updated pages on the Web. The <META> tag allows you to prevent most robots from indexing your Web page. This is useful when you have created a Web page for a specific audience, such as your family or company, and do not want other people to access the Web page.

Use the noindex value to prevent robots from indexing a Web page and the nofollow value to prevent robots from indexing any Web pages linked to the page. The nofollow value is useful when

your Web page includes links to Web pages created by friends or colleagues who do not want their pages indexed.

If you later decide that you want robots to index either your Web page or any linked Web pages, make sure that you remove the appropriate value(s) from your HTML document.

If your Web page has already been indexed, you may want to remove the Web page from a search tool. Most search tools include a Web page that allows you to remove your Web pages from their index.

PREVENT ROBOTS FROM INDEXING A WEB PAGE

```
<HTML>
<HEAD>
<TITLE>Smith Family Home Page</TITLE>
<META NAME="robots"  CONTENT="noindex, nofollow">
</HEAD>
<BODY>

<H1><CENTER>Welcome Smith Family Members and Friends!</CENTER></H1>
<P>The Smith Family has grown over the years, and now we have created a Web site
in touch and update each other about family events.
<BR>It will be updated regularly, and anyone who would like to post some family-relat
should contact the
<A HREF="mailto:webmaster@smithfamily.com">Webmaster</A>.</P>

<H3>New Addition!</H3>
<P>There is a new addition to the Smith family! Mike and Janet Smith have given birth
baby boy named Justin. He is doing very well. Congratulations!</P>

</BODY>
</HTML>
```

Welcome Smith Family Members and Friends!

The Smith Family has grown over the years, and now we have created a Web site to keep in touch and update each other about family events.
It will be updated regularly, and anyone who would like to post some family-related news should contact the Webmaster.

New Addition!

There is a new addition to the Smith family! Mike and Janet Smith have given birth to a baby boy named Justin. He is doing very well. Congratulations!

1 Between the <HEAD> and </HEAD> tags, type **<META NAME="robots"** and then add a blank space.

2 Type **CONTENT="noindex,** to prevent robots from indexing your Web page. Then add a blank space.

3 Type **nofollow">** to prevent robots from indexing any Web pages linked to your Web page.

■ When users view your Web page, the information you specified to prevent robots from indexing the page will not appear.

WEB PRESENCE PROVIDERS

Web presence providers are companies that make Web pages available on the Web. Web presence providers store Web pages on computers called Web servers. Web servers monitor and control access to Web pages.

To find a Web presence provider that suits your needs, try performing a search for "Web hosting" or "Web services" in a search tool or check your local yellow pages. You may also want to ask other Web page authors which Web presence provider they recommend.

TYPES OF WEB PRESENCE PROVIDERS

Internet Service Providers

Internet service providers are companies that offer people access to the Internet. Most Internet service providers offer at least 5 Megabytes (MB) of space on their Web servers where customers can publish their Web pages free of charge. Many Internet service providers also offer additional options for a fee. These options may include extra mailboxes for e-mail messages, improved technical support and CGI script hosting.

Commercial Online Services

Commercial online services such as America Online will publish Web pages customers create free of charge. Many commercial online services offer easy-to-use programs to help people create and publish Web pages.

Free Web Presence Providers

Many companies on the Web will publish your Web pages for free. These companies offer a limited amount of storage space and may place advertisements on your Web pages. Free Web presence providers may also offer limited technical support and impose restrictions on the size and content of your Web pages. Companies such as Yahoo! GeoCities (geocities.yahoo.com), Tripod (www.tripod.lycos.com) and Xoom.com (xoom.com) are examples of free Web presence providers.

Dedicated Web Presence Providers

Dedicated Web presence providers are companies that specialize in publishing Web pages for a fee. Dedicated Web presence providers are flexible and offer features that other Web presence providers do not offer such as advanced support for multimedia. Popular dedicated Web presence providers include Hostess Web Hosting (www.hostess.com), pair Networks (www.pair.com) and DreamHost (www.dreamhost.com).

Your Own Web Server

Purchasing your own Web server is the most expensive way to publish Web pages and requires you to set up a full-time connection to the Internet using a connection such as a DSL (Digital Subscriber Line) or a cable modem. Setting up and maintaining your own Web server is difficult but will give you the greatest amount of control over your Web pages.

CHOOSE A WEB PRESENCE PROVIDER

Technical Support

A Web presence provider should have a technical support department to answer your questions. You should be able to contact the department by telephone or by e-mail. A good technical support department will respond to questions you send by e-mail within a day.

Traffic Limit

When users view your Web pages, information transfers from the Web server to their computers. The amount of information that transfers depends on the number of users who view your Web pages and the total file size of your pages. Most Web presence providers limit the amount of information that can transfer in one day. If the limit is exceeded, you may have to pay extra. You should choose a Web presence provider that allows at least 50 Megabytes (MB) of information to transfer in one day.

Reliability

Make sure the Web presence provider you choose is reliable. A Web presence provider should be able to tell you how often their Web servers shut down. You may also want to ask a Web presence provider for customer references that you can contact. Keep in mind that all Web presence providers occasionally shut down their servers for maintenance and upgrades.

Storage Space

Most Web presence providers limit the amount of storage space you can use. Choose a Web presence provider that allows you to store at least 5 Megabytes (MB) of information. If your Web pages contain many large multimedia files, such as sounds and videos, you may want to consider a Web presence provider that will allow you to purchase additional storage space.

Available Bandwidth

Bandwidth is the amount of data that can be transferred in a set amount of time. A Web presence provider's bandwidth is determined by the speed of its connections to the Internet. A high bandwidth can help decrease the amount of time users spend waiting to view your Web pages. Keep in mind that the maximum bandwidth of a Web presence provider is not as important as the amount of bandwidth that is available. You should ensure that a Web presence provider has enough available bandwidth to suit your Web site's needs.

Access Logs

A good Web presence provider will supply you with statistics about your Web pages, such as where your users are from. You may also be able to view any error messages users have seen when viewing your Web pages, such as "Page Not Found." These statistics can help you determine if you need to make changes to your Web pages.

WEB PRESENCE PROVIDER CONSIDERATIONS (CONTINUED)

Domain Name Registration

Your Web page address, or domain name, is usually the name of your Web presence provider followed by the path to your Web pages on their Web server. For a fee, most Web presence providers will register a personalized domain name for you. A personalized domain name is easy to remember and will not change if you switch to another Web presence provider. Visit the www.networksolutions.com Web site to determine if the domain name you want to use has already been registered.

Secure Web Servers

Many Web presence providers offer secure Web servers, which allow you to publish Web pages that request confidential information from users, such as credit card information. Secure Web servers use software to encode confidential information that transfers between users and the Web server.

Shopping Software

If you plan to use your Web pages to sell products on the Web, consider a Web presence provider that offers shopping software. Shopping software helps you create Web pages that accept orders, verify credit card numbers, generate invoices and organize product shipments.

Web Server Features

When choosing a Web presence provider, consider the Web server features that the provider offers. For example, if your Web pages include forms that require custom CGI scripts, the Web server you use must allow you to upload and use your own CGI scripts. If your Web pages include advanced features such as streaming multimedia files, the Web server must support these features for your Web pages to work properly.

Database Access

Consider choosing a Web presence provider that lets you use a database on the Web server. A database program gives users access to a large amount of information. Databases can be used to implement applications that manipulate large amounts of data, such as Web-based bulletin boards and online shopping systems.

Shell Access

Shell access allows you to edit Web pages directly on a Web server. This is faster than editing the pages on your computer and then transferring the updated pages to the Web server. Shell access lets you edit your Web pages from any computer connected to the Internet, which is useful if you plan to update your Web pages from more than one location.

TRANSFER WEB PAGES TO A WEB SERVER

Y ou must transfer your Web pages to a Web server to make the pages available on the Web.

You need a File Transfer Protocol (FTP) program to transfer your Web pages to a Web server. Popular FTP programs include WS_FTP Pro for Windows and Fetch for Macintosh. In the example below, we use WS_FTP Pro version 6.5.

Before you can transfer Web pages to a Web server, you must set up a connection to the Web server. You only need to set up a connection to a Web server once. After you set up a connection, you can connect to the Web server at any time.

To set up a connection to a Web server, you must know the address of the server, your user ID and your password. If you do not know this information, contact your Web presence provider.

Many FTP programs allow you to save your password, which prevents you from having to retype your password each time you transfer Web pages to your Web server. When you save your password, anyone who uses your computer will be able to connect to your Web server, so you should not save your password if other people will have access to your computer.

SET UP A CONNECTION

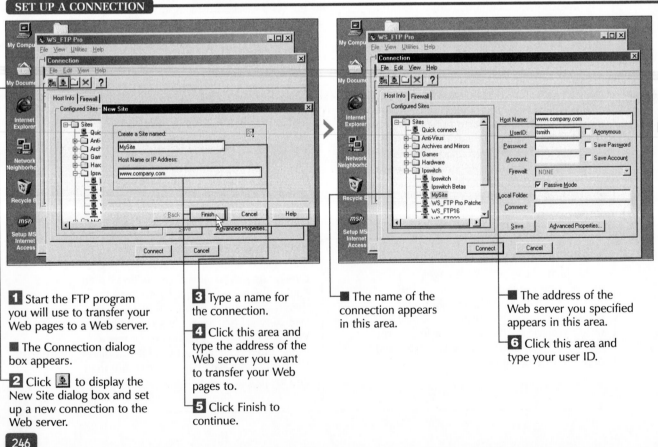

1 Start the FTP program you will use to transfer your Web pages to a Web server.

■ The Connection dialog box appears.

2 Click 🔳 to display the New Site dialog box and set up a new connection to the Web server.

3 Type a name for the connection.

4 Click this area and type the address of the Web server you want to transfer your Web pages to.

5 Click Finish to continue.

■ The name of the connection appears in this area.

■ The address of the Web server you specified appears in this area.

6 Click this area and type your user ID.

Extra

You can obtain the latest version of WS_FTP Pro at the www.ipswitch.com Web site. Fetch is available at the www.dartmouth.edu/pages/sofdev/fetch.html Web site.

You can create a new folder to store and organize your Web server connections. In the Configured Sites area of the Connection dialog box, click the folder you want to store the new subfolder. If you want to create a main folder, click the Sites folder. Then click ☐ to create the folder. In the New Folder dialog box, type the name of the new folder and then click Finish.

FTP programs allow you to set up multiple connections. This is useful if you want to use one connection to transfer your Web pages to a Web server and another connection to download files from a different Web server. Perform steps 1 to 9 below for each connection you want to set up.

You can delete a connection you no longer need. Click the connection in the Configured Sites area of the Connection dialog box and then click ☒ to delete the connection. Click Yes in the dialog box that appears to confirm the deletion.

CONNECT TO WEB SERVER

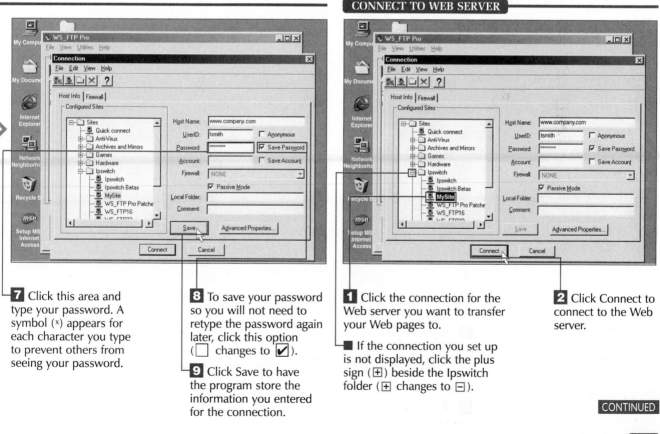

7 Click this area and type your password. A symbol (×) appears for each character you type to prevent others from seeing your password.

8 To save your password so you will not need to retype the password again later, click this option (☐ changes to ☑).

9 Click Save to have the program store the information you entered for the connection.

1 Click the connection for the Web server you want to transfer your Web pages to.

■ If the connection you set up is not displayed, click the plus sign (⊞) beside the Ipswitch folder (⊞ changes to ⊟).

2 Click Connect to connect to the Web server.

CONTINUED ▶

TRANSFER WEB PAGES TO A WEB SERVER (CONTINUED)

Once you have connected to a Web server, you can transfer information to the server.

You can transfer a single file, multiple files or an entire folder to the Web server at once. Before you transfer files and folders to a Web server, you must locate the folder on the server you want to transfer your files and folders to. This folder is often named "public." If you do not know the name of the folder, contact your Web presence provider.

If your connection to the Web server is idle for an extended period of time, the server

may automatically disconnect you. This helps ensure that the Web server's resources are available for other people who need to access the server.

If you later make changes to the Web pages stored on your computer, you must transfer the updated pages to the Web server. The updated Web pages will replace the old Web pages on the server. When you transfer updated pages, a message may appear indicating that the updated pages will replace the old pages.

TRANSFER WEB PAGES TO A WEB SERVER

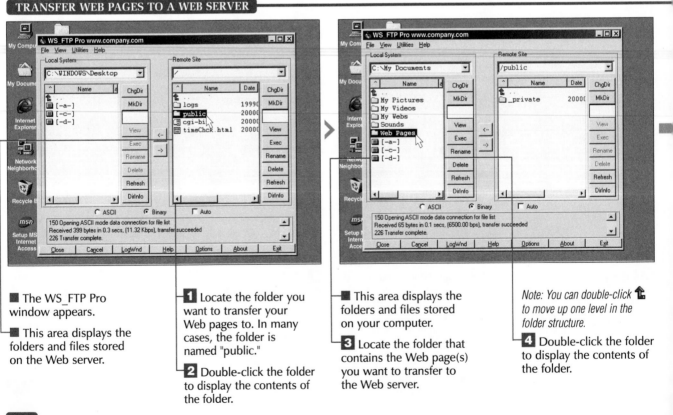

■ The WS_FTP Pro window appears.

■ This area displays the folders and files stored on the Web server.

1 Locate the folder you want to transfer your Web pages to. In many cases, the folder is named "public."

2 Double-click the folder to display the contents of the folder.

■ This area displays the folders and files stored on your computer.

3 Locate the folder that contains the Web page(s) you want to transfer to the Web server.

Note: You can double-click 🔼 *to move up one level in the folder structure.*

4 Double-click the folder to display the contents of the folder.

Extra

You should check all references to files on your Web pages before transferring the pages to a Web server. For example, if an image on a Web page is stored in the same folder as the Web page, make sure you specified just the name of the image (example: banner.gif). If the image is stored in a subfolder, make sure you specified the location and name of the image (example: images/banner.gif).

Before transferring your Web pages to a Web server, you should make sure the Web page file names all have the .html or .htm extension and do not include spaces or special characters, such as * or &. You should also check with your Web presence provider to ensure that you have used the correct name for your home page.

If you have accidentally transferred a file to the Web server, you should delete the file from the server. This helps save storage space on the Web server. To delete a file from the Web server, select the file in the right pane of the WS_FTP Pro window and then click the Delete button. Click Yes in the dialog box that appears to confirm the deletion.

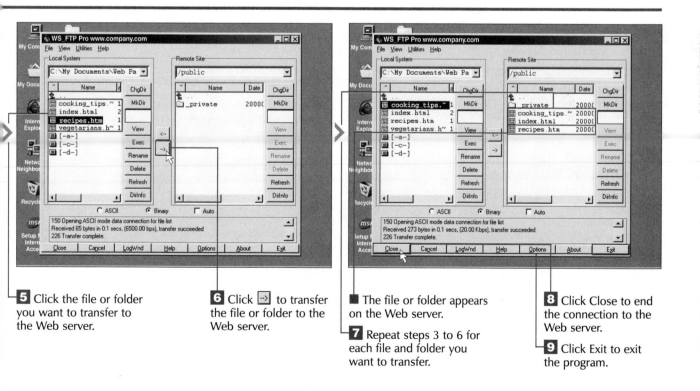

5 Click the file or folder you want to transfer to the Web server.

6 Click → to transfer the file or folder to the Web server.

■ The file or folder appears on the Web server.

7 Repeat steps 3 to 6 for each file and folder you want to transfer.

8 Click Close to end the connection to the Web server.

9 Click Exit to exit the program.

TEST YOUR WEB PAGES

Once you have published your Web pages, you should test the pages to make sure that they look and work the way you planned. Verify that users will be able to easily browse through your information. You should also make sure that your Web pages have a consistent design and writing style and do not contain any formatting or layout errors.

TEST YOUR WEB PAGES

Check Links

Check the links on your Web pages to make sure that they will take users to the intended destinations. Visit the linked Web pages regularly to make sure that they still exist and contain useful information. Users will become frustrated if they select a link that is no longer relevant or displays an error message.

Use a Validation Service

A validation service can check your Web pages for HTML errors. Validation services are useful even if your Web pages appear to work properly, since invalid HTML code may cause future problems. Validation services are available at the validator.w3.org and www2.imagiware.com/RxHTML Web sites.

Try Different Transfer Speeds

Determine how long your Web pages will take to appear at different transfer speeds. Many people use modems that transfer information at 56 Kbps, but slower modems are still common. Web pages with large file sizes may take a long time to transfer.

Turn Off Images

Some users turn off the display of images to browse the Web more quickly, while others use text-based Web browsers that cannot display images. You should view your Web pages without images to ensure that users who do not see images will find your pages useful.

View at Different Resolutions

The resolution of a monitor determines the amount of information that will appear on a screen. View your Web pages using common resolutions, such as 640x480 and 800x600, to determine if your information will fit properly on most screens.

View in Different Web Browsers

View your Web pages in different Web browsers. Each Web browser will display your Web pages in a slightly different way. Test your Web pages with the two most popular Web browsers–Microsoft Internet Explorer and Netscape Navigator.

View on Different Computers

Web pages can look different when displayed on different types of computers, such as a PC or Macintosh. View your Web pages on different computers to ensure that the pages will appear the way you planned and that multimedia you added to your Web pages will work correctly.

PUBLICIZE YOUR WEB PAGES

O nce you have published your Web pages, you should let people know about the pages. There are several ways to publicize your Web pages.

PUBLICIZE YOUR WEB PAGES

E-mail Messages

Most e-mail programs offer a feature, called a signature, that allows you to add the same information to the end of every e-mail message you send. Include a link to your Web pages in your signature to publicize the pages in all your e-mail messages.

Exchange Links

If another Web page discusses topics similar to yours, ask the author to include a link to your Web pages if you do the same. This allows people reading the other Web page to easily visit your Web pages.

Join a Web Ring

A Web ring is a group of related Web sites that are all linked together. Each site in a Web ring publicizes the other sites in the ring. Use a search tool such as Yahoo! (www.yahoo.com) to find a Web ring related to the topic of your Web pages.

Web Page Advertisements

Many companies set aside areas on their Web pages where you can advertise your Web pages. The LinkExchange helps you advertise your Web pages free of charge. The LinkExchange is located at the adnetwork.linkexchange.com Web site.

Newsgroups

Post an announcement about your Web pages to discussion groups on the Internet called newsgroups. Make sure you choose newsgroups that discuss topics related to your Web pages. Many people announce new and updated Web pages in the comp.infosystems.www.announce newsgroup.

Mailing Lists

Send an announcement about your Web pages to carefully selected mailing lists on the Internet. A mailing list is a discussion group that communicates through e-mail. You should read the messages in a mailing list before sending an announcement to ensure that the members will be interested in your Web pages. A directory of mailing lists is available at the www.liszt.com Web site.

Search Tools

Submit your Web pages to search tools to help users find the pages. Popular search tools include AltaVista (www.altavista.com) and Yahoo! (www.yahoo.com). You may also want to submit your Web pages to specialized search tools that feature Web sites about a specific topic, such as HumorSearch (www.humorsearch.com).

To submit your Web pages to many search tools at once, visit the www.submit-it.com or www.submiturl.com Web site.

TROUBLESHOOT YOUR WEB PAGES

I f your Web pages do not appear the way you expect when you display the pages in a Web browser, there are several common HTML errors you can check for to troubleshoot the problem. Locating errors in a Web page can be difficult, since Web browsers display pages containing incorrect HTML code as best as they can rather than generating error messages.

COMMON ERRORS

Typing Errors

Typing errors are the most common errors in HTML code. Web browsers usually ignore HTML tags and attributes they do not recognize, so mistyped HTML code is usually ignored. For example, if you type `<A HERF="webpage.html">` for a link instead of `<A HREF="webpage.html">`, the link will not appear on your Web page.

Missing Quotation Marks or Angle Brackets

If you forget to type a closing quotation mark for a value or a closing angle bracket for a tag, Web browsers will not know where the information for the value or tag ends. This may cause Web browsers to omit a section of your Web page or display the HTML code on your Web page.

Missing End Tags

While some end tags are optional in HTML, such as the `</P>` tag, others are necessary to properly display elements. For example, if you leave off the `</FONT>` tag, Web browsers will not know when to stop formatting text on your Web page using the font settings you specified.

Incorrect Path

When adding some elements to your Web page, such as a link or an image, you must specify the location and name of the file for the element. If you specify the incorrect path, Web browsers will not be able to locate the information.

Incorrect Extension

If you specify the incorrect extension when adding an element such as an image or sound to your Web page, the element will not appear on the page. For example, if you use the .gif extension for an image that is saved using the .jpg extension, a Web browser will not be able to locate and display the image file.

Unsupported HTML Code

Even if your HTML code does not contain errors, your Web page may not appear correctly in a Web browser if the browser does not yet support the code you are using. For example, some features of style sheets are not yet fully supported by Web browsers.

Missing Images

If an image does not appear on your Web page, check the file name of the image. Make sure you spelled the name correctly, using the correct uppercase and lowercase letters. You should also verify that you are using the proper extension in the file name and that the image is saved in a format that Web browsers support, such as JPEG or GIF.

Sounds or Videos Do Not Play

A Web browser's ability to play sounds and videos depends on the plug-ins that are installed for the browser. A plug-in is software that adds features to a Web browser. If you are having difficulty playing a sound or video, make sure that your Web browser has the correct plug-ins. You should also verify that you successfully transferred the sound or video file to your Web server and that you specified the correct path for the sound or video file in your HTML code.

The Web Browser Cannot Find Your Web Page

If an error message appears stating that your Web page cannot be found, you may have placed your Web page in the wrong directory on the Web server. Contact your Web presence provider to confirm where you should store your Web pages. You should also make sure that you have given your home page the correct name. Home pages are usually named index.html.

The Web Browser Displays Your HTML Code

If you did not save your Web page with the .html or .htm extension, some Web browsers will display your HTML code. Check that you did not accidentally give your Web page the .txt extension. Some word processors may automatically add the .txt extension to your Web page file. You should also make sure that you used the <HTML> tag on your Web page. Without this tag, a Web browser may not recognize your document as a Web page.

The Web Browser Displays a Blank Screen

If your Web browser displays a blank screen, you may have a missing or incorrectly typed end tag for a large element such as a table (</TABLE>) or frameset (</FRAMESET>). You should also check HTML tags that appear in the head section of your Web page. For example, if the <STYLE> tag is incomplete or misspelled, your Web page may appear blank in a Web browser window.

INTRODUCTION TO XML

**Like HTML, Extensible Markup Language (XML)
is a computer language that builds on previous
languages, including SGML. XML provides a
more flexible method for creating Web documents
than HTML.**

WHAT IS SGML?

Standard Generalized Markup Language (SGML) is
a very powerful and complex language that allows
authors to create their own custom markup languages.
Using SGML, an author can specify the types of
information contained in a document and create rules
to ensure that the document maintains a rigid format.
This ensures that any user or program accessing the
document will understand the content and structure
of the document, making the document easier to
work with and share.

SGML is a complex system that has been in
development for over 20 years. Due to its complexity,
SGML is not widely used. Organizations that use
SGML include governments and companies that
regularly process large amounts of text data.

WHAT IS XML?

XML is a subset of SGML that was developed with
a strong emphasis on creating documents for the
Web. XML is much easier to learn and use than
SGML, yet still allows authors to access some of
the power of SGML.

Like SGML, XML allows authors to create their
own markup languages that define the content
of documents. XML uses a tag system similar to
the tags used in HTML, though XML allows authors
to create and define rules for their own tags. For
example, when creating a document that lists
addresses, an XML author may want to create tags
such as <street>, <city>, <country> and
<zip> to structure the XML document.

XML AND HTML

HTML was originally created as a simple markup
language for specifying the structure and content of
information in Web documents. As the Web and Web
browsers became more popular, HTML evolved into
more of a formatting markup language used to specify
the layout and appearance of Web documents.

XML allows Web authors to once again focus on
structure, leaving the formatting of documents to
other methods, such as style sheets.

HTML can be regarded as a subset of XML and will
coexist with XML on the Web. HTML documents
will continue to be the primary method of creating
Web pages for years to come.

CREATING XML DOCUMENTS

XML documents are text documents that are often created using a text editor or word processor. In its simplest form, an XML document consists of processing instructions, markup tags and data. There are programs available, called XML editors, that can help you create XML documents. Microsoft XML Notepad is an XML editor for Windows-based computers that is available at the msdn.microsoft.com/xml/notepad Web site.

Microsoft XML Notepad

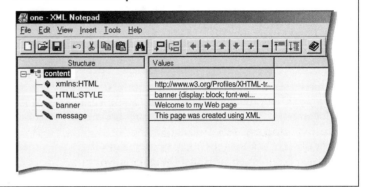

EXTENSIBLE STYLESHEET LANGUAGE

One of the disadvantages of using XML documents on the Web is that XML itself does not provide a method for telling Web browsers how to display information. The World Wide Web Consortium (W3C) recommends using Extensible Stylesheet Language (XSL) to format XML documents for display in Web browsers and other processing programs. XSL is not yet widely supported by Web browsers. You can find more information about XSL at the www.w3.org/TR/xsl Web site.

CASCADING STYLE SHEETS

Since XSL is not yet widely supported, Cascading Style Sheets (CSS) are commonly used to apply formatting to XML documents. Using CSS with an XML document is similar to using style sheets with an HTML document. Since many Web browsers already support CSS, this method provides an immediate way to specify the formatting and layout for an XML document.

DOCUMENT TYPE DEFINITION

The Document Type Definition (DTD) for an XML document is the set of specifications for the custom markup language used in the document. A DTD identifies the type of information each tag in the document can enclose.

Once an XML author has created a DTD for a document, the author can share the DTD with other programs and users. For example, a company may want to share a DTD with its suppliers so that the company and suppliers can easily exchange information using the same markup language. There are many DTDs available on the Internet. For example, DTDs are available at the www.xml.org/xmlorg_registry Web site.

INTRODUCTION TO XML (CONTINUED)

PROCESSING XML DOCUMENTS

Documents you create using XML are of little use unless there is a program available that can process the documents. Currently, most processing programs are custom programs that XML authors create specifically for their documents. Using a customized processing program ensures that the program will be able to recognize the tags an author created.

In the future, many more standard programs such as word processors, spreadsheets and presentation programs will be able to create and process XML documents. These programs may allow authors to create XML documents without having to learn XML, similar to the way visual editors do not require authors to learn HTML.

WEB BROWSERS AS PROCESSING PROGRAMS

Unfortunately, most Web browsers do not yet fully understand XML and thus cannot process XML documents. This may change as new versions of Web browsers are released. Even when more Web browsers are able to process XML documents, creating XML documents will likely continue to be more difficult than creating HTML documents.

XML does not contain formatting instructions that a Web browser can use to determine how to display information as a formatted Web page. As a result, unless other methods are used, Web browsers that support XML currently display the code for an XML document rather than formatted elements. Since the XML specifications are not yet final, this may change in the future.

THE XML SPECIFICATION

The World Wide Web Consortium, referred to as the W3C, is made up of hundreds of organizations that have an interest in the future of the World Wide Web. The W3C sets the standards for various areas of the Web, such as HTML and XML. When the W3C issues a set of standards, they are referred to as specifications. These specifications help ensure that different technologies all use a common set of rules when accessing and creating content for the Web. The current XML specification is version 1.0 and is available at the www.w3.org/TR/1998/REC-xml-19980210.html Web site.

BENEFITS OF USING XML

Flexibility

Since XML allows authors to create their own tags to suit their needs, XML provides more flexibility than HTML. Authors do not need to rely on predefined tags to structure their documents.

Versatility

XML's emphasis on using tags to define the structure of a document allows Web authors to create versatile documents that can be easily modified for different audiences or processing programs. For example, editors and layout artists can both view the same document in different ways by using different DTDs. Each DTD will define rules for the same tags from the original document, but will give the tags different meanings.

Standardization

Many Web page authors dislike the lack of standardization offered by HTML. Since individual Web browsers all differ in the HTML tags they support and how they display supported tags, a Web page can look very different when viewed in different Web browsers. XML resolves this issue by giving authors control over the way their documents are presented rather than allowing Web browsers to determine how documents appear. The author of an XML document creates custom tags and then defines rules for the tags that processing programs must follow.

WHY LEARN XML NOW?

XML is now the preferred method for creating Web documents according to the W3C. Though XML is not yet fully supported by Web browsers, this will likely change in the next few years. Learning XML now will allow you to take advantage of the advanced features offered by XML as they become supported.

XML RESOURCES

There are many resources you can consult to learn more about XML, including *XML: Your visual blueprint for building expert Web pages* (ISBN 0-7645-3477-7), published by IDG Books Worldwide, Inc.

Web Sites		Newsgroups
Everything XML www.intraware.com/everything/xml/index.html	*The XML Cover Pages* www.oasis-open.org/cover/xml.html	comp.text.xml microsoft.public.xml
XML.com www.xml.com	*XML-L Mailing List* listserv.hea.ie/lists/xml-l.html	
The World Wide Web Consortium www.w3.org		

CREATE AN XML DECLARATION

To create an XML document, use a text editor or word processor, such as Microsoft WordPad or Corel WordPerfect. The first step for creating an XML document is entering an XML declaration.

An XML declaration is a processing instruction that appears on the first line of an XML document. The XML declaration provides information about the document for the Web browser or other program that will process the document. Processing instructions are enclosed in question marks and in greater than and less than symbols, such as <?XML?>.

The XML declaration is composed of several declarations, including a *version declaration*, an *encoding declaration* and a *standalone declaration*.

The version declaration tells the processing program which version of XML was used to create the document. The current version of XML is version 1.0.

The encoding declaration identifies the encoding scheme for the XML document to the processing program. The encoding scheme for a document depends largely on the language used in the document. For documents written in English, the encoding scheme UTF-8 is often used.

The standalone declaration tells the processing program whether the document requires the use of another document. If the document does not need to access information from another document, specify a value of yes for the standalone declaration.

CREATE AN XML DECLARATION

1 Start your text editor or word processor.

■ In this example, we use Microsoft WordPad.

2 Type **<??>**.

3 Click between the question marks.

4 Type **xml** to identify your document as an XML document.

5 Type **version=""**.

6 Click between the quotation marks.

7 Type the number for the XML version you are using.

Extra

The version, encoding and standalone declarations are optional, though it is considered proper form to at least include the version declaration. If you do not specify a version, encoding or standalone declaration, your document will use the following default values.

DECLARATION	DEFAULT VALUE
version	1.0
encoding	UTF-8
standalone	yes

XML version 1.0 is currently the only version of XML. As with HTML, features will be added and removed to create new versions of XML in the future. As new versions are created, the version declaration will become increasingly important, since processing programs will need to know which version of XML a document conforms to.

Currently, few Web browsers can process XML documents, although this will change as new versions of Web browsers are released. Microsoft's Internet Explorer version 5 or later is commonly used to view XML documents. You can obtain the latest version of Internet Explorer for free at the www.microsoft.com/ie Web site.

Document - WordPad
File Edit View Insert Format Help

`<?xml version="1.0" encoding="UTF-8"?>`

Document - WordPad
File Edit View Insert Format Help

`<?xml version="1.0" encoding="UTF-8" standalone="yes"?>`

8 Type **encoding=""**.

9 Click between the quotation marks.

10 Type the encoding scheme for the XML document.

11 Type **standalone=""**.

12 Click between the quotation marks.

13 Type **yes** to specify that the document does not require the use of another document.

CREATE ELEMENTS

The body of an XML document is composed of elements. An element consists of data surrounded by a start tag and an end tag.

Unlike HTML, XML allows you to create your own tags for elements. This provides you with greater flexibility, but means that processing programs must be able to interpret the tags.

The main element in an XML document is known as the root element. The start and end tags you assign to the root element surround all the other elements in the XML document, similar to the <HTML> and </HTML> tags in an HTML document.

Create other elements inside the root element by assigning start and end tags to the element and

then entering data between the tags. The elements you create should divide your document into structural sections. For example, create elements such as titles, subtitles and introductory text.

Save your XML document as a text document, using the .xml extension. You can then view the document in a Web browser. The browser will display the contents of the XML document. To have a Web browser display an XML document as a Web page, you must use another method, such as cascading style sheets. To use style sheets with XML, see page 262.

CREATE ELEMENTS

```
Document - WordPad
File  Edit  View  Insert  Format  Help

<?xml version="1.0" encoding="UTF-8" standalone="yes"?>
<content>

</content>
```

```
Document - WordPad
File  Edit  View  Insert  Format  Help

<?xml version="1.0" encoding="UTF-8" standalone="yes"?>
<content>
    <banner>
        Welcome to my Web page
    </banner>
</content>
```

1 Type the start tag you want to use for the root element of the document.

2 Type a corresponding end tag for the root element.

3 To create an element, click between the start and end tags for the root element.

4 Type the start tag you want to use for the new element.

5 Type a corresponding end tag for the element.

6 Type the text for the element between the start and end tags.

Extra

Displaying an XML document in a Web browser is useful for detecting any errors you may have made while creating the document. If a Web browser detects an error, the browser will display an error message and provide information about the location and type of the error.

IF YOU TYPE:

```
<?xml version="1.0" encoding="UTF-8" standalone="yes"?>
<content>
    <banner>
        Welcome to my Web page
    <message>
        This page is created using XML
    </message>
</content>
```

THIS ERROR MESSAGE APPEARS:

The XML page cannot be displayed

Cannot view XML input using XSL style sheet. Please correct the error and then click the Refresh button, or try again later.

End tag 'content' does not match the start tag 'banner'. Line 8, Position 3

```
</content>
--^
```

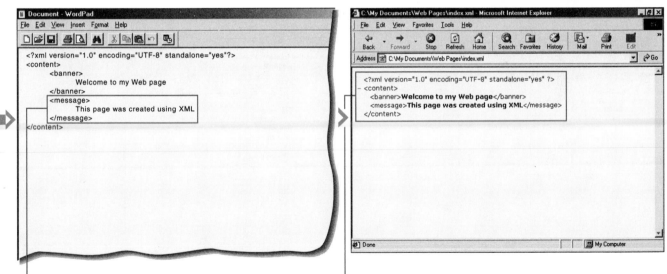

7 Repeat steps 3 to 6 for each element you want to create.

■ In this example, we create a page title and main text for the document.

8 Save the XML document as a text document with the .xml extension.

9 Display the XML document in a Web browser as you would display an HTML document in a Web browser.

■ The contents of the XML document appear.

Note: To display the contents of the XML document as a Web page, you must use another method, such as cascading style sheets. For more information, see page 262.

USE CASCADING STYLE SHEETS WITH XML

I f you want Web browsers to display your XML document as a formatted Web page, you must use a method such as *cascading style sheets* to help the browser interpret the contents of the document.

To use style sheets with an XML document, first create an xml-stylesheet processing instruction to identify the type of style sheet you are using to Web browsers. Then use XHTML to add style sheet information to the XML document. For more information on XHTML, see the top of page 263.

Before a Web browser can understand XHTML code, you must define an XHTML namespace. A namespace tells Web browsers where they can find information about the code in an XML document. To define an XHTML namespace, use the xmlns attribute to specify the location of the namespace. The W3C Web site provides a predefined XHTML namespace you can use.

Use the <HTML:style> tag to set up a style sheet using XHTML. You can then specify styles for the elements in your XML document as you would specify styles for elements in an HTML document.

USE CASCADING STYLE SHEETS WITH XML

```
index - WordPad
File  Edit  View  Insert  Format  Help

<?xml version="1.0" encoding="UTF-8" standalone="yes"?>
<?xml-stylesheet type="text/css"?>
<content xmlns:HTML="http://www.w3.org/Profiles/XHTML-transitional">

        <banner>
                Welcome to my Web page
        </banner>
        <message>
                This page was created using XML
        </message>
</content>
```

```
index - WordPad
File  Edit  View  Insert  Format  Help

<?xml version="1.0" encoding="UTF-8" standalone="yes"?>
<?xml-stylesheet type="text/css"?>
<content  xmlns:HTML="http://www.w3.org/Profiles/XHTML-transitional" >
        <HTML:style>
                banner {

        <banner>
                Welcome to my Web page
        </banner>
        <message>
                This page was created using XML
        </message>
</content>
```

1 After the XML declaration, type **<?xml-stylesheet type="text/ css"?>** to specify that you want to use a style sheet.

2 In the start tag for the root element, type **xmlns:HTML="http:// www.w3.org/Profiles/ XHTML-transitional"** to define the XHTML namespace.

3 Type **<HTML:style>** to mark the beginning of the style sheet.

4 Type the tag for an element you want to define styles for.

5 Type **{** to begin the style sheet properties for the tag.

XHTML is an attempt to convert HTML into a format that conforms to XML. This involves rewriting HTML, using the stricter set of rules provided by XML.

The current version of XHTML is version 1.0. This version combines the features of HTML version 4 with the rules of XML version 1.0. For example, XHTML uses the same tags as HTML, but requires that the tags be lowercase and that every tag use a closing tag, including tags that do not have closing tags in HTML.

XHTML is specifically designed to work with multiple types of processing programs, making it useful for creating documents that will be viewed on non-traditional devices, such as mobile phones, handheld computers and television set top boxes. Using non-traditional devices to access the Web is becoming increasingly popular.

For more information on XHTML, visit the www.w3.org/TR/xhtml1 Web site.

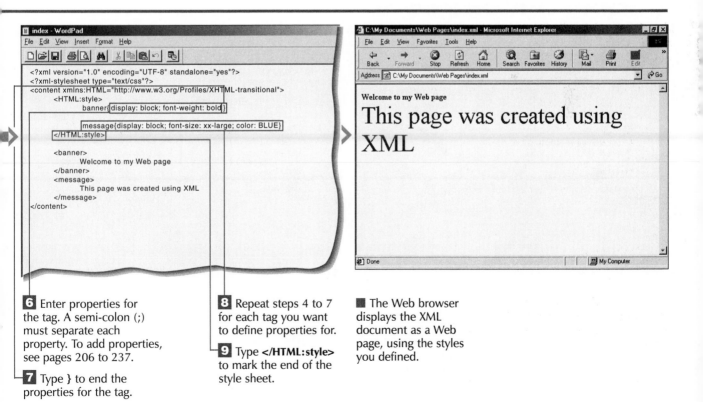

6 Enter properties for the tag. A semi-colon (;) must separate each property. To add properties, see pages 206 to 237.

7 Type } to end the properties for the tag.

8 Repeat steps 4 to 7 for each tag you want to define properties for.

9 Type **</HTML:style>** to mark the end of the style sheet.

■ The Web browser displays the XML document as a Web page, using the styles you defined.

CREATE A SIMPLE DOCUMENT TYPE DEFINITION

A major advantage of using XML is that it allows you to create your own custom tags that suit your specific needs. Create a Document Type Definition (DTD) to define rules for the tags you create.

A DTD appears at the beginning of an XML document, directly below the XML declaration. In a simple XML document, the <!DOCTYPE> tag contains the rules for every tag in the document. Use the <!ELEMENT> tag to specify the type of information each tag can contain.

When an XML document's content conforms to the specifications in its DTD, the XML document

is considered valid. Any content that does not conform to the DTD is considered invalid and may prevent the document from being processed by a Web browser or other processing program.

Some XML documents use external DTDs rather than internal DTDs as shown below. An external DTD is stored in a separate file rather than appearing at the beginning of an XML document. External DTDs are useful when you want to use the same set of rules for several XML documents.

CREATE A SIMPLE DOCUMENT TYPE DEFINITION

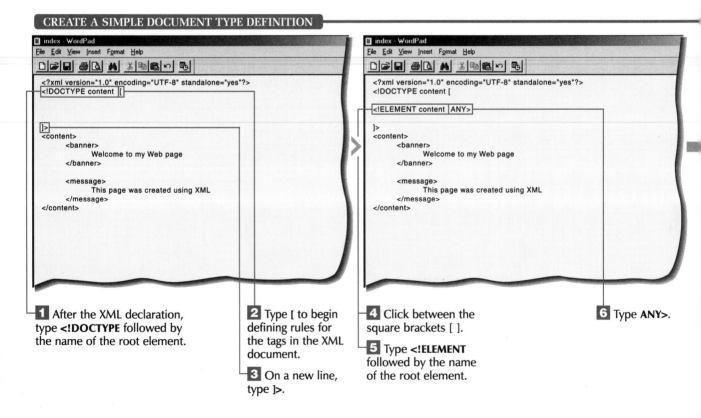

1 After the XML declaration, type **<!DOCTYPE** followed by the name of the root element.

2 Type **[** to begin defining rules for the tags in the XML document.

3 On a new line, type **]>**.

4 Click between the square brackets [ ].

5 Type **<!ELEMENT** followed by the name of the root element.

6 Type **ANY>**.

Extra

The `<!ELEMENT>` tag specifies the type of information that individual tags in your document can contain. Each element can use the following two major types of information.

ANY

Specifying the ANY type for a tag allows the tag to enclose any type of information, including text and other tags. The ANY type is usually only used for the root element.

#PCDATA

PCDATA stands for Parsed Character Data. Specifying the #PCDATA type for a tag allows the tag to enclose text but not other tags.

Web browsers do not yet support DTDs. You can display an XML document that contains a DTD in a Web browser, but the browser will not be able to detect any errors you may have made while creating the DTD. There are tools available on the Internet that you can use to validate a DTD you created. For example, use the cgi.w3.org/cgi-bin/xmlschema-check Web site to validate online XML documents.

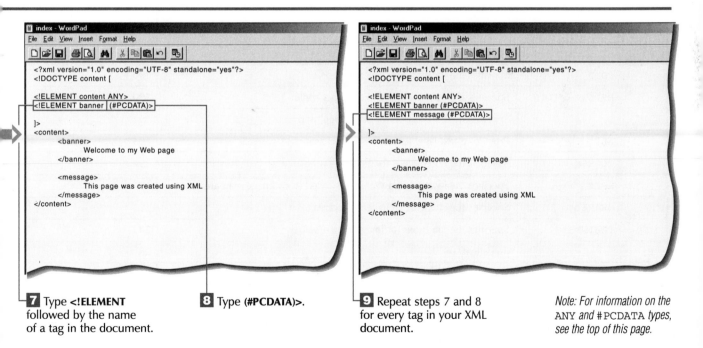

7 Type **<!ELEMENT** followed by the name of a tag in the document.

8 Type **(#PCDATA)>**.

9 Repeat steps 7 and 8 for every tag in your XML document.

Note: For information on the ANY and #PCDATA types, see the top of this page.

HTML TAG SUMMARY

TAG/ATTRIBUTE	DESCRIPTION	PAGE REFERENCES
MOST TAGS		
CLASS	Divides tags into groups for applying styles	202
ID	Identifies a specific tag	201
STYLE	Applies a style locally	200
TITLE	Adds tool tips to elements	181
<!DOCTYPE>	Identifies the HTML version used on a Web page	13
<A>	Creates a link	74, 76
ACCESSKEY	Adds a keyboard shortcut to a link	86
HREF	Specifies the location of linked information	74, 76
NAME	Names a Web page area	76
TABINDEX	Specifies the tab order for links	87
TARGET	Specifies a window or frame for a link	84, 148
<APPLET>	Adds a Java applet to a Web page	190
ARCHIVE	Specifies the location of a Java archive file	191
CODE	Specifies the location of a Java applet	190
HEIGHT, WIDTH	Specifies the height and width of a Java applet	190
<AREA>	Specifies the information for one image map area	194
ALT	Provides a text label for an image map area	195
COORDS	Specifies the coordinates for an image map area	194
HREF	Specifies the location of a Web page linked to an image map area	194
SHAPE	Specifies the shape of an image map area	194
TABINDEX	Specifies the tab order for image map areas	143
<B>	Bolds text	26
<BASE>	Sets the default window or frame for links	84, 148
TARGET	Specifies the window or frame links will open in	84, 148
<BASEFONT>	Changes the appearance of all text	30
SIZE	Changes the size of text	30
<BIG>	Makes text larger than the surrounding text	31

TAG/ATTRIBUTE	DESCRIPTION	PAGE REFERENCES
<BLOCKQUOTE>	Creates a block quote	37
<BODY>	Identifies the main content of a Web page	12
ALINK, LINK, VLINK	Changes the color of links	85
BACKGROUND	Adds a background image	46
BGCOLOR	Adds a background color	34
BGPROPERTIES	Specifies that a background image will not move when a user scrolls	182
BOTTOMMARGIN	Changes the bottom margin	35
LEFTMARGIN	Changes the left margin	35
MARGINHEIGHT	Changes the top and bottom margins	35
MARGINWIDTH	Changes the left and right margins	35
RIGHTMARGIN	Changes the right margin	35
TEXT	Changes the color of text	32
TOPMARGIN	Changes the top margin	35
 	Starts a new line	18
CLEAR	Stops text from wrapping	48, 110
<BUTTON>	Creates a button	137, 164
TYPE	Specifies the type of button	137, 164
<CAPTION>	Adds a caption to a table	91
ALIGN	Changes the alignment of a caption	91
<CENTER>	Centers elements on a Web page	27, 45
<CODE>	Identifies text as computer code	36
<COL>	Creates a non-structural column group in a table	92
ALIGN	Changes the horizontal alignment of data	98
BGCOLOR	Adds a background color	96
CHAR	Specifies a character to align	99
SPAN	Specifies the number of columns in a column group	92
VALIGN	Changes the vertical alignment of data	98

HTML TAG SUMMARY

TAG/ATTRIBUTE	DESCRIPTION	PAGE REFERENCES
<COLGROUP>	Creates a structural column group in a table	92
ALIGN	Changes the horizontal alignment of data	98
BGCOLOR	Adds a background color	96
CHAR	Specifies a character to align	99
SPAN	Specifies the number of columns in a column group	92
VALIGN	Changes the vertical alignment of data	98
<DD>	Identifies a definition in a definition list	43
<DEL>	Strikes out deleted text	27
<DIV>	Divides a Web page into areas for applying styles	204
CLASS	Identifies the style to use in a Web page area	205
<DL>	Creates a definition list	43
<DT>	Identifies a term in a definition list	43
<EM>	Emphasizes text using italics	27
<EMBED>	Adds a sound or video to a Web page	114, 118
ALIGN	Wraps text around a video	119
AUTOSTART	Plays a sound or video automatically	114, 118
HEIGHT, WIDTH	Specifies a height and width for sound controls or a video	114, 118
HIDDEN	Hides the controls for a sound	115
LOOP	Plays a sound or video continuously	114, 118
SRC	Specifies the location of a sound or video	114, 118
<FIELDSET>	Organizes form elements into groups	140
<FONT>	Changes the appearance of text	29, 30, 32
COLOR	Changes the color of text	32
FACE	Changes the font of text	29
SIZE	Changes the size of text	30
<FORM>	Creates a form	122
ACCEPT-CHARSET	Specifies character sets a Web server must support	123
ACTION	Specifies where a Web browser will send user information	122

TAG/ATTRIBUTE	DESCRIPTION	PAGE REFERENCES
ENCTYPE	Specifies the format for transferring form information	122, 134
METHOD	Specifies how form information is transferred over the Internet	122
TARGET	Specifies where the confirmation message for a form will appear	123
<FRAME>	Specifies information for one frame	144
BORDERCOLOR	Changes the color of the borders for a frame	153
FRAMEBORDER	Hides the borders for a frame	153
MARGINHEIGHT	Changes the top and bottom margins for a frame	154
MARGINWIDTH	Changes the left and right margins for a frame	154
NAME	Names a frame	145
NORESIZE	Prevents users from resizing a frame	151
SCROLLING	Hides or displays scroll bars for a frame	150
SRC	Specifies the location of the Web page that will appear in a frame	145
<FRAMESET>	Creates a set of frames	144
BORDER	Changes the thickness of frame borders	152
BORDERCOLOR	Changes the color of frame borders	152
COLS	Creates columns of frames	144
FRAMEBORDER	Hides frame borders	152
FRAMESPACING	Changes the thickness of frame borders	153
ROWS	Creates rows of frames	144
<H1> to <H6>	Creates a heading	20
ALIGN	Changes the alignment of a heading	20
<HEAD>	Identifies the head section of a Web page	12
<HR>	Adds a horizontal rule to a Web page	52
ALIGN	Changes the alignment of a horizontal rule	53
NOSHADE	Removes the 3-dimensional effect from a horizontal rule	53
SIZE	Changes the thickness of a horizontal rule	52
WIDTH	Changes the width of a horizontal rule	52
<HTML>	Identifies a document as an HTML document	12

HTML TAG SUMMARY

TAG/ATTRIBUTE	DESCRIPTION	PAGE REFERENCES
`<I>`	Italicizes text	26
`<IFRAME>`	Creates an inline frame	156
ALIGN	Wraps text around an inline frame	157
HEIGHT, WIDTH	Specifies a height and width for an inline frame	156
MARGINHEIGHT	Changes the top and bottom margins for an inline frame	157
MARGINWIDTH	Changes the left and right margins for an inline frame	157
NAME	Names an inline frame	156
SCROLLING	Hides or displays scrollbars for an inline frame	157
SRC	Specifies the location of the Web page that will appear in an inline frame	156
`<IMG>`	Adds an image to a Web page	44
ALIGN	Aligns an image with text or wraps text around an image	48, 50
ALT	Displays alternative text when an image does not appear	44
BORDER	Adds a border to an image	47
DYNSRC	Adds an internal AVI video to a Web page	119
HEIGHT, WIDTH	Specifies a height and width for an image	58, 59
HSPACE, VSPACE	Adds space around an image	51
ISMAP	Creates a server-side image map	195
LOWSRC	Specifies the location of a low-resolution version of an image	64
NAME	Names an image for a JavaScript	170
SRC	Specifies the location of an image	44
TABINDEX	Specifies the tab order for images	143
USEMAP	Specifies the name of an image map	192
`<INPUT>`	Creates form elements	124, 128, 130, 134, 136, 138, 139
ACCEPT	Specifies the types of files users can send	135
ACCESSKEY	Adds a keyboard shortcut to a form element	131
CHECKED	Selects a check box or radio button automatically	128, 130
DISABLED	Prevents users from using a form element	127
MAXLENGTH	Specifies the maximum number of characters for a form element	124

TAG/ATTRIBUTE	DESCRIPTION	PAGE REFERENCES
NAME	Identifies a form element in the form results	124, 128, 130, 134, 137, 138, 139
READONLY	Prevents users from editing information in a form element	127
SIZE	Specifies the size of a form element	124, 134
SRC	Specifies the location of the image for a graphical submit button	138
TABINDEX	Specifies the tab order for form elements	143
TYPE	Specifies the type of form element	124, 128, 130, 134, 136, 138, 139
VALUE	Identifies a form element	125, 128, 130, 136, 139
<INS>	Underlines inserted text	27
<KBD>	Identifies text users should type	36
<LABEL>	Labels a form element	142
FOR	Identifies the form element for a label	142
<LAYER>	Positions elements	237
HEIGHT, WIDTH	Specifies a height and width for a layer	237
LEFT	Specifies a position for a layer from the left edge of a window	237
TOP	Specifies a position for a layer from the top edge of a window	237
Z-INDEX	Controls the order layers overlap	237
<LEGEND>	Adds a title to a group of form elements	140
ALIGN	Aligns the title for a group of form elements	140
<LI>	Identifies an item in an ordered or unordered list	38, 40
TYPE	Specifies a bullet style for a list item	41
VALUE	Specifies the number for a list item	39
<LINK>	Links an external style sheet to a Web page	199
HREF	Specifies the location of an external style sheet	199
REL	Specifies the relationship of an external style sheet to the Web page	199
TYPE	Specifies the format of an external style sheet	199
<MAP>	Creates an image map	192
NAME	Names an image map	192

HTML TAG SUMMARY

TAG/ATTRIBUTE	DESCRIPTION	PAGE REFERENCES
<MARQUEE>	Creates a marquee	176
BEHAVIOR	Specifies how text will scroll	176
BGCOLOR	Adds a background color to a marquee	177
DIRECTION	Specifies the direction text will scroll	176
HEIGHT, WIDTH	Specifies a height and width for a marquee	177
HSPACE, VSPACE	Adds space around a marquee	177
LOOP	Specifies the number of times text will scroll across the screen	176
SCROLLAMOUNT	Specifies the amount of space text will move at a time	176
SCROLLDELAY	Specifies the amount of time between each movement of text	176
TRUESPEED	Overrides the minimum SCROLLDELAY value	177
<META>	Provides information about a Web page	159, 186, 188, 238-242
CONTENT	Specifies custom information about a Web page	159, 186, 188, 238-242
HTTP-EQUIV	Provides instructions for a Web server	159, 186, 188, 241
NAME	Identifies the type of information	238-240, 242
URL	Specifies the location of a Web page that will appear automatically	186
<NOBR>	Keeps text on one line	17
<NOEMBED>	Displays alternative text when a browser does not support the <EMBED> tag	115
<NOFRAMES>	Displays alternative text when frames do not appear	147
<NOSCRIPT>	Displays alternative text when a JavaScript does not run	160
<OBJECT>	Adds an object to a Web page	115, 119, 191
CLASSID	Specifies the location of an object	191
DATA	Specifies the location of an object	115, 119
HEIGHT, WIDTH	Specifies a height and width for an object	119, 191
<OL>	Creates an ordered list	38
START	Specifies a starting number for an ordered list	39
TYPE	Specifies a number style for an ordered list	38
<OPTGROUP>	Divides a form menu into submenus	133
LABEL	Specifies a title for each submenu	133

TAG/ATTRIBUTE	DESCRIPTION	PAGE REFERENCES
<OPTION>	Creates a menu option on a form	132
SELECTED	Selects a menu option automatically	132
VALUE	Identifies a menu option in the form results	132
<P>	Starts a new paragraph	16
ALIGN	Changes the alignment of a paragraph	16
<PRE>	Retains the spacing of text	22
<Q>	Identifies a short quotation	37
<SAMP>	Identifies sample text	36
<SCRIPT>	Adds JavaScript to a Web page	158
DEFER	Informs browsers that a script will not generate Web page content	159
LANGUAGE	Specifies the scripting language for a script	159
SRC	Specifies the location of an external script	161
TYPE	Specifies the scripting language for a script	158
<SELECT>	Creates a menu on a form	132
MULTIPLE	Allows users to select more than one menu option	133
NAME	Identifies a menu in the form results	132
SIZE	Specifies the number of options visible in a menu	132
TABINDEX	Specifies the tab order of form elements	143
<SMALL>	Makes text smaller than the surrounding text	31
<SPACER>	Adds a block of space to a Web page	185
ALIGN	Wraps text around a block of space	185
HEIGHT, WIDTH	Specifies a height and width for a block of space	185
TYPE	Specifies the type of space	185
<SPAN>	Divides text into sections for applying styles	205
CLASS	Identifies a section of text for a style	205
<STRIKE>	Places a line through text	26
<STRONG>	Emphasizes text using bold formatting	27
<STYLE>	Creates an internal style sheet	196
<SUB>	Subscripts text	28

HTML TAG SUMMARY

TAG/ATTRIBUTE	DESCRIPTION	PAGE REFERENCES
`<SUP>`	Superscripts text	28
`<TABLE>`	Creates a table	88
ALIGN	Wraps text around a table	110
BACKGROUND	Adds a background image	97
BGCOLOR	Adds a background color	96
BORDER	Adds a border	90
BORDERCOLOR	Specifies a color for a border	90
CELLPADDING	Changes the amount of space around the contents of cells	104
CELLSPACING	Changes the amount of space between cells	104
FRAME	Specifies which external borders to display	106
HEIGHT, WIDTH	Specifies a height and width for a table	100
RULES	Specifies which internal borders to display	106
`<TBODY>`	Creates a body row group in a table	94
ALIGN	Changes the horizontal alignment of data	98
BGCOLOR	Adds a background color	96
CHAR	Specifies a character to align	99
VALIGN	Changes the vertical alignment of data	98
`<TD>`, `<TH>`	Creates a data cell or header cell in a table	88
ALIGN	Changes the horizontal alignment of data	98
BACKGROUND	Adds a background image	97
BGCOLOR	Adds a background color	96
CHAR	Specifies a character to align	99
COLSPAN	Spans a cell across columns	102
HEIGHT, WIDTH	Changes the height and width of a cell	101
NOWRAP	Keeps text in a cell on one line	108
ROWSPAN	Spans a cell down rows	102
VALIGN	Changes the vertical alignment of data	98

TAG/ATTRIBUTE	DESCRIPTION	PAGE REFERENCES
<TEXTAREA>	Creates a large text area on a form	126
ACCESSKEY	Adds a keyboard shortcut to a large text area	131
COLS	Specifies a width for a large text area	126
DISABLED	Prevents users from using a large text area	127
NAME	Identifies a large text area in the form results	126
READONLY	Prevents users from editing information in a large text area	127
ROWS	Specifies a height for a large text area	126
TABINDEX	Specifies the tab order of form elements	143
WRAP	Specifies how text will wrap in a large text area	126
<TFOOT>	Creates a footer row group in a table	94
ALIGN	Changes the horizontal alignment of data	98
BGCOLOR	Adds a background color	96
CHAR	Specifies a character to align	99
VALIGN	Changes the vertical alignment of data	98
<THEAD>	Creates a header row group in a table	94
ALIGN	Changes the horizontal alignment of data	98
BGCOLOR	Adds a background color	96
CHAR	Specifies a character to align	99
VALIGN	Changes the vertical alignment of data	98
<TITLE>	Creates a title for a Web page	12
<TR>	Creates a row in a table	88
ALIGN	Changes the horizontal alignment of data	98
BGCOLOR	Adds a background color	96
CHAR	Specifies a character to align	99
VALIGN	Changes the vertical alignment of data	98
<TT>	Displays text in a monospaced font	36
<U>	Underlines text	26
<UL>	Creates an unordered list	40
TYPE	Specifies a bullet style for an unordered list	40

STYLE SHEET PROPERTY SUMMARY

PROPERTIES	DESCRIPTION	PAGE REFERENCES
background	Adds a background color or image to elements	220, 222
background-attachment	Specifies if a background image will remain stationary	221
background-image	Adds a background image to elements	221
background-position	Specifies a starting position for a background image	221
background-repeat	Specifies how a background image will repeat	221
border	Places a border around elements	226
border-bottom	Specifies a bottom border for elements	227
border-color	Specifies a color for borders	227
border-left	Specifies a left border for elements	227
border-right	Specifies a right border for elements	227
border-style	Specifies a style for borders	227
border-top	Specifies a top border for elements	227
border-width	Specifies a thickness for borders	227
bottom	Positions elements with respect to the bottom edge of elements	234, 236
clear	Stops text from wrapping around elements	228
color	Changes the color of text or other elements	215
display	Changes the display of elements	229
float	Wraps text around elements	228
font	Changes multiple font settings at once	211
font-family	Changes the font of text	210
font-size	Changes the font size of text	212
font-style	Italicizes text	207
font-variant	Displays text in small caps	213
font-weight	Bolds text	206
height	Specifies a height for elements	223
left	Positions elements with respect to the left edge of elements	234, 236

PROPERTIES	DESCRIPTION	PAGE REFERENCES
letter-spacing	Adds space between letters	217
line-height	Adds space between lines of text	216
list-style	Specifies a bullet or number style for lists	230
margin	Changes all four margins for elements at once	225
margin-bottom	Changes the bottom margin for elements	225
margin-left	Changes the left margin for elements	225
margin-right	Changes the right margin for elements	225
margin-top	Changes the top margin for elements	225
padding	Adds space around all four sides of elements	224
padding-bottom	Adds space to the bottom of elements	224
padding-left	Adds space to the left side of elements	224
padding-right	Adds space to the right side of elements	224
padding-top	Adds space to the top of elements	224
page-break-after	Adds a page break after elements	233
page-break-before	Adds a page break before elements	233
position	Specifies an absolute or relative position for elements	234, 236
right	Positions elements with respect to the right edge of elements	234, 236
text-align	Changes the alignment of text	214
text-decoration	Adds a line to text, makes text blink	208, 211
text-indent	Indents the first line of text	209
text-transform	Changes the case of text	213
top	Positions elements with respect to the top edge of elements	234, 236
vertical-align	Specifies a vertical alignment for inline elements	232
width	Specifies a width for elements	223
word-spacing	Adds space between words	217
z-index	Controls how positioned elements overlap	237

WHAT'S ON THE CD-ROM DISC

The CD-ROM disc included in this book contains many useful files and programs that can be used when creating Web pages. You will find a Web page providing one-click access to all the Internet links mentioned in the book, as well as several popular programs you can install and use on your computer. Before installing any of the programs on the disc, make sure a newer version of the program is not already installed on your computer. For information on installing different versions of the same program, contact the program's manufacturer.

SYSTEM REQUIREMENTS

While most programs on the CD-ROM disc have minimal system requirements, your computer should be equipped with the following hardware and software to use all the contents of the CD-ROM disc:

Windows

* A Pentium or faster processor.
* Microsoft Windows 95 or later.
* At least 32MB of RAM.
* At least 200MB of hard drive space.
* A double-speed (2x) or faster CD-ROM drive.
* A monitor capable of displaying at least 256 colors or grayscale.
* A modem with a speed of at least 28,800 bps.
* DirectX version 3.0 or later.

Macintosh

* Mac OS 8.1 or later.
* At least 32MB of RAM.
* Virtual Memory turned on, set to 64MB.
* At least 200MB of hard drive space.
* A double-speed (2x) or faster CD-ROM drive.
* 604 PowerPC (200 MHz or better).
* A modem with a speed of at least 28,800 bps.

AUTHOR'S SOURCE CODE

The CD provides files that contain all the sample code used throughout the book. You can browse these files directly from the CD-ROM or you can copy them to your hard drive and use them as the basis for your own projects. You should open the files using a text editor such as WordPad, for Windows users, or SimpleText, for Macintosh users.

WEB LINKS

This CD contains a Web page that provides one-click access to all the Web pages and Internet references in the book. To use these links you must have an Internet connection and a Web browser, such as Internet Explorer, installed.

ACROBAT VERSION

The CD-ROM disc contains an e-version of this book that you can view and search using Adobe Acrobat Reader. You can also use the hyperlinks provided in the text to access all Web pages and Internet references in the book. You cannot print the pages or copy text from the Acrobat files. An evaluation version of Adobe Acrobat Reader is also included on the disc.

INSTALLING AND USING THE SOFTWARE

This CD-ROM disc contains several useful programs.

Before installing a program from this CD, you should exit all other programs. In order to use most of the programs, you must accept the license agreement provided with the program. Make sure you read any Readme files provided with each program.

Program Versions

Shareware programs are fully functional, free trial versions of copyrighted programs. If you like a particular program, you can register with its author for a nominal fee and receive licenses, enhanced versions and technical support.

Freeware programs are free, copyrighted games, applications and utilities. You can copy them to as many computers as you like, but they have no technical support.

HTML:
Your visual blueprint for
designing effective Web pages

GNU software is governed by its own license, which is included inside the folder of the GNU software. There are no restrictions on distribution of this software. See the GNU license for more details.

Trial, demo and evaluation versions are usually limited either by time or functionality. For example, you may not be able to save projects using these versions.

For your convenience, the software titles on the CD are listed alphabetically.

Acrobat Reader

For Microsoft Windows 95/98/NT/2000 and Macintosh. Evaluation version.

This disc contains an evaluation version of Acrobat Reader 4.0 from Adobe. You will need this program to access the book files also included on this disc. For more information about using Acrobat Reader, see page 282.

AscToHTM

Version 3.2 for Microsoft Windows 95/98/NT. Shareware version.

AscToHTM is a utility that converts plain text files to HTML format suitable for posting on a Web site. AscToHTM automatically detects bullets and tables and can automatically add links and JavaScript to generated Web pages.

AscToHTM is a shareware program from JafSoft Limited. AscToHTM is fully functional for 30 days, after which time you are required to register it with the author.

The latest version of AscToHTM is available at www.jafsoft.com.

BBEdit

Version 5.1.1 for Macintosh. Demo version.

BBEdit is an HTML editor for the Macintosh operating system. BBEdit includes many features, such as multi-level undo, a spell checker and the ability to work with files located on remote Web servers.

BBEdit 5.1.1 is a demo version from Bare Bones Software. BBEdit has full functionality, except that the ability to save files is disabled.

The latest version of BBEdit and a collection of BBEdit Plug-Ins & Extensions are available at www.bbedit.com.

BBEdit Lite

Version 4.6 for Macintosh. Freeware version.

BBEdit Lite is the freeware version of the popular BBEdit HTML editor. BBEdit Lite includes many features, such as the ability to find and replace text in multiple files and easy access to HTML tags.

BBEdit Lite is freeware from Bare Bones Software.

The latest version of BBEdit Lite and the full version of BBEdit are available at www.bbedit.com.

Communicator

Version 4.7 for Microsoft Windows 95/98/NT and Macintosh. Commercial version.

Communicator is a suite of applications from Netscape that include the popular Web browser, Navigator. Communicator also includes other Internet related applications including the Winamp music player, the Messenger e-mail program and the AOL Instant Messenger communication program.

Communicator is a fully functional program from Netscape. There is no charge for its use.

The latest version of Communicator, as well as support files and additional components are available at www.netscape.com.

CuteFTP

Version 4.0 for Microsoft Windows 95/98/NT/2000. Shareware version.

CuteFTP is a program used to transfer files between computers that are connected via the Internet or an internal network. CuteFTP offers advanced features such as the ability to schedule file transfers and search FTP sites for specific files.

CuteFTP is a shareware program from GlobalSCAPE, Inc. CuteFTP is fully functional for 30 days, after which time you are required to register it with the author.

The latest version of CuteFTP is available at www.cuteftp.com.

WHAT'S ON THE CD-ROM DISC

Gif·glf·giF

Version 1.24 for Microsoft Windows 95/98/NT. Version 1.53 for Macintosh. Evaluation version.

Gif·glf·giF is a program that allows you to create animations for your Web pages. Animations can be created from screen captures, making Gif·glf·giF suitable for creating instructional Web pages.

Gif·glf·giF is a shareware program from Pedagoguery Software Inc. Gif·glf·giF is fully functional for 30 days, after which time you are required to register it with the author.

Additional versions of Gif·glf·giF are available at www.peda.com.

GoldWave

Version 4.16 for Microsoft Windows 95/98/NT/2000. Shareware version.

GoldWave is a program that lets you record, create and alter audio files. GoldWave can also be used to copy tracks from audio CD discs and convert them to formats that can be saved on a computer.

GoldWave is a demo program from Boutell.Com, Inc. GoldWave is fully functional, except that you are limited to using 150 commands per session.

You can download support files and additional components for GoldWave at www.goldwave.com.

HomeSite

Version 4.5 for Microsoft Windows 95/98/NT/2000. Evaluation version.

HomeSite is a full featured HTML editor that is well-suited for use with other Web-related coding languages, such as Active Server Pages and VBScript. HomeSite also includes strong Web site management features.

HomeSite is an evaluation program from Allaire. It is fully functional for 30 days, after which time you are required to register it with the author.

You can download the latest version of HomeSite, as well as participate in message forums with other HomeSite users at www.allaire.com.

Internet Explorer

Version 5.01 for Microsoft Windows 95/98. Version 4.5 for Macintosh. Commercial version.

Internet Explorer 5 is Microsoft's latest Web browser. It offers new and improved features that make browsing the Web faster and easier. Internet Explorer also includes a VBScript engine which can be used to create and test VBScript scripts.

Internet Explorer is a fully functional program from Microsoft Corporation. There is no charge for its use.

You can download support files and additional components from the Internet Explorer Web site at www.microsoft.com/windows/ie.

Mapedit

Version 2.63 for Microsoft Windows 95/98/NT. Shareware version.

Mapedit is a program that generates the HTML code required for including image maps on Web pages.

Mapedit is a shareware program from Boutell.Com, Inc. Mapedit is fully functional for 30 days, after which time you are required to register it with the author.

Additional versions of Mapedit are available at the Web site www.boutell.com.

Paint Shop Pro

Version 6.0 for Microsoft Windows 95/98/NT. Evaluation version.

Paint Shop Pro is an image editing and creation program. Paint Shop Pro can be used to capture images from a computer screen or digital camera and then edit the images, adding special effects such as shadows.

Paint Shop Pro is an evaluation program from Jasc Software, Inc. Paint Shop Pro is fully functional for 30 days, after which time you are required to register it with the author.

You can download additional components and access technical support for Paint Shop Pro at www.jasc.com.

HTML:
Your visual blueprint for
designing effective Web pages

QuickTime

Version 4.1 for Microsoft Windows 95/98/NT/2000 and Macintosh. Commercial version.

QuickTime is a program that allows you to play audio and video files on your computer. QuickTime allows you to play over 200 different types of audio and video files.

The QuickTime player is a free program from Apple.

The latest version of QuickTime is available at www.apple.com.

RealPlayer

Version 7.0 Basic for Microsoft Windows 95/98/NT/2000 and Macintosh. Plug-in.

RealPlayer lets you play audio and video files compatible with RealPlayer. RealPlayer also allows you to listen to or view streaming media from sources such as radio stations on the Internet.

RealPlayer is a free program from Real Networks.

You can download additional components and access technical support for RealPlayer at www.real.com.

WS_FTP Pro

Version 6.0 for Microsoft Windows 95/98/NT/2000. Trial version.

WS_FTP Pro is a program used to transfer files between computers that are connected via the Internet or an internal network.

WS_FTP Pro can automatically resume downloading files that were interrupted while being transferred and can be used from the command line.

WS_FTP Pro is a trial program from Ipswitch, Inc. WS_FTP Pro is fully functional for 30 days, after which time you are required to register it with the author.

The latest version of WS_FTP Pro is available at www.ipswitch.com.

TROUBLESHOOTING

We tried our best to compile programs that work on most computers with the minimum system requirements. Your computer, however, may differ and some programs may not work properly for some reason.

The two most likely problems are that you do not have enough memory (RAM) for the programs you want to use or you have other programs running that are affecting installation or running of a program. If you get error messages while trying to install or use the programs on the CD-ROM disc, try one or more of the following methods and then try installing or running the software again:

* Close all running programs.
* Restart your computer.
* Turn off any anti-virus software.
* Close the CD-ROM interface and run demos or installations directly from Windows Explorer.
* Add more RAM to your computer.

If you still have trouble installing the programs from the CD-ROM disc, please call IDG Books Worldwide Customer Service at: 800-762-2974 (outside the U.S.: 317-572-3342).

USING THE E-VERSION OF THE BOOK

You can view *HTML: Your visual blueprint for designing effective Web pages* on your screen using the CD-ROM disc included at the back of this book. The CD-ROM disc allows you to search the contents of each chapter of the book for a specific word or phrase. The CD-ROM disc also provides a convenient way of keeping the book handy while traveling.

You must install Adobe Acrobat Reader on your computer before you can view the book on the CD-ROM disc. This program is provided on

the disc. Acrobat Reader allows you to view Portable Document Format (PDF) files, which can display books and magazines on your screen exactly as they appear in printed form.

To view the contents of the book using Acrobat Reader, display the contents of the disc. Double-click the BookPDFs folder to display the contents of the folder. In the window that appears, double-click the icon for the chapter of the book you want to review.

USING THE E-VERSION OF THE BOOK

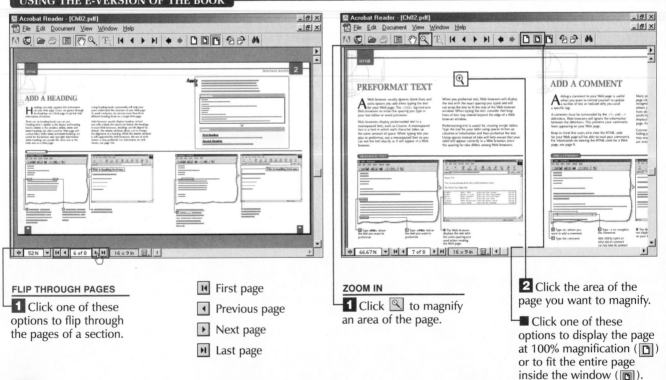

FLIP THROUGH PAGES

1 Click one of these options to flip through the pages of a section.

◄ First page
◄ Previous page
► Next page
► Last page

ZOOM IN

1 Click 🔍 to magnify an area of the page.

2 Click the area of the page you want to magnify.

■ Click one of these options to display the page at 100% magnification (🗋) or to fit the entire page inside the window (🗔).

HTML:
Your visual blueprint for
designing effective Web pages

Extra

To install Acrobat Reader, insert the CD-ROM disc into a drive. In the screen that appears, click Software. Click Acrobat Reader and then click Install at the bottom of the screen. Then follow the instructions on your screen to install the program.

You can make searching the book more convenient by copying the .pdf files to your own computer. Display the contents of the CD-ROM disc and then copy the BookPDFs folder from the CD to your hard drive. This allows you to easily access the contents of the book at any time.

Acrobat Reader is a popular and useful program. There are many files available on the Web that are designed to be viewed using Acrobat Reader. Look for files with the .pdf extension. For more information about Acrobat Reader, visit the Web site at www.adobe.com/products/acrobat/readermain.html.

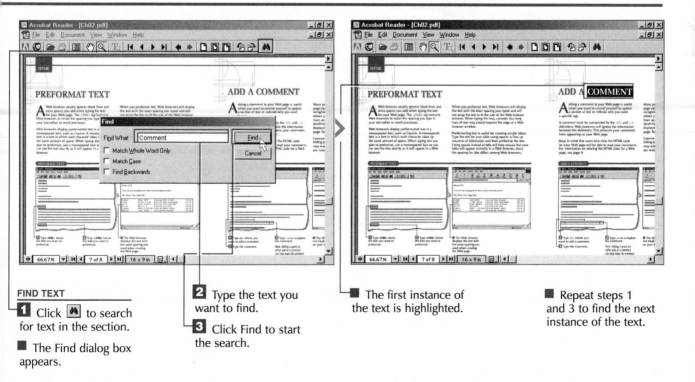

FIND TEXT

1 Click 🔍 to search for text in the section.

■ The Find dialog box appears.

2 Type the text you want to find.

3 Click Find to start the search.

■ The first instance of the text is highlighted.

■ Repeat steps 1 and 3 to find the next instance of the text.

APPENDIX

IDG BOOKS WORLDWIDE, INC.
END-USER LICENSE AGREEMENT

READ THIS. You should carefully read these terms and conditions before opening the software packet(s) included with this book ("Book"). This is a license agreement ("Agreement") between you and IDG Books Worldwide, Inc. ("IDGB"). By opening the accompanying software packet(s), you acknowledge that you have read and accept the following terms and conditions. If you do not agree and do not want to be bound by such terms and conditions, promptly return the Book and the unopened software packet(s) to the place you obtained them for a full refund.

1. License Grant. IDGB grants to you (either an individual or entity) a nonexclusive license to use one copy of the enclosed software program(s) (collectively, the "Software") solely for your own personal or business purposes on a single computer (whether a standard computer or a workstation component of a multi-user network). The Software is in use on a computer when it is loaded into temporary memory (i.e., RAM) or installed into permanent memory (e.g., hard disk, CD-ROM or other storage device). IDGB reserves all rights not expressly granted herein.

2. Ownership. IDGB is the owner of all right, title and interest, including copyright, in and to the compilation of the Software recorded on the CD-ROM. Copyright to the individual programs on the CD-ROM is owned by the author or other authorized copyright owner of each program. Ownership of the Software and all proprietary rights relating thereto remain with IDGB and its licensors.

3. Restrictions On Use and Transfer.

(a) You may only (i) make one copy of the Software for backup or archival purposes, or (ii) transfer the Software to a single hard disk, provided that you keep the original for backup or archival purposes. You may not (i) rent or lease the Software, (ii) copy or reproduce the Software through a LAN or other network system or through any computer subscriber system or bulletin-board system, or (iii) modify, adapt or create derivative works based on the Software.

(b) You may not reverse engineer, decompile, or disassemble the Software. You may transfer the Software and user documentation on a permanent basis, provided that the transferee agrees to accept the terms and conditions of this Agreement and you retain no copies. If the Software is an update or has been updated, any transfer must include the most recent update and all prior versions.

4. Restrictions on Use of Individual Programs. You must follow the individual requirements and restrictions detailed for each individual program in the "What's On The CD-ROM Disc" section of this Book. These limitations are contained in the individual license agreements recorded on the CD-ROM. These restrictions may include a requirement that after using the program for the period of time specified in its text, the user must pay a registration fee or discontinue use. By opening the Software packet(s), you will be agreeing to abide by the licenses and restrictions for these individual programs. None of the material on this disc(s) or listed in this Book may ever be distributed, in original or modified form, for commercial purposes.

5. Limited Warranty.

(a) IDGB warrants that the Software and CD-ROM are free from defects in materials and workmanship under normal use for a period of sixty (60) days from the date of purchase of this Book. If IDGB receives

HTML:
Your visual blueprint for
designing effective Web pages

notification within the warranty period of defects in materials or workmanship, IDGB will replace the defective CD-ROM.

(b) IDGB AND THE AUTHOR OF THE BOOK DISCLAIM ALL OTHER WARRANTIES, EXPRESS OR IMPLIED, INCLUDING WITHOUT LIMITATION IMPLIED WARRANTIES OF MERCHANTABILITY AND FITNESS FOR A PARTICULAR PURPOSE, WITH RESPECT TO THE SOFTWARE, THE PROGRAMS, THE SOURCE CODE CONTAINED THEREIN, AND/ OR THE TECHNIQUES DESCRIBED IN THIS BOOK. IDGB DOES NOT WARRANT THAT THE FUNCTIONS CONTAINED IN THE SOFTWARE WILL MEET YOUR REQUIREMENTS OR THAT THE OPERATION OF THE SOFTWARE WILL BE ERROR FREE.

(c) This limited warranty gives you specific legal rights, and you may have other rights which vary from jurisdiction to jurisdiction.

6. Remedies.

(a) IDGB's entire liability and your exclusive remedy for defects in materials and workmanship shall be limited to replacement of the Software, which may be returned to IDGB with a copy of your receipt at the following address: Disc Fulfillment Department, Attn: HTML: Your visual blueprint for designing effective Web pages, IDG Books Worldwide, Inc., 10475 Crosspoint Boulevard, Indianapolis, Indiana, 46256, or call 1-800-762-2974. Please allow 3-4 weeks for delivery. This Limited Warranty is void if failure of the Software has resulted from accident, abuse, or misapplication. Any replacement Software will be warranted for the remainder of the original warranty period or thirty (30) days, whichever is longer.

(b) In no event shall IDGB or the author be liable for any damages whatsoever (including without limitation damages for loss of business profits, business interruption, loss of business information, or any other pecuniary loss) arising out of the use of or inability to use the Book or the Software, even if IDGB has been advised of the possibility of such damages.

(c) Because some jurisdictions do not allow the exclusion or limitation of liability for consequential or incidental damages, the above limitation or exclusion may not apply to you.

7. U.S. Government Restricted Rights. Use, duplication, or disclosure of the Software by the U.S. Government is subject to restrictions stated in paragraph (c) (1) (ii) of the Rights in Technical Data and Computer Software clause of DFARS 252.227-7013, and in subparagraphs (a) through (d) of the Commercial Computer—Restricted Rights clause at FAR 52.227-19, and in similar clauses in the NASA FAR supplement, when applicable.

8. General. This Agreement constitutes the entire understanding of the parties, and revokes and supersedes all prior agreements, oral or written, between them and may not be modified or amended except in a writing signed by both parties hereto which specifically refers to this Agreement. This Agreement shall take precedence over any other documents that may be in conflict herewith. If any one or more provisions contained in this Agreement are held by any court or tribunal to be invalid, illegal or otherwise unenforceable, each and every other provision shall remain in full force and effect.

INDEX

Numbers and Symbols

* (asterisk), for frames, 144
#PCDATA (Parsed Character Data) data type, 265
  code, for inserting spaces, 19
/* */ comment delimiters, 199
<!-- --> comment delimiters, 23
@font-face command, 211
@import command, 199
<!DOCTYPE> tag, 13, 264
<!ELEMENT> tag, 264-265

A

<A> tag, 74-75, 76-77, 86
absolute
     positioning, of elements, 236-237
     URLs, 74
ACCEPT attribute (<INPUT> tag), 135
ACCEPT-CHARSET attribute (<FORM> tag), 123
access
     counters, 183
     logs, 244
ACCESSKEY attribute
     <A> tag, 86
     form tags, 131
ACTION attribute (<FORM> tag), 122-123
active links, 85, 218
ActiveX, 191
alert messages, display, using JavaScript, 167
align
     captions, in tables, 91
     data, in tables, 98-99
     elements, vertically, using style sheets, 232
     headings, 20-21
     horizontal rules, 53
     images, with text, 50
     paragraphs, 16-17
     text, using style sheets, 214
ALIGN attribute
     <CAPTION> tag, 91
     <EMBED> tag, 119
     <H1> to <H6> tags, 20-21
     <HR> tag, 53
     <IFRAME> tag, 157
     <IMG> tag, 48-49, 50, 54-55
     <LEGEND> tag, 140
     <P> tag, 16-17
     <SPACER> tag, 185
     table tags, 98-99, 110-111
ALINK attribute (<BODY> tag), 85

ALT attribute

ALT attribute
     <AREA> tag, 195
     <IMG> tag, 44-45, 65
alternative
     information, provide, for frames, 147
     text, provide
          for images, 44-45
          for Java applets, 190-191
          for JavaScript, 160
          for sounds or videos, 115
anchors, for links, 76
animated GIF images, 180
ANY, data type, 264-265
<APPLET> tag, 190-191
applets, Java, 190-191
ARCHIVE attribute (<APPLET> tag), 191
<AREA> tag, 194-195
ARPANET, 2
asterisks (*), use to specify sizes of frames, 144
attributes, for tags, overview, 8. *See also specific attribute*
author, specify, for Web pages, 240
AUTOSTART attribute (<EMBED> tag), 114-115, 118-119

B

<B> tag, 26
background
     colors
          add, using style sheets, 222
          change, 34
               for marquees, 177
     images
          add, 46
               to tables, 97
               using style sheets, 220-221
          obtain, 220
          starting position, specify, using style sheets, 221
     make transparent, for images, 68-69
     property, 219, 220-221, 222
     sounds, add, 115
BACKGROUND attribute
     <BODY> tag, 46, 182
     table tags, 97
background-attachment property, 221
background-image property, 221
background-position property, 221
background-repeat property, 221
bandwidth, 244
banners, add to Web pages, 45
<BASE> tag, 84, 148
<BASEFONT> tag, 30
baseline, of text, 232
BBEdit, 11

286

HTML:
Your visual blueprint for
designing effective Web Pages

INDEX

HTML:
Your visual blueprint for
designing effective Web Pages

INDEX

HTML:
Your visual blueprint for
designing effective Web Pages

I

HTML:
Your visual blueprint for
designing effective Web Pages

293

HTML:
Your visual blueprint for
designing effective Web Pages

HTML:
Your visual blueprint for
designing effective Web Pages

HTML:
Your visual blueprint for
designing effective Web Pages

U

INDEX

HTML:
Your visual blueprint for
designing effective Web Pages

Read Less, Learn More™

Visual

New Series!

The visual alternative to learning complex computer topics.

For experienced computer users, developers, network professionals who learn best visually.

Extra

Apply It

"Apply It" and "Extra" provide ready-to-run code and useful tips.

Title	ISBN	Price
Active Server™ Pages 3.0: Your visual blueprint for developing interactive Web sites	0-7645-3472-6	$24.99
Apache Web Server 2.0: Your visual blueprint to network administration with Apache	0-7645-3520-X	$24.99
HTML: Your visual blueprint for designing effective Web pages	0-7645-3471-8	$24.99
JavaScript™: Your visual blueprint for building dynamic Web pages	0-7645-4730-5	$24.99
Linux®: Your visual blueprint to the Linux platform	0-7645-3481-5	$24.99
Perl: Your visual blueprint for building Perl scripts	0-7645-3478-5	$24.99
Unix®: Your visual blueprint to the universe of Unix	0-7645-3480-7	$24.99
XML™: Your visual blueprint for building expert Web pages	0-7645-3477-7	$24.99

Over 9 million *Visual* books in print!

with these two-color Visual™ guides

The Complete Visual Reference

For visual learners who want an all-in-one reference/tutorial that delivers more in-depth information about a technology topic.

"Master It" tips provide additional topic coverage

Title	ISBN	Price
Master Active Directory™ VISUALLY™	0-7645-3425-4	$34.99
Master HTML 4 & XHTML 1 VISUALLY™	0-7645-3454-8	$34.99
Master Microsoft® Access 2000 VISUALLY™	0-7645-6048-4	$39.99
Master Microsoft® Office 2000 VISUALLY™	0-7645-6050-6	$39.99
Master Microsoft® Windows® Me Millennium Edition VISUALLY™	0-7645-3496-3	$34.99
Master Microsoft® Word 2000 VISUALLY™	0-7645-6046-8	$39.99
Master Office 97 VISUALLY™	0-7645-6036-0	$39.99
Master Photoshop® 5.5 VISUALLY™	0-7645-6045-X	$39.99
Master Red Hat® Linux® VISUALLY™	0-7645-3436-X	$34.99
Master Windows® 95 VISUALLY™	0-7645-6024-7	$39.99
Master Windows® 98 VISUALLY™	0-7645-6034-4	$39.99
Master Windows® 2000 Professional VISUALLY™	0-7645-3421-1	$39.99
Master Windows® 2000 Server VISUALLY™	0-7645-3426-2	$34.99

The Visual™ series is available wherever books are sold, or call
1-800-762-2974.
Outside the US, call
317-572-3993

ORDER FORM

IDG BOOKS

TRADE & INDIVIDUAL ORDERS
Phone: **(800) 762-2974**
or **(317) 572-3993**
(8 a.m.–6 p.m., CST, weekdays)
FAX : **(800) 550-2747**
or **(317) 572-4002**

EDUCATIONAL ORDERS & DISCOUNTS
Phone: **(800) 434-2086**
(8:30 a.m.–5:00 p.m., CST, weekdays)
FAX : **(317) 572-4005**

CORPORATE ORDERS FOR 3-D VISUAL™ SERIES
Phone: **(800) 469-6616**
(8 a.m.–5 p.m., EST, weekdays)
FAX : **(905) 890-9434**

Qty	ISBN	Title	Price	Total

Shipping & Handling Charges

	Description	First book	Each add'l. book	Total
Domestic	Normal	$4.50	$1.50	$
	Two Day Air	$8.50	$2.50	$
	Overnight	$18.00	$3.00	$
International	Surface	$8.00	$8.00	$
	Airmail	$16.00	$16.00	$
	DHL Air	$17.00	$17.00	$

Subtotal _____

*CA residents add
applicable sales tax* _____

*IN, MA and MD
residents add
5% sales tax* _____

*IL residents add
6.25% sales tax* _____

*RI residents add
7% sales tax* _____

*TX residents add
8.25% sales tax* _____

Shipping _____

Total _____

Ship to:

Name_____

Address_____

Company_____

City/State/Zip_____

Daytime Phone_____

Payment: ☐ Check to IDG Books (US Funds Only)

☐ Visa ☐ Mastercard ☐ American Express

Card # _____ Exp. _____ Signature_____